Unstrung heroes

Fifty guitar greats you should know

Schiffer Publishing Ltd

4880 Lower Valley Road • Atglen, PA 19310

Pete Braidis

Other Schiffer Books on Related Subjects:

Ball's Manual of Gretsch Guitars: 1950s. Edward Ball.
ISBN: 978-0-7643-4643-9

Electric Guitars. Robert Goudy. ISBN: 978-0-7643-0964-9

The Ultimate: An Illustrated History of Hamer Guitars.
Steve Matthes and Joe Moffett. Foreword by Rick Nielsen,
Introduction by Paul Hamer, and Afterword by Jol Dantzig.
ISBN: 978-0-7643-4352-0

Vintage Electric Guitars: In Praise of Fretted Americana.
William G. Moseley, Jr. Photography by Bill Ingalls, Jr.;
Foreword by Jeff Carlisi. ISBN: 978-0-7643-1361-5

Designed by Justin Watkinson
Type set in TitanText/Zurich BT/Helvetica Neue LT Pro/Minion Pro
ISBN: 978-0-7643-5088-7
Printed in China

Published by Schiffer Publishing, Ltd.
4880 Lower Valley Road
Atglen, PA 19310
Phone: (610) 593-1777; Fax: (610) 593-2002
E-mail: Info@schifferbooks.com

For our complete selection of fine books on this and related subjects,
please visit our website at www.schifferbooks.com. You may also write
for a free catalog.
    This book may be purchased from the publisher.
    We are always looking for people to write books on new and related
subjects. If you have an idea for a book, please contact us at proposals@
schifferbooks.com.
    Schiffer Publishing's titles are available at special discounts for
bulk purchases for sales promotions or premiums. Special editions,
including personalized covers, corporate imprints, and excerpts, can
be created in large quantities for special needs. For more information,
contact the publisher.

This book is 100% dedicated to my late mother, Mary Ellen Braidis, who wouldn't understand much of the content in here, but would understand that it came from my heart that also happens to miss her each and every day and will never stop doing so. Not a day goes by that I don't think of her, whether it's in a laugh or a cry. I only wish I knew for sure if she knew about this book. I'm thinking she does.

THIS IS FOR YOU THEN, MOM.

Contents

CHAPTER 1

Why Another Book About Guitar Players?

So, *why another book about guitar players?* you may ask.

Well, my thinking was that a book on the world's best zither players may not be a smashing success, so I went with an instrument I knew very well: the guitar.

This book takes a very different approach, however, and does not include the usual suspects when it comes to guitar greats. I will explain why.

In 1982, when I was in eighth grade, my Dad came home from work and gave me an acoustic guitar and told me I was going to my first guitar lesson that night. I was less than pleased to be doing this against my wishes, and that it had just been sprung on me. My mom and dad convinced me it was a good idea as I had started to fall in love with music the previous year, and within just that one year, I had already built up an advanced knowledge of exactly what I was listening to.

After my first few guitar lessons, which involved learning the strings and a few chords and being taught such riveting songs as "Jingle Bells" and "Three Blind Mice," it eventually got to the point where I could bring in a rock song to learn. I went with "Tom Sawyer" by Rush, and once I got those first few chords down, I was actually making music.

Alex Lifeson of Rush was why I kept playing guitar. He was and is a fascinating and highly unique player, rarely settling for common structures. Lifeson was a good guy to emulate because my style became quite odd, largely due to a decision to use weird chords and an understanding I was never going to be a traditional lead guitarist. It's not that I don't understand lead players— as you read this book, you'll see that I do. It's just that the innate talent it takes to create a solo and play it properly was not with me, so I opted for rhythm guitar, which is just as important, really.

Seeing concerts would become a very big deal and on December 13, 1982, I witnessed Rush and Rory Gallagher at the Spectrum in Philadelphia. Since Rory was the opener, he was the first live performer I'd ever heard and saw (as well as the first guitar player); I was blown away instantly—and he remains a guitar god to me to this day. I have seen close to 400 concerts now (my 23rd Rush show was this summer), and live music is still the best way to hear your favorite performers.

My purpose for writing this book is to let people know that while Eric Clapton, Jimi Hendrix, Jimmy Page, Eddie Van Halen, Carlos Santana, Randy Rhoads, B. B. King, George Harrison, Pete Townshend, Stevie Ray Vaughan, Prince, Keith Richards, Chuck Berry, etc., are all phenomenal players, we already know all about them.

Many books have covered these guys endlessly, so I wanted to take a different approach and reach out to players that I thought were every bit as good as those legends, if not better. Underrated, undervalued, under-appreciated—whatever the phrase or phrases may be—I just see them as too "under the radar." When it comes to describing these guitarists and certain songs, riffs, or ideas, I can only use so many adjectives, so if you see some of the same ones popping up often, so be it. I suppose describing a solo like a "perfectly ripe tomato" might've been an option, but I chose descriptions like awesome, killer, amazing, breathtaking, and the like, which I think captured my enthusiasm better.

When you hear a few guys arguing in a bar over drinks about who the best guitar player is, you're likely to hear the names Page, Hendrix, Clapton, Van Halen, etc., but if *I* were there going on about some of the names in this book, most likely I'd get a quizzical, drunken "Who are *they?*" I'd very much love for people who read this book to investigate the catalogs of these incredible guitarists and learn all about the genius of players such as Terry Kath, Frank Marino, Kyoji Yamamoto, Rik Emmett, Davey Johnstone, Nili Brosh, Wendell Richardson, and all the others featured.

My favorite guitar player is Ritchie Blackmore of Deep Purple and Rainbow, and my favorite band is a tie between Rush and Thin Lizzy (I can never decide). The guitar harmonies in Thin Lizzy still amaze me to this day. On any given day I might play Echo & Bunnymen, Miles Davis, the Strokes, Adele, Slayer, Daft Punk, Frank Sinatra, or the Byrds. Why listen to just one style? You never know what you might find.

This book may not change the world, but it is a really good way to learn more about guitar players of all types, why they play, and who influenced them. I also tried in my interviews to ask some non-typical questions that led to some great stories and responses. Not only did I do a lot of research, but I already knew most of what I needed to know being such a fan of these players—and then got to learn a whole lot more.

I tried my best to avoid a lot of technical terms, although some of that does pop up here and there. Hopefully, this book will make reading about these players and their styles and choices of guitar and equipment easy to understand and not too confusing—I think I achieved that.

I do mention a lot of US and UK chart information because that stuff is ingrained in my head, and I also wanted to point out the success that these artists did have that may not be common knowledge. And, as an MTV nut since I was thirteen years old, I asked some questions when possible about those glorious days of cranking out music videos when MTV actually played music all day long as opposed to now, where you can watch…nothing. Too, I always feel a sense of humor is a nice touch and these conversations have plenty of that. It should be easy enough to tell a phone interview from an email interview by the flow of the conversation, and both work well.

It's been quite the journey writing this book and it has taken well over a year. I have gotten the chance to interview some of my all-time musical favorites and ended up becoming friends with quite a few of them. (I *am* a nice guy after all.)

Some may not care for my choices or think I didn't include so-and-so or forgot about someone they feel was obvious or I didn't represent enough players from a certain style of music; but keep in mind, I reached out to far more players than those appearing in this book, and some simply didn't get back to me (for whatever reason). That doesn't mean they wouldn't have been interested, or maybe they weren't, but in some cases I don't know if they ever saw the requests. The players who did respond were truly wonderful people and there wasn't one single interview that was disappointing. And I'm not stuck on older players. I did reach out to some modern, current players, but only a few were accessible to me, which was a shame.

There are players from hard rock, heavy metal, jazz, country rock, blues, progressive rock, pop, new wave, funk, Motown, folk rock, Singer/Songwriters, new age, fusion, and afro-pop represented in this book. I most certainly do not listen to just one style of music, and I would think few people do that. I tried to get more country, jazz, and R&B players, but it didn't quite work out.

My hope is anyone reading this will understand my love of music, for without music, I wouldn't be here today, and that is a fact.

In conclusion, thanks for buying this book, and I really hope you learn about these ultra-talented guitar players, seek out their music, and spread the word, because they so dearly deserve that attention. I loved doing this project and consider it a blessing that I was given the opportunity to do so.

As they say…rock on.

CHAPTER 2

Berton Averre

(Born December 13, 1953, Van Nuys, CA)

Get the Knack. **If you were into music and alive and breathing in 1979, you knew this album and this phrase. They were no one-hit wonder as many critics have lumped them into that category over the years. These guys were seriously accomplished musicians of the highest degree. The Knack was one of the very best power pop/new wave bands that existed.**

The Knack was put together in 1978 with Averre (lead guitar, keyboards), Doug Fieger (vocals, guitars), Bruce Gary (drums) and Prescott Niles (bass). The band's demos were rejected by numerous labels, but they kept at it and became a hit on the Sunset Strip scene, and some big names came on stage and jammed with the guys. Suddenly, labels started to care and a bidding war broke out with the band signing to Capitol Records.

The much-hyped debut album *Get the Knack* went to #1 in 1979 for five weeks in the US, selling over 2 million and more than 6 million worldwide. Of course, "My Sharona" was the single that everyone was talking about, and topped the US singles charts for six weeks. This song about teenage angst and lust had that signature stuttering riff that guitarist Berton Averre became so damn good at. Then there's that guitar solo. Averre's solo is the stuff of legend and it still resonates.

It's pretty mind-blowing that he was able to get away with such a tricky, yet lyrical solo of significant length in a pop/rock song that went to #1. I dare say it's one of the greatest solos of the '70s. In fact, I just said it. The risqué "Good Girls Don't" narrowly missed the Top 10 as the second single and out and out rockers such as "Frustrated" and "Let Me Out" were sheer brilliance. All the musicians are proven worthy on these cuts. A cover of Buddy Holly's "Heartbeat" is done up Knack-style, "That's What the Little Girls Do" and the shuffle of "(She's So) Selfish" are also top shelf. Averre's guitar playing and writing are perfectly executed.

The Knack were eventually accused of being misogynistic (the lyrics kinda were at times), contrived, and stand-offish towards the media. A backlash developed that was totally unjustified. The album was recorded for a measly $18,000 and yet Mike Chapman's production is crystal clear. The album was the fastest-selling debut since *Meet the Beatles* from the Beatles in 1964, and wouldn't ya know it? "My Sharona" was the fastest-selling single since "I Want to Hold Your Hand" by those very same Beatles also in '64.

The sophomore album …*but the little girls understand* came out in 1980 and the knives were out from the critics. The album sold respectably, going Gold and hitting #15, and produced a Top 40 hit in "Baby Talks Dirty." Yes, that song has a similar riff and feel to "My Sharona" and yes the lyrics are about sex, but this is still a cool tune. The riff drives the song, the drive gets harder with the chorus, and the solo has different shapes and fills. Very creative guitar work and hooks galore once again. A minor hit was also scored in "Can't Put a Price on Love," which is downbeat, but a nice change with smooth hooks and ultra-tasty guitar.

Other cool tunes included "It's You," "I Want Ya," "Tell Me You're Mine," "The Feeling I Get" (talk about paying homage to the Phil Spector sound), and a great cover of the Kinks' "Hard Way," which is power pop bliss with a stellar solo. "Mr. Handleman" showed a nice Beatles influence with catchy chords and piano, but yeah, those lyrics were a bit much. Still, this was no clunker, although far from the debut's quality.

In 1981, *Round Trip* was a flop barely scraping the Top 100 and the single "Pay the Devil (Ooo, Baby, Ooo)" only hit #67. Sadly, they wouldn't tour much for this one, the label losing interest. Phil Jost was added on keyboards to boost the sound.

Yet again, we had another sorely misunderstood album. The single wasn't so hot, but "Radiating Love," "Boys Go Crazy," "Another Lousy Day in Paradise" (superb power pop), "She Likes the Beat," and "Africa" all were of a good fashion, and Averre's guitar playing yet again was doing all the right things. The sounds he used were a little different this time around, and the playing remained inventive, especially on "Africa," which was a really tricky solo with some unusual sounds. The group called it quits at year's end, re-formed in 1986, and played club gigs for a few years before Gary left in 1989, replaced first by Pat Torpey, then Billy Ward.

A comeback album, *Serious Fun,* surfaced in 1991, and "Rocket O' Love" was even a Top 10 rock radio hit and for good reason. "One Day at a Time" was the real gem on the album, but the album sank quickly after their label Charisma went under and the group split again, only to re-form a few years later with Ward back.

Now with the awesome Terry Bozzio on drums (ex-Frank Zappa, Missing Persons, Jeff Beck), a really fun album called *Zoom* came out in 1998. Sweet '60s melodies enrapture the songs. The playing, mix, and production are pristine. "Can I Borrow a Kiss" should be a #1 hit twenty times over and "Mister Magazine" isn't far behind. The fans loved it, but *Zoom* didn't get the support it so deserved. Bozzio soon gave way to David Henderson who played on *Normal as the Next Guy* (2001) and Torpey returned during those sessions and would remain until 2010, when Fieger sadly died of cancer (Gary had tragically died as well in 2006), and the group folded.

Averre has since become involved in writing and playing for musical theatre including three musical comedies with writer Tom Schulman, further showing his talents (and he's also a fine keyboardist by the way).

The Knack was a collective batch of excellent musicians and songwriters and anyone who understands the art of musicianship should well appreciate these guys. Berton Averre is a key reason why people wanted to get the Knack. If you haven't before, I suggest you do. There's still time!

I was very pleased to catch up with Berton just prior to Christmas 2014 and had a chance to ask him some questions.

Who were the players that were an influence on you when you began playing guitar?

The usual gang of immortals: Hendrix first and foremost, then Clapton, Page, Beck. Two players who really inspired and influenced me who don't get as much mention would be Johnny Winter and Michael Bloomfield. Johnny could pretty much smoke anyone, and Bloomfield conveyed the intensity and angst of the blues better than any other white guy, in my opinion.

What types of guitars have you preferred over the years? I know a Les Paul must be one of them!

I am first, last, and foremost a Les Paul player. When recording, Strats have their place (of course), as well as a Rickenbacker 12-string, a Tele...but I'm a humbucker guy.

"My Sharona" simply has one of the finest guitar solos of the '70s. I don't know how you got all that work into a #1 hit along with that jumpy riff. The riff reminds me of Jimmy Page in how he would have one note on the low E string and skip over a string to the D string for the other note on "Immigrant Song" or "The Wanton Song." And there are those warm power chords too. Take me through how you came up with all of it!

Well, first off, the riff in "Immigrant Song" is beyond great. There's the aggression, almost to the point of violence. The visceral experience of it reminds me of my reaction as a twelve year old to "Talk Talk" by the Music Machine, or the "Oop bip bip oop bip bip yeah!" in Love's "Seven and Seven Is." Right there is the choreographed anarchy that people are foolish enough to believe was invented by punk. And, yes, I think that sense of, well, bashing your head against the wall for fun sneaked into the riff in "My Sharona." But to be honest the actual inspiration for it was a lot more recent.

I was a huge fan of Elvis Costello and the Attractions, and the drum breakdown in "Pump It Up" killed me—now that I think of it, it was taking me back to "Talk Talk," etc. I channeled the idea of organized pounding and somehow that came out in an octave riff (maybe "Immigrant Song" is in my DNA). The aggression in the staccato I think was most what I was trying to convey. The Knack was just starting to gig in Hollywood, which was fueling Doug and me to crank up our songwriting output.

I had the riff and the turnaround chords (the C to Bb), and brought it into a rehearsal. I showed it to Prescott (our great bass player), and suggested to Bruce (our epic drummer) that it was more a tom and snare thing, as opposed to straight time (hi hat/kick/snare, you know). We just jammed it, and Doug started scat singing over it. He said, "Hey, that's great, let's go home and write it," which we did. In the early days our best work tended to happen with the two of us sitting in a room, bouncing ideas off each other. Chords, lyrics, structure all came out in the collaboration of "Sharona." Doug started doing the stutter thing (probably off of Daltrey in "My Generation") to "My Sharona," who was a girl he was coveting at the time. (He eventually got her, big surprise.)

As for the solo, Doug liked my playing and I suppose saw it as a feature of the band. He's the one who suggested an extended solo (most all of the solos in our songs are integrated to-the-point parts of the song, which I've always felt is very much a good thing), and he's the one who came up with the chords bed. Interesting in that, after the tension/release of the song, the solo and accompaniment is very much a departure. Kind of like the extended coda on "Layla," I guess. However he/we had the good sense to return to the hook to end the song.

The solo developed over months of playing the song in the clubs. I do remember Doug's instruction when I recorded it for *Get the Knack*: "Just burn." So I did. At one point—about three-quarters of the way through the solo—I do this descending thing. It's right after the whip gliss on the E string after the extended highest (ever-so-slightly flat) bent note.

Anyway, I thought it was sloppy and I did a disgusted dump down the fret. Mike Chapman goes "What are you doing?! Why did you stop?!" I said, "I fucked up." He goes, "No you didn't, it's great!" I said, "Well, pick it up from there, punch me in." They did and I finished up. So, taking into account that one interruption, it was basically a one-take solo. You have to understand, we recorded that album pretty much live in the studio (that might have been the only overdubbed solo), and we were pretty damn well rehearsed.

The guitar work throughout the debut album is what led me towards you guys. "That's What the Little Girls Do," "Frustrated," "Let Me Out"—it's all so well-thought out by all involved. How hard was it to craft these songs into shape?

Well, like I said, Doug was always about guitar parts in a song being organic to the song, as opposed to "here's where the guitarist starts riffing." I concurred, and was happy to oblige. One thing I always felt was a great feature in a solo was melody. I know that sounds obvious, but if you can work in a major melody, as opposed to simply rock and roll in a blues scale, you're golden. Listen to Jeff Beck on the first album, Hendrix on "May This Be Love." The first Hendrix song I ever heard was "The Wind Cries Mary," and at that tender age—before I learned to play really well—what struck me was that the solo was in a major key. It was a total game changer. So, if you listen to those songs you mention, you'll hear major key melodies, even in the rockers.

I feel the second album... but the little girls understand... was very good and never understood the criticism. "Baby Talks Dirty" has some killer riffs and chords and even though it has that similar feel to "My Sharona," I feel it stands on its own. "It's You," "I Want Ya" and the Kinks cover "The Hard Way" were all probably better choices as first single though. How did you guys feel about "Baby Talks Dirty"?

I'll be frank. I don't like this album very much. There are songs on it I think are really good, but as a whole, I like our other records better. As for "Baby Talks Dirty," Doug was really behind the song, but the three of us weren't too happy with it. I agree that another choice for first single would have been better. There were people who didn't like our band, and were poised to trash us. As hard as it was to come back strong after having such a big hit as "Sharona," releasing a song that sounded as if it was an attempt at echoing it, didn't make it any easier.

Round Trip had some gems too. "Another Lousy Day in Paradise" should've been a smash and is power pop perfection. But "Africa" has a zany solo that seems to have some jazz fusion in the mix. It's fantastic guitar work, seriously. Were parts of that solo double-tracked as well? And how did the whole band feel about this one? It's also very funky and danceable—a real departure.

I think we did much of our best work on this album. "Sweet Dreams" is quite possibly my favorite Doug Fieger song. "Another Lousy Day" was one of those songs that Doug and I cranked out sitting in a room together and bouncing ideas as they came. The riff was if I remember correctly a nod to "Pleasant Valley Sunday."

As for "Afrika" (Doug insisted on the "k" spelling), the whole band was quite happy with it. Prescott was a funkmeister who turned me on to Earth Wind and Fire, and my Fender Rhodes part on that was inspired by "Get Away." Bruce relished the opportunity of working out. Doug really dug it and channeled a bit of Jim Morrison for it. I did enjoy doing another keyboard song, as well.

As for the solo, yes it's two-part with lots of harmony and intersecting parts swooping down over each other. Doug's suggestion on this one was along the lines of "It should sound like noise, not like a guitar solo." He was kinda high at the time. I chose not to follow this stricture. I wanted to show what I could do: noise has its place, but I wanted people to listen to it more than once.

Here's a cool thing that happens in that solo you might not be aware of, because it's a bit lost in the multilayered parts. We had the great reeds player Tom Scott come in to add things and one of the ideas was to have him cop and play unison with one of my lines. It's very cool, and I remember he enjoyed it, because the quirkiness of a guitar part made for odd work on a sax, and it gave him one more tiny piece he might be able to use at a later date.

"Rocket O' Love" was a big radio hit from Serious Fun *in 1991 and then the label went under. Bummer I assume?*

Well, they had pretty much bagged on us before the label went belly up. Their big campaign to bring the record home was the ballad on it, "One Step at a Time." We kept waiting for that magic moment when they released it and gave us their big push. Never happened. I understand the record biz has a million stories very much like that.

Zoom *may have been one of your best. "Can I Borrow a Kiss" would have been a #1 hit in a just world. There's some real '60s melodies in the music as well, especially "Mister Magazine." You guys had to have been proud of this one.*

I agree. I really like this record. "Mister Magazine" is just one more great Doug Fieger song. "Can I Borrow a Kiss" had an interesting story. Doug brought me this chorus that he had written. I thought, yeah, that's a great chorus, and as a surprise to him I constructed the verses to support it. It's a story song, in that it recounts something that actually happened to Doug in his misspent youth. So when he gave me the backstory of the chorus, I wrote it for him. I was well into writing musical theatre by then, and so writing for a character came naturally to me, I think.

I know you've also done work in theater and musicals—was that as different as it sounds or were there some similarities to being in a band you could rely on?

It's very much a different field. One can write in a rock style, of course, but the demands of the craft are much more pressing. In rock, you bash out a song, and if it's good, it works, fine, you're done. In musical theatre, the needs of the story have to be served. The characters have to be served. Tone has to be consistent. The lyricist has to write in the language of the character. Most important, perhaps, a song has to *develop*, because it's replacing a segment of story. My example is this.

A rock song's verse is basically "Look at that girl." The chorus is "I really want to have her." The second verse is "Wow, just *look* at that girl!" The second chorus is "I really *really* want to have her." You get the idea. The same song as musical theatre is more like this. First A Section: "Look at that girl, I really want to have her." Second A Section: "And this is what I'm going to do to get her to want me too, because I really want to have her." B Section (bridge): "But what if I try, and she doesn't want me? Will I be able to survive that?" Third A Section: "I don't care, I want her too much, I'll risk it all. Here goes nothing!"

Final silly question I ask most players: my cats would like to know if you could rename a Knack album or song after any type of cat, what would you come up with?

At the risk of alienating you, I'm afraid it would be *"But Dogs* Understand." By the way, might I suggest that in response to that question, there is no need to rename a song for a cat. One already exists: "Siamese Twins."

*Thank you so much for getting back to me. You are an extremely gifted player and thanks for the great music. Merry Christmas and Festivus (*Seinfeld *joke if you get it; if not, never mind...).*

A Festivus for the Rest of Us! Thanks Pete!

Recommended solo: "My Sharona" from *Get the Knack* with the Knack (1979)
Further info: www.theknack.com and www.bertonaverre.com
Photo credit: Frank Zinn

CHAPTER 3

Martin Barre

(Born Martin Lancelot Barre, November 17, 1946, Kings Heath, Birmingham, West Midlands, UK)

Martin Barre has been the guitar player in Jethro Tull since December 1968. Although Jethro Tull became one of the biggest bands of the 1970s, remained a fairly big act in the 1980s, and became a steady touring machine from the 1990s on, for some unknown reason, Barre has never received the proper accolades as a guitarist. Sure, Tull fans know how damn good he is, but do enough other people know? Not really.

Barre joined Tull following the departure of original guitarist Mick Abrahams who wanted the band to be more of a pure blues outfit, something flautist/vocalist/acoustic guitarist Ian Anderson was not interested in. A battle of wills ensued and Abrahams quit despite the success of the debut album *This Was*. After Black Sabbath's Tony Iommi briefly filled in (he left not feeling comfortable in Tull and of course went on to super-stardom with Sabbath), Martin got the gig and made his live debut with the band on December 30, 1968.

Tull opened some European dates for Jimi Hendrix in 1969 and then both Vanilla Fudge and Led Zeppelin later that year—yikes. Asked to write a "hit single" by management, Anderson came up with the laid-back jazz/pop of "Living in the Past" a UK Top 3 smash (and later in 1972) a near-US Top 10 hit. The song was in 5/4 time making it an oddity, but Barre's quaint playing added to the song's delightful feel. The album *Stand Up* came out later that year, topping the UK charts and reaching the US Top 20. The searing blues/rock cut "Nothing is Easy" allowed all the members to let loose (bassist Glen Cornick and drummer Clive Bunker included) and Barre's solos are deft and puncture the sound. Other classics included the classical piece "Bouree" (originally by Bach), the Middle-Eastern flavored "Fat Man" and the downbeat blues raunch of "A New Day Yesterday."

In the year 1970, *Benefit* was another huge success and featured the awesome "To Cry You a Song," as well as the classic "Teacher" that appeared only on the US version but was a hit single in the UK and featured some memorable riffing by Barre. *Benefit* made the edges of the US Top 10 and also saw the addition of John Evan on keyboards. The band would appear at the massive *Isle of Wight Festival* late that year.

The sound expanded and with new bass player Jeffrey Hammond. With Hammond on board, Tull would issue *Aqualung* in 1971, their first Top 10 LP in the US, which sold over 3 million copies. Although Tull would go on to do even better albums, *Aqualung* was indeed a masterpiece. A semi-conceptual album (though Anderson says it is NOT prog rock), it features one great after another, most notably "Aqualung," "Locomotive Breath," "Cross Eyed Mary," "Hymn #43," and the epic "My God." While the lyrics and overall themes are brilliant, these songs simply don't exist without Barre's guitar playing. The riffs on "Aqualung" and "Locomotive Breath" alone are among the most famous in rock history. And live, these songs become monoliths.

With new drummer Barriemore Barlow, Tull expanded musically and, in 1972, poked fun at the progressive rock genre a little too well with the *Thick as a Brick* album, which was one song stretched over both sides of the album. A highly unusual US #1 album, *Thick as a Brick* is ingenious and the playing by all members is incredible. *A Passion Play* was a more baffling effort—yet another one-song concept album that made little sense to anyone, but nonetheless went to #1 in the States confirming the band's enormous stature in the rock world.

The critics were not kind to this album, and Tull responded with a song-based album in 1974 with *War Child* that hit #2 and provided one of their biggest hits in the US in the quirky "Bungle in the Jungle." The pleasant acoustic number "Skating Away (On the Thin Ice of the New Day)" was a huge radio hit as well. Overall, *War Child was* a very good album and Barre's playing is a highlight as usual. Songs such as "Back-Door Angels" and "Queen and Country" are rather unheralded.

Another Top 10 album titled *Minstrel in the Gallery* followed in 1975 and the title cut was a minor hit. This eight-minute track has some seriously violent guitar work by Barre who lets loose with a torrent of riffs and solos that many metal guitarists have copped through the years. No, this isn't heavy metal per se, but it is damn ferocious, and the playing is through the roof. The sixteen-minute piece "Baker St. Muse" is a very involved track, and there are also some lovely acoustic folk-oriented songs and more that mix hard rock and prog only as Jethro Tull could. The subsequent tour included five sold-out nights at the Forum in Los Angeles and saw David Palmer added as second keyboardist.

New bassist John Glascock appeared on the lousy 1976 album *Too Old to Rock n' Roll: Too Young to Die*, which was a letdown thematically and musically (despite the great title cut and "Crazed Institution"), but then Tull released their 1977 masterpiece *Songs from the Wood*.

One of the band's finest albums, the record perfectly marries hard rock, progressive rock, and folk. The heavy riffs of "Hunting Girl," the folk overtones of "Songs from the Wood" and "Jack in the Green," the festive Christmas song "Ring Out, Solstice Bells," and the harsh, metallic sounds of "Pibroch (Cap In Hand)" are all works of excellence. The album went Top 10 Gold and 1978's *Heavy Horses* also went Gold containing the nine-minute title track that was a spirited song and the thunderous hard rock of "No Lullaby" alongside the whimsical folk of "One Brown Mouse."

In 1979, *Stormwatch* ended the great run, and Glascock had fallen ill, which put a damper on things (he would soon pass away). David Pegg of Fairport Convention replaced him for the tour and would stay until 1995. *Stormwatch* sports brilliant guitar work from Barre and "Orion," "Old Ghosts," the forceful ten minutes of "Dark Ages" and the moving instrumental "Elegy" all show that this was a band still firing on all cylinders. After the tour however, Barlow, Evan, and Palmer were all gone.

In 1980, *A* (which started life as an Anderson solo album) was a foray towards more techno-oriented material driven with loads of synths and seriously bad white jump suits but still had great cuts like "Black Sunday." Virtuoso musician Eddie Jobson (ex-Frank Zappa, Roxy Music, UK) playing violin and keyboards and a stellar drummer in Mark Craney made this a powerful, interesting, and rather unusual lineup.

Barre was never out of ideas and 1982's *Broadsword and the Beast* (introducing new keyboards maestro Peter John-Vettese and drummer Jerry Conway) was a meeting of hard rock, prog and even some medieval themes. "Beastie," "Broadsword," and "Fallen on Hard Times" all stood out with some of the music on the heavy side, especially the ferocious "Beastie." This was to be Tull's last Top 20 album in the US and last grandiose tour complete with giant pirate ship. Arrrggghh, ye maties!

In 1984, *Under Wraps* completely lost the plot with cheesy programming and electronics and Anderson blew out his voice due to the tough keys the songs were recorded in, and the tour had to be cancelled halfway through. This album still had good songs buried beneath the electro-cheese.

A major comeback was achieved with 1987's *Crest of a Knave*, a Gold album that had classics such as the ZZ Top-styled hard rock of "Steel Monkey," the twelve minutes of genius that is "Budapest" (one of the group's finest moments), the rocker "Jump Start," the note-perfect rocker "Farm on the Freeway" (Barre lays down some creative riffs and solos) and the laid-back Dire Straits sounds of "Said She Was A Dancer." Hilariously, Tull would win a Grammy Award in the metal category. While Barre has laid down some monster riffs through the years, one would think the flute would be a dead giveaway that heavy metal did not exactly describe Tull.

Tull carried on releasing the solid *Rock Island* in 1989, the blues-based *Catfish Rising* in 1991, the Middle-Eastern influenced *Roots to Branches* in 1995 (featuring the propulsive "Dangerous Veils" with Barre's crushing guitar work on full display), and 1999's *J-Tull.com*. In 2003, the wonderful *Jethro Tull Christmas Album* was released and was to be the last studio album. A plethora of extensive deluxe edition remasters of the back catalogue have followed with 5.1 surround sound mixes by Porcupine Tree's Steven Wilson and continue to this day.

Though Tull toured extensively each and every year, they have been inactive since 2011 with Anderson focusing on a solo career and Barre doing the same. Martin has issued numerous solo albums worth inspecting such as *Stage Left* (2003), *Away with Words* (2013), and *Order of Play* (2014). Barre has also recently been playing oft-neglected Tull songs on tour with an excellent band that is a real treat for Tull diehards. It is criminal more people aren't aware of the fact that Jethro Tull are far more than just one man's musical vision. Without Martin Barre none of it would've been the same.

In February 2015, Martin was kind enough to answer my questions making this book all the better.

Who were some of the early players who influenced you when you began playing?

My dad gave me LPs of Barney Kessel, Wes Montgomery, and other jazz artists he liked when he heard I wanted to play guitar. Although I wasn't too keen on the style, it was a great introduction to music, in the days when there was little to reference to in guitar players. My first big influence was Leslie West of Mountain who we toured with in the middle 1970s. Mainly it was because they were a great band and communicated so well on stage. I learned mostly about the attitude towards music, although I loved his playing. Nowadays I enjoy people like Joe Bonamassa, Robben Ford, and the many country players who have dazzling techniques and good imagination.

What type of guitars have you preferred through the years?

I started on Gibsons until the vintage value exceeded the practicality of having them on the road. I had met and become great friends with Paul Hamer and used his guitars up to the time he left the company. I have used Ibanez, Tom Anderson Manson, and now PRS guitars. The PRS I am very happy with, they are a complete instrument tonally and 100% road friendly; tough and reliable.

The year 1969 was a huge year for you: you recorded your first single with the band, which became a smash despite an odd time signature in "Living In The Past," also had a follow-up hit in "Sweet Dream," did your first album with the band Stand Up, which still sounds fantastic and has some blazing guitar on "Nothing Is Easy" and "A New Day Yesterday." Do you have any thoughts about that whirlwind year and the Stand Up album?

The early years of Jethro Tull will always be the most precious memories. There was a naivety to the band, yet we were learning our "trade" on the fly and having wonderful times on the road. It was very exciting to be a musician in the early '70s. To think of sharing gigs with Hendrix, Zappa, Led Zeppelin, the Eagles, and many more is incredible.

Could you describe the guitar work on the song "Minstrel in the Gallery"? I still get a thrill hearing the torrent of riffs and the power of both you and Barrie Barlow on drums. This is my favorite playing of yours on a Tull song.

Minstrel was a groundbreaking album for us in the level of playing and musicality. There was still the contrast between acoustic and electric, but this time it was a great success. Barrie, John, and Jeffrey were so inventive with their contribution.

Songs from the Wood is many a Tull fan's favorite album and mine as well. Whether it's the heaviness of "Pibroch (Cap in Hand)" and "Hunting Girl" or the lighter, folksier songs like the title cut and the Christmas song "Ring Out, Solstice Bells," everything flows perfectly. Do you have fond memories of that album?

Songs from the Wood was in the era of David Palmer, who brought so much to the band in his arrangements and personality. He was a brilliant person to have in the studio. The music was challenging but very satisfying to record.

Crest of a Knave was a big comeback album and there were a lot of different styles in your playing on that one. There are so many classic songs including "Steel Monkey," "Farm on the Freeway," and "Budapest." Was that a special time for you guys after some experts had predicted the end of the band?

The absence of keyboards gave me a huge space to create music within; it was a perfect opportunity to play lots of guitar. It was an important album, as it re-instated the importance of the guitar in the music of Jethro Tull.

How crazy was it to win the hard rock/heavy metal Grammy in 1989? It's been much discussed, and great you won, but it was a bit odd, although your riffs and playing lend themselves to hard rock...

The category created by the Grammy committee was unfortunate as hard rock did not cross over into heavy metal.

  However, it was our time, and I was very proud of the award. At the end of the day, people thought we deserved something!

Your most recent solo studio album Away with Words *is beautifully produced and played. You must be pleased with the results and reaction to the album?*

Away with Words was a project I had in mind to do many years ago. It was self-indulgent and I loved recording it!

  Acoustic instruments are a very important to my writing and playing and even though it doesn't represent what the Martin Barre Band play live, I felt it was a good and worthy project. It was important to redress the balance with the live CD *Order of Play* and now we are working on recording my own songs.

A final silly question I ask most players: if you could rename a few Tull songs or albums after a cat or breed of cat what would you come up with? I've gotten some amusing answers and my cats want to know!

I have already named instrumental pieces after our cats and dogs: Murphy (the dog) and Morris Minus and Tom (the cats). Next up is "Fatcat "(the cat!!).

Recommended solo: "Minstrel in the Gallery" from *Minstrel in the Gallery* with Jethro Tull (1975)
Further Info: www.martinbarre.com
Photo credit: Martin Barre (from his personal collection)

CHAPTER 4

Jennifer Batten

(Born November 29, 1957, New York City, NY)

One of the most creative guitarists out there, regardless of genre, Jennifer Batten has accomplished more than most guitar players could have ever dreamed.

Starting to play around age eight, she became a blues and hard rock fan and was eventually able to establish an intriguing two-hand tapping technique and developed a variety of unusual sounds through various techniques and effects.

Jennifer attended the Musician's Institute (formerly known as the Guitar Institute of Technology) in the late '70s and, upon leaving school, she established herself on the session scene by 1980.

Nothing could have been huger than being selected as the lead guitarist for Michael Jackson, and in 1987, Jennifer landed that gig after being one of many who auditioned. The *Bad* tour was her first with the King of Pop and she nailed the songs, adding her own flair (and even wearing some bizarre outfits). Of course, the penultimate moment was the solo in "Beat It" each night, and despite the immense pressure and the cumbersome costume she had to wear (with mask), each and every night she pulled it off with aplomb. While there wasn't much in the way of lead guitar on certain songs, Jennifer's excellent rhythm skills allowed her to focus on other aspects of her playing. Another song she got to wail on was "Dirty Diana."

Unsure if that would ever happen again, when MJ returned to the road for the *Dangerous* album in 1992, Jennifer was thrilled to learn that yes, she would be back in the same role once more with some excellent new songs to play such as "Black or White" and "Jam." The tour lasted until late 1993 and also included a record-viewed appearance at halftime of Super Bowl XXVII between Dallas and Buffalo that was far better than the game, which was another blowout. This performance forever changed the NFL's thinking on their previously abominable halftime shows that bordered on dinner theater.

In 1996–1997, despite saying he'd never tour again, Michael took to the road all over the world, but curiously, only played two US shows; both in Hawaii. Once more, Jennifer got the call and was at her best, knowing the material like the back of her hand at this point, but working furiously hard each night in massive soccer stadiums.

Michael would not plan a tour again until 2009 and passed away less than a week before the jaunt was to begin. Though Jennifer was not to be the guitar player this time, another talented female lead guitarist in Orianthi had been selected. Batten's legacy with MJ, however, was secure.

Jennifer released a solo album in 1992 called *Above Below and Beyond* and would also issue *Momentum* in 1997 and *Whatever* in 2007. Batten also has had two music books published: *Two Hand Rock* and *The Transcribed Guitar Solos of Peter Sprague*.

So, playing with MJ was pretty damn big, yes? Well, so was playing with Rock and Roll Hall of Fame guitarist Jeff Beck! Jennifer joined Jeff's band in 1998 and played on the album *Who Else!* in 1999 and toured as part of Jeff's band that year. The album saw Jeff trying new things including techno rock and looping, and it worked surprisingly well, especially on the wild cut "What Mama Said," which Jennifer co-wrote. Other cuts such as "THX 138," "Psycho Sam" and "Brush with the Blues" were highlights and the instrumental album made the US Top 100.

In 2001, the album *You Had it Coming* was released featuring the same basic approach as the last album, and it was a damn good one. Jennifer wrote the album's massive sounding opener "Earthquake" and it is appropriately titled. Other standouts were "Nadia," "Rosebud," "Suspension," and the Grammy winner "Dirty Mind" (complete with Imogen Heap panting on it). Jennifer and Jeff had two polar-opposite styles, yet two very alike minds. Somehow this worked incredibly well and led to some raucous live shows. After another tour, Jennifer would move on.

She has continued to play live on her own and has also done tribute shows to the music of Michael Jackson. Jennifer will always be remembered for her work with both Michael Jackson and Jeff Beck, but will also be fondly thought of when it comes to groundbreaking guitarists and what she has done for females around the world: no longer staying in the shadows, willing to break new ground as guitar players. Much respect is due.

In January 2015, Jennifer was kind enough to answer in detail a number of questions I had, especially the fact that she got to work for so long with one of the biggest musical legends of our time…

Who were some of your main influences as you began really getting into the instrument?

I started playing guitar when I was eight years old, so at that time my influences were the Beatles and The Monkees. When I reached my teenage years, I really got into the blues. I would take almost all of my allowance that was supposed to be for many different things, and spend it almost all on blues records. I would go down to the basement of a local store that had the cheap albums called cut-outs. Any album that had a gash in the cardboard was very cheap. I picked up records by BB King, John Lee Hooker, Sonny Terry, and Brownie McGee. That was a fantastic education for several years. Then, when I discovered Jeff Beck, it was all over. He became and still is my favorite guitar player. Little did I know when I was a teenager that I would end up in his band!

At that time his biggest selling record *Blow by Blow* was playing on the radio. Many years later, after I graduated from the Guitar Institute of Technology, I memorized all of his guitar solos on that record and his following record called *Wired*. I went through plenty of different phases with music as I grew older, but Jeff was always a constant. When I was going to guitar school the big guitar players at that time were Larry Carlton, Lee Ritenour, Al Di Meola, and George Benson. I was extremely interested in jazz in that time period. I spent a lot of time listening to Joe Pass and Wes Montgomery. Jaco Pastorius' debut record came out at that time as well, and I became a huge fan of Weather Report.

For a long time after school was out, I stayed interested in jazz and fusion guitar players and added Steve Morse to my favorites list. Eventually I got more interested in mainstream rock 'n' roll with Van Halen and George Lynch of Dokken.

What have been your preferred guitars through the years live and in the studio?

In my teenage years I was buying a Les Paul through my allowance my father was giving me. It took many years to pay that off! But as everyone knows, it's a very heavy guitar, so it's really not practical to have around your neck for too many hours at a time. When I went to the guitar school I got a Gibson Birdland jazz guitar, and when I had to send it back to Gibson because of a bad neck, I used my father's L4 Gibson for the duration of the school year.

Within the next few years following the school, I bought a couple of Stratocasters, and I used those for many years. I also had a 335 at one time. I think it's good to check out a lot of different guitars to see what really resonates with you. When I got the tour with Michael Jackson, I signed on with Ibanez and played their very lightweight, thin body guitars. I stayed with that company for seven years and experienced seven different guitars with bad necks. So, after one of the builders told me I just had bad luck with necks, I decided to jump ship and join on with Washburn. I stayed with them for about fifteen years, until Line 6 came out with the James Tyler Variax guitars.

These guitars have the highest technology electronics available. There are probably at least fifty virtual guitar models you can have access to, and they sound really good. So for instance, you can kick in the Stratocaster mode and the five way pickup selector will give you all great Stratocaster sounds. You can also access Telecaster sounds, Rickenbacker, jazz guitars and even acoustic models within the same guitar. One of the main reasons I was interested in that guitar was the acoustic models, plus there is a dial where you can instantly change tunings because it's all virtual. They also have computer software so you can essentially customize each of your guitar models should you choose to. But, I really customize the physical portion of that guitar and did a lot of experimenting to make it comfortable for me. Currently, I'm headed back to Washburn, but I have asked them to take electronics out of my Line 6 guitar and insert it into the new guitar they are building me.

One thing I've noticed when I've heard you tackle well-known songs is how amazingly you make the vocal melodies come through the guitar and you don't even stick to it note for note, yet the song is still recognizable. Two of my favorites I've seen you do are "Smells Like Teen Spirit" and "Wanna Be Startin' Somethin'." Arranging is something you must take pride in—how did you come up with the idea for the Nirvana song?

I have been doing a solo film show for many years now. I wanted to be able to do a low-maintenance kind of gig where I was not in charge of a bunch of other players. So I came up with the idea of making films for all of my songs and playing along with them in sync. I only have three CDs out and have made films for just about all of the songs, and I get sick of playing them all the time. So, I started adding cover songs and noticed that people really react favorably when it's a big hit song that I'm covering that they recognize.

My own music is a lot more esoteric. I have chosen a wide variety of songs to cover because I am aware that as a solo act, you really need to pull out all the stops to keep an audience engaged for ninety minutes. So, not only have I done some Michael Jackson medleys over the years but I wanted to add songs that people would not expect from me. At the time Nirvana was big I really wasn't much of a fan, but all these years later having heard those songs so many times on the radio, it kind of makes you nostalgic. So I decided to take a stab at "Teen Spirit" and really enjoyed the challenge of covering the melody. It can be extremely challenging covering a song like that, which was done by a vocalist. The melody is very simple but to just play the notes is not enough. If you listen to how it is sung and phrased, it is very lazy and almost drunk sounding, so I tried to choose a vocal sound as well as use my tremolo bar to manipulate the sounds to sound as vocal as is possible on a guitar. The thing I really like about Nirvana in general, is the use of dynamics where the verse is very quiet in the chorus comes in like a machete.

A new song that I have added to my films show is the Britney Spears tune "Oops! I Did It Again." I mainly chose that because of the video I was making for it. It just came to me one night how funny the title of the song is. Everybody knows that title but may not know the rest of the lyrics. So I got the idea to use clips from YouTube of people falling on stage every time it got to the "Oops" chorus. I chose that song just because of that visual connection. I really enjoy looking at the audience's faces when the choruses come up. I think it's very important to learn how the singer sang each phrase exactly, which can be very time-consuming to get all the detail of what they do. And then I can add my own creativity and change it up a bit from night to night.

Landing the Michael Jackson gig in 1987 for the Bad tour was beyond massive. How were you told you got the gig?

The funny thing about that question is I was never actually told I got the gig!

When I got the call to do it after I had auditioned, I was told to come down and then rehearsed with the band to see how it went. Week after week I would go to rehearsal all day but it was never confirmed that I was good to go. Eventually I got a passport processed and a ticket to Tokyo, so I thought things were looking pretty good. I was told they auditioned about 100 people so I feel very, very lucky that I was chosen. All these years later, I was recently shown my audition video as well as a paper that was with it where Michael was making notes on people. He put two stars next to my name and the word GREAT capital letters. It was so cool to get access to that after all these years.

Can you even accurately describe what that first gig was like (I think it may have been at the Tokyo Dome?) if possible?

No, it wasn't at the Tokyo Dome because that building had not been completed yet in 1987. It was another Tokyo stadium. I remember being very nervous during the day, but it was only fear of the unknown. Honestly, we had rehearsed so much that when we hit the stage I am glad to report, that it was just second nature and we just had fun.

I must admit, I loved the outlandish outfit you wore on that tour—it looked like a Mexican wrestler and an ancient spirit! Did you have any say in that, and how in the world did you play with that thing on?

I had a lot of different costumes over the ten-year period I was with Michael. Some of them were very challenging to perform in. On one tour I had three- or four-foot Viking horns on my head. They also tried attaching a dragon to my back. It was so heavy I felt like my back was going to break. And people said I did not look happy when I was wearing it, so that didn't last very long thankfully. On the last tour I really had to have the perspective that it was more of a theater production than anything else. I wore what was essentially an S&M mask of leather with a leather strap under my chin and another across my nose. The only good thing about that ghastly costume was that there was a wig attached to it.

Prior to that costume, I would have to spend two-and-one-half hours in the makeup room getting my hair done up for that outrageous blonde Amazon look. Yes, I did have a little bit of say about my costumes. For instance, I was asked in the beginning how I felt about wearing high heels. I don't like them one bit, and the costumers were very accommodating and made me flat boots instead. But, aside from little details like that, I did not want to complain about a thing because it was all part of Michael's vision in creating a spectacular show to wow the audience. I was just glad to be there.

Although I'm sure it's been asked, how did you approach the solo on "Beat It"? It's so revered and so famous that it was important not to stray too far, but you still managed to add your own inflections in there. Also, what were among your favorite songs to play guitar on through the tours?

I think that solo is one of the greatest solos of the '80s for sure. Anything I did that strayed from the original was not intentional. It's a difficult solo to get every nuance out every night. One of the challenges I had was that we tuned down to a low C, two whole steps below the recorded key. So, I had really heavy strings to accommodate for being detuned that far. Not only that, but we played the song much faster than Eddie had actually recorded it. In my opinion the speed kind of sucked the life out of that solo but I did what I could with it. If the song had been recorded as fast as we played it live I guarantee that he would have played a different solo.

I think quite a few people don't realize just how musical Michael was, and how talented. How would you describe the musical side of Michael that you saw?

Michael was an all-around creative being. He was just one of those rare humans that got way more than his fair share of talent. There will never be another guy who was so good at so many different aspects of creativity. His music was just a foundation for all of his other creativity, which included dance and detailed visions for every aspect of his shows and videos. People often ask how involved he was with writing music. As far as I know, aside from maybe dabbling with various instruments he didn't really play any. So to compensate, he did everything with his voice. He could beat box drums on a demo, and then layer the rest of the parts from the bass to the harmonies to the main melody on top of that beatbox. He would then hire musicians to replace his voice with real instruments. You can hear an example of his beat boxing in the song "Stranger in Moscow."

On the Dangerous and HIStory world tours, were you able to inject more of your own playing in there by that point or was it fairly strict? You also got to play with amazing musicians on each tour—even Sheryl Crow on the Bad tour. Bubbles never came on stage did he?

Bubbles never came on stage during a show but most likely did at a few rehearsals. He was brought to Japan and I saw him backstage quite a bit. He was also brought on a little bit of the American tour along with his trainer.

Yes, it was such a blessing to play with musicians of that quality. Greg Phillinganes was the musical director [*an amazing keyboardist, Greg would go on to long stints with Eric Clapton and Toto*] and was just one of those guys who were born talented. His mother told me that he was picking songs off the radio when he was four years old. And being able to play with Ricky Lawson really enhanced my sense of groove over that first year and a half. We were all very lucky to have each other and kept in touch many years after the tour was done. Sadly, the last time we all got together was for a memorial for Ricky Lawson who passed away around Christmastime 2013. Prior to that, we had all gotten together for a private viewing of the DVD that was released for the 25th anniversary of *Bad*. Looking back, I am so thankful that we were able to do that. I think we all realized that we were blessed to be a part of such a huge chunk of musical history.

I saw you in Philly in 1999 when you were with Jeff Beck. How did that come about and do you have fond memories of that era which included two albums and tours? I loved your tradeoffs with Jeff on "Blue Wind"; that was killer!

Playing in Jeff Beck's band was not a dream I ever had. My goal when I went on the second Michael Jackson tour was to meet Jeff and get an autograph. That was it. I didn't meet him on that tour and I got to go into the studio where he was recording his rockabilly album. It was very exciting to be in his presence as he had been the ultimate guitar hero since I was a teenager, and I had spent so many hours learning his solos.

When I met him, my first record had just been released. I had also just been given a couple copies of a video from a piece I did for London MTV where I was playing "Flight of the Bumblebee." So, when I met him I gave him my newly released CD as well as a copy of that video.

I got my autograph and soon went on my way thinking I would probably never see him again. But, a couple months later he called me up and said he had finally gotten a chance to listen to my CD and he wanted to record a CD with me. I was shell-shocked from that conversation for quite a while. As it turned out, it was actually five years before we joined forces. He called me up to come play a short tour in Italy. My time with him lasted three years and two CDs. It was an amazing education in many ways, because he said a good portion of what I would do was trigger guitar synthesizer sounds. So I had to be a geek and learn how to program immediately. It was also very enlightening just hanging out with him for hours on the bus and hearing his perspective and his thoughts about music. He's just one of those guys who never sits still and wants to always explore. He listens to everything and never wants to repeat himself. He said there was no reason to record a new album unless there was something very new to be said.

Your solo album has a song called "Ass Whoopin'" that is a killer. It actually reminds me of Jeff Beck, and take that as a compliment! Will there be anything new on the horizon from you?

Thanks. Most of the songs on my *Whatever* CD were written during my stay with Jeff. He always wants new material so I spent all of my free time writing for him. Basically, whatever didn't end up on his album ended up as *Whatever*. I am currently spending all of my time either working on instructional DVDs for truefire.com, or working on arrangements and charting out songs for live two hours.

The whole thing with the digital age and how everybody can steal your music with no repercussions makes it completely impossible for me to afford to record another record. That's not to say that it won't happen at some point, but the idea of spending $10,000 or $20,000 to put new music online as a "gift" for people doesn't fly with me. I suppose also in the not-too-distant future that there will be holograms of us all that we can send off to different stages while we stay home in our slippers.

Another thing I am working on, which I hope to launch this summer, is touring a crash course for the millennial musician. It will be a very intense four hours jam-packed with information and demos that will help people become self-empowered in navigating their lives as creative people. There is a lot more to being a musician than making CDs.

Last silly question I ask most everyone: if you could rename an MJ or Jeff Beck song with a cat theme what would you come up with? My cats are curious.

How about "Brush with the Mews"

Recommended solo: "Ass Whoopin'" from *Whatever* solo album (2007) and "Beat It" live with Michael Jackson
Further info: www.jenniferbatten.com
Photo credit: Brent Angelo
Jennifer was placed in the *Guitar Player Magazine* Hall of Fame in November 2015 and in 2016 is touring with guitar legends Uli Jon Roth (also in this book) and Andy Timmons on the *Ultimate Guitar Experience Tour*.

CHAPTER 5

Eric Bazilian

(Born July 21, 1953, Philadelphia, PA)

Eric Bazilian has been playing guitar since he was nine years old. To say the least, he got pretty damn good at it.

Also adept at playing mandolin, piano, his first instrument at age five, Bazilian is plenty accomplished musically. While attending the University of Pennsylvania (and earning a BA in physics) he formed his first significant band called Baby Grand with keyboard-playing friend Rob Hyman and vocalist David Kagan, produced by pal Rick Chertoff. Baby Grand landed a major label deal with Arista Records and issued two albums to little notice, though both deserved a better fate. The excellent song "Never Enough" from the first Baby Grand album would later be covered by Patty Smyth and became a hit in 1987. It's an early example of the distinctive writing that has spanned a glorious career for Bazilian.

After Baby Grand folded, Bazilian and Hyman formed the Hooters in Philadelphia in 1980, a musical act that would encompass new wave, reggae, ska, pop, folk, and rock to wonderful effect. The Hooters built up a rabid following as the Philly new wave scene of the early '80s was bursting with talent and many bands wound up getting signed by major labels.

In 1983, after years of incessant gigging, the indie label Antenna Records issued the band's debut mini-album *Amore*. By the time of *Amore*, the band's lineup was Bazilian, Hyman, guitarist John Lilley, bassist Rob Miller, and drummer David Uosikkinen. Miller would be replaced by Andy King in 1984, with Fran Smith Jr. taking over in 1987.

Many of the tracks from *Amore* became local smashes on Philly rock radio stations and eventually major labels took notice; Columbia signed the band issuing the debut album *Nervous Night* in spring 1985. The album sold over 2 million copies in the US and produced four hit singles beginning with the ingenious "All You Zombies," a tune reworked from the *Amore* album. The song involved reggae, pop, and rock with highly intelligent lyrics and a truly outstanding guitar solo from Bazilian that involved some tasty slide work. The moody solo perfectly accented the music.

"Zombies" became a hit single and MTV favorite and was followed by the huge pop hits "And We Danced" (#21), "Day by Day" (#18) (which featured a very speedy, tricky run at the end of its solo) and "Where Do the Children Go" (reaching #38 with a guest vocal by Patty Smyth). The title track, "South Ferry Road" and the infectious "Hanging on a Heartbeat" were among the other excellent songs.

The Hooters played some of the biggest gigs any band in the world could have dreamed of, appearing at *Live Aid* on July 13, 1985, in their native Philadelphia at JFK Stadium (the same site where, as an unsigned band, they got to perform on a bill headlined by the Who with Santana and the Clash on September 25, 1982) as well as the *America Rocks* concert in New Orleans, Louisiana, to commemorate the restoration of the Statue of Liberty and Ellis Island and the major *Conspiracy of Hope Concert* for

Amnesty International on June 15, 1986, in East Rutherford, New Jersey, which saw their set include a truly mesmerizing rendition of the Beatles classic "Lucy in the Sky with Diamonds" rearranged on mandolin and synthesizers. Not only that, they also performed at ex-Pink Floyd bassist/vocalist Roger Waters's first solo presentation of *The Wall* on July 21, 1990, which also happened to be Bazilian's birthday.

They also played at MTV's New Year's Eve concert in 1985, at the MTV Video Music Awards in 1986, and were named Best New Band of the Year by *Billboard Magazine*.

The Hooters' 1987 album *One Way Home* went Gold and produced further hits in the dark "Johnny B," and the clever, infectious TV evangelist-bashing "Satellite" as well as the Celtic/folk workout "Karla with a K," perhaps the band's finest hour, and an example of their amazing compositional skills. Again, the musicianship here was extraordinary. "Fightin' on the Same Side" and two six-minute cuts in "Graveyard Waltz" and the title song were other highlights. The band would also headline a show at the Spectrum in Philly aired live as it happened on MTV on Thanksgiving Night in 1987.

The year 1989 saw the release of *Zig Zag*, a tragically unrecognized album that failed to achieve the sales of previous records, stalling outside the Top 100. Nonetheless, the folk tune "500 Miles" became a worldwide hit and "Brother, Don't You Walk Away" also scored airplay along with the ode to Philly "Beat up Guitar." The deal with Columbia ended in 1990, but the band had a great run and Bazilian's guitar playing on the first three Hooters albums is way beyond what the average pop or rock band was doing in the mid to late '80s.

With Mindy Jostin added on violin and guitar and a new deal with MCA, the band issued *Out of Body* in 1993. Though the album sold poorly in the States, it did well worldwide where they began focusing their touring. The energetic "Twenty-Five Hours a Day" was the album's best known song and "Private Emotion" would later become a hit for Ricky Martin (!). The Hooters called a time-out in 1995.

Bazilian not only released two fine solo albums in *The Optimist* (2000) and *A Very Dull Boy* (2002), but became one of the most sought-after writers in the business. Eric penned and produced Joan Osborne's 1996 Top 10 smash "One of Us," which was also nominated for a Grammy. He has also written for (among many others) Bon Jovi, Journey, Robbie Williams, Patty Smyth, the Calling, Cyndi Lauper, Scorpions, and Billy Idol.

The Hooters reunited in 2001 for a one-off show at the Spectrum in Philly with the same lineup as had gone on hiatus in 1995 (minus Jostin), but made the reunion permanent in 2003, and the following year they were presented with a Lifetime Achievement Award from the Philadelphia Music Awards.

A new studio album *Time Stand Still* was issued in 2007 featuring the live favorite "I'm Alive" as well as a sterling mandolin-soaked adaptation of Don Henley's "The Boys of Summer," which has been a much-deserved fixture at concerts ever since. Tommy Williams was added to the lineup in 2010 adding further guitar and mandolin, and the band sounds every bit as good as before in 2014 vocally and musically.

Eric Bazilian is a wonderful musician because he understands what goes where and why. His skills as a writer/arranger/vocalist and instrumentalist call out for notice and accolades. It remains a pleasure to hear a true guitar player in every sense of the word such as Eric. Is it any wonder why so many big name musicians continue to seek Eric out because of his musical ability and writing? Nope!

In September of 2014, I was able to spend a good amount of time chatting to one of Philadelphia's greatest representatives in music:

Who were some of the people that inspired you at the start when you wanted to play guitar?

Here's the deal: I was one of those kids who was ten years old when the Beatles played the *Ed Sullivan Show* and I had already started playing guitar when I was eight or nine years old. So, I was already playing a bit when I saw the Beatles and that was all she wrote. George (Harrison) was the "it" guitar player, although I came to appreciate what a genius John Lennon was just in how he played that riff in "I Feel Fine" where he picked up his pinky and then the 7th was played on the D string. I then moved on to the Kinks with Dave Davies and his groundbreaking solo on "You Really Got Me," and of course the Stones with both Brian Jones and Keith Richards. Then the floodgates really opened with what I call the "holy trinity" of Jeff Beck, Hendrix, and Clapton. In the late '60s it just broke wide open with the blues thing and also Mike Bloomfield—the first blues guitar solo I ever figured out was "Blues In Chicago." And, I cannot underestimate the effect that Roger McGuinn had on me with the Byrds.

That's funny because I was going to ask later on if the Byrds were any kind of an influence on the Hooters, or yourself.

They were huge! In fact, I got my first Rickenbacker 12-string June 25, 1966. I got a blonde one instead of a sunburst because I was just a little bit more into Roger—although he was still Jim at that time—McGuinn then George Harrison at that time. McGuinn: no one played the 12-string like that, then or since. The Mike Campbells and Peter Bucks of the world, they do a variation of that, but there was a finesse that he had and a fire that no one else has ever had on that instrument. Ya know, "8 Miles High," "Why," "I See You," I mean I saw him perform those songs numerous times—up close, front row, real personal—my eyes saw what he was doing, but my brain couldn't register it.

He had such an influence on me and Rickenbackers in general—in fact, I'm looking at my rack o' Ricks right now. I have three 12-strings from 1966.

On that note, what is your guitar of choice?

Up until the past year it's been a '56 Les Paul Goldtop. I got my first one in 1967 right when Les Pauls were starting to emerge on the popular scene. Mike Bloomfield was playing one, Clapton was a big one and Todd Rundgren in his band at the time Woody's Truck Stop—he got his first one. And a friend of mine from Philly Nick Jameson who produced and played in Foghat also got one around that time.

By chance, I was walking to school one day and there's this old guy who's probably about thirty (old to me then) carrying a Les Paul without a case. I said, "Excuse me sir, is that a Les Paul?" and he said, "No son, it's a Gibson." Now, the '55 and '56 Les Pauls are notorious because the decals on them faded quickly, so he didn't know what he had. You really had to squint to see the Les Paul decal. As far as he was concerned, it was just a Gibson. So I bought it from him for $150. And that very guitar was my go-to until January of 1976.

I was in a van going to a studio in Montreal to make my first album with Baby Grand and we were in an accident. They towed the van and I grabbed the first two guitars I could before they took us to the hospital because I did not trust that situation. The two guitars I happened to grab were my Rickenbacker 12-string and my Martin. We didn't see the van again until much later and my Les Paul and my Strat were gone.

I knew that story was going to have a heartbreaking ending!

Yeah, it was heartbreaking. I found another Les Paul a few months later—a mint '55 at House of Guitars in Rochester, NY. I paid what I thought was a fortune at the time for it. I never liked it and it never felt quite right to me. Maybe it was too clean, maybe it was because it was an early '55 and it didn't have a Tune-O-Matic bridge, but for whatever reason, I never used it, so I ended up selling it in the early '80s. Then, in 1991, I was at House of Guitars in LA and they had just gotten in a '56; they opened the case and I said, "That's mine!"

And you've had it ever since?

Yeah, it was a separated-at-birth twin—it wasn't the same guitar as the other one, but it had a dark back which was very rare for the '50s. If I had to have one guitar, this would be it. It's just exquisite. Although live my guitar choice is a Les Paul Junior and I play those in concert with the Hooters. I like a one pickup guitar.

Did you use that this summer? I saw you guys in Philly in June and thought I saw you playing one.

Yes I did. I have three of them: a '58, a '59, and a '60.

It has such a nice, rich sound—I love those.

Yeah, they're great. Live I like it better because the volume control is right by my pinky and I tend to use volume control a lot. And I only use a bridge pickup in general. I must say…there is a '52 Telecaster that has been living here at my studio and that's sort of become a go-to as well. My standard line is I make a Les Paul sound like a Tele and a Tele sound like shit! I've never been much of a Tele guy, but I like this one. It's magic. A friend of mine left it here because he didn't want to bring it to his place in New York and I've now had it for seven or eight years. I don't mind playing valued guitars live—I mean why own it if you're not going to use it? That being said, there are some I'll never use live or even take out of the case! [Laughs]

Could you describe the solo on "All You Zombies"? I know that's one of your most famous songs, but it's very distinctive, especially with the slide and some of the runs that you use. Do you remember how you came up with it?

That's funny, because I have a very clear visual memory of that. I cut that solo at Studio Four in Philadelphia. I played Paul Junior on that—the same one you saw me play in June this year. I was mostly using an AC-30 amp for solos on *Nervous Night*, but I plugged into my Marshall and it was a pretty clean sound if I recall and everybody's ears in the control room kind of perked up, and that was a one-take solo.

That solo was only one take?

Yep. It was a little on the Joe Walsh side. Some other solos were only one or two takes on that album. "Day by Day" was the same thing.

That's another great one, especially the speedy run at the end there that you do.

[Laughs] Yeah, that was real fancy! That Les Paul Junior is the only guitar on that *Nervous Night* album.

Just the one guitar for the whole album?

I did one overdub with a Telecaster on "And We Danced" on a 16th note delay but otherwise, every guitar on that record is a Les Paul Junior.

Once "All You Zombies" hit MTV around May 1985 I was so thrilled to see a band I considered mine getting all that play nationally. Were you aware of the impact it was having or were you just doing the videos and then too busy with touring and recording to notice? I'm guessing you had to have known.

MTV? Absolutely! That year, both *Live Aid* and MTV were very key to our success.

And the video for "Satellite" got heavy play in '87 and caused a bit of controversy, but I don't think people got what you were saying there.

I don't think WE got what we were saying! [Laughs]

That is my favorite song of yours and it broke you briefly in the UK where it went Top 25.

Thanks for saying that about the song! And yes, that was our brief fifteen minutes in England.

Why was it that song that hit there when you had hits all around the world?

I do not know; I don't get it. We even played *Top of the Pops* with Paul McCartney!

And then One Way Home *did well here. I see no shame in a Gold album, but obviously it wasn't the 2 million of* Nervous Night.

They took back our Gold album on *One Way Home*!

What? Can they do that?

They did—they took it back, because after the returns it did not quite go Gold.

[Laughs] I'm always speechless at the record industry.

But *Nervous Night* did indeed go Double Platinum.

Yes it did and One Way Home *went Gold but not Gold!*

Yes, an honor-Gold but not Gold. Faux Gold!

Then there was Zig Zag, *which I thought was as good as the others but didn't sell so hot, and I was worried the label would panic and drop you guys.*

That's the album that really got us going in Scandinavia, where we remain big. It all started with *One Way Home*—more in Germany and a little in Scandinavia. In fact, "Johnny B" was a huge hit in Germany and "500 Miles" in Scandinavia.

Did you feel "Johnny B" was a little too dark as a first single from the album in the US?

Yes I did, I would've gone for "Satellite" first, personally, although my favorite on that album remains "Karla with a K."

That is such a wonderful, wonderful song. As the third single, it seemed as though there wasn't proper support.

Yeah, the label pulled the plug on that one. I think it was a mistake doing a live video for that one, too.

Wasn't that from the MTV concert on Thanksgiving here in Philly?

Yeah, and I think in itself that was ill-advised. We weren't ready to headline an arena show at that point. The band was ready, but our production wasn't. We were using the same stage that we'd been using in theaters and it didn't fill that stage at the Spectrum.

I wanted to ask you about Live Aid. What an amazing, head-spinning experience that must've been?

It was surreal, I'll tell ya that. By the time we started, it was finished.

It was around ten minutes or so.

Ten minutes that shook our world!

And you made Philly proud.

And then Sir Bob left us off of the DVD!

Yeah, some artists were not on there like Santana, Rick Springfield, and Led Zeppelin. Was this by choice for you guys or by exclusion?

Not our choice—it was his choice. The legendary thing he said when he saw the lineup for Philly was, "Who the fuck are the Hooters?"

Yes, I recall that idiotic quote.

The week that the *Live Aid* DVD came out (in November 2004) Bob Geldolf actually opened for us in Germany.

Oh, the irony! I love it.

His demeanor was sheepish shall we say. We were very polite to him.

Did he know who you were?

Oh yeah! He was opening for us.

The Amnesty International concert show from June 1986 was another massive event you were involved in. MTV showed the entire twelve-hour concert and your whole thirty-minutes set, though only two are on the DVD. You did a stunning re-arrangement of "Lucy in the Sky with Diamonds" that was well worth me being late for a barbecue that day! It showed all of your diversity and talent.

Oh, thanks so much. That went over very well but I was barely on camera!

And, let's not forget another biggie when the Hooters played Roger Waters' The Wall *concert in Germany in 1990...*

Oh yeah! We first met Roger around 1988 when we played London at the Town & Country Club and I was hanging at the stage after the show talking to some people and our tour manager came up to me and said, "Eric, you better come upstairs to the bar." I said, "Okay, give me a few minutes," and he said, "No. You really want to come up now." I get upstairs and there's Roger Waters extending his hand for a shake and he says, "Hi Eric, I'm your fan"!

Then a week before *The Wall* concert we're touring Japan and we get a call from Roger asking if we'd play the show in Berlin.

On that short of a notice?

On that short of a notice. We got on a plane and flew over for that one day. He initially wanted us to do a set before the show. It was to be us, Ronnie Hawkins and the Hawks, and the Chieftains. How's that for eclectic?

Makes sense in a way because some of you guys helped The Band cover "Atlantic City" by Springsteen on their album Jericho.

Yeah, that came out great and we [the Hooters] just played that in Atlantic City! Anyway, Roger was a sweet man and he ended up asking us to do "Mother" as part of *The Wall* with Levon Helm from The Band and Sinead O' Connor. He also gave us a part in the opening of the show and at the end he had us go up to the top of the scaffolds. We were on one scaffold and the Scorpions were on another and fireworks started going off and it was actually my birthday, so what a birthday that was!

And there's another connection; you have written with The Scorpions for years now, which would surprise many people.

Yes I have; three albums now. In 2003, for whatever reason they contacted me and I flew out for a week and we really hit it off and kept going.

The last few albums that you've worked on with the band have seen them refocus on who they were, especially Sting in the Tail.

I agree, but there was that album *Humanity-Hour 1*.

I actually liked that album!

I did too, but Desmond Child had that whole concept thing, which was brilliant, but the idea didn't catch on.

Being a part of that amazing '80s new wave scene in Philly with The A's, Robert Hazard and the Heroes, Beru Revue, Tommy Conwell & the Young Rumblers, and so on—that had to have been fun.

I wish I had appreciated it more then, but we are all so caught up in it. It was like Liverpool in the '60s. So much was happening and we were working so hard.

It will never happen again.

No, it won't. It's safe to say that can't happen again—probably anywhere. It was another time. That's just the way it is now in the industry.

I always thought the song we talked about earlier "Karla with a K" sounded like a mix of Cajun and Celtic, and I love the mandolin that lends so much.

I truly enjoy mandolin and you are very accurate on that description and I have no idea how we came up with that mix. The instrumental part of that has been used as a beer commercial in the UK. We played an anniversary show in the 2000s for WMMR-FM in Philly and Jethro Tull were also on the bill and when we started playing that song, Ian Anderson came rushing out and said, "Oh my God what is that song? My wife loves that!"

Has Don Henley ever commented on your version of "The Boys of Summer"?

Apparently it's his favorite cover.

It should be—it's fantastic. I'm so happy I got to talk to you and it was a real pleasure.

You know what's ironic? Some of my best guitar work isn't on any Hooters albums.

On your solo albums then?

You know I have solo albums?

Yes, you have two.

Well played then! [Laughs]

I thank you. One final moronic question: my cats want to know if you could rename a Hooters song or album after a cat what would it be?

Let's see…*Nervous Cat*…no…*One Way Cat*…no…

I think I have one!

Whaddya got?

"Kitty with A K"?

Hey—that's pretty good.

I'll say you came up with it.

What about *Cat Stand Still*?

That's pretty bad.

You're right [laughs]. Oh—you know a solo I really like? The one on "I'm Alive" from *Time Stand Still*.

That's a dynamite solo—fits the song.

I wrote the bulk of that song one day in Sweden in the summer of 2005 and the lead vocal and guitar solo were done that day from the demo. I'm a firm believer in keeping everything—there's a reason why.

Such a great set opener too.

Live we still kick ass. The band is more on fire than ever before.

Recommended solo: "All You Zombies" from *Nervous Night* with the Hooters (1985)
Further info: www.ericbazilian.com and www.hootersmusic.com
Photo credit: Heiko Roth/Rock and Royalty

CHAPTER 6

Eric Bell
(Born September 3, 1947, East Belfast, Northern Ireland)

Eric Bell is an Irish guitarist of the utmost class. Getting his professional start in the late '60s he briefly played with Them at the end of Van Morrison's time with that group and also played with several other acts, including Shades of Blue, before landing in the lucrative (but creatively stifling) Irish showband circuit with The Dreams.

Everything changed in 1969, when bassist/vocalist Phil Lynott and drummer Brian Downey needed a guitar player for the new band they were forming in Dublin, Ireland. Bell liked what they said and, along with keyboardist Eric Wrixon, joined the original lineup. It was Bell who came up with the band name Thin Lizzy, altering it from a robot named Tin Lizzie in the comic book *The Dandy*.

By 1970, the band issued their first single "The Farmer" to little notice. The single was in a very limited pressing and the murky production didn't help. The b-side "I Need You" was a better song but the band was clearly just getting started.

Wrixon was deemed expendable and the remaining trio carried on ferrying into London for more visibility and better paying gigs. A meeting with influential BBC DJ John Peel was pivotal and Peel helped the band on their way. A deal with Decca Records followed after hard work in the clubs. Neither the debut album *Thin Lizzy* or the EP *New Day* (both 1971) made an impact, and the musical direction was muddled. One listen to the guitar work, however, and you knew there was something special there. "Ray Gun" is one of the few rock songs on the album and Bell lets his guitar do the talking.

In 1972, *Shades of a Blue Orphanage* flopped and, again, the direction of the band was unclear: folk, Celtic, hard rock, blues, etc. Yet, a song such as "Brought Down" was so good and the guitar playing supreme, that you wondered, what were they exactly? Who was Thin Lizzy? What style of music did they really want to play and play best? Well, music fans found out in November 1972 with the non-album single "Whisky in the Jar" where everything changed. A guitar-heavy adaptation of a traditional Irish folk song, "Whisky" topped the Irish charts and became a worldwide smash, also reaching the UK Top 10. The song came about from rehearsals and wasn't anything they thought too seriously about at first.

Suddenly the band were on *Top of the Pops,* but they weren't thrilled that it was with something they'd considered more of a lark than anything else. Truth be told, it's pretty damn brilliant. Bell's guitar work is exemplary and the intro alone is steeped in a fusion of folk, Celtic, and rock and worked all angles to perfection. His piercing solo achieves a perfect sense of place and tone. Throw in Lynott's ever-developing bass work, his distinctive vocals, and Downey's astonishing drumming, and it's clear that this was no throwaway.

The band's follow-up single "Randolph's Tango" sadly failed to capitalize on the success, despite being an inventive, charming gem from Lynott's pen. The guitar solo is a thing of beauty, deftly played. Bell adds in a Spanish-flavored solo that seems to get better with each note, taking the listener to exhilarating heights. There are quick runs, beautifully picked single notes and strumming that is a mixture of different flavors. It's baffling that this song was only a hit in Ireland where it made the Top 15 as it is an example of the brilliance of Lynott's charismatic writing and Bell and Downey's playing.

The year 1973 also saw the issue of *Vagabonds of the Western World* by far and away the best of the Bell era Lizzy albums where the band finally saw things coalesce. Hard rock and blues rule the day here on great material such as the title cut, "The Rocker" (check out this solo which also has some great use of vibrato), "Gonna Creep Up on You," "Little Girl in Bloom" (once again check out the haunting vibrato) and "Slow Blues" where Bell really lets loose with some vicious playing.

Yet again, however, the album failed to find an audience and coupled with troubles with life on the road, frustration over the band's career, musical differences, and in desperate need of a break, Bell left the band in January 1974 (after an incident that occurred during the band's New Year's Eve show in Belfast, Northern Ireland).

After clearing his head, he formed the Eric Bell Band for a short while before joining the Noel Redding Band (led by ex-Jimi Hendrix Experience bassist Redding) for several albums. He also reactivated his own band and played in the '80s with Mainsqueeze who toured extensively in Europe and backed up Bo Diddley on the live album *Hey...Bo Diddley in Concert* in 1986.

There was also a brief reunion of the original Lizzy lineup of Lynott, Downey, and Bell for the raucous "Song for Jimi" released as a flexi-single in 1981 where the old fire and chemistry were evident. It felt loose and alive and all three members went for broke and just jammed in honor of the late Jimi Hendrix.

Bell (along with ex-Lizzy guitarists Gary Moore, Brian Robertson, and Snowy White) guested with Thin Lizzy on their 1983 farewell tour and appears on the double-live album from that tour *Life* in 1983 playing "The Rocker."

Eric also took part in the Gary Moore-organized tribute to Phil Lynott in 2005 celebrating Phil's life and music as well as the fact that a statue of the late Lizzy leader was now in Dublin Square. A DVD of the show *One Night in Dublin: A Tribute to Phil Lynott* was released featuring many ex-Thin Lizzy members, including Bell.

With his own band, Bell has continued to gig and record in the 1990s and 2000s with *Belfast Blues in a Jar,* the most recent album in 2012. This album has some seriously sweet guitar playing as Eric remains true to his musical beliefs and is really worth purchasing.

In October 2014, I was thrilled to be able to get involved in a chat with Eric about his career and playing. He had some great responses to my questions:

Who were some of the guitar players that got you interested in playing the instrument? I assume blues players were close to your heart.

Some of the guys that gave me an interest; most of them a bit quirky. I love that type of playing. Hank Marvin from the Shadows. Bo Winberg from the Spotniks. The guitarist who played on "El Paso" by Marty Robbins and on the album *Gunfighter Ballads* by Robbins. Django Reinhardt, Wes Montgomery, then the Beatles...who made us all learn new chords. Then the Stones came along, and I got my first taste of blues. A student guy in Belfast loaned me records of Howlin' Wolf, Sonny Boy Williamson, Buddy Guy, etc. It took me a long time to understand, and I used to lay in my bedroom in darkness and listen to the blues. I loved Hubert Sumlin, early B. B. King, early Buddy Guy.

What are your guitars of choice?

My first decent guitar was a Gibson 300, when I was playing with Irish showbands...I always wanted a Stratocaster as well. One night with a few drinks too many I swapped my Gibson for a white Strat with the guitarist who was on the same bill. Then, when Thin Lizzy started, I bought the sunburst Stratocaster, which I still play and love. I've also fancied a Gretsch Anniversary, one of the lime green ones.

"Whisky in the Jar" was something I know you had a push/pull relationship with as it became a smash hit in 1972–1973, but the guitar playing is simply awesome. How did you create the guitar parts for it? It's very detailed and unique.

"Whiskey in the Jar." By far the most difficult song to try and get ideas for. It took me about six weeks to make up the intro alone. I ended up approaching the intro as Irish pipes being played rather than the guitar. Then the repeated riff...it took about two weeks to find...I was singing ideas for that riff on buses, tubes, out walking, etc., and it eventually came to me as I was on my way home in a taxi. Once I had the riff, the guitar solo just seemed to create itself.

"Black Boys on the Corner" has my favorite solo by you—the song just screams bad-ass. Do you recall recording that one? The tone is special.

Yeah, Philip came up with that raunchy riff for "Black Boys." I spent a while trying to get a good tone, as a lot of it was played on the bass strings of the guitar. A lot of players don't seem to use the bottom strings much, and play a lot on the top three strings.

The follow-up single to "Whisky" was "Randolph's Tango," a gorgeously constructed song with a solo that sounds very Spanish and Latin influenced to me. I find it to be stunning and another side of your playing that doesn't get discussed.

"Randolph's Tango." I found when playing with Thin Lizzy it was a very big challenge to keep coming up with ideas...Philip would come up with a very basic idea for a song sometimes and I would end up playing everything I knew on the guitar and it still didn't work. So, this sort of would wake up my imagination...I always tried to play something that would sound natural in the song. So, when it was a song like "Randolph's Tango," I heard the type of solo I came up with as a blues or rock-type solo just wouldn't have worked.

That whole Funky Junction Play Deep Purple *thing from 1972 was a bizarre situation—how do you look back on that now?*

Funky Junction...some guy came into our management one day and said he would pay X amount of money if we would record an album of Deep Purple songs. We went for it and had to fly two guys over from Dublin, one that sang like Ian Gillan of Deep Purple and one that played Hammond Organ like Jon Lord. At the time we couldn't give it away...I think now it's a sort of collectors' item.

Was leaving Lizzy in early 1974 a necessity? It sounds like the road, the industry, and the fact that Vagabonds of the Western World—*easily your best album to that point—hadn't been the hit it should've been played a role.*

Yeah, I had to leave Thin Lizzy, otherwise I would have ended up a junkie, an alcoholic, or a basket case. At the time we were gigging so much, I just didn't take care of myself and had bad trips on acid, and my girlfriend left for another man, and I was living in a horrible one-room in London. Also, I felt the band was slowly turning into a pop-type band. It came to a head in my hometown Belfast, when at the gig (New Year's Eve, 1973), I just freaked out, threw my guitar up in the air, kicked over the two 4 x 12 cabs and staggered off. Which is why I'm still around.

In 1981, the "Song for Jimi" flexi-single was issued. It came out incredible—was that a loose jam and how did that feel after all that time?

"Song for Jimi." Lizzy's management phoned me and said Philip wanted me to play on a song he wrote about Hendrix. I met him down in some London studio, we hadn't seen each other for quite a while, and after we settled down we started playing this riff together. It all felt a little bit like the old days—the old Thin Lizzy; but it was just a one off.

I know you and Mainsqueeze backed up Bo Diddley on a live album that was released in 1986—what was it like playing with the man?

Bo Diddley...a real gentleman and a child-like enthusiasm. I would sit with him in the back of the coach a lot, he was a real funny guy. He bought a digital keyboard when we were touring the UK and opened the cardboard box it was in. He gave me two colored stickers from the box and I stuck them on the head of my guitar...they are still there.

Do you feel you're where you need to be with the Eric Bell Band now?

The beauty of having your own band I find is I can play and experiment at gigs the way I feel on the night and when it works, there's nothing like it. Seeing people enjoying what you do as well.

Silly bonus question I ask most everyone. If you could rename a Lizzy song or album after a cat or type of cat, what would it be? My cats want to know—ha ha.

Yeah...I love cats...my favorite animal! What about "Black Cats on the Corner" ???

Recomended solo: "Randolph's Tango" non-album single with Thin Lizzy (1973), also on 2 CD Deluxe Edition remaster of *Vagabonds of the Western World* (2010)
Further info: www.eric-bell.com
Photo credit: Stephen Davidson

CHAPTER 7

Mick Box

(Born Michael Frederick Box, June 9, 1947, Walthamstow, London, England)

Mick Box has dedicated his life to British hard rock/prog rock outfit Uriah Heep and has been with the band since their inception in 1969.

Originally known as Spice, Uriah Heep changed their early musical style from a hard R&B to the then-burgeoning prog rock movement accenting Box's wah-wah heavy guitar, Ken Hensley's organ, and David Byron's stunning vocals.

Critics despised the band with one reporter from *Rolling Stone Magazine* saying she'd commit suicide if the band ever made it. Not sure if she followed through, but Heep did indeed become a huge success.

From 1971–1975 the band's classic lineup achieved numerous sold-out tours as well as four consecutive Gold albums in the US. Box's distinctive wah-wah heavy sound, Ken Hensley's swirling organ and critical songwriting, David Byron's operatic vocals (he was an influence on Queen's Freddie Mercury), Gary Thain's dazzling bass lines, and Lee Kerslake's tasteful, yet powerful drumming (as well as the band's unusual four-part harmony vocals) created a sound that was highly unique.

Heep's debut album *Very 'Eavy, Very 'Umble* is one of the first heavy metal or heavy rock albums and the pummeling epic "Gypsy" with Box's guitars duking it out with Hensley's swirling organs and Byron's vocal histrionics are way ahead of their time. "Bird of Prey" from *Salisbury* offers similar evidence, and *Look at Yourself* provided the ten-minute "July Morning" a masterstroke of light and shade, whimsy and power, and melancholy and madness.

The albums *Demons and Wizards* (with the US Top 40 hit "Easy Livin'," "The Wizard," "Circle of Hands" and the downtrodden "Rainbow Demon") , *The Magician's Birthday* ("Sunrise," "Sweet Lorriane," and the crazed ten-minute title cut that also sports a lengthy jam between Box and Kerslake that gives any '70s rock guitarist a run for their money), *Uriah Heep Live*, *Sweet Freedom* ("Stealin'," "Pilgrim," and the title cut) and *Wonderworld* ("So Tired," "Suicidal Man," and "Dreams") all were from this time period and made the US Top 40 and led to sellout tours.

Following Thain's dismissal due to drug issues (he would sadly die within a year) in 1975, John Wetton (ex-King Crimson, Roxy Music) stepped in. That year's *Return to Fantasy* was a Top 10 UK album, and with songs such as the creepy title song, "Shady Lady," "Showdown," and the sinister headbanger "Devil's Daughter," Heep had put out a fine, fine album. Inconsistency would follow, however.

But after a poor follow-up album with *High and Mighty* in 1976, Byron was booted for drinking issues (he would pass away in 1985) and Wetton departed (resurfacing later in Asia). With new singer John Lawton and ex-David Bowie bassist Trevor Bolder, Heep would issue three commercial LPs (including the excellent *Firefly* in 1977) that saw their US and UK popularity drop, but soar worldwide. *Firefly* had some really choice material including the menacing "The Hanging Tree," the beautiful "Wise Man," and the sweeping title song. *Innocent Victim* and *Fallen Angel* were far less successful musically.

However, 1977's "Free Me" became a huge hit single in many territories and saw the band pursuing an Eagles-styled country rock sound (only on this song), which, if nothing else, showed how versatile Box's playing was.

Kerslake and Lawton left in 1979 with singer John Sloman and drummer Chris Slade (later in the Firm, AC/DC, and Asia) up next for a highly questionable album in 1980 called *Conquest*. Hensley soon left and Heep split for a while before resurfacing with a shocking comeback album in 1982 with *Abominog*.

Now sporting a polished, heavy AOR sound like Foreigner, Heep entered the MTV-era sounding fresh and vibrant (and scoring an MTV hit with the melodic gem "That's The Way That It Is") as Box's guitar playing remained at a high level with Mick adapting his style for crisp, tight solos and no '70s excess. *Abominog* is so good; it truly marked a rebirth for the band. The material was colorful and lively filled with synthesizer flourishes, propulsive rhythms, and exciting vocals. The crossover track "On the Rebound" was a great cover of a Russ Ballard tune that somehow successfully managed to mix dance and hard rock, while "Sell Your Soul," "Too Scared to Run," "Chasing Shadows," and "Think it Over" are molten classics that shine and burn with Box's guitars fresh and csytalline. The album was their best selling in years and revived their sagging fortunes in the US.

Vocalist Pete Goalby, keyboardist John Sinclair, bassist Bob Daisley (ex-Rainbow and Ozzy), and Kerslake crafted another fine effort in 1983 with *Head First* including the radio hit "Other Side of Midnight" and arena rockers like "Stay on Top" and "Rollin' the Rock." Daisley then went back to Ozzy, and Bolder returned for the overproduced (and costly) album *Equator*. Despite being a disappointment, *Equator* had some good songs, like the Gothic rocker "Night of the Wolf" and "Poor Little Rich Girl." "Party Time," however, went into Spinal Tap territory and not in a good way and was a career nadir.

By 1986, Heep were relegated to the same clubs they started in. Hardly anyone knew or cared they were still together, but Box remained defiant through very difficult times.

In December 1987, Heep would play ten sold-out shows in the then-USSR and *Live in Moscow* (1988) proved they still not only had it, but were perhaps as good as ever with the core of Box, Bolder, and Kerslake joined by fantastic singer Bernie Shaw and keyboardist Phil Lanzon. This lineup would remain intact for twenty years. The year 1989's *Raging Silence* was a good start to reclaiming their pride, but 1991's *Different World* was a little shaky and the band's label went belly-up, not helping matters. Once again, many gave up Heep for dead.

In 1995, the *Sea of Light* album was the beginning of a career renaissance for the band. Since then, they somehow have managed to release some of the finest albums of their career with some of their very best playing and writing. The opening cut "Against the Odds" should be the name of a Heep documentary. This song defines everything that is right about the band and Mick Box. Shaw's vocals soar with power and grace, Lanzon's organ and keyboard work pumps along in tandem with Box's ferocious guitar riffs, while Bolder's dazzling fretwork on bass and Kerslake's otherworldly drumming propel the song and its defiant lyrics to heights no band that old should be able to accomplish. The guitar solos on this track are enough to raise the hairs on any listener's neck and grabs one right out of their seat. It is an example of how criminally underrated Mick Box is as a guitarist. The whole album is a revitalized Heep no longer confused about who they should be.

The opener on 1998's *Sonic Origami* (another great album) "Between Two Worlds" is of a similar spine-tingling vein. The solo is filled with every ounce of emotion as Shaw's vocals provide, and the results are magic. Somehow from the wreckage, Heep and Box were now flying.

Kerslake retired in 2007, and Russell Gilbrook added a serious dimension of power on drums when he joined. *Wake the Sleeper,* a 2008 album was arguably one of the best of their career with the title track with Box playing like a man possessed. "Overload" and "War Child" pack a sonic wallop that few bands their age could hope to equal as well.

Into the Wild (2011) and the 2014 release *Outsider* continue the excellence, although Bolder sadly lost a battle with cancer in 2013 and Davey Rimmer has taken over since. There has been no slippage at all in the playing and writing department. In fact, Uriah Heep and Box may be better now than they were at the height of their popularity in the early-mid '70s. If not, they're both damn close.

To appreciate Mick Box's guitar work isn't hard to do. He never wanted to be a guitar hero and has always put the band ahead of himself for over four decades, and there have been some very painful years. Those who know of Heep and Box, however, are well aware that this man's talents haven't been properly recognized, as well as his determination and dedication. He's just overwhelmingly good and underappreciated.

Here is a brief chat I had with Mick in May 2014 just prior to the release of *Outsider*:

My favorite solo of yours is on "Against the Odds" from the Sea of Light *album. I find that jaw-dropping and one of your finest moments. Could you describe how you arrived at composing that solo?*

I wanted to write an exciting guitar part that you could sing the melody. For the most part I achieved that but some of the fast stuff you would have to be an auctioneer to able to sing it. A good solo must have an entrance, a memorable bit in the middle, and a good end.

What would be some of your personal favorites among your solos on Uriah Heep songs?

"Salisbury" and on and on! It's impossible for me to choose, so I let the fans do that.

Who are a few other players from yesterday or today you admire and enjoy listening to?

Jeff Beck is my favorite guitarist of all time. Others I enjoy are Ritchie Blackmore, who is right up there, too. Paul Kossoff, Django Reinhardt, Eddie Van Halen, Les Paul, Jimi Hendrix and so on.

Where are you at in your head when you take the stage each night and what guitar do you favor the most for live playing?

I am in a happy state and raring to go. The guitar I favor for live playing is my Carparelli S4 guitar, color white.

If you could name a cat after a Uriah Heep album or song, what would it be (my cats want to know—ha ha)?

That's easy! "*Look Cat Yourself*"!

Recommended solo: "Against the Odds" from *Sea of Light* with Uriah Heep (1995)
Further info: www.Uriah-heep.com
Photo credit: Christie Goodwin

CHAPTER 8

Nili Brosh

(Born August 13, 1988, Rishon LeZion, Israel)

Nili Brosh is a guitar virtuoso and a Berklee School of Music graduate, who graduated Summa Cum Laude in 2009. (That's really good in case you are unaware.) Not just Rodney Dangerfield *Back to School* good, but seriously good!

With a world of talent, it wasn't very long before she was able to start making a name for herself and quickly escalated into a musical force to be reckoned with.

Born in Israel in 1988, she moved to the US with her family at the age of twelve and started to develop a passion for playing guitar after seeing her brother Ethan become a very accomplished musician. After graduating from college, she issued an instrumental album titled *Through the Looking Glass,* in 2010, which was extremely impressive, and showcased her skills as a player, arranger, and writer. Pieces like "The House of Tomorrow," "Placebo," "Typsy Gypsy," and "High Strung" are amazing examples of her technical proficiency.

Musically, things are very much in the vein of the guitar greats like Joe Satriani, Steve Vai, Yngwie Malmsteen, and such, but this isn't just some pale imitation or shredding exercise. These songs have musical depth to them and Brosh's playing is dynamic and adventurous. The riffs are at times mountainous, the solos incredibly lyrical, and her tone is marvelous. This was just the start though.

Brosh became part of the band Seven the Hardway in 2011, which included guitar great Tony MacAlpine and, as a result, she was asked to join MacAlpine's band that proved to be a perfect fit as she and another virtuoso were able to trade riffs and solos and harmonize as well with perfect execution. Bassist Bjorn Englen and drummer Aquiles Priester are also in the band, making it an exceptional showcase of talent.

In 2013, she joined her brother's Ethan Brosh Band for touring duties opening for Yngwie and also played with the band Vigilant. The year 2014 saw her once more touring with MacAlpine but also issuing her second album *A Matter of Perception,* which is 100 times the album her debut was, and that is high praise indeed, trust me.

This latest effort includes the mesmerizing "Silence of Saturday," which is an exquisite slice of playing with some complicated patterns and tricky runs as well as devastating harmonies. Other highlights include "Double Entendre," "Exit Strategy," and "Adaptable Creatures." The most impressive aspect about Nili's playing is that she has feel, something usually lacking in this musical genre. Yes, she can play those speedy runs if need be, but that's really not a critical part of her playing. She's got a great attitude and continues to grow each year with her guitar work.

Brosh also plays part time with the Iron Maidens, one of the finest tribute acts out there, who have been around since 2001 paying homage to the brilliant Iron Maiden. These women not only look amazing but play amazing, and when it comes to Iron

Maiden songs, you best play well or you will be laughed off the stage. Seeing as the girls have been doing this for over a decade, it's safe to say they have been acknowledged for their musical chops. Seeing and hearing Nili play tracks like "Powerslave" and "The Trooper" is a blast, and when she has the time to play with these girls it's awesome.

Nili Brosh is an amazing player with great technical skills and a knowledge of guitar complexities that is a result of her hard years of schooling and work. Her gender doesn't mean squat; she's awesome. Got a problem with that, guys? No? Good!

In February 2015, Nili and I had an informative chat and the words went as follows:

Who were some of your influences growing up that made you want to play guitar?

My two earliest influences are my brother Ethan and Nuno Bettencourt. Ethan turned me on to Extreme when I was very young, and listening to both the record *Pornograffitti* as well as Ethan's own playing made me think the guitar was a very cool thing.

What are the models of guitars you've preferred through the years of playing?

In my teenage years I had a Charvel model 4 and a BC Rich ST-III, on which I learned my shredder-friendly music growing up. Later on, I had an endorsement with a company called Inspire Guitars, which makes amazing custom guitars, and finally I went on to endorse Ibanez, who provide me the 7-string guitars I play today. I play two RG Prestige guitars (the 1527M and the 2727FZ) as well as the RG Premium 927QM.

You rock the pink sneakers—that's your trademark right? Just don't set them on fire like Hendrix!

Ha, I guess it's become a trademark of sorts in the last few years. I've always liked neon stuff and Converse sneakers, so the first time I saw a combination of the two, I just had to have them! I'm not much of an impulse buyer, but when I see something that grabs me that much, I can't help myself. I now have a neon yellow pair as well.

Was releasing Through the Looking Glass *an amazing thing? After all, you had only recently graduated at that point. Was any of that material written while at school?*

I think it was an amazing thing whose amazingness I wasn't really aware of at the time. I just thought of it as "what is." I had some songs that I had written in high school and early college, and I wanted to make them into a record. I took my best shot at it, and that's what you hear in *Through the Looking Glass*.

Is playing with the Iron Maidens fun? The band is so tight playing fairly complex material, it seems fun has to be part of the equation. And, those solos that have been laid down through the years are very well written and must be played properly. That is truly one of the best tribute acts out there.

Playing with the Iron Maidens was really fun! I'm glad you're enjoying that band. I think it is very cool that you can get a group of girls together who all love Maiden enough to learn that kind of music down to its tiniest nuance. I felt compelled to do the same when I was in that band, so I did my best to learn all the solos as close as possible to the originals, and really pay tribute to Maiden as best I could.

Are there any artists you like past or present that would surprise people (I can't imagine all you listen to is the style of music you play!).

Hmmm...the Backstreet Boys! But I've gotten asked this question several times by now, so maybe some readers wouldn't be so surprised!

Can you take me though the composing of "Silence of Saturday" from your new album A Matter of Perception*? I have listened to this piece many, many times. The composition, the tone, and your harmonies are just fantastic. This is a very musical piece; no noodling just for noodling's sake, which can plague the genre. I really feel your new album is stellar.*

Thank you! I wish there was more of a story behind it, but "Silence of Saturday" was honestly one of those songs that kind of just "wrote itself," at least as far as the melody and harmony are concerned. The arrangement was what took a long time—I had that electronic drum groove in the intro and outro for a long time, but wanted to expand on that direction, so my co-producer Sabi Saltiel and I worked on those extra parts and effects for a few months. The funny thing about this song—and not many people know this—is that I almost scrapped it entirely. I really didn't like it at first, for whatever reason, and almost took it off of the record. I'm definitely glad I didn't—I love it now, and I'm glad so many people are enjoying it as well.

Playing in Tony MacAlpine's band is a seriously great gig and you two blend fantastically. How great has that been for you, and has it sharpened your skills even further?

Thanks again! It has been enormously helpful for my playing. I wasn't anywhere near where I am now before I met Tony, and he's responsible for a large part of my development. It's not as if I had taken lessons from him per se, but just being around him and playing with him on a regular basis shaped my improvement in a natural kind of way—without necessarily trying. I just played the music and my skills and style evolved through it. It's not to say the gig or the parts were easy, but I was just trying to do my job as best I can, and my playing transformed as a result.

A silly, final question I ask most players: my cats would like to know if you had to rename one of your albums or songs with a cat theme, what would you come up with—ha ha?

Hmm...how about *A Matter of Purrrrception*?

Recommended solo: "Silence of Saturday" from *A Matter of Perception* solo album (2014)
Further info: www.nilibrosh.com
Photo credit: Kamil Kowalski

Craig Chaquico

(Born September 26, 1954, in Sacramento, CA)

Craig Chaquico was born to play guitar. He began playing at age ten and was already playing professionally by age fourteen. In between that timeframe, however, Craig and his father were involved in a terrible accident caused by a drunk driver that left young Craig with numerous injuries, including both arms broken. Somehow, only able to use his thumbs, he began playing guitar again while rehabbing and, once the slow healing process was over, he was better than before.

Spotted by Paul Kantner of Jefferson Airplane at the age of sixteen, he was invited to do studio and live work and, in 1971, played on the Kantner/Grace Slick album *Sunfighter*. By 1974, he had been invited to join the newly christened Jefferson Starship debuting on the album *Dragon Fly*, which contained the rockin' hit "Ride the Tiger," a hard rock song where Chaquico laid down a vibrant, wicked solo that truly clawed like a tiger and was unlike anything the Airplane/Starship had done before. There are some serious scales being played here. Year 1975's *Red Octopus* album was a huge success, including the Top 5 single "Miracles" and the album saw Chaquico contributing writing, including the fan favorite "Fast Buck Freddie."

Throughout the '70s and '80s Jefferson Starship racked up a batch of Top 20 hits, some of which were in the easy-listening vein like "With Your Love," "Count on Me," and "Runaway," and they were all fine songs for what they were. Each album during this period (*Spitfire* from 1976, *Earth* from 1978, and *Freedom at Point Zero* from 1979) had plenty of great album cuts and Chaquico's guitar playing was exceptional.

It was *Freedom at Point Zero* that produced the Top 20 hit "Jane" a commercial slice of hard rock sliding in that Toto/Foreigner/Journey vein and doing it well. Craig's soloing on here, both in the mid-section and the outro remains memorable, and really introduced him to a lot of new fans with his playing.

With 1981's *Modern Times* LP the band released three excellent singles starting with the memorable "Find Your Way Back" a Top 30 hit that received heavy rotation with its video (complete with Craig on double-neck guitar and single moustache!) on the brand-new MTV. Chaquico's lead work on this track is exemplary, including guitar harmonies and a searing high-pitched sound.

Even better was follow-up single "Stranger" that is filled with eerie guitar fills throughout (accompanied by a thudding bass/drum pattern) and a truly vicious solo that is one of Chaquico's finest moments. Seriously, when it ends you want to applaud! The third single "Save Your Love" wasn't much of a hit but perhaps it's because Chaquico unleashes a solo of fury that burns like no tomorrow for about the last three minutes of the song's six-minute length that went beyond the average short-attention span listener. I tell ya, this solo is one of the finest you will hear in rock guitar playing.

There would be more hits over the next few years, but Jefferson Starship would fold and Starship came into being in 1985. While this ultra-commercial outfit had a series of monster hits, some of these songs were to say the least a little cheesy. The most notorious would be 1985's #1 hit "We Built This City" and 1987's #1 hit from the cringe-worthy film *Mannequin*, "Nothing's Gonna Stop Us Now" (at least it wasn't from *Mannequin 2: On the Move*). There was another #1 hit in 1986 with the sappy tune "Sara."

Here's the thing: do these songs make me wince? Yes, but seeing as I didn't play on three #1 hits, I'll just say it was successful, wasn't it? In 1989, *Love Among the Cannibals* was released and the sales were fading. Still, a big hit came with "It's Not Enough" that rose to #12 on the charts and was a quality pop/rock song. But Craig was already looking forward and ready for new musical outlets. Chaquico left in 1990 and the group folded shortly thereafter.

Craig then formed the hard rock band Big Bad Wolf which released one self-titled album that howled into obscurity. Craig's guitar playing on the album was choice as one would expect, but the material was generic and the production and mix cloying and sterile. Much better was ahead for the man.

Then things changed dramatically as Craig ventured into the world of acoustic music starting with 1993's *Acoustic Highway*. It was 1994's *Acoustic Planet,* however, that would become his best-known solo work, garnering a Grammy nomination and topping the new age charts. This album and the style of music it had have been copied numerous times since. *Acoustic Planet* still stands out as an important recording and here one can find a variety of sounds from Chaquico's guitar playing that are pleasing but also creative. Among Craig's other solo works are albums such as *A Thousand Pictures* (1996), *Four Corners* (1999), *Midnight Noon* (2004) and *Follow the Sun* (2009).

Craig continues to mine a solo career with great success and 2012's *Fire Red Moon* shows his playing is as classy as ever. Craig is also actively involved with the American Music Therapy Association (AMTA) and is a member of Bikers for Charity. On top of that, he also has his own signature guitar with Carvin.

I was able to participate in a fantastic, detailed interview with Craig in August of 2014 and here it is:

Who were your main influences when you started getting into the instrument?

Well, it would be cowboys around the campfire, summer camp stuff first and acoustic guitars and folk songs. Then Surf music, the Beatles, Rolling Stones, Bob Dylan, and the Monkees TV show, which was kinda like the Beatles' movies. Then the radio and the little switch on my brother's radio that went from AM mono to FM stereo to KZAP-FM in Sacramento. Then babysitting for my big brother and putting on his headphones and listening to Jimi Hendrix for the first time. His kids were having pillow fights and racing around the house, but I was in my own world just me and Jimi Hendrix and "Third Stone from the Sun," etc. My big brother's record collection, which included Chet Atkins, Wes Montgomery, and other jazz, and then my own record collection that started with my very first album from Quicksilver Messenger Service with the black and silver cover and a Rick Griffen drawing.

I seriously started listening non-stop to Pink Floyd, Cream, Santana, Led Zeppelin, Jefferson Airplane, Hot Tuna, Grateful Dead, Grand Funk Railroad, Allman Brothers, Johnny Winter and Rick Derringer, Joe Walsh's James Gang, Big Brother and the Holding Company, Mountain, Bad Company, anything with guitars, guitars, guitars, especially power trios or any albums with long songs in one key I could just play along with over and over and improvise—which was kinda like practicing over and over only way more fun than just scales.

What are your preferred guitars of choice on stage or in the studio and were you happy with the results of your signature Carvin guitar?

At first my preferred guitars in the studio and on all of the first four multi-platinum albums of Jefferson Starship were vintage Les Pauls and Stratocasters and Fender Bassman amps. Maybe the occasional Tele, ES-335, Firebird, Dan Electro, Rickenbacker, jazz Bass, Precision Bass, Martins, Guild 12-strings, Twin, Princeton, Champ, Marshall, Dumble amps, as if they were all colors on a painter's palette that I explored to see what was so unique about each.

After a huge riot in Germany where most were destroyed and/or perhaps stolen, I had to replace them. I decided not to replace them with more rare vintage guitars and amps. Live and learn. So after investigating several great guitar companies like Dean, BC Rich, and newer Fenders and Gibsons, which I still really like, I fell in love at first sight with Carvin and it was a marriage made in heaven ever since.

I went to writing and playing more on acoustic guitar when I left what was left of Starship that basically consisted of a singer and a manager who made a majority two-thirds corporate decision and told me to forget writing anything myself anymore because "rockin' guitar songs" were "out of fashion." My wife became pregnant soon thereafter and the acoustic guitar became more welcome around the house, but Carvin didn't really offer an actual production acoustic guitar yet.

A rep for Washburn I ran into at Bananas At Large in San Rafael, CA, let me borrow one of his guitars, a one-of-a-kind Festival Series prototype. He died right after he gave it to me a few weeks later. Then I started writing on it and recording and changing a few things on it. Washburn heard my first acoustic guitar totally instrumental #1 solo CD being played on the radio and liked how I modified their festival series and asked to use those modifications for a Craig Chaquico signature model.

I agreed only if they agreed to plant a tree for every guitar made, which they did as the sticker inside every CC guitar explained, but they later ended up being mass-produced off-shore as part of another corporate decision and the quality really went downhill almost right from the start. I remember walking into a music store on the road and seeing one of those lesser quality versions on the wall and after playing it I almost threw up. So Carvin worked with me on a design that I've been happy with ever since. They are still the very best guitar company that I know of, but who knows what happens in the corporate world these days?

I know you are a big believer in the healing power of music (and so am I, trust me). Can you describe the importance the guitar and music in general played as you recovered from that terrible car accident when you were just twelve years old or so?

Music was a welcome companion during a frighteningly difficult time. The first thing I asked for was my little acoustic guitar and my doctor encouraged me to play because I think she knew I loved it and that it would be good for my circulation, dexterity, and to keep my muscles from atrophying while everything was healing in casts for months at that age. I wrote a song all on one string when I was twelve that later ended up on a Grammy-nominated, #1 album, thirty years later and named it after my doctor, Elizabeth. Since it was all on the one e-string I could only reach with little fingers sticking out of the casts, I called it "E-lizabeth's Song"—later "Center of Courage." But I think she also knew it would be good for my spirit and soul, which it was. So during my bed stay and then my wheelchair, therapy, crutches, and corrective shoes, guitar helped me through a difficult and frightening time. When my solo album on the acoustic guitar first came out, I went back to the same hospital to play for the doctor who healed me, and for the staff and other kids and family who were also in a scary place, to let them know that music was an inspiration and great escape as well as a light at the end of the tunnel. Anything is possible.

I found out about the American Music Therapy Association and how they work with musicians and doctors to bring music and healing powers to people in hospitals who can't go out and see music themselves. So ever since then I've been able to play little mini FREE solo concerts on tour with just me, and an acoustic guitar and a backing track, for geriatric patients, pediatric patients, psychiatric patients, criminally insane, Down Syndrome patients, and Alzheimer's patients. I was a national spokesperson for a while.

I played at Nordoff-Robbins in New York and saw the kids respond there. I played for Patch Adams, who Robin Williams later played in a movie. Alzheimer's patients who wouldn't respond to anything were shown to have periods of lucidity after listening to music. It's something about rewiring the brain that has been damaged by illness or head injuries. People who have forgotten how to speak can first learn to hum and then sing along with songs from their childhood. People who can't walk can first learn to move in time to music and begin to dance.

An older man who didn't recognize his family or respond to photos or language listened to some music he and his wife listened to when they were younger and dating. When he heard the first few notes, he smiled, looked at his wife, and a tear came to his eye and they danced. That period of lucidity lasted beyond the length of the song and led to more recovery.

I was picked up at the airport in Minneapolis, and the driver, Curt, told me of his friend Lee, who was in the hospital after being hit by a drunk driver (like my dad and I were), and he couldn't come out to see me play, so I mentioned that if Curt worked out the red tape and gave me a ride I would go in and play for Lee instead after my show. The staff found us a room and I played to just a few folks and Lee couldn't move much in a wheelchair with a halo brace on his head and shoulders, but he could move in his imagination and I'll never forget the light in his eyes that danced about even though his body couldn't yet.

Less than a year later, I received a handwritten letter in some shaky script from Lee himself that expressed how much the concert meant to him and that he listened to my music while recovering so he wanted his first letter to be to me. Whew! A year later to the day, when I was back in town playing, he was being released out of the Center of Courage rehab wing of the hospital and we talked about it on the radio and a Harley guy with a sidecar volunteered to pick Lee up and take him to my concert. I was inspired to dedicate the song that I wrote in the hospital on one string since it was the only string I could reach with my hands in casts and my fingers only sticking out so far. "E-lizabeth's Song" was named after my doctor but dedicated to Lee and Maria (...a wheelchair basketball player who also comes to my shows).

When I was playing at the House of Blues in New Orleans and not wearing my stage pass backstage, a big bouncer ran up to me and kinda freaked me out. I figured I would be kicked out of my own concert again. But he heard my story on stage about "E-lizabeths Song" and told me of his own beloved grandma who had a stroke and they said would never speak again. They played her my music, and it helped kick-start the healing. After rocking, humming, singing a few words for a while she now is able to speak to her grandchildren and laugh at the original prognosis before the application of the music doses.

You joined Jefferson Starship when you were very young. How imposing and exciting was all that for you back then?

It was a reality check to be an audience member at Altamonte looking at some of my future bandmates, along with other musical heroes like David Crosby and Graham Nash and spotting the Grateful Dead as a fan, and then within a year being in the studio with some of them and yet still having to ride my bicycle to school and keep my grades up and do my homework or my parents wouldn't let me play guitar.

In high school we would tell our parents we were staying at each other's' houses for the weekend and then go to San Francisco to see bands at Winterland or Golden

Gate Park. Usually, one mom would call another and all hell broke loose when we got home. We'd get grounded and have to stay in our bedrooms where we played along with the music we got turned on to when we did our great escapes to the Emerald City and saw the magical bands of Oz or owlsly depending.

I ended up playing on the senior lawn at La Sierra High School in a power trio with one of my fellow fugitives and music and art class sophisticates, Rick Eberly, on bass, who later illustrated *Guitar Player Magazine* as an amazing cartoonist! We weren't seniors, but we sort of got a temporary pass if we played during lunch. Cream, Hendrix, etc. No folk songs or ballads whatsoever...or vocals.

My English teacher, Jack Traylor, who unbeknownst to us students was already a well-known folksinger and lyricist by members of the Jefferson Airplane, saw me—a lowly sophomore—on the senior lawn and asked me to stay after school. Uh-oh, I thought, I'll be pushing an egg across the senior lawn with my nose, but instead, he pulled out a Martin and started playing me songs and asking me to join HIS band. Grace Slick and Paul Kantner with other SF musical luminaries came to our little club dates where I lied about my age and wore a fake mustache to be able to play in bars where alcohol was being served. Forget the condiments. Sometimes the fake mustache would fall in the soda glass and I would freak out about the hairy caterpillar-looking creature in the ice cubes till I realized it was actually part of my alter ego, super hero, crime fighting costume. The glue also would fluoresce bright green under a black light we also later discovered and had trouble explaining well enough to keep that gig.

Soon I was being asked to play guitar on some of Grace Slick and Paul Kantner's solo albums, along with other Bay Area friends and heroes like John Cipollina, Pete Sears, David Crosby, Graham Nash, the Pointer Sisters, and Jerry Garcia. I remember playing on a basic track where I was to play rhythm and leave the solo for Jerry to overdub the next day. Of course I got carried away eventually after a few takes and blew through the reserved "senior lawn" guitar solo myself, figuring they would just erase my sophomore solo before Jerry came to play. When he showed up and did his own solos on various cuts, they forgot to mute my solo. I later heard that when he heard the track for the first time, he asked to hear it again and said, "Why not let the kid have another solo?" I always wanted to give him a high 4½ ever since whenever I saw him, but even though we played onstage together for hundreds of thousands of people at the Oakland Coliseum, or the SNACK concert in the park, or other free concerts in Golden Gate Park, we never really ever hung out at all. BUMMER!!!!

Personally, my favorite era of Jefferson Starship was during your tenure especially the years of 1978-1983. "Jane" remains an all-time hard rock classic and "Stranger" still blows me away when I hear it now. Do you recall how you came up with the solos for those two songs, especially "Stranger"?

I'll never forget those days. We had lost Grace and Marty and our *incredible* drummer John Barbata after the riot in Germany, along with all my guitars and amps. But as "one door closes, another opens," from my song on *Freedom At Point Zero* where we introduced Mickey Thomas and Aynsley Dunbar with new producer Ron Nevison (UFO, Led Zeppelin, the Who, Bad Company) and engineer Mike Clink (later Guns N' Roses, Slash, Aerosmith, Whitesnake, Steve Vai, et al.), so needless to say GUITARS were greatly encouraged as well as my songwriting, "Jane" being a prime example as well as the idea I had when I first heard Mickey in a club and thought that he was like a cross between Stevie Wonder, Michael Jackson, Robert Plant, and Paul Rogers to my ear. YEAHHH for guitars and Craig too thanks to that new debut line-up!!

But our nervous fidgety manager came in and timed my solo in "Jane" with a stopwatch, saying it was too long at twenty-eight seconds. Bullshit! Dunbar and the whole band except maybe Mickey backed me up and we left the full "long" solo intact and our manager said it would never be played on the radio with that solo in it. ("Free Bird" was another musical universe and stellar performance(s) either way, so I couldn't really point to that).

Every time I hear "Jane" on the radio today, thirty-plus years later, I have to smile because we all fought for every second of that solo. Our manager had insisted that no hit song on the radio had ever had "long" solos like that anymore and he was right. When I met the guys from Metallica at an awards show, they told me that when they were in high school they really liked "Jane" because it was the only song on the radio that "had a long guitar solo"—relativity theory.

Lucky for me this all coincided with the addition of Aynsley Dunbar on drums and Ron Nevison as a producer, both of whom I already had admired and respected with amazing work prior to Starship. Aynsley played with Zappa, Journey, later Whitesnake, and had a real rock foundation. Ron Nevison had producing credits with Led Zeppelin, Bad Company, UFO, and a lot of guitar-based bands. Later Heart and other groups as well...He really encouraged my style of guitar playing, along with Pete Sears who always wrote songs that featured lots of guitar, even more than the songs I wrote, with "Stranger" being one of them. Thank you, Pete!

I remember to this day Mike Clink (who later produced Guns N' Roses and Whitesnake and Steve Vai and others) and Ron were in the studio while I played various versions of the solo in "Stranger," all of which were improvised (whereas on "Jane" I had already written the solo pretty much note-for-note, and I went in and did that solo in two takes we'd mixed together with the beginning of one and the end of the other. It took longer to get the right tone and mic placement than to play the solo). "Stranger," however, was a combination of probably five or six takes that I wasn't 100% happy with any of them yet, and Ron and Mike both told me to take a break and come back in a half an hour.

Instead, I peeked through the glass from a corner of the studio into the control room and saw them meticulously taking notes of the best parts of my solo and when I came back they had constructed a terrific solo that I later learned how to play. So much of the credit could probably be given to their style of production with years of recording guitar players and their ears for composition and being able to select the pieces from what I was doing off the top of my head without thinking about it. Sometimes that's the best of both worlds.

I remember the solo on "Save Your Love." When it was over I almost didn't know where I was and couldn't remember a note I played and wanted to redo it and everybody in the studio was shaking their head telling me to come back and listen to what just happened. I couldn't remember what I played but I really like that song because we left that LONG solo the way it was from the one take. Ironically that was the night John Lennon died and it came across the TV right in the control room during the football game as we finished listening to that solo for "Save Your Love" and we all unanimously decided that the recording session was over for the night. But that solo lives on.

How in the world did you guys get involved with the Star Wars Holiday Special *in 1978? It's awesome and hilarious at the same time!*

We had been known for sci-fi lyrics. I have always been a huge sci-fi fan. *Star Wars* was so groundbreaking and inspiring when we heard they wanted us to appear and submit a song we jumped at the chance.

I had just written a song already called "Light The Sky On Fire" about UFOs, alien visitations, and influences, after reading sci-fi since I was a kid and in the hospital, loving *2001 – A Space Odyssey* when it came out after hearing about it for years in the sci-fi mags, and having read the book prior to the film, *Star Trek* TOS, and just reading *Chariots of the Gods* by Von Daniken that spoke of all the stuff you see on *Ancient Aliens* now only back in '78. It had lyrics alluding to carvings on pyramids and temples, the amazing scientific mathematical astronomical knowledge needed for such, the incredible efforts needed to construct the ones in Egypt and South America, what are they doing there and why, and the legends of visitors from the sky that will return someday. Although I felt the song wasn't performed as well in the studio as it was later LIVE, it seemed to look good on paper, as did the #1 Jefferson Starship appearing on the #1 TV network on the #1 sci-fi movie franchise.

After seeing *Star Wars*, I realized sci-fi movies would never be the same, and compared to the TV production of *Star Trek* TOS, which I still love and was light-years ahead of course. The same goes with the state of the art TV variety shows like the #1 award-winning Carol Burnett broadcasts and productions. The same experienced, proven, TV production style went into the #1 *Star Wars Holiday Special* but without any of the ground breaking NEW technology and production style of the first *Star Wars* hit movie. This was in between the first and second film, and George was hard at work on it instead of micro-managing TV shows I THINK??? This was all before Yoda and Luke's dad, etc. I can see why it looked great on paper.

We never saw any of it till it came out. The rest is history. Literally, Lucas Films will never release it, which is unfortunate for me since I wrote the song that appears in it as a cult classic and something that has been viewed by millions of earthlings.

I did manage to somehow also get a song on a satellite that is still in Earth orbit as part of the space arc project. There is an edited version of my song, "Just One World," from my #1 Grammy-nominated *Acoustic Planet* album (...that title has been ripped off more than a few times since) as part of other recordings and artwork from earth. Chuck Berry is on *Voyager* and his music has left the solar system. I can see aliens coming back to earth after hearing Chuck Berry, maybe seeing the *Star Wars Holiday Special*, and hearing my song in orbit and then making contact with us saying, "...nice stuff, Earthers! Please send more Chuck Berry!"

Were you surprised at the amazing reaction and success of the Acoustic Planet *album in 1994? And what led to that style of making music for you?*

More surprised than anybody I'm sure! I hit #1 in *Billboard*. Grammy nominated. WOW! I'm grateful my dad saw that before he died as well as me turning him on to the Grateful Dead.

Anyway, after leaving the "corporate day job" of the kind of corporate hit-making machine with no actual band that the Starship seemed to be striving for, after everybody I enjoyed playing with had already left, I made a hard rockin' album with huge vox and a killer singer, Rolf Hartley, with electric guitar-heavy songs like Jane. We called ourselves Big Bad Wolf.

"My, what big amps you have! What big guitars! What big vox!" "All the better to eat you with!" just like the book says. Which was pretty much what we heard from record execs "eat me" or "fuk you, good luck, you suk." So, it was never released in the USA either. It should have been on the *Star Wars Holiday Special* if it was never going to be released. It was recorded in '90, right when I left Mickey Thomas and the manager, that later became Mickey Thomas's Starship or something?

Either way, the grunge thing was breaking big-time and that kind of changed the "state of the art" again for everybody. So our music was considered too dated at that point as all the bands like us were being dropped, much less signed. Although in Europe and Japan it found an appreciative audience, not so in the USA as we were passed on by all the greats after me spending a year, non-stop, in my and Rolf's studios and funding the whole recording, demo, and showcasing process after "quitting my day job." Yikes!

Then, my wife became pregnant and suddenly the acoustic guitar seemed much more welcome around the house and my fear level grew that I may never find gainful employment as a guitarist from Sacramento in the music business again.

The keyboard player for Jerry Garcia's live touring band at the time, Ozzie Ahlers, was kind enough to play some of the sampled vox we used in the Big Bad Wolf live shows appropriately ("pay no attention to the man behind the curtain") by playing samples and additional keys. He was also producing music for the *GUMBY Movie,* and the story I heard was that Joe Satriani had to bail at the last minute for some sessions and I ended up playing all the electric guitar solos for *GUMBY* instead.

So when I started to play the music on acoustic guitar while Kyle was in the womb, I asked Ozzie what he thought about maybe coming over to my studio and helping me write and produce. He was my first choice on keys, but I was clearly his second choice to Joe on guitar, third if you count Jerry Garcia I guess? Anyway, we were passed on by a huge new age label based where I lived in Mill Valley, five minutes from my own studio in the redwoods. They said they heard some new age, but if I sounded more new age like George Winston, or Kitaro, or Ottmar Liebert they would sign me because they heard a lotta other influences like rock, jazz, blues. They said change my style or try those other labels if I wanted a shot? So I went to the jazz side of the label Starship was on and they said they heard some jazz, but if I sounded more like George Benson they would sign me but they heard new age, rock, and blues so they said change my style or try those other labels. I recall an exec actually said I was "playing the wrong model of guitar" to give me a shot.

Hmmmm…So I went to a rock shred label and guess what? If I sounded more like Steve Vai, etc. and the same thing with the blues, if I sounded more like Clapton or Robert Cray, etc., etc., etc.—that's what I would hear and it was pretty depressing, but lucky for me somebody up there likes me because an Earth angel named Nadine Condon, who also wrote a GREAT insider book about the biz, and worked with Jefferson Starship as a publicist, played my demo cassette for the #1 indie new age label, Higher Octave Music, and Matt Marshall and Dan Selene and William Aura liked it JUST THE WAY IT WAS! It became the #1 indie new age album of the whole year in *Billboard*. Now, a million CDs later and Grammy nomination, and #1s, I've been told at one time all those other labels who passed on me were telling new artists that if they sounded more like Craig Chaquico they would give them a shot. Nobody is more surprised or more grateful then me now to still be playing music from five decades. "…the most famous guitarist from Sacramento that nobody has ever heard of."

I must ask: "We Built This City." As hated as it is loved, do you still have fond memories of recording it? After all, it did hit #1…

Weeeellllll, yes… I figured if I played any guitar on it at all it might ruin it though. So in the video you see me in it just for a second standing there with the guitar over my shoulder till I swing it around and play THE ONE guitar part in the whole song till the vamp at the end. A basic C chord on 4 strings of just tonic and 5ths I think. Sort of a pop version of a real power chord. Then at the end I got to play but figured it may fade early anyway but I still tried to think, "Okay, what would a great actor like Tommy Lee Jones do if this was a movie instead of a song? Or Jackie Chan? That didn't work out so I thought, "What would Jeff Beck play if he was allowed this once in a lifetime opportunity?" So, hopefully there is a statute of limitations on almost obvious influences, but that song did go to #1. Also voted the #1 worst song too I think, which is bullshit because I know we recorded a few much worse than that.

A final silly question I've asked most guitarists I've interviewed: If you could rename a Jefferson Starship or Starship song/album after a cat what would it be called? My cats want to know—ha ha.

Red Octopussy!

Recommended solo: "Save Your Love" from *Modern Times* by Jefferson Starship (1981)
Further info: www.craigchaquico.com
Photo Credit: Kaye Runner

CHAPTER 10

Bruce Cockburn

(Born Bruce Douglas Cockburn, May 27, 1945, Ottawa, Ontario, Canada)

Some singer/songwriters just strum a few chords on acoustic guitar and do little else. That's fine, because their voice and their writing are usually the most important factor. There are, however some singer/songwriters who also happen to be fantastic musicians and Canada's Bruce Cockburn is one such fellow.

Cockburn is one of rock's finest writers as evidenced by his decades of songs, many of which are thought-provoking and in their own way, akin to poetry. Cockburn's skills as a guitar player are every bit as important in his music and he has proven through the years to be quite a dazzling player, rarely doing conventional guitar parts on either acoustic or electric guitar.

In the mid-1960s, Bruce attended the prestigious Berklee School of Music in Boston, Massachusetts, and then played in various bands in the late '60s before becoming a solo artist and signing his first record contract. The debut album *Bruce Cockburn* (1970) had songs, such as "Man of a Thousand Faces" and "Spring Song" that showcased everything great about Bruce: his acoustic guitar work, his voice, and his writing. *High Winds, White Sky* featured the affecting title cut and "Let Us Go Laughing" as highlights that again accented Bruce's musical attributes with sparse arrangements. The year1972's *Sunwheel Dance* featured the exultant title piece that is one of the finest acoustic guitar workouts one could ever hope to hear. I dare you not to feel something special when listening to this musical touchstone. "Dialogue With the Devil (Or Why Don't We Celebrate)" was six-and-one-half minutes of amazing lyrics, acoustic guitar, and vocals that many fans find to be one of Cockburn's strongest compositions. The buoyant "For the Birds" is a true gem and the mind opens to the beauty of our feathered friends in flight to music like this.

With *Night Vision* in 1973, Cockburn hit pay dirt yet again and the acoustic instrumental piece "Foxglove" is nothing short of transfixing. Bruce's dexterity and sense of light and shade with the chords makes this another beautiful listening experience. Throw in some tricky runs and picking and, yeah, you've got yourself another one of the greatest acoustic guitar instrumentals ever written right here, and it's over in a flash—just one minute and twenty-four seconds. This album also featured the nearly eight minute epic instrumental "Islands in a Black Sky" (just listen to the acoustic guitar playing here! It's not only breathtaking, but one can clearly hear the influence on Michael Hedges among others) and "You Don't Have to Play the Horses."

Salt, Sun and Time was next up in 1974 and sported "Never So Free," the title song (a quiet, tranquil acoustic instrumental) and the charming "Christmas Song" as Bruce continued an amazing run of albums that were consistently fantastic. In 1975, Joy Will Find a Way was released and the song "Burn" (great chorus) proved to be a real highlight and "Joy Will Find a Way (A Song About Dying)" featured an exuberant, African feel to the music and this was far from a downer and instead was simply a statement about how death is indeed a part of life. The longing of "January in the Halifax Airport Lounge" was truly beautiful. And, don't forget about the moving "Starwheel." In 1976, In the Falling Dark provided "Little Seahorse," "Water into Wine" and "Lord of the Starfields," which has some powerful music added to a religious theme.

Further Adventures Of had "Rainfall," "A Montreal Song," and "Outside a Broken Phone Booth with Money in My Hand" with the latter certainly having an amusing title, but here Bruce started introducing more electric guitar and lively bass and drum patterns.

In 1979, Dancing in the Dragon's Jaws proved to be a big turning point for Bruce. This album became his first to chart in the US climbing all the way to #45. "Wondering Where the Lions Are" roared into the US Top 25 on the singles charts in 1980, becoming a surprise hit and a much-deserved one. There are beautiful acoustic guitars and delicate rhythms and use of percussion with subtle backing vocals that make the colors come to life in this wonderful song that has remained a classic. So many other songs on this album including "After the Rain," "Hills of Morning," and "Badlands Flashback" prove this record to be one of Cockburn's finest hours. An appearance on Saturday Night Live in 1980 confirmed that America had finally caught on.

Humans was another winner in 1980, including "Fascist Architecture," "Grim Travellers" and especially "Tokyo," which is one of his very best compositions. "Rumours of Glory" was also a minor US hit and the closing six-minute cut "The Rose Above the Sky" is a true Cockburn prize with mysterious lyrics and excellent instrumentation. In 1981, Cockburn released Inner City Front which had some infectious material such as the snappy new wave sounding "Wanna Go Walking" that echoed the likes of Joe Jackson and the jazzy touches of the instrumental "Radio Shoes" could be Steely Dan or Billy Joel. The musicianship is supreme here and it's cool to see Bruce going into different avenues. However, some '80s production interferes (drum machine, synth washes) at times. The album is uneven but when it's good, it's really good as in the nearly eight-minute stunner "Loner," which has some wild violin work by Hugh Marsh as Bruce now had a seriously great backing band.

In 1983, The Trouble with Normal was released and saw a move towards mostly political themes and musically a Caribbean influence surfaced. It was 1984's Stealing Fire, however, that saw Cockburn reach new heights. This album was politically fueled as well, especially in regards to Central America, which Bruce had visited recently. The anger at the senselessness of the situation was obvious in the lyrics to many songs and other topics were dealt with that were just as hot. Stealing Fire is nothing short of a tour de force for Cockburn. Making it even better is the music on the album which fuses Latin, rock, pop, and folk. "Dust and Diesel," "Nicaragua" and "Peggy's Kitchen Wall" are all awesome. Musically, Bruce was throwing in some vibes that sounded like the police, Peter Gabriel, and Talking Heads and was clearly paying attention to new musical styles as well as standing on his own.

The chilling "Lovers in a Dangerous Time" is a work of genius and Bruce's lyrics paint a picture attached to seductive rhythms and alternative rock sounds like the Chapman Stick. A striking video became an MTV hit as did the clip for the venomous "If I Had a Rocket Launcher," which briefly made the US singles charts and also made the US Top 20 at rock radio. Bruce's muted electric guitars add to the atmosphere of "Lovers in a Dangerous Time" and the chorus is enrapturing. With Miche Pouliot on drums, Fergus Marsh on bass and stick, Jon Goldsmith on keyboards, and Chi Sharpe on percussion, Bruce had tremendous support musically. Lyrically, it gets no better than the line, "But nothing worth having comes without some kind of fight/Got to kick at the darkness til it bleeds daylight," which would later be appropriated by U2 on their song "God Part II" in 1989.

The year 1986's *World of Wonders* featured the classic "Call it Democracy" as well as "People See Through You." The greatest hits album *Waiting on a Miracle: Singles 1970–1987* featured the new song "Waiting for a Miracle," which became one of Bruce's most important and beloved songs, and it is always requested to be performed at his shows where the solo acoustic version takes on new significance.

Big Circumstance (1988—this included the Canadian Top 10 hit "If a Tree Falls" that was a spirited pro-environmental track with some wailing country rock electric guitar using a lot of tremolo), *Nothing But a Burning Light* (1991), the classy seasonal album *Christmas* (1993—just listen to "Silent Night," "It Came Upon a Midnight Clear," and the way too brief but pretty acoustic instrumental of "Joy to the World") and *Dart to the Heart* (1994) kept the quality going.

Charity of Night was next in 1997 and proved to be one of Cockburn's finest. The strange visages that are created from the cinematic lyrics (some of which are spoken Lou Reed-style) detailing mystery, lust, deception, and who knows what else, are truly something here and then there's the acoustic guitar and voice. "Pacing the Cage" is as deep as it gets dealing with the rut that life can see one settle into in need of an escape. "Night Train" is a cool song, grooving along with a shuffle aided by Rob Wasserman on bass and a classy black-and-white video and was to become yet another hit single in Canada.

Further studio albums have all been worth the wait with *Breakfast in New Orleans, Dinner in Timbuktu* (1999), *You've Never Seen Everything* (2003), *Speechless* (2005), *Life Short Call Now* (2006—this also featured a large string orchestra) and the folk/country-oriented *Small Source of Comfort* (2011) that included some intriguing instrumentals, such as "Parnassus and Fog" as well as lyrical material in "The Iris of the World" and the warped, bizarre "Call Me Rose," where ex-President Richard Nixon is reincarnated as a single mom living in the slums. Why not?

All of Bruce's live albums are excellent, and in the last few years a critically acclaimed documentary called *Bruce Cockburn Pacing the Cage: The Feature Documentary* was a major boon for fans in 2013 and even better was Bruce's long-hoped-for book *Rumours of Glory: A Memoir* released in November 2014, along with a career-spanning box set of eight CDs and one DVD also called *Rumours of Glory*.

Bruce was additionally made a member of the Order of Canada in 1982 and promoted to Officer twenty years later. In 2001, he was inducted into the Canadian Music Hall of Fame and the following year was inducted into the Canadian Broadcast Hall of Fame. Bruce also has six honorary doctorates and he received the Queen Elizabeth II Diamond Jubilee Medal in 2012. Cockburn has sixteen Gold albums and three Platinum albums in Canada and has placed twenty-one singles on the charts in Canada while putting nine albums on the US charts with *Stealing Fire* charting the longest, for thirty-one weeks.

On July 2, 2005 Bruce performed an excellent solo acoustic set at the Live 8 concert in Toronto, Ontario, in Canada (actually in Barrie, Ontario) and his version of "Waiting for a Miracle" was a highlight of the day. Besides his gifts as a writer on many topics, from religion to Central America to the environment, and his talents as a singer, Bruce Cockburn is one of the very finest guitar players to grace this planet. A good amount of people know that, but so many more should because this man has the goods. Need I say more?

I was truly honored to speak with Bruce in April 2015 on a glorious, warm, sunny day made all the better by getting to converse with this talented man…

Who were some of your musical influences as you began a musical career?

The music that made me want to start playing guitar was the original rock and roll. The big influences for me were Buddy Holly and the Crickets and Scotty Moore from Elvis Presley's band. That was the music that made me want to be a guitar player, but I soon discovered other models of players, like Wes Montgomery and Gabor Szabo, who had a series of albums in the early '60s as part of Chico Hamilton's band, and he had a real interesting style that appealed to me a lot. And also at the same time I discovered the old blues guys. Mississippi John Hurt was a big influence with his fingerpicking, as well as Mance Lipscomb and Brownie McGhee.

I wanted to comment on the fingerpicking because I enjoy that aspect of your playing so much. In the early days did you use much open tuning?

No, no open tuning in the early days; it was all standard tuning. I guess I should qualify that because I did do a lot of drop D tuning by just lowering the E string. Now since then, I've used quite a few different tunings. One is to drop the G string to F sharp. Another one is the DADGAD with an E on the bottom instead of the D, which I call EGAD.

Egads! [Laughs]

[Laughs]

You should copyright that.

I should, but I'll just add it to the folklore. [Laughs] There's also an open C tuning that I learned from listening to the Reverend Gary Davis on some things but not a lot.

That's extremely interesting. One of the first songs I heard from you when I was in high school—and my friend's stepfather had the Sunwheel Dance *album—was the title cut that is one of my most treasured guitar pieces by you. Do you remember the origins of that one?*

I do actually. In the late '60s I had run into a guy named Fox Watson, and I also ran into him a few times after that. Fox was from North Carolina and he had this beautiful style of playing fiddle tunes kind of slowed down in open tunings and it was a really nice effect and I had never heard anybody play like that. He really worked at it for a while and I kind of adopted some of that, and my first real attempt was the piece "Sunwheel Dance" and a little while later, I also had a piece called "Foxglove" which was named after Fox Watson.

I was going to ask about "Foxglove" because that is my second favorite guitar piece you have after "Sunwheel Dance."

"Foxglove" is in that open C tuning I mentioned earlier and "Sunwheel Dance" is actually in a D tuning, and I think that's the only piece I've ever done in that tuning. I was trying to do what Fox was doing to allow the melody to kind of appear over top the alternating bass. It's the same principle as Mississippi John Hurt's playing, but it was applied differently in this case. I think "Foxglove" comes closer to the style that Fox was doing than "Sunwheel Dance" does, but I was trying to create something that sounded like a fiddle tune, so that was "Sunwheel Dance."

That is really fascinating stuff there. I actually see sunshine on a front porch when I hear that song if that makes any sense to you at all.

Yeah, it kinda rolls around and feels sunny and it has a nice tune.

And I do know that instrumentals have to have names and they don't necessarily reflect what the piece is.

Yes, it's after the fact.

But sometimes they do make sense and here the title works. "Foxglove" was one I didn't quite get, but now I understand it. That album Night Vision *also had a long piece called "Islands in a Black Sky" that is amazing. The pieces that were instrumental; were they always intended as instrumentals or were there spots where lyrics were attempted but abandoned?*

They were always intended as instrumentals. When I write songs, the lyrics always come first, so I'm looking for music to fit those lyrics. When it's an instrumental piece, it's intended to be just that. I don't recall ever writing an instrumental piece that then became a song—I can't swear I've never done it, but I don't remember ever doing it!

The piece is long but never gets dull, which is not easy to do with long instrumentals. And it does sound as though it was intended to be instrumental.

It was, and it was a case of trying to incorporate improvisation because first and foremost I'm not an improviser, although I love improvised music. I end up writing these pieces and the pieces want to be repeated the way I wrote them. Once in a while I'm able to come up with something that gives me the space to be able to improvise and that was one example.

"Foxglove," although short seems the perfect length.

That was a composed piece and it is what it is, like "Sunwheel Dance" and a lot of the other stuff that I've written. There are moments when I come up with something that allows for improvising to happen but sometimes that works out by accident and I'm happy about that. There's a piece on *High Winds, White Sky* called "Ting/The Cauldron," which is me and two percussionists, and that is an improvised piece of music. Nothing was planned about that; we just got in the studio and played. I see that one differently than all the others because of that fact that there was no planning and no overriding scheme. "Islands in a Black Sky" was composed with a space in the middle for me to be able to improvise over that E drone in standard tuning.

And do you look back fondly on these pieces, or do they just seem from another time in another part of your career?

I don't play them anymore, but I don't regret them! [Laughs]

I hope you don't regret them because I like them so much! [Laughs] *Something like "Dialogue With the Devil," did you come up with all those lyrics prior to the music?*

Pretty much. There was a little give and take, and there's always that lyrical structure before I get into the music area.

"Lord of the Starfields" is an often talked about song, but that is really quite a lyric and the music couldn't possibly go any better with it than it does.

I don't remember exactly what I was thinking when I wrote the music. Some of what I say will be repeated from my book, but in this case I was at a friend's cabin well north of Toronto and I went alone walking at night and it's just a gravel road and there's no light and it's very remote and the towns around there are small.

I'm walking down this gravel road and though there was no moon, there was a sky full of stars, enough that you could make out the shapes of the trees on each side of the road and see where you were putting your feet and just walking in that atmosphere; I started thinking about God and that wonderful sense of the depth of things that you get sometimes from standing under the night sky. There are things that are so far away and there's a feeling that you are experiencing a brush with infinity. I started thinking about the starfields and I wanted to write a song like the ones in the Bible, so that was what happened.

There is a lot of stunning imagery in that song.

I've always attempted to write songs that had some substance to them. There's a range there as there are some silly songs and this would be a case in point of a song where I said something that I felt needed to be said and not that the world needed another guy talking about God, but in my heart I felt I needed to say these things. I don't think there any rules; I think you should be able to write about whatever is in your heart, and in this case, I did that.

When "Wondering Where the Lions Are" broke big in the States in 1980 from Dancing in the Dragon's Jaws, *were you surprised at, after flying under the radar in the US, that song in particular was such a big hit? And how did you find out how well that was doing in America?*

Well, I had a new record deal with Millennium Records at the time and it was felt among the circle of people I was dealing with at the time that that song had a chance at radio and I was going, "Yeah, whatever." Then I thought, "These guys know more about this than I do, so let's try it." And it worked. It worked probably based on the song and the promotion and effort that were made in getting it onto radio, at least in the States.

In Canada it was less surprising, I guess, because I did have a track record and though I'd never really had a big national hit, I did have a lot of songs that had gotten regional airplay. So that became—after ten years of recording—the one that was the big national hit. Of course, once it started to click in the States, all the Canadian radio stations were checking in to see what their American counterparts were doing and that enhanced it further in Canada, too.

The song that was more surprising that got on the air was "If I Had a Rocket Launcher" because there seemed to me no chance in hell that was ever going to be on the radio!

That defied logic! As a young kid in high school I was watching MTV all the time and that song got significant exposure that I look back at now, and think, "How was that possible?"

It did get a lot of airplay, but the thing was they hadn't figured out what they were yet. In 1984, MTV was still looking around for things and I don't know who got them to play that. Somebody must've made a phone call, but they did play it and that was a good thing.

I forget whether "Rocket Launcher" or "Lovers in a Dangerous Time" was first, but the next single around 1986 was "Call it Democracy" and that was a hit in Canada but not in the States. That got no exposure on MTV at all; they just flat-out refused to play it. They refused to play the video on the premise that it showed the logos of corporations and it was against their policy to gratuitously show corporate logos.

Ha! How ironic!

No kidding! And it was a white lie because they just didn't like politics at that time.

You had mentioned "Lovers in a Dangerous Time," which is my favorite song of yours, and that video holds up with the lighting, the color, and the imagery, although there are some hokey things in it.

Thanks for that, but it's the least favorite of all my videos.

Really? Oh no! [Laughs]

I like the song, but it was our first video and we were trying for something, and I look at it and it's like a bunch of hippies dancing around.

Well, it does have its artsy-fartsy pretentions; I won't deny that! [Laughs] *I do like it though and always have and, if I recall, you're playing a Flying V in that clip.*

I could be, but I don't remember!

Did you play a Flying V often?

I did in that period. I had a couple of Flying V's. I had an orange one and a blue-green one and they actually, they were really nice guitars and I kinda wish I still had one now, but I traded them for other things I needed. I went through a lot of electric guitars. In the early '80s I was playing Flying V's and electric guitars a lot.

"Lovers in a Dangerous Time" also features some nice Chapman Stick work, if I've always been hearing that right.

Yes, that's right. A lot of the music on that album was the result of collaborating with Fergus Marsh, who was a great bass player and a heavy Chapman Stick player who got heavier working with me because I made him use the top end of it. He was coming from the Tony Levin school of playing…

I was just about to mention how that sound was very much like Levin's.

Yeah, it was a really cool sound, but what intrigued me was the idea that you could put a Chapman Stick and a guitar together and you had this section of guitars coloring the whole sound spectrum. We put a lot of work into that album, working out guitar parts and Stick parts that meshed.

Both Peter Gabriel and King Crimson had a lot of Chapman Stick in their sound, and there you go: Tony Levin in both bands.

Yep.

Stealing Fire was actually your biggest selling album in the US as it spent something like thirty weeks on the charts.

I'd say so; that's probably true.

"Lovers in a Dangerous Time" is a very special song as is "Waiting for a Miracle," which I believe originated from a greatest hits album in 1987.

Yes, it was written in time for it to be on that compilation, but it was never on any studio album.

I like the original but the solo acoustic version is where I think it works best.

It goes over very well when I play it that way.

Going back to "Wondering Where the Lions Are," you did perform that on Saturday Night Live *in 1980, right?*

Yeah, we did do that on there.

Was that a little awkward for you to have been on such a big TV show?

I had done a number of local TV shows, but never anything of that scale, and it was my big national TV debut. It was one of only a few aside from a few big pop shows. The experience was harrowing. I don't like performing on TV anyway, but it's a very artificial atmosphere.

I guess it doesn't bother me as much now as it did then, but it seemed like such a fake atmosphere. It was stressful. The audience is looking at everything else going on and only marginally tuned into the music. There's no feedback from the audience and you have all these people running around talking on headphones yelling, "Hurry up, hurry up"! You get no chance to fix anything or if you screw up, there's no way of coming back on later in the show with some corny way of making people forget about it! I was feeling a lot of that.

The atmosphere in the studio was quite tense because a lot of the main characters on the show left soon after that and you could feel that tension between the cast and the producers. Nobody was mean to us or anything like that, but it was strange. The other band on the show was the Amazing Rhythm Aces, so we each played one song only.

There is an intriguing song on the Humans *album called "Tokyo" I'd like to ask you about.*

I was flying home from Tokyo and I wrote it. That was basically it. It's an impression of Tokyo. I'd been on a tour of Japan and I can't recall if that was the first or the second tour of Japan for me in the late '70s. That one and "Grim Travellers" were both the product of the same flight from Japan and the same note taking basically.

I was on my way to the airport in Tokyo to catch my flight home and we were stuck in freeway traffic as anyone always is there and the highway was divided and there was a canal that went down the middle of the two directions of lanes. The guardrail was broken and there was a crane parked in the opposite lane that was in the process of pulling this car from the canal.

I had a good chance to look at this. Someone could've been in that car or maybe they were moved by that time; I don't know, but the guardrail had been broken very recently. So, someone had gone off this freeway five stories high and had fallen into the canal with their car and it was kind of shocking, because in places like that where you are so dependent on the people around you to get you through your day because you can't even read or speak the language or understand a street sign—I just found myself feeling very vulnerable about a situation like that and very open to everything that is around me. I was in a state of heightened openness that it was pretty shocking to think that somebody might be dead right there.

And it had been a beautiful trip up to that point and other than working really hard, which is what everyone in Japan does anyway, it was magical. There were really interesting images and encounters, so this incident gave it a different twist and I started writing that on the plane. I just started with that and impressions of Tokyo like gray-suited guys pissing against the wall, which you see every day. Every day at 6 o'clock they hit the bars after work and get shitfaced and then they take the train home and in between work and the train, they're pissing on the walls!

That's some lovely imagery there. [Laughs]

[Laughs] Well, that's what I was getting at and the *pachinko* parlors and such. All that stuff went into it and put some perspective on the trip.

You had a late '90s album called Charity of Night *which has some of your most memorable songs on it. I won't pretend to quite know what's going on in the title cut.*

Well, here I may be repeating myself because it's in the book, but I don't mind talking about it. That song "Charity of Night" was about three events that are widely separated in time. It refers to the timeframe in the verses, and the spoken word part of it describes those events. I was in all of these events, but in the second verse, I put "she" in the verse as the pronoun instead of "he" because I wanted to create this unfolding love story because in the last verse they get together. So, there's a "he" in the first verse, a "she" in the middle, and they get together in the last verse and there's the two of them. That was the idea and the chorus is the idea of living with all these memories and the way in which life goes and flows and ebbs.

"Pacing the Cage" and "Night Train" are also excellent songs. I really feel it's one of your very best albums.

It's my favorite album along with the one that followed it *Breakfast in New Orleans, Dinner in Timbuktu.*

You also had Rob Wasserman on bass. Was that him in the "Night Train" video? I can't recall.

No, he was actually quite disappointed that he couldn't make the filming of that video. We couldn't work it out, but we wanted him in it. He didn't want people thinking that it was someone else playing the bass part on that song. [Laughs] He played on the whole album and I think it was Gary Craig on drums.

In 2005 you played the Live 8 concert in Toronto, which was a great cause.

It's interesting playing those big shows. I'm more comfortable in smaller places, but it's still good.

And did you get the call from Bob Geldof?

No, it would've been my management that got the call. I met him once sometime in the '80s but that was it.

With the box set, the book from your memoirs, and the Pacing the Cage *documentary, you have certainly been giving the fans a lot to digest.*

I've regurgitated a lot myself! It was a strange period of reminiscing. The box set exists because of the book, and it's a collection of all the songs that are in the box plus the extras. That was my manager Bernie Finkelstein's idea to do that and it was a good one. But there wasn't enough of dredging up the past, so the book added some more to it. [Laughs]

[Laughs] *With the book, was there a point where you said I just can't write anymore; I've lived too damn long!*

It was a chore and it was hard. The first 100 pages went quite easily and I had to have a friend help later as a co-writer, but most of the early part of it was me. My friend Greg King contributed overall to the shape of the book, but he's to blame for the amount of politics in the book. [Laughs]

I would've only put some in, but he pushed some parts in that direction because that's what he was interested in. I was happy with that, but I wouldn't have thought of that myself. It took three years to write the book. I wasn't writing songs or anything; every spare moment was dedicated to the book.

That book started around the time my second daughter was born and here I am trying to be a new Dad again and write the book and make a living with my career all at the same time and it was very hard. But it got done, and I'm glad that it did.

So it's safe to say you wouldn't do it again? [Laughs]

[Laughs] Not soon, until I forget how hard it was; maybe after that!

I can sympathize. I've been working on this book for a year. And when you're consumed by fitting the book into the little spare time you have, it's tough all right. In your case, we're not talking about a five-year career; we're talking about decades.

Almost fifty years of stuff. The mandate from the publisher was that they wanted a spiritual memoir; that's what they wanted initially. But they were unable to define what they meant by that, so it changed. And this became about my life entirely, although a lot got left out. It covered such a span, it could've been thousands of pages. Luckily, we were able to contain ourselves and limited it to around 500 pages.

We don't want you writing a Stephen King novel! Now, you're also in the Canadian Music Hall of Fame, which had to have been a nice honor.

It was! It was one of the nicest things that has come my way in my career. I'm not much at all for awards shows. I don't like the principles and the atmosphere, and I'm not into self-promotion. This, however, was a very nice honor. I had mixed feelings because on the one hand it was exciting, but it was also me thinking, "Aren't you supposed to be dead for an award like this?" [Laughs] Was it a kiss-off or something? But it turned out very nice and it was a big deal.

The biggest aspect was that I had to write a speech for national television and that was terrifying. That was all I could think about at first. The women that sang did very nice versions of my songs and there was this neat little film that they showed and all these people saying nice things about me. I was nervous though. I was fine when I made the speech as it turned out. As I was walking across the stage up to the lectern, it all fell away and I said, "I've been through this before, just be natural," and it went well. What was I worried about? [Laughs]

Well, it is unnatural and many people are fearful of public speaking. My final question: what guitar models acoustics and electric have you preferred through the years?

In the beginning it was actually Fox Watson who convinced me to get a Martin D-18. I was playing a Martin 00-18 at the time and I ended up giving that to my then-wife who, with my blessing, gave it to a friend of ours who is another fingerpicking guitar player and he still has it. It's a beautiful guitar and it has aged incredibly, so I kind of regret not having it now. The D-18 kept me in good stead for a long time.

And later into the '70s I got into handmade stuff. I had a Larrivee for a while and a Wren for a while made by David Wren and that got burnt in a fire at a rehearsal space. Then I floundered around for a while and I had a Yamaha that was slightly customized for me and I didn't like it at all. Eventually I got Manzer guitars by Linda Manzer who makes beautiful instruments. She apprenticed for Larrivee originally. I have two 6-strings and one 12-string that she made, as well as an electric charango that she made,which I think was the first one she made.

As for electric guitars, I have a bunch of them, and I don't get to play them as much because circumstantially what I've been doing for quite a few years has primarily been acoustic. I have a 1960s Gibson ES-175 and I've got a D-18 from 1959, which is the year I started playing and I don't use it very often. It doesn't have a pickup in it and I have a no-name guitar from 1959, which I had to have because, as I've said, that was the year I started playing. You might see someone like Jimmy Reed playing it back then. It's very cool to have and it sounds great.

I've got a few Charvel Surfcasters that I played a lot in the '90s and a bunch of others.

Any Fender guitars?

Yeah, I have a Jazzmaster and a Jazzmaster 12-string. I don't think I've ever used the 12-string anywhere but I've played it at home. The Jazzmaster you can hear on *Nothing But a Burning Light*, and that's the guitar you hear the most on that album. I also have a National Resolectric which I like a lot. I have a Les Paul studio which is a recent acquisition and I bought it because it wasn't like a regular Les Paul.

I really don't relate to those Les Pauls. They're good guitars and everything but I never really felt I could get what I wanted to out of those. I have an old S. S. Stewart Archtop too from way back that was another cheapo but that one you can hear on *You've Never Seen Everything*. It's an indulgence; the electric guitars are a musician's collection as opposed to a collector's collection because none of it's really collectible. There's always something wrong with them which make them affordable by being unusable! [Laughs]

Recommended solo: "Sunwheel Dance" from *Sunwheel Dance* solo album (1972)
Further info: www.brucecockburn.com
Photo credit: Kevin Kelly

CHAPTER 11

Dennis Coffey

(Born November 11, 1940, Detroit, MI)

Dennis Coffey has played on some of the most amazing songs any guitar player (or any musician for that matter) could have ever dreamed.

Coffey began playing guitar in his early teens in Detroit, Michigan, and played on his first session at age fifteen in 1955. He was a member of the Royaltones who scored a couple of minor hits in the early '60s and this band would also back up some fairly big names.

It wasn't until 1967, when Coffey became part of the renowned Funk Brothers that his career began to escalate. The Funk Brothers was the name given to the studio collective that played on all those wonderful songs at Motown Records. Coffey played differently from the other guitar players in the stable, such as Robert White, Eddie Willis, and Joe Messina. Coffey brought a mix of funk, rock, and soul into the songs and was very important for his use of effects that were only used sparingly on songs but had a lasting impact. Among the things Coffey brought in were the use of Echoplex, some fuzzy distortion, and a lot of wah-wah.

Coffey played on the Temptations' late '60s/early '70s hits such as "Cloud Nine" (a Top 10 hit in 1968), "Run Away Child, Running Wild" (a Top 10 hit in 1969 with Dennis's very distinctive wah-wah guitar running throughout) and the seriously awesome "Psychedelic Shack," another Top 10 hit in 1970, which continued a string of fantastic albums and singles where the Temptations found a gritty, funky sound that even rocked a little adapting to the times and singing about street life and a real world where things weren't so rosy.

And that wasn't all Coffey played on with the Temptations, also laying down sweet, understated licks on "Ball of Confusion (That's what the World is Today)" that landed at #3 on the charts later in 1970. Also, make sure to check out the full six-minute version of "Psychedelic Shack" that surfaced in 2003 on a compilation album that features some extended jamming and more of that groove you can't get enough of.

Coffey also played guitar on Diana Ross & the Supremes' #1 classic "Someday We'll Be Together" which went to #1 in late 1969 and would not be the same without those guitar figures. It was also the last of a crazy 12 #1 singles for the Supremes and was the last to feature Ross, who would leave in early 1970. It's hard not to think of all that when hearing this masterpiece of a song, just like it's hard to imagine it without those sly guitar parts that most casual listeners probably paid little notice to.

Freda Payne's classic "Band of Gold" also features Coffey on guitar although it is Ray Parker Jr. playing the lead. This very interesting song hit #3 in 1970 in the US and #1 in the UK. Also that year, Coffey could be heard playing on Edwin Starr's "War." The Temptations had already recorded the song for the *Psychedelic Shack* album but were very reluctant to put the song out as a single due to the heavy nature of the topic and the times. The legendary songwriting team of Norman Whitfield and Barrett Strong wrote this track and Whitfield, in particular, wanted it out as a single, so Starr volunteered to record it and took it to #1. The horns and guitars duke it out in a marvelous production that Whitfield executed brilliantly. The song, of course, would take on a new life in 1986 when Bruce Springsteen & the E. Street Band returned it to the Top 10 with their own powerful take.

Coffey also played that familiar intro to another Temptations classic on "Just My Imagination (Running Away with Me)" that went to #1 in 1971. Coffey would enjoy solo success with the divinely funky instrumental "Scorpio" that became a surprise Top 10 smash in 1971 selling over a million copies. The scratchy guitar and nasty funk make this a must-hear song filled with irresistible grooves, beats, and rhythms. The mid-section breakdown becomes a jungle strut with bongos and drums interlocked in a wicked groove and then fellow Funk Brother Bob Babbitt lays down a juicy bass solo. In January of 1972 Coffey had the distinction of becoming the first white performer on the infamous music/dance show *Soul Train*. Now that's respect.

Credited to Dennis Coffey and the Detroit Guitar Band, Coffey scored another instrumental hit with "Taurus," which cracked the Top 20 in 1972. The guitars are more prominent here and have a bit more bite. Yet again this is all about groove, rhythm, and funk, and it's deliriously good fun as were the albums Coffey put out, like the Top 40 album *Evolution* in 1971, as well as *Goin' for Myself* (1972), *Electric Coffey* (1973), and the 1974 releases *Dance Party* and *Instant Coffey,* with the latter including the great jazzy freak-out "Outrageous (The Mind Excursion)."

Coffey also did some film work scoring *Black Belt Jones* in 1974 and found success as a producer with Gallery's massive hit from 1972 "Nice to Be with You." This ultra-catchy song became a Top 5 US single, sold over a million copies, and featured Coffey as coproducer and arranger.

Dennis also discovered talented singer/songwriter Sixto Rodriguez who was signed to Sussex Records, the same label that Coffey was on. Coffey plays lead guitar and co-produced and arranged the debut album *Cold Fact*. Though the album flopped in 1970, as did the follow-up *Coming from Reality* in 1971 (which Coffey also had a hand in, though he did not play on this one), Rodriguez as he was now known became a cult figure in Australia where he had a great deal of success.

After disappearing, Rodriguez became something of a myth in various countries where his music continued to sell, such as South Africa, Zimbabwe, and New Zealand. Rumors of his death were false and he resurfaced in the 2000s to acclaim, which led to the Oscar-winning documentary film *Searching for Sugar Man* in 2012 in which Coffey appears. Rodriguez now regularly tours around the world to great crowds. What an amazing story, and it couldn't have happened without Dennis Coffey having discovered him with Mike Theodore!

Dennis is still very much getting it done—playing as well as ever and delivering the funk as he wishes here in 2015.

In February of 2015, I was happy to speak with Dennis about his career then and now, and just listening to him telling me all these amazing stories and musical moments was a blast.

I see you're still out there gigging, including last night. How is the current live situation working out with gigs?

Well, I've got over 5,000 Facebook friends, so they all need to show up at the gigs! [Laughs]

Facebook is a waste in some ways, but it definitely can help with promoting things. Moving on, who were some of the players, even if they weren't guitarists, who got you started with music?

Well you know what? My mom said I could deem what was going on in every song on the radio at about two years old. Her side of the family was very musical. My dad bought me a guitar at a pawn shop when I was very young for like $15 and it was a Harmony acoustic guitar. When I went up north, I had two cousins and they both played guitar and sang country music and I used to go up there every summer for a week up in the Copper country in Michigan. They showed me a few chords and that was what got me up and running.

Through the years what models of guitars have you preferred?

It's always been Gibson. It's interesting because when I played on my first record at fifteen years old, it was the song "I'm Gone" by Vic Gallon. I was in high school and got the call to play on the record. I had to get a band together with some guys my age and older. The bass player was twenty-one, so he drove to the session and we cut the two sides of the single and Vic sang and played acoustic guitar and within three or four weeks I was hearing myself on country radio.

And what did your parents think?

My mom saw me doing garage bands and how much I practiced, so she was supportive. I was lucky enough that by the age of sixteen, I was doing a few gigs a week in wedding bands and playing teen clubs.

Where did the funk playing come from?

I started playing Jimmy Reed stuff and then we got in to playing Doo Wop songs. Then I started learning B. B. King and the Blues and Sun Records songs from Elvis Presley and Carl Perkins. About six or seven years ago, I played at a Gibson event at the Gibson Guitar Factory and I actually saw Sonny Burgess, who was the first artist on Sun Records, play with what was left of the original Sun Records rhythm section about an hour's worth of rockabilly. When you heard them play this stuff, you really got it and said, "Hey, this where it all comes from."

I got a chance to meet Scotty Moore and since then I've done two or three gigs with James Burton.

Wow, there's some serious, serious players! Was it around 1967 or so when you became part of the Funk Brothers team for Motown Records?

Yeah, it was right around '67 or '68. I went into the service for a few years; I had volunteered for the draft and I was in the 101st Airborne Division. When I came out of the service, I was recording down in South Carolina with Maurice Williams and other people, and I had a record out when I was still in the Army as Clark Summit. They made up that name.

So that was your pseudonym? [Laughs]

I don't even know where they came up with that. I think it was a town in Pennsylvania. [Laughs]

It is, it's not far from here! So what led to the Motown work?

Well, I was playing with the Royaltones in the early '60s and I recorded with Daryl Banks and there was the Volumes—all that Northern soul stuff. The first million-seller I was on was "Handy Man" with Del Shannon around 1964 or so. So I did all those kinds of things and more work with Del. Then I started working at the Golden World label for Eddie Wingate doing sessions for J. J. Barnes and Edwin Starr and those guys.

Then Motown bought Golden World Studios and in that timeframe I got a call from James Jamerson—the Funk Brothers bass player—and he knew I was playing in a lot of soul clubs at the time. He introduced me to Hank Cosby who was Stevie Wonder's producer and he was a contractor for all the musicians at Motown. Essentially he said that Motown had decided to create a producer's workshop in the upstairs of Golden World Studios for the purpose of letting the producers experiment when they weren't on the studio clock and therefore not on a union scale.

So, they told me they'd put me on a retainer once a week and I think it was two-and-one-half hours from 7 to 9:30 and I'd be in this workshop. A lot of producers would come through the workshop and Norman Whitfield came in there one day and he was producing this song "Cloud Nine" by the Temptations, and he put the music chart up and I saw the part and I said I thought I could put this wah-wah sound on there with my pedal and took it out of my bag. He heard that and said, "That's it! That's what I want!" and within two weeks I was playing on "Cloud Nine" with the Temptations and that's how it all started!

I am assuming it was usually the musicians as a collective working on these songs and then the band or vocal group or whatever would do their thing. Was there any interaction with the Temptations between you guys and them?

No, the basic thing that happened most of the time was usually we were there with the arranger and the producer. They had these master rhythm charts and we had to read them and divide up the guitar parts, put some hot licks in it and create a feel to make a hit single. We churned out one song an hour.

There were other Temptations smashes at this time in the late '60s/early '70s such as "Ball of Confusion," "Runway Child, Running Wild" and "Psychedelic Shack"—in fact, I only recently heard the full six-minute version of that song and there were quite a few other elongated songs that were of a jam-like nature at this time.

Yeah, that was Norman Whitfield taking Motown on a 180-degree turn because he was very savvy and went out in the clubs and was very tuned into the whole psychedelic movement with all those protest songs and such.

It really was an amazing thing. He seemed determined to make Motown current and hip and not be stuck in a time warp doing the same old things over and over again. He didn't want to be dated or out of fashion. It was very forward-thinking.

Yeah, and I was the guy to help him do it because I was the guy with the wah-wah pedal and I had the Echoplex. "Ball of Confusion"—he just said to create something in the front, count it off, bam! And off we went. That stuff was all done in real time—there were no overdubs or anything like that.

Is that right?

Oh yeah. Any of the things I did like "Friendship Train" with that intro for Gladys Knight & The Pips and "Psychedelic Shack" with the Temptations or even "Just My Imagination" with the Temptations...those wild intros I created on the fly. I just counted it off, read the chart and it was time to go.

That's so awesome. Those distinctive guitar parts of yours on songs like "Smiling Faces" from the Undisputed Truth and the Dramatics song "In the Rain." I mean, I can clearly hear your playing, even if it's just in a few spots on those wonderful songs. It sure sounds like the Echoplex to me, but I may be off there.

You're right, that is indeed the Echoplex on "In the Rain."

When did you first use the Echoplex and realize it could be used to your advantage?

I was working with the Royaltones and we had an old PA and needed an echo sound, so we used an Echoplex they had for a microphone echo. That's what was big in the '50s. Somewhere down the road I ended up buying one and ran a guitar through it, and that's kinda how that started.

You had mentioned Edwin Starr earlier and you played on "War" correct?

Yes indeed, and I also played on his hit "Stop Her on Sight (S.O.S.)" before "War" for Golden World Records.

The Temptations recorded "War" first in 1970, but did not want to issue it as a single because of the topicality of it, so Edwin Starr did his version later that year and took it to #1 with your guitar parts! What part did you play on the song?

I'm playing that high part you can hear with that fuzztone running throughout the choruses.

I thought that was you, I wasn't sure though! Another legendary song you played on was what turned out to be the last #1 single for Diana Ross & the Supremes, "Someday We'll Be Together." Again, what part was yours there?

I'm doing that vibrato part on the verses and choruses that rings. And then I do the backbeat on the choruses.

Did you have any idea that the Supremes were about to implode? It almost sounds like a farewell song.

I only saw her (Diana Ross) a few times, so I had no idea. She was shy but very nice to me. I would see her talking to Berry Gordy about things but didn't know what. At that point, I was pretty much doing double sessions every day, which would be from 11:00 a.m. to 2:00 p.m. and 3:00 p.m. to 6:00 p.m. and then head over to Golden World and do the workshop from 7:00 p.m. to 9:30 p.m. By 10:00 p.m., I was at Tower Studios doing work for Freda Payne, Chairmen of the Board and all those people.

I was going to ask about the Freda Payne session as well. How did playing on "Band of Gold" happen? This was yet another monster hit.

I had a choral sitar by that point and that was a written part so I just went in and did my thing on that song.

Moving on to your solo career, there was of course "Scorpio." I love that song and I always found it interesting, because here you are, a guitar player, and you allowed the rhythm section to breathe and take over in the mid-section for a couple of minutes.

I learned that from Norman (Whitfield). He was always doing those breakdowns and I used the Funk Brothers except for (James) Jamerson because he was unavailable, so I used (Bob) Babbitt and he laid down that amazing bass solo.

The whole thing is just so funky and dyn-o-mite. [Laughs] *Were you shocked when it became a Top 10 single in 1971? That was a million-selling smash after all.*

What happened was the album was out for a year and didn't do squat. So I'm in the middle of doing the *Goin' for Myself* album with an orchestra thinking nobody wants a guitar band and Ron Mosely calls me up from New York—and he was the National Promotion guy for Sussex Records—and he says, "Man, these clubs are just pounding 'Scorpio' so whatever you're doing just stop and do a three guitar band song or just stop in total, because I'm going to rework 'Scorpio'." That's just what he did and the thing just took off.

And then "Taurus" became a Top 20 hit and I kinda liked that one even better because of the odd guitar sounds and that it was a little more guitar based.

Ya know, Kim Thayil from Soundgarden told me that too. He said hearing "Taurus" got him started on playing guitar.

Wow, that's high praise because he's awesome.

Yeah, it's cool! [Laughs]

I believe you were also the first white act to perform on Soul Train in 1972.

Absolutely; I was before Elton John. Nobody seems to be able to find the tape. And, I performed live with no pantomiming. In fact, I brought the whole band in there and the place was so crowded that nobody could move. One of the guys that worked at that station said, "We've got 25% more people than can fit in this place because they knew you were gonna be here playing!"

And do you recall meeting Don Cornelius at all?

Oh yeah, sure. I met him in Chicago one time and then I saw him in Los Angeles when my second wife and I were looking for a house out there. We saw him on the strip somewhere like the Hyatt Regency or something and he sent us over a bottle of champagne, which I thought was pretty cool.

Yeah, that's very cool and quite thoughtful. Now, throughout the '70s into the early '80s you continued to release some fine albums like Instant Coffey, *which I really liked that had more of a jazz direction.*

Yeah, that was James Jamerson who had an influence on that album.

You had a really nice solo catalog and you weren't afraid to embrace a little disco or music that was danceable either and other styles that I thought showed versatility.

I didn't mind at all. Now, I still do the funk and the Motown and I mix it all together and I sing and also do traditional jazz with upright bass and I enjoy it all because it's different.

I had the chance to play with Les Paul before he passed away. A couple months before that happened I went to the Rock and Roll Hall of Fame and played with Larry Carlton and Joe Bonamassa and John Pizzarelli. It was the 50th anniversary of the Gibson ES-335 and was a tribute to Larry Carlton. So I did that and then I was invited to play with Les Paul as a tribute to him. There were twelve guitar players there, including Duane Eddy and the Ventures, and it went right up through to myself, James Burton, Billy Gibbons, and then Richie Sambora and Slash. We were all there paying tribute to Les Paul and we all did a couple of songs and each of us soloed with Les—it was great.

You also played in the early days of Funkadelic; is that right?

I just recorded on that first album and the first song I recorded with George Clinton was "I Wanna Testify" with the Parliaments.

I love that song. I just cannot get over all these songs you've been a part of. You also played guitar on Stevie Wonder's excellent version of the Beatles classic "We Can Work it Out."

Yeah, I think I was part of the backbeat on that one. Did you know Stevie produced "It's a Shame" by the Spinners? He produced that record and I'm on that one too. The two Funk Brothers couldn't get the drum parts quite right so Stevie grabbed the sticks from the guys and played the part himself! [Laughs]

I knew he produced the song but I didn't know the rest of that. I love him even more now! And you also played with Marvin Gaye on the I Want You *album from 1976.*

I'm on that whole album. It was me and Ray Parker Jr. doing the guitars on that album.

Ray is great, too. There was so much detail and so much going on these singles and albums you played on and the guitars were never very prominent in the mix.

Yeah, that's true.

Did you ever feel a little disappointed in that, that maybe just a little tweak here or a slight boost or emphasis on a certain part might've been better? Or was it just to play the best parts for the betterment of the songs?

You know what, I was a hired gun and I was so busy I had no time to think about it. At Motown I was playing on so many hits, then I'd go down to Muscle Shoals in Alabama or record in Nashville or Miami for Atlantic Records and Jerry Wexler from Atlantic tried to hire me on board, but I was making too much money at Motown so I couldn't leave.

You didn't go with Motown when they moved to Los Angeles correct?

That's right. I didn't move out there with them. I was always independent on a retainer for the producer's workshop, so they didn't have me under contract. Back in the day what I did was I recorded an instrumental version of the Isley Brothers "It's Your Thing." Mike Theodore and I were partners and we were doing production together. Mike sent one copy to Clarence Avant and I handed one to Hank Cosby.

Clarence responded and he loved it and he gave us a deal. So we were getting ready to go into the studio and all the contracts were signed. A few months later Hank told us that Berry Gordy loved it and wanted to sign us to Motown but it was too late as we were now with Sussex, or Maverick, as they may have been called at the time.

The whole Rodriguez thing fascinates me to this day. With that first album Cold Fact, *did you look at it like it was just another album or, despite the lack of sales that would follow, did you have any inkling to how good he was?*

That was a thing where Mike Theodore and I discovered him. His manager called us and like the movie said, we went and saw him at a place called the Sewer and we signed him up and arranged and produced that album. I play all the guitar parts except for the acoustic guitars, which were played by Rodriguez. I also played bass on the song "I Wonder." The first four songs, we recorded him by himself because he was so shy and added the band later.

Because he was so talented you had to have felt pretty good doing this album.

We all believed in him, but it took so long for him to be recognized. I opened for him in London and Birmingham in the UK last spring in packed houses. Just those two shows though.

That's fantastic. It's wild that he had this huge following in the '70s and beyond in places like Australia, New Zealand, and South Africa, but nobody knew he was here until the film.

It was ironic because he'd call me at all hours of the night and he'd be reading *Billboard* saying I can't believe who is doing well and making money. He was struggling and making nothing at the time. Thirty years later he was saying the same things but now he was living it!

Such an amazing story and proof that never giving up can work out sometimes.

It's something all right.

You put out a solo album recently a few years back.

That was a self-titled album in 2011. I toured for that including London, Paris, and all over, and I played US festivals like Bonnaroo and South by Southwest twice.

Bonnaroo, huh? That's pretty wild.

Yeah, I also played the Long Beach Funkfest. I played in Chicago, Philly, and Cleveland, and all over and finished it here in Detroit.

You're still using the trusted Gibsons right?

Yes! What happened was my Motown was a Firebird Gibson and my jazz/funk guitar was a Gibson Byrdland, which I started using again tonight. It's got fifty years of funk in it and we had some funky things going on last night!

Sounds like a great time.

It was. And after the Les Paul gig, Gibson decided that they would give me a new guitar, and they gave me a 355 pretty much to my specs and what I wanted on it, so I use that sometimes for recording and for concerts. I did a few concerts with the Les Paul Trio as well in New York after Les passed away and I played with them again in his hometown of Waukesha, Wisconsin.

I'd say you have had one helluva career.

And I've been sampled an awful lot and gotten paid in a pretty good deal. LL Cool J is one among about twenty others.

It's nice to see you playing festivals where a younger crowd can see you perform.

We get young people all the time at my gigs because I change things up every night and throw in different styles. I'm there to play and these young guys I play with play their asses off. I just count the songs off and there they go.

Speaking of younger musicians, you have collaborated recently with Mayer Hawthorne who I like quite a bit.

There's a great video of us doing "All Your Goodies are Gone." And when I played in London recently he flew over to join me and I had Amy Winehouse's band behind me and a few female singers. It was a wild show.

I think he gets it and that was a great collaboration on an old Parliaments tune. Recorded and mixed beautifully, too.

He does get it, although it's funny because he tried to dictate how I would play and I told him, "The only one that ever did that to me was Stevie Wonder and you're not going to do that!" [Laughs] I went along with whatever he wanted though, so it worked out.

Does it soak in all these years later about everything you've played on?

It does, but my newest thing is doing gigs with a straight-ahead jazz band, and the other night the place was packed for our first gig. I played with Jerry Mackenzie and he used to play and record with Stan Kenton. We had a good time.

It's been a pleasure talking to you because growing up I always wanted to know who those guys were playing on those songs. I knew who sang them, but I was more interested in the musicianship. Motown and Philadelphia International had so many amazing players.

They had a good scene there with Philly International. When I got the Funk Brother Pioneer award in Philly, we went over to that studio that Gamble and Huff owned.

That is a huge part of Philly's musical history, trust me.

They made great records. I always looked at it like you had Motown, Philly International, and Stax Records, but Motown was the powerhouse with Berry. Berry told me that he couldn't have started Motown anywhere but Detroit because of the city, and he was such a visionary.

Where else could it have been but Detroit?

Nowhere else, but Philly was right behind and so was Stax. Motown was the tops though.

Recommended solo: "Taurus" from *Goin' for Myself* solo album
with the Detroit Guitar Band (1972)
Further info: www.denniscoffeysite.com
Photo credit: Doug Coombe

CHAPTER 12
Ian Crichton
(Born Ian Stevenson Crichton, August 3, 1956, Oakville, Ontario, Canada)

Saga is one of the greatest bands to ever come out of Canada and there have been plenty of great musical acts from the Great White North. Saga also has had one of the finest guitarists anywhere in Ian Crichton, who has been there with the band for their entire nearly four decade career.

Starting life as Pockets and thankfully ditching that horrible name, they became Saga and issued their self-titled debut album in 1978 through indie label Maze Records. The band consisted of Michael Sadler (vocals/keyboards), Ian (guitar), Ian's brother Jim (bass/keyboards), Peter Rochon (keyboards), and Steve Negus (drums). The material was a mix of progressive rock, hard rock, and AOR. Snappy opener "How Long" had percolating synths mixed with riff-heavy guitars and an almost Queen-like guitar breakdown in the mid-section. Epics such as "Ice Nice" and "Tired World (Chapter Six)" were quite progressive and Ian's guitars were something that leapt out at the listener. No pun intended, but "Ice Nice" is one cool song. Highly unusual in arrangement and very proggy and even jazzy, laced with drabs of electric piano and synths that lull the listener into a dreamy state, things get ripping in the solo section to the outro.

The next album *Images at Twilight* was more of the same and that was a good thing. "Mouse in a Maze" and "It's Time" (Chapter Three) are among the best cuts, and Greg Chadd replaced Rochon in the band as well.

In late 1980, Saga issued *Silent Knight,* which was their finest moment yet. With Jim Gilmour (keyboards) replacing Chadd, the band crafted more symphonic songs, including the chilling epic "Don't Be Late" (Chapter Two), which became a surprise hit on the fledgling MTV the following year. Eerie vocoders, floating beds of synths, quietly muted guitars, and a hushed vocal all give way to a propulsive finale where the guitars on keyboards blend as one (and three different members are playing them) in Yes-like fashion with trade-off solos and Ian Crichton's work is masterful. Hard to believe something like this could be as popular as a music video, but these were the glory days of MTV in 1981. The network also played "Careful Where You Step." The album went Gold in Canada and thanks to MTV, Portrait Records gave the band a major label deal.

Worlds Apart was a fantastic album from start to finish, and Rupert Hine's production was perfect for the band entering the mainstream while retaining their signature sound. In 1982, "On the Loose" became a surprise US Top 30 single aided by a clever video that acted as a mini-movie, accenting the song's cinematic sound. The mid-section features a sweeping solo by Ian in tandem with the galloping keyboards. His familiar staccato lines are amazing and can be heard on the popular follow-up single "Wind Him Up," also a US hit and MTV favorite. Ian's picking as well as his ability to bend a note are always a thrill to hear and a key to the Saga sound. The otherworldly "No Stranger (Chapter Eight)" brought a conclusion to the story being told since the first album dealing with Einstein. A crackling solo and rollicking drumming make this an exciting piece of music. "Amnesia" and "Time's Up" are other highlights. The album also made the US Top 30 and went Gold and they won a Juno (Canadian Grammy).

In 1983, *Heads or Tales* featured some more classic material in the edgy "The Flyer" (a minor US hit single) and "Catwalk" (just listen to these riffs by Ian), which both found favor on MTV and a bit on the radio, and the album made the US Top 100. And again they went Gold in Canada as well as Germany where they had a rabid fan base. And by the way, the unedited eight-minute version of "Catwalk" has an insane solo by Ian that is ridiculously good and one of his finest moments. How did this not make the original album??? "Scratching the Surface" and "The Pitchman" (listen to the guitar picking on this song!) were also fine examples that the band were creatively on fire.

In 1985, the band stopped working with Hine as producer and the end result was the commercial styling of *Behavior*. The album still had serious merits and the single "What Do I Know?" was a subtle, beautifully conceived song with a guitar solo of sheer eloquence. The solo allows the song to go a different place melodically. An attractive video received fair MTV play and the song made the US Top 25 at rock radio, but it should've reached higher heights. Many of the songs on this album are emotional and quite captivating such as "You and the Night" (almost exclusively driven by keyboards and electronic percussion, Ian comes in with a sweet solo echoing the likes of David Gilmour) and the lengthy "(Goodbye) Once Upon a Time," written by Sadler about his recently late father. This was to be the band's last album to chart in the US.

Internal issues led to both Negus and Gilmour leaving and a new deal with Atlantic followed. Curt Cress came in on drums and *Wildest Dreams* came out in 1987 and flopped. A shame, as the album saw a continuation of the melodic themes of the previous album, but an over-reliance on programming, midi-guitar, and synthaxe stripped away a lot of the heart of the band. Despite this, "Only Time Will Tell" was a pleasant single that sadly got buried, and yet again the guitar playing was wonderful. The album, however, was weak overall, but "We've Been Here Before" was a prize.

When Negus and Gilmour returned in 1993, the band started to return to their hallmark sound and incorporated modern elements with *Security of Illusion*. Listen to the crunch of "Mind over Matter"; it rocks, and Ian's guitar playing is going new places. Each album in the '90s saw the band working out different things—some good, some not. Glen Soble took over on drums in 1997, but with Negus back, the band began a series of striking albums that really defined who Saga always were starting with the excellent *Full Circle* in 1999 with "Remember When" (Chapter 9), "Time Bomb," and "Uncle Albert's Eyes" (Chapter 13) strong tracks featuring that stunning guitar work from Ian Crichton. *House of Cards* (2001) and *Marathon* (2003) were such strong albums.

Crichton also appeared on Asia's album *Aura* in 2001, playing on five cuts including the song "Come Make My Day" which he co-wrote and the nine-minute epic "Free" that also featured ex-Asia members Steve Howe and Pat Thrall on guitar.

Things got even better with *Trust* (2006) and *10,000 Days* (2007), both with new drummer Brian Doerner. *10,000 Days* was the final album for Sadler who announced he was retiring after the tour for the album. This was one of the band's best albums ever produced thanks to tracks such as: "Lifeline," "Book of Days," "Corkentellis," and "More Than I Deserve." If this was the swan song, then so be it. Doerner suffered a heart attack and couldn't start the tour so Chris Sutherland filled in until Doerner was well.

In 2008, Rob Moratti was plucked from obscurity to sing after a YouTube search failed and 2009's *Human Condition* proved to be even better despite the major hole of Sadler's absence. Moretti's voice was different but incredibly rich and strong. The album was a heady mix of prog and hard rock bordering on fusion and metal at times as shown on "Human Condition," a blistering track where Ian was able to wield his axe venturing into fusion/metal/prog territory, not too dissimilar to Dream Theater. The guitar playing is beyond intense. "Crown of Thorns" is also devastating and "Let it Go," "Hands of Time," and "Step Inside" are all wondrous and Ian's guitars are something else.

Sadler returned in 2011 and *20/20* (with new drummer Mike Thorne), while not as good as its predecessor, was another example of this band's commitment to excellence and Ian Crichton's guitar wizardry. "Six Feet Under," "Anywhere You Wanna Go," "Till the Well Runs Dry," and "Ellery" all prove they were as good as ever, and *Sagacity* from 2014 (their 21st album) was another amazing release proving that some bands (although not many) end up better in their old age much like Uriah Heep or Rush. It would place in the Top 20 in Germany.

"Let It Slide" shows that modern Dream Theater touch, yet the main sound is still very much Saga and how Ian Crichton continues to come up with the goods time and again is a mystery. His guitar work on this song is stellar and "Go with the Flow" and "Let It Slide" are fantastic. This whole band is underrated, but Ian Crichton is such a pleasure to listen to, and he plays some beautiful acoustic passages on "Go with the Flow" and then in comes the changes and right back again.

Look, the lifelong Saga fans (and there's a ton in Canada, Puerto Rico, and Germany, among other locales) know how stunning a player Ian Crichton is. It would be nice if more rock fans were aware of his excellence.

Ian is such a wonderful guy and here are his responses to some questions from an interview in January 2015:

Who were some of the guitar players that influenced you over the years, especially when first starting out?

I started playing at thirteen years old; at that time all the greats were rising: Clapton, Hendrix, Beck, Page, Blackmore, and it was very exciting to me, all these guys playing their twist on guitar and pioneering at the same time. By age fifteen, I could play well, learning from figuring out what they were playing, then came the John McLaughlin's, Al Di Meola's, etc.—fusion was here, but I most loved progressive rock as these bands were so different from each other.

What are the favored types of guitars of yours through the years and why?

I'm a Stratocaster guy, bought my 1964 in 1969, it did the first 5 Saga CD's mainly. I also used a '77 Les Pro, and all the Gibson line from the '50s–'60s and Fender of course are favorites, but there are a lot of smaller company makers that are great now. I've been playing Musicman and also Lado for the last twenty-five years, but when it comes to recording, the Strat still comes out, I stopped using it on the road for fear of damage or theft.

One very significant part of your sound is that staccato playing style, which is also a part of the signature sound of Saga. What led you to developing that and how tricky was it to perfect as well as use properly within the band's music?

That was the fusion side coming out. In a rock genre, the keyboard lines in Saga are tricky on guitar. Lines that are easier on guitar are tricky on keys. It's always been a great exercise playing lines that are written on keys.

MTV played a huge role in Saga's US success in the early 1980s. I still remember seeing the video for the amazing "Don't Be Late" very often the first few years. I know the band later thanked MTV for helping Saga land a major label deal with Portrait Records in 1982. When did you become aware of MTV and the fact your videos were getting played so often?

Right from the beginning, we heard there was a lone station playing music videos in the States and we did two videos in Toronto. There was really not very much product for them [MTV] to play from other artists...yet, they played us over and over, which lead to the CBS deal with Portrait. MTV was on everywhere by then and they played us heavily for a decade.

Along those lines, why is it "On the Loose" became such a big hit in the US? It's a great song, but it has a long instrumental mid-section; it rocks and it certainly isn't commercial, yet it became a smash. The well-directed MTV video helped a lot, but why was it only this song that became such a big hit here, or is it just one of those hard-to-explain things?

Well we had a few hits, "Wind Him Up," "The Flyer," "Only Time Will Tell," and others, but "On the Loose" was the biggest—the middle section I played is melodic, so it worked in a hit song, had it been a "go for it solo," it would have been edited.

Can you take me through the solo on "Catwalk"? The full eight-minute version in particular is my absolute favorite of yours and that's saying something because I am so fond of your guitar work.

Back then I used a 1 x 12 Mesa boogie combo and a Roland Jazz 120 chorus amp, all of the guitars were played off the bed track takes, half the solos also. We partitioned the instruments with office—movable walls. Baffles, it was recorded at Farmyard Studio in England, which was a farm-studio, a lot of ambience! The end solo was a one-take thing live. The producer Rupert Hine really wanted it on the record; I was so-so about it, but people have mentioned that to me many times.

I feel that most of your recent albums such as House of Cards, Trust *and* 10,000 Days *are easily among your finest. It's so refreshing to hear bands like yourselves who have been around so long still crafting high-quality albums that aren't just product. With the current musical climate, how tough is it to put in so much work these days knowing sales will be what they will be?*

Good question, been dealing with that for over twenty years and it's just got worse. Nowadays it's competing with free sites. Hit number 1 artists are selling 500k. At the end of the '80s we sold 450k just in the States, and were looked at like...these guys aren't going anywhere anymore. Funny, sort of isn't it? But we love new music and people who are into Saga appreciate this; it makes live shows better and current.

The album with Rob Moratti singing called The Human Condition *has some mind-blowing material, like the title track, which is very close to Dream Theater-styled metal/prog/fusion and "Crown of Thorns." How much of a challenge was it writing without Michael Sadler there?*

That CD I went nuts on; Michael had left and the challenge of replacing his voice was daunting. In the end we chose just a great vocalist, then came the writing. I was writing for eight months or more. There is a lot of music still around from that, we chose the tunes and worked with Rob on the Saga way of things and he did a great job. It was a different-sounding band though—but refreshing after so many years. I'm fond of that record, but it didn't work live, and a few years later Michael came back. On we go.

With the new record Sagacity and cuts such as "Let it Slide" the band and you are showing no signs of slowing down and there is a willingness to keep experimenting. Has your approach to writing and soloing changed in recent times?

Not changed but developed I'd say. I know "On the Loose" was a big hit, but for me later material was better. I still write the same way, which is in my studio at home in the basement. I can produce a song (idea) in a day or three. I always come to the Saga table with thirty to thirty-five song ideas. Having said that, Jim Gilmour does the same; it's a picky band and our ideas combined usually make up one Saga song.

Final silly question I ask most players: If you had to change a Saga album or song to be named after a cat theme what would you come up with? My cats are curious (and no, you can't use "Catwalk"!).

"Minou"—which is pussy in French…as in cat. She followed my daughter to school when Kaitlyn was six years old. Twenty-one years later she passed and is missed. We now have Mini and she's six years old.

Recommended solo: "Catwalk" from *Heads or Tales* with Saga (1983)
*especially the extended version on the remastered version of the album
Further info: www.sagaontour.ca
Photo credit: Alexander Mertsch

CHAPTER 13
Rik Emmett
(Born Richard Gordon Emmett, July 10, 1953, Toronto, Ontario, Canada)

Toronto guitarist/vocalist Rik Emmett came to prominence with hard rock outfit Triumph (who formed in 1975 with drummer/vocalist Gil Moore and bassist/keyboardist Mike Levine) and released two albums through the Canadian label Attic Records. The title cut of their sophomore album *Rock and Roll Machine* featured an extended guitar solo spotlight for Emmett that attracted a lot of attention and featured guitar pyrotechnics that rivaled Eddie Van Halen.

RCA Records in the US signed the band in 1978 and issued the US version of *Rock and Roll Machine* that featured tracks from both Canadian LPs including the prog rock epic "Blinding Light Show/ Moonchild," which was a stunning achievement at such an early stage for the band.

In 1979, *Just a Game* broke the band, eventually going Gold and providing the Top 40 hit "Hold On," as well as the moody rocker "Lay It on the Line." Both Emmett's singing and playing were outstanding and Rik also had a classical guitar piece called "Fantasy Serenade" on the album, which showed his versatility. Triumph's first Top 40 album was 1980's *Progressions of Power* that would prove to be their heaviest, and included the party anthem "I Live for the Weekend" that featured five glorious minutes of Emmett shredding away. The instrumental acoustic piece "Finger Talkin'" was another *ahem*, triumph.

The group hit the big time with 1981's *Allied Forces*, which went Platinum and produced a string of radio hits, including the spirited "Fight the Good Fight" one of Emmett's finest vocal and guitar songs, the headbanger "Allied Forces" and the inspirational "Magic Power," which went on to be one of the band's most enduring songs. Another guitar piece "Petite Etude" offered classical shadings. *Never Surrender* was a Gold album in 1983 and the title cut contained one of Rik's most complex guitar solos. The band would perform in front of over 300,000 fans at the US Festival '83 later that year.

In 1984, the band signed to MCA and developed a more commercial sound on the Gold LP *Thunder Seven*. Yet again, Emmett made every moment count and the gorgeous acoustic instrumental "Midsummer's Daydream" became a fan favorite, while the blues instrumental "Little Boy Blues" closed the album in fine fashion. "Time Goes

UNSTRUNG HEROES

By" sported one of his finest solos laid down thus far. An elaborate stage/laser show accompanied the 1985 tour and led to the live LP *Stages*.

In 1986, *Sport of Kings* album made the Top 40 and garnered the band's biggest hit with "Somebody's Out There," which was a US Top 30 single. "Embrujo" was Emmett's guitar piece, but the album's melodic, keyboard based sound lessened the heaviness, although a few cuts like "Play with the Fire" and "Hooked on You" rocked. Fans and those in the band were not thrilled with the new direction and the label was adding to the problem. The band even added keyboardist/guitarist Rick Santers on the tour, an obvious nod to how much technology went into the album.

In 1987, *Surveillance* sold disappointingly but still had gems including "Headed for Nowhere" that featured a guitar battle between Emmett and Steve Morse (ex-Dixie Dregs, then in Kansas, later in Deep Purple), "Long Time Gone," and "Never Say Never." Only a Canadian tour would follow in 1988, and then Emmett quit the band due to internal friction and squabbles, and the group split.

In 1990, Rik released his first solo album and would enjoy success in his native Canada with several albums, including *Absolutely* in 1990 and *Ipso Facto* in 1992. He eventually focused on everything from jazz to blues to solo acoustic, flamenco, and classical.

Rik now plays solo acoustic gigs, full band gigs, and as an acoustic duo with Dave Dunlop who is a phenomenal player as well in his own right. Rik and Dave offer a night of Triumph songs rearranged (including some astounding harmonies on guitar), solo tunes, covers, and pretty damn funny tales from Rik.

Accolades have deservedly been given to Emmett, including Smooth Jazz awards in 2005 and 2006 as Guitarist of the Year. With Triumph, Rik was inducted into the Canadian Rock Hall of Fame in 1993, the Music Industry Hall of Fame in 2007, and the Junos Hall of Fame (Canadian Grammys) in 2008. For the first time in decades Rik, Gil, and Mike reunited to accept these awards in 2007 and 2008.

This led to two reunion live shows (with Dunlop on board as well) at the Sweden rock and Rocklahoma Festivals in summer 2008. The band rehearsed for months and worked very hard at capturing the old chemistry again and it was certainly there and documented on the live CD/DVD *Live at Sweden Rock* in 2012. The songs were played in a different key, but Emmett's playing and vocalizing were flawless.

Sadly, no further shows happened, but Rik continues to work at a heavy rate in his solo career, including an acoustic trio dubbed P.R.O. that includes Rik and guitarists Pavlo and Oscar Lopez utilizing a Mediterranean and Latin sound as well as duo gigs with Dunlop, solo performances, and full band concerts.

Emmett also teaches music at Humber College in Toronto and is artistic director of the annual Songstudio Songwriting Workshop. His dedication to the guitar, his virtuosity, and willingness to play a multitude of styles sets him apart from many who play the instrument. While Rik is anything but an obscure name, it is long past time to recognize one of the finest guitar players to ever touch the instrument.

In May 2014, Rik and I had a very long, enjoyable and, at times, quite amusing chat. I did my best to pick the highlights:

Hey Rik, you should be flattered because of my top three favorite players; you're the one still living!

[Hearty laugh] Well, half-living anyway!

You and I both trust me. What age was it when you realized your love for the guitar?

I was of that generation that had seen the Beatles on *Ed Sullivan* and then I started miming to 45s in my friend's garage strumming a tennis racket, and then when I was nine or ten my Grandfather gave me a guitar that was his sister's that was in his closet.

It was an old catalog guitar and had a couple of palm trees stenciled on the front. It was a piece of shit, but it was like, "Here's your ticket to the universe—now you have your passport"! And that was the beginning for me.

I loved music but I played a lot of sports and it wasn't until I tore my knee up at seventeen where I said to myself, "Okay, maybe sports is not your future." And I knew between ten to seventeen years old that I had a gift and I believe from gifts opportunities come. So, people started saying, "hey you're good; maybe you should join our band and you should be our singer" and those things started happening because now you're displaying a certain level of talent, but so what? At some point you have to start putting in the hard work.

And that's where it changes to another level.

Yeah, and seventeen was where I started doing some woodshedding to see if maybe I could become professional. I got my union card pretty early on as I played in wedding bands and things and I was a jobbing guy when I was still in school. I was in a country and western band at one point and I was burning the candle at both ends.

Who are some of the players of the past or even today that you respect and enjoy listening to and were perhaps influences as well?

I respect all guitar players that take it seriously and chase it. What I mean by that is, it is an infinite challenge to create music, and in the face of the infinite, are you doing conscientious work that has a nice spirit to it, that's coming from a really humble place and you're putting the music out ahead of you? I really love anybody who seems to be doing that, so I would be just as happy watching a guy like Brad Paisley as I would a guy like Kurt Rosenwinkle; you know what I mean?

I teach at a jazz college so you can imagine the range of influences I'm confronted with on an ongoing basis of players who are really deep and good. The guys that I can tend to sort of gravitate towards are the melodic players, like Robben Ford, Larry Carlton-lyrical kinds of players, you know?

But the guys who influenced me when I first started there was the Beatles as I mentioned, but then that whole thing with Clapton and Hendrix and you mentioned that those guys are the ones magazines and books still talk about and put on the cover and it's because there was this cultural shift that occurred from guys playing guitar in pop bands in the background to the point where it was like now; you can be a hero out front and push the envelope, you know?

Clapton was my guy more than Hendrix, although I loved Hendrix because he was more of a laid back, bluesy, tasteful kind of guy and I liked the character of that playing a lot. And that led me to all those British players in progressive rock bands so Steve Howe (of Yes and Asia)—he really became my guy. I love his playing and he was eclectic as he enjoyed Chet Atkins and I was now deeply into that school of guitar playing.

However, I wasn't really proficient so I wasn't going to be playing all those weird time signatures because I truly did like pop songs. I remained relatively accessible and joining Triumph—that's what Triumph was predicated on: being accessible, but also being heavy with hard rock and just a hint of progressive rock.

Oh, you did have progressive rock in there like "Blinding Light Show/ Moonchild" for example.

Yeah, there was just a hint! And that was because of me more than the other guys as they would've been happier making Ted Nugent-type hard rock and being in a band that was kinda like Kiss or whatever. They liked very straight-up kind of stuff as did I. Every musician has certain kinds of tastes. Gil loved blues and rock 'n' roll and Mike listened to a lot of stuff, like the Eagles and that laid-back California style.

Now that surprises me, but at the same time I wouldn't expect that everyone in Triumph only liked styles that sounded like Triumph.

Sure, and the point of all of this is that a band is going to meet on common ground, and the common ground for those guys was nowhere near as progressive as where mine might've been with a different ensemble, but that's okay. That's what you do: you meet on common ground and it can work.

I was watching MTV right from the start in 1981, and they played you guys to death, really for much of your career. It was especially so in those early days. Were you aware of that at the time?

Oh yeah, but part of that too was that MTV was based out of New York and we were signed to RCA Records and RCA thought "hey, this could be good," and then RCA [Laughs], this is kind of a funny story…when our *Just a Game* album came out in 1979, RCA—bless their pointy little head—they had recently come out with this VHS machine and there was a war going on with Sony who had Betamax.

So, RCA had this brilliant idea that they were going to put their machines in every record store that they possibly could and they were going to put VHS tapes on replay of bands playing and very few of the RCA acts cottoned to how this might have a pretty cool impact, and we had already done four music videos for the *Just a Game* album and RCA was running these videos on all their VHS machines in stores across America. So, consequently, here comes MTV and they've got nothing to play, like maybe a couple Mike Nesmith videos, so they were like *ooohhh*, here's four songs from Triumph and they've got flashing lights, flashpots, a neon logo sign, and MTV wanted something that would jump off the screen.

I also think we were one of the first acts to do a Saturday Night Concert Special with them. We said, you pay and put a production crew together, and we'll play a place like Baltimore and we played at Towson State's arena. The deal was, you shoot the video and you pay for it and we'll sign off, and you can clip out songs if you want and air it and keep it in rotation. They were all over that like stink [Laughs] because that was great for them.

You were always in solid rotation on MTV. I still remember seeing "A World of Fantasy" for the first time in 1983 and being excited and of course "Somebody's Out There" in 1986 was heavily played and became your biggest hit single in the US.

Yes it was, and in the end they also really played "Follow Your Heart." That was the first rock video that used steady-cams (in 1985). I can remember sitting around in a production meeting and we had a gig in Providence, Rhode Island, or someplace like that, and keeping the crowd around after the show so that we could shoot this video. The guy would wear the steady-cam like a harness with the camera suspended in front of him, and wherever he went, there would be this incredibly smooth tracking shot. So we said, you've got to come up the main aisle of the arena and right up on the stage, so we had to build ramps so that he could do these shots. It was a dad and his son that had come up with this technology and we hired them for that video and so that was the first rock video that had those smooth tracking shots using the steady-cam.

That became so commonplace afterwards with all those Def Leppard and Bon Jovi videos that looked exactly the same.

Yep, it was much copied. Plus, we always had a big lightshow from the beginning, which became de rigueur as well. So it was, oh yeah, we'll do the live promo shoot with the big production and all the lights in the background.

The one guitar solo of yours that I remember the most is "Never Surrender." The verses are almost choppy in a reggae-ish vein and then there's this midsection with that ominous bass line that is followed by a harmonic you do with some tremolo and then this menacing solo follows. How did that come about? That's the one solo I'd like your thoughts on.

It's hard to remember how things generate. Part of it is, we'd already done the *Allied Forces* album and "Fight the Good Fight" and "Magic Power" had done well at Album Rock Radio so we knew we didn't have to lock ourselves into singles necessarily, and that our songwriting could be a little more epic and a bit longer. This all grew out of the fact that Led Zeppelin had done "Stairway to Heaven," which was like a symphonic story almost, and it went through all these stages and the guitar solo was the real kicker, where the song got into its highest gear. So there were a lot of bands like Styx, Kansas, Journey that could create songs with a soft intro and then kick up into another gear and have a different feel for the bridge and the guitar solo.

Back on the *Just a Game* album the "Lay It on the Line" solo had been a departure. I always thought, could you make a song where if there wasn't a bridge, could the solo itself function as a bridge? In my songwriting classes I tell students I think bridges should sort of be like vacations. You know, you have a song, you have its form, you have its structure—but when you hit the bridge you give the listener a chance to go someplace else. Have it be a complimentary place, but nevertheless have it be a vacation from the form that keeps on repeating. As for "Never Surrender," I had written the lyrics, but Gil came up with that groove. And in a way it had the same feel as "Fight the Good Fight."

I've always thought those tunes were comparable in that epic style.

[Sounds out the feel] Yeah, and it had the funky, syncopated half-time vibe. And Zeppelin was a precursor to that sort of writing where John Bonham would change things up with his drumming. Straight-forward, but the feel would be syncopated or a half-time almost swing-style beat. So, yes, when you say reggae, that's pretty much it. It had a weird feel that turned it around in a way. We weren't the kind of band that would sit around and write a piece of music and say, yes this is what we're doing. To us, we just memorized it and played it.

Having given you all that background, when that bass line came in, it started the next chunk. Sort of like breaking it all apart and building it back up. Remember that Fleetwood Mac song where it just came to a stop and that bass line came in heading to the finish?

Do you mean "The Chain"?

Yes, "The Chain"! I always loved shit like that; songs that had a really cool part setting up something special and signifying a change. So that was the idea for Mike Levine with the bass riff, which lends itself to the question: how do you get from half-time to double-time? How do you get from the plodding kind of reggae feel to that energetic rocking section? When you play live that's really what the audience wants. They want that rock and roll or double kick or anything that kicks the energy up. That was us just trying to have that sort of epic thing that would go over well in concert.

And go figure—it was a huge radio hit.

Yeah, and it was kinda long too. I still play it now in my solo shows, but not in the key of D Minor anymore, actually I think it was E Minor—that's crazy! Now I do it in B Minor.

Well, you don't want to hurt yourself in special places...

[Laughs] Indeed!

In 1987 from the Surveillance *album on "Headed for Nowhere," you and Steve Morse got to duke it out on guitar. What was that like? That had to have been something very memorable.*

Wow, Steve is just an unbelievable guitarist—beyond the beyond. The story that I like to tell about that session is that he'd come into town and stayed at my place and we'd done a day of writing together and I think we played a gig—maybe he was there two or three days, I forget! In the studio, we set him up so he was in the control room and the amp was out on the floor, and he does a take, and me and the producer have our jaws right on the floor. The guy is just drop-dead, amazingly good.

So he finishes a couple of takes and he's standing there shaking his head and frowning and he says, "I'm really sorry guys." And we said, "What the fuck are you talking about?" And then he says "I just can't seem to get it together today, I don't really have it." [Laughs heartily] Then I say, "Are you kidding me? Will you lighten up?" I mean, he is so good that he's his own worst critic sometimes, and being in the room with him was an honor, and then playing and writing with him was a tremendous treat. When you talk about physical gifts, an ability to pick a guitar and create flowing, running lines Steve Morse is clearly one of the world's best guitar players.

I was fortunate enough to meet him at a Dixie Dregs show in Philly in 1992 and he is so humble and so very nice.

He may even be too humble and again that comes back to what I was saying earlier that if somebody is humble in the face of it, that's a pretty good thing. That means that they're going to keep after it. Steve landed that gig in Deep Purple back in '94 and, I haven't kept up with too much of his solo work and life has a habit of getting in the way of things, but I haven't seen him in years and I always liked him, and what you just described that humility; that's one of the nicest things about him.

One of my favorite guitar pieces of yours is from your Triumph days called "Midsummer's Daydream." Was that to show the light and shade of Triumph on the albums as well as a chance to play what you felt as opposed to what was expected?

Well, the story of guitar pieces on Triumph albums was because when we were doing the first album Mike was more or less functioning as the producer in the earliest days, and we were desperate for material. The record company had said, okay, make us an album and let's get started and we had maybe 2 songs [laughs]! It was like, what are we gonna do? So I had a song from the band I had been in before Triumph and that was "Blinding Light Show" which was in E Minor and a section in 7/4 that we changed to 4/4 for Triumph so that was in the mix and yet we were still short on material.

Mike asked if there was anything else and I said I had a classical guitar piece that's in E Minor, so if "Blinding Light Show" broke down in the middle of the song, we could place the classical guitar piece in there and then we could come back in with a rip-roaring rock solo and then have the last verse and Mike said, "That's a great idea, that's great." So that was "Moonchild" from the first album we ever made in 1976. After that, every time we were in pre-production in the studio Mike would come to me and say, "You're gonna do a guitar piece, right?" I said, "Oh, right! Sure, I guess." [Laughs] It then became standard that on every album there would be a guitar piece, usually classical or acoustic.

And I looked forward to what piece you would have on each album.

For me it was a huge bonus being in a rock band that I was gonna get the opportunity to be doing something like this because one of my favorite albums in High School had been *Fragile* by Yes. That album had "Mood for a Day" and I just thought it was so great to have this rock album with these long progressive rock pieces, but besides that each guy got a solo piece and it was very nice of Mike and Gil to give me that latitude.

As for "Midsummer's Daydream" I was left to my devices on the *Thunder Seven* album a lot. At the time the other guys were busy with their own lives and also dealing with getting the band away from RCA Records to MCA, so I could book the studio and spend the whole day messing around with various ideas so I was doing things like that vocal piece "Time Canon" and "Midsummer's Daydream" was a piece where I had been fooling around with a Drop D tuning and then I thought that I wanted something that's kind of lilting and memorable so the melody would be relatively simple to follow but harmonically not too complex. Ya know, a 1 a 4, 1, 5 chord and a 6 every now and then, and would have some nice, challenging little licks in it.

If you think back on the way acoustic guitars showed up on albums, you think of *Led Zeppelin* (the first album) where Jimmy Page did "Black Mountain Side" and that was an odd-tuning thing so it wasn't like I was inventing the form or anything. When you're in a rock band you sort of know that everything is gonna be minor keys with some hard rock riffs and some ominous sounding things. So if you're looking to break up the flow, you're either going to mystical weird or real major key, real diatonic. I think "Midsummer" was just a question of me writing it in summer and wishing I was sitting under a tree with a blade of grass stuck between my teeth and just playing my guitar.

When I was writing guitar pieces for Triumph albums I would be thinking you've got to have a little bit of flashy technique so you can get your guitar transcription into *Guitar Player Magazine*. [Laughs] By the same token you know there's some people who might've had too much to drink and have been banging their heads in the second row can say, "No, this is cool. I can follow this for now." You just don't want to go too far.

On *The Yes Album* by Yes, Steve Howe had "Clap" which was a live recording and I thought this guy's been doing it so long, that I could pull it off too. It can be done if your guitar piece has the right kind of vibe. "Clap" and "Mood for a Day" were very influential pieces to me.

Even still at each Yes concerts fans look forward to those pieces being played live. You can also hear a clear Chet Atkins influence on "Clap."

Oh yeah, for sure. And he's even using a pick on that, a hybrid style picking where Chet would've been doing it with a thumb pick. For me, I ditch the pick and just use my nails.

Of the solo shows which do you prefer?

No preference really, but I did play a solo performance down in Texas last week and I hadn't done one of those in a while, so I was a bit nervous about having no support to bounce off of but it went very well. When you've been around as long as I have and played so many gigs in different circumstances and formats you start to realize it doesn't matter how many musicians are on stage or how big the crowd is. The circumstance will create its own freedoms and limitations.

I do really enjoy the duo shows with Dave Dunlop. We really play off each other well and he has worked out a 2nd part on Triumph pieces like "Midsummer's Daydream," "Fantasy Serenade" and "Petite Etude." It's all harmonized and when we do those shows I can play those pieces in a heavily arranged way for two guitars.

Any hopes for future Triumph activity?

I don't think so, no. We did those two reunion shows in 2008 and there was something that was bringing the idea of reconciliation and a re-forming of the brotherhood full circle and the gigs cemented that. I think that was enough for Gil. He's back to running Metalworks Studios and the school and his production company. His family was younger than Mike and I. He still has teenagers to spend time with and the whole thing of a drummer getting back in shape—it took about six months and we rehearsed every single day and afterwards I think he said, "Well that was a lotta work!" I think he felt that was enough.

So maybe those two gigs were a blessing that they even happened at all?

For sure, as there was a lot of psychological baggage for everybody but especially for me in a lot of ways. So I think to have gotten them out of the way was big. It's not like there are no conversations as we often have promoters coming to us, but the offers haven't been overwhelming enough for Gil to go through it all again. And in the end it's up to him as he owns the Triumph brand, the label so if he doesn't want to do it's not gonna happen. But that's okay.

And what is your guitar of choice?

Lately I've been playing Gibson Les Pauls for rock shows with a kind of '60s neck reissues that are chambered so they're lighter. In a way I like that because part of me... because I had that Framus Ackerman in Triumph which was like a Les Paul but had a block in the middle like a 335 and I've always been a jazz archtop kind of guy. I was playing a 335 for a while, and I saw a video that had been shot of me from a while ago and it looked like I was playing a guitar that had been bought for me by my Uncle and I was a little kid—it dwarfed me. I'm not a tall guy I'm only five-foot-eight! I might have four or five Les Pauls in my collection.

Having said that, Godin has a Montreal Premiere guitar which is a thin-line semi-hollow body. I think I might be trying that because my other favorite is a Godin 5th Avenue, a full-blown archtop, floating pickup. It's a pure jazz guitar and I use that for acoustic shows. It's halfway between the Gibson 175 and Johnny Smith. I've endorsed a lot of Japanese and American guitars but these Godin guitars are really great guitars, very nicely done and at a very reasonable price. I will leave you with an anecdote now.

Anecdotes are good, go for it!

I was playing in Buffalo around 2001 at a festival and George Benson was playing nearby and I was to play at the Tralf Music Hall. The promoter for the festival I was in was telling me he had a dream to get Jeff Beck, Eric Clapton and Carlos Santana jamming on a stage together. That was why he was throwing his weight behind this show and he worked with PBS locally.

So I knew he liked the idea of collaborations and I told him that the *Breezin'* album by George Benson was the soundtrack to my honeymoon. I said that if there's anyway George could come and jam I would be thrilled and up for it. He wrote a note and stapled it to the check as payment for the gig and wrote to George that he should come to the Tralf.

I get towards the end of my set and get a note sent to me that George is here and ready to jam and at this point I am now tremendously fuckin' nervous and saying, "Oh no! What have I done?" because I wasn't thinking it was going to happen. I come back out for the encore and tell the audience that George Benson is here and he's going to play and the audience goes nuts. Two white spotlights are circling around, and he comes towards the stage with two linebacker-sized bodyguards and he goes up the side and my keyboard player starts playing "On Broadway" and then George gives me a big hug, and I'd never even met him before, and screams "Give me the gun!"

And I'm thinking, what the hell does he mean? He said it again. I then found out he was saying Godin, because he had seen me playing earlier doing some acoustic playing with my Godin which was an acoustic/electric. And that's what he wanted to play—the Godin, so I screamed to the roadie, "Give him the gun"!

So I've got these great pictures of George playing this guitar which was so small on him, because he's in good shape and has a big chest and he looks all hammy playing my guitar and I have pictures of that as well as he and I playing together. I gave that guitar to Dave Dunlop and he now plays it. It was like a dream come true. At one point I wanted to modulate the song up and I instructed the band, because Benson's version modulates up half-steps a few times and at the moment I kick it up George starts singing in the old key! That got hairy for a moment and we went back to the original key.

And as well-known as he is, George Benson is somewhat underrated because the average person doesn't know of him like he would Jimmy Page, Eric Clapton, Eddie Van Halen, etc.

To me George Benson isn't underrated because I rate him very highly, but I hear what you're saying there. I sometimes do a covers gig just for fun and I had to learn "Reelin' in the Years" by Steely Dan and that solo is crazy by Elliot Randall. Holy shit is that ever a great solo! There's another great player that people should know about. The lead guitar parts are so clever and tricky. That's another guy under the radar.

I think he's brilliant. He was even in Asia for a while in the late '90s.

Was he? I did not know that.

Well, it wasn't the classic lineup, but he was a part of the band led by Geoff Downes with John Payne.

You know, they pitched to me at one point.

Asia? Is that true?

Yeah, it was. They only had a few European festivals on the books, but Steve Howe wasn't there and I got calls from both Carl Palmer and John Wetton. And I heard these very cultivated British voices on the phone saying [does decent British accent] "I think it would be really fantastic if you joined the group, you'd be the perfect guy." I had to pass though as there weren't enough gigs to put in all that work.

This must've been in 1990 when three of the four from the original lineup re-formed and released Then and Now.

Yes, that's exactly when that was.

They ended up choosing Pat Thrall.

Did they? He was a good choice.

And another player I revere is Terry Kath—just a genius to me almost none better than him.

You know, that solo in "25 or 6 to 4" is just outrageous. That guy could play and do things that were just so special. I've covered that one too and trust me that is no easy chore. He was a very special player and that band was great, especially blending in the horns.

Ya know, another offer that came my way around that time in 1990, was Damn Yankees. I got a call from Jack Blades when that was formulating and I had talked to Tommy Shaw a couple of times about other things. And he's a very good player and talented. So Jack calls me and he said, "Oh, we got Tommy and we got Ted Nugent..." and I said, "Stop! You've got more than you need in the guitar department and why would you want a Canadian in something called Damn Yankees"? Jack is nobody's fool and he figured out that if you get the right writers together, you'll get really great material and now you'll have a great shot at getting on the radio.

And they had so many radio hits.

Tommy and Jack worked very well together and they're pretty good writers and can sing their asses off so it worked.

In conclusion, I ask a silly question. If you had to rename a Triumph album after a cat what would it be? My felines want the scoop.

Oh boy. The *Surveillance* album cover, the eye was like a cat's eye. So, I'm thinking *Cat's Eye.*

Well, there we go, although I was hoping for something like Allied Kitties.

Hey, I'm taking this seriously buddy! [Laughs]

Recommended solo: "Never Surrender" from *Never Surrender* with Triumph (1983)
Further info: www.rikemmett.com
Photo credit: Doug Lewis

CHAPTER 14

Dave Flett

(Born David Flett, June 2, 1951, Alberdeen, Scotland)

Here is another reason why this book exists. Anything but a household name, yet a truly excellent player, Dave Flett is a fella who deserves far more recognition. Dave began his career playing with several different acts in his native Scotland, and while those acts didn't go anywhere, his playing wasn't in vain. He was recommended for the gig in Manfred Mann's Earth Band and nailed the audition in 1975 in time for a big fall tour of North America.

Flett's first album with the Earth Band was 1976's the *Roaring Silence,* which became their biggest seller ever in the US, as a phenomenal rendition of Bruce Springsteen's "Blinded by the Light" became a surprise Top 10 single. This lengthy treatment of seven minutes long features a landmark solo from Flett using some odd phasing effects and a serene style of playing that avoids pretense and flash. The song is still heard every day on the radio and in bars to this day, and the solo stands out in a major way. The intense prog rock and jazz fusion of songs such as "Songbird," the epic "Singing the Dolphin Through" and the bizarre "Waiter, There's a Yawn in My Ear" feature

challenging licks and solos throughout that are most impressive. There were also classical themes underneath these songs adding a tricky touch as well.

The next album was *Watch* in 1978 and that record had memorable songs like the dreamy, wistful "California" that also happens to include an emotional, ripping solo that takes the song to another dimension. This is such a wonderful guitar solo, it is highly recommended. Other highlights were the UK hit "Davy's on the Road Again," the prog of "Drowning on Dry Land/Fish Soup" and the intense "Chicago Institute" where Flett unleashes a wild, furious solo.

Flett departed in 1979, but later that year he was brought into the world of the legendary Thin Lizzy, joining the band for a Japanese tour and a follow-up Christmas tour of the UK. Lizzy needed a new guitarist in the wake of the sudden departure of Gary Moore during a US tour that year. Lizzy leader bassist/vocalist Phil Lynott, guitarist Scott Gorham and drummer Brian Downey brought in Midge Ure of Ultravox to complete the US tour but added Flett for the next round of dates that allowed Ure to concentrate more on keyboards.

The dates were excellent and Flett really fit in. Several new songs were introduced, including "Didn't I" and "Sweetheart," both of which would end up on 1980s *Chinatown* LP. Ultimately, Dave wasn't asked to stay on board for some reason and Lizzy selected blues-based player Snowy White. Dave did do a guest spot with Lizzy at a gig in the summer of 1981 in his hometown of Aberdeen, which was a special moment.

Dave more or less retired from music and became an addictions counselor in Florida, which he still excels at to this day, but still had enough music going through him to provide a solo album *Flying Blind* in 2014, which came out rather well. A song on the album titled "Stolen Identity" is based on a strange real-life incident that occurred when a man in Costa Rica posed as Dave and began an investment scam. Luckily, this dirtbag was caught, but the experience understandably shook Dave. We know who the real Dave Flett is; a damn good guitar player and great guy who hopefully anyone reading this will now know a little bit more.

In November 2014, I was able to talk to the actual Dave Flett!

Who were some of the guitarists that influenced you or that you admired growing up?

As a kid, I loved listening to the Shadows because of Hank Marvin's playing, e.g., tracks such as "Apache" and "Wonderful Land." However, I didn't start playing until I was around seventeen. A friend at school played me *Disraeli Gears* by Cream and all bets were off. I had discovered the key to life, which was Eric Clapton's guitar playing. Shortly afterwards, I heard Carlos Santana and his playing resonated with me in much the same way as Clapton's playing had done. Then there was Paul Kossoff of Free and Peter Green from Fleetwood Mac. They had such an amazing feel to their playing that it was impossible not to be moved.

What guitars have you preferred the most over the years?

Because I was a Clapton nut, it was all about Gibsons. When I joined Manfred Mann's Earth Band, I used a '63 SG Les Paul, then a reissue Flying V, then a Black Beauty which I bought from Rick Derringer. I then moved to Fender Strats because they made it harder to achieve a good tone. Crank a Gibson up to 10 and it will always provide an acceptable tone, whereas the Strat makes you work for it. Jeff Beck is without a doubt "the master of the Stratocaster." These days I've added Joe Satriani and Andy Timmons Ibanez models as well as Paul Reed Smith models.

Can you take me through the solo on "Blinded by the Light" with Manfred Mann's Earth Band? That is a landmark guitar solo that still sounds fresh today and has great feel and an interesting tone. Was that something you guys knew would hit big?

Believe it or not, it was my first time in a recording studio. I couldn't get used to wearing headphones and not hearing my guitar blasting out of a Marshall cabinet. I had also just been given an MXR 90 to try out and used it on the recording. When I kick in the phaser mid-solo you can hear an obvious volume drop. I didn't want this solo used because of that, but Manfred felt it made the solo "real." He was of course right. I also used a Crybaby wah pedal left open in different positions which provided interesting tonal variations.

We had no idea that the song would make such an impact, although it did feel like a good song at the time. What is even more bizarre is that many radio stations played the version that included the guitar solo, instead of the shorter, edited version.

Cuts like "Songbird" and "Waiter, There's a Yawn in My Ear" were very fusion/progressive rock-oriented. That's some pretty tricky stuff and you more than held your own. Is that a style you had played prior to these songs?

Round about the time I joined the Earth Band a lot of my friends were listening to jazz rock fusion. I was exposed to Chick Corea, Billy Cobham, Stanley Clarke, and John McLaughlin. The closest I had come to that genre was hearing Genesis and Yes. Because my style is blues-based, I was definitely out of my comfort zone playing tracks such as "Songbird" and "Waiter." Since I didn't have a good disciplined guitar technique or any musical/theoretical training, I had no alternative other than to turn the amp up to 10 and go for it.

"Chicago Institute" has an amazing solo. Were you given the chance to explore as you saw fit creatively with that? And was that solo constructed or improvised?

If my memory serves me well, after we had recorded the backing tracks for *Watch,* the band, except for myself and Manfred, took off for a summer break with their families. Therefore, I was given free rein to experiment with all the guitar parts and sounds on the album. The solos were always improvised, but sometimes I might use the beginning of one solo and the end of another to create the final solo. However, they were never "constructed" per se.

"California" was a song that showed your light and shade in your playing. Pretty and simple acoustic work and then a ripping solo. I am still really impressed by that solo all these years later at how it captured the moment in an intense way that the rest of the song wasn't about.

As soon as Manfred played me that song I felt an emotional connection to the lyric, so I wanted to pull something special out of the bag. The solo couldn't be "pretty" or textbook. It needed to express the exact sentiment of the lyric and to change moods as the story unfolded. That was the plan, plain and simple.

How exciting was it to be a part of the Black Rose tour with Thin Lizzy in late 1979? Did you jell with the guys (Phil, Brian, Scott, and Midge)? It sounded like it from the bootlegs I've heard.

This was the first time Thin Lizzy had been to Japan so I felt the pressure was on. However, it was reassuring to know that Phil and the guys trusted in my abilities enough to go ahead with the Japanese tour. It was a great experience playing "Jailbreak," "Still in Love with You," "The Cowboy Song," etc., onstage next to Scott and Phil. We got along well and they made me feel like one of the guys. For a British rock guitarist, it doesn't get any better.

During the time with Lizzy I know you got to play new songs with them live such as "Didn't I" and "Sweetheart" that ended up on the Chinatown album. That must've been a good sign if you were asked to play on new material.

They actually had me playing those tracks when I went for the audition. It's always a bit risky to introduce new material to a live show. The fans know what they want and new material, if not up to snuff, can throw them. It felt good to be playing tracks on which no other guitar players had left their stamp. Again it was a bit risky but they were obviously confident I could handle it. The new tracks were well received.

Could you describe your new solo album Flying Blind *and how you felt it came out?*

I left the music business years ago and turned my efforts to providing mental health therapy in Florida. But one day I found that someone in Costa Rica was passing himself off as the guitar player on "Blinded by the Light." I felt serious concern at the prospect of music fans being conned by an impostor, so I wrote a song describing how it felt being the victim of identity theft. That song is "Stolen Identity" and it started the ball rolling. I revisited some old demos, called in a few favours from pals, old and new, and the result was *Flying Blind.*

Because I was producing my first solo record, I committed myself to creating an album of songs—which are each different in tone and pace—and which all feel familiar, but fresh. I also wanted the album to be about songs and not just guitar solo after guitar solo. To achieve this end I enlisted the talents of Tony Manna (keyboards, vocals, engineering, and co-producing) who I feel gave me an album to be proud of.

Silly question I ask most players: if you could rename a Manfred Mann song or album from your time there after a cat what would you come up with? My cats are curious!

I guess "California" could be "Cataphonia" or "The Mighty Quinn" could be "The Mighty Mouser"!

Recommended solo: "California" from *Watch* with Manfred Mann's Earth Band (1978)
Further info: www.daveflett.com
Photo credit: Ueli Frey

CHAPTER 15

Vic Flick

(Born Victor Harold Flick, May 14, 1937, Worcester Park, Surrey, England)

Flick. Vic Flick.

Now say that like it's Bond. James Bond (get it?).

If you don't know Mr. Flick's name, let me introduce you to him.

Vic began playing in the late '50s doing Skiffle with the Bob Cort Skiffle Group and, at one point, they toured with Paul Anka. Also on that bill was the John Barry Seven whom Flick would join in 1958. With the John Barry Seven, Flick wrote the track "Zapata" that features some amazing note bending by Flick and a distinctive twang; and also played with the band on the new theme song for the popular British TV series *Jukebox Jury* on the song "Hit and Miss" in 1960, which would remain the theme until 1967. Flick also played with the John Barry Seven on "Walk Don't Run" in 1960.

Flick also did sessions throughout the early to late '60s apart from his work with the John Barry Seven, including appearing on songs by Nancy Sinatra, Petula Clark, Engelbert Humperdinck, Cliff Richard, Adam Faith, John Layton, and Eddie Shapiro.

Among the most well-known tunes he was included on Faith's "Poor Me" (the shortest running time for a #1 hit in the UK's history at a robust 1:43!) as well as Peter and Gordon's worldwide #1 smash "A World Without Love" (written by Paul McCartney and John Lennon) where you hear his excellent playing on 12-string guitar. Others were Petula Clark's legendary "Downtown" which topped the US charts in 1965 and is one of the best pop songs ever (not to mention playing a role in a hilarious *Seinfeld* episode), and the Walker Brothers' masterful version of "Make it Easy on Yourself" that topped the UK charts and made the US Top 20 in 1965. Try to find a more emotional yet controlled vocal like Scott Walker does on this song—good luck.

There's plenty more. Vic played on two colossal Tom Jones hits: "It's Not Unusual" (1964) and "What's New Pussycat?" (1965), as well as Tom's gems "Green Green Grass of Home" (1967, and this isn't a happy song if you're paying a modicum of attention to the lyrics), and the psychedelic-tinged "Delilah" (1968). We also had Vic playing on Sandie Shaw's UK chart-topper "Puppet on a String" and Humperdinck's "Release Me," which was the biggest selling single in the UK in 1967 (and also a #1 hit there and Top 10 in the US).

Vic also played on the awesome "Black is Black" by Los Bravos, which hit the Top 5 in the US and #2 in the UK in 1966. And how cool is it that Vic's distinctive guitar tones are heard on the worldwide sexed-up smash "*Je t'aime…moi non plus*" by Serge Gainsbourg and Jane Birkin, which was a saucy number with Procol Harum-sounding organ (no joke intended on the organ part) and choppy guitar and drums with strings, while Gainsborg and Birkin tell each other such subtleties as "*Je vais et je viens, entre tes reins*" ("I go and I come between your loins"). This song has lived in infamy in film soundtracks and commercials (Do the product companies have any idea what this song is saying?) and it's made all the sleeker with Vic's guitars. Austin Powers has probably shagged a few babes to this song.

The most notable of Vic's contributions to music are rather significant. He played all the guitars on "Ringo's Theme (This Boy)" on the soundtrack of the Beatles film *A Hard Day's Night* in 1964 and it appears on the accompanying album of the North American release. Watch the scene in the film and you know immediately that it's Vic Flick on guitar.

And perhaps you've heard of "James Bond Theme." Yes, that is indeed Vic Flick playing the beyond legendary guitar parts on that sinister piece of music that has become a staple of both cinema and music through the decades. "James Bond Theme" first appeared in the film *Dr. No* in 1962 and was written by Monty Norman who did the score for the film. However, the arrangement was handled by John Barry, who of course Vic had played with. Barry has since scored eleven Bond films.

Vic played the theme on his 1939 English Clifford Essex Paragon Deluxe guitar and used a Vox AC15 amp giving it that odd surf rock cum jazz twang. Spy music never sounded so good. Flick would also play on these James Bond film scores: *From Russia with Love* (1963), *Goldfinger* (1964), *Thunderball* (1965), *You Only Live Twice* (1967), *On Her Majesty's Secret Service* (1969), *Diamonds are Forever* (1971), and *License to Kill* (1989). Vic played on the infamous Shirley Bassey song "Goldfinger" from the film of the same name which was a US Top 10 hit in 1965 and is one of the most notorious of all the Bond theme songs. Vic also played on "Diamonds Are Forever" sung by Bassey in 1971.

In 1972, Vic played with Gilbert O' Sullivan on Gilbert's monster hit "Alone Again (Naturally)" that spent six weeks at #1 on the US singles charts. Vic also issued a solo album called *West of Winward* in 1968 and the title cut is an excellent song with that familiar guitar twang and a hip horn arrangement aided by groovy organ and drums sounding wonderfully of its time.

Among the other film credits for Flick are impressive contributions to *The Ipcress File* (1965), *Midnight Cowboy* (1969), *The Return of the Pink Panther* (1975), and a series of Merchant-Ivory films, including *Autobiography of a Princess* (1975), *The Europeans* (1979), *Quartet* (1981), and *Heat and Dust* (1983).

Vic has also done music for television on famous shows, such as *The Avengers* and *The Prisoner*.

In 1999, Vic teamed up with composer Nic Raine and with the Prague Philharmonic Orchestra recorded the album *Bond Back in Action*. A solo album titled *James Bond Now* was released in 2003 featuring interpretations of Bond movie classics and three new songs, and in 2008, Vic wrote an autobiography called *Vic Flick Guitarman: From James Bond to the Beatles and Beyond*. The year 2012 saw Vic honored by the Academy of Motion Pictures Arts and Sciences for *The Music of Bond: The First 50 Years* which paid homage to all of the great music from these films through the decades.

Vic Flick deserves not only respect but his own agent code. Is 008 taken?

In March of 2015, I was pleased to spend the afternoon chatting with Vic about his career accomplishments and he could not have been nicer. It went like this:

Who were some of the influences for you as you began playing? I'm curious because there weren't a lot of guitarists at the time.

Yes, that's true; there weren't very many players at the time. There was Barney Kessell, Django Reinhardt, Charlie Christian who was a very fine player. Tal Farlow was a big influence on me as he was a great player. His passion was painting names on boats and yachts, but he was a great player. I listened to a lot of the rhythm players in big bands like Count Basie.

Rhythm is always important and especially back then as lead guitar playing was quite rare. The guitar was really just another part of the rhythm section, especially in big band and swing music.

Well that's right. Guitars were usually given to singers with rubber strings because they couldn't play.

You wrote the song "Zapata" for the John Barry Seven, which is a great piece of music. Was getting the chance to play and occasionally write with that group a turning point in your career?

Not the writing so much, but John Barry needed three pieces more to go on an album called *String Beat,* so Les Reed wrote one, I wrote one and we might've fallen one short there. That album was a turning point in that sense because I sat there in a chair with an amp behind me playing all these string parts and it was like an audition for all the top fixers in England. It was quite nerve-racking at the time, but soon the phone started ringing for all these sessions.

So this became a branching off in a way?

Yes, because in London there were lots of guitar players coming up but not that many who could read music and charts and such. I could because of my background in piano. My father set me to the piano when I was young and I was able to transfer that ability to guitar, and to this day, I still sometimes read on piano first.

When sessions started coming in how did it work? Were you part of a roster?

You had these fixers or contractors, as they're called over here in the States, and they would see you as someone who could read and play and this led to jobs. It was a slow process; but, before long, you'd do three or four sessions a day. I admire my wife for being with me for fifty-four years now because back then she knew how hard I was working. If you said no to a job for whatever reason, you might get bumped way down on the call list, so I was taking pretty much what jobs were available.

There was one fiddle player who said he was going on holiday for two weeks and Charlie Katz who was one of the big fixers in London called him forgetting he was on holiday. The guy answered the phone and Charlie said, "I thought you were away somewhere"? The fiddle player then said, "No, I just wanted two weeks off." So Charlie said, "You want two weeks off, you've got them!" The poor fiddle player didn't get another call for nearly a year. So there was a little bit of a "fear" element. [Laughs]

[Laughs] *Ouch! The fiddler made a goof! (Yes, that was a bad pun, Ed.)*

I remember at EMI Studios (now Abbey Road); there were all these engineers in white coats, which was an odd sight.

Like being in a lab.

Exactly, that's right.

With Tom Jones I know "Big" Jim Sullivan played on a lot of songs at the time and did both of you guys play on songs with him?

There was myself, "Big" Jim Sullivan, Bryan Daly, Judd Proctor, Les Thatcher, Joe Moretti, and a young Jimmy Page who did a few sessions as well. We all sat around and, when we turned up for a job, it would be a combo of any of us, or one of us.

It was kind of like a roster.

Yes, it was a roster, but there were other players too. With Tom Jones I played on "It's Not Unusual" and "Green Green Grass of Home" and songs like that.

"Green Green Grass of Home" is actually a rather morbid song.

It is and so is "Delilah." I did a lot of work with Tom Jones. I think I'm on "What's New Pussycat?" but at the time you really didn't make a note of anything. You went to work and put your hours in whether it was 10–1, 2–5 or 7–10 p.m. Sometimes you didn't even know who the singer was and other times a singer wouldn't even be there. Jonesy (Tom Jones) was there most of the time and we had some good times with him.

A lot of times we didn't know who some of the singers were because there were so many new names. Some stuck and others were never heard of. Most of the time you could tell who would be successful but not all of the time. It was a very energetic and innovative time for music.

And you played on "Downtown" by Petula Clark.

Yes, I did and I played on quite a few by her. She was a good singer and a good person. She went through her au natural business walking around with nothing on. Not in the studio, but in her house! She would show up for sessions in chiffon clothes that you could see through. It was a very interesting time.

That would be an inspirational session for me.

It was all rather cabaret wasn't it?

You were also on that tremendous version of "Make it Easy on Yourself" by the Walker Brothers. Your sound is very distinctive on that one.

I did quite a few with the Walker Brothers, including that one.

Now, with all the sessions you did at the time, are you able to remember a particular song like that and how you felt about it as you played your part?

We did a lot of work at Phillips Studios in London and what I remember was that it was difficult to park there! The Walker Brothers and Dusty Springfield also recorded there and I worked with her. I also had worked with her long before she became famous. She's passed now, of course, as have a lot of those I worked with, Peter. Life goes on I suppose.

I've learned that, trust me. You also played on that great Peter and Gordon song "A World Without Love," which went to #1. Was that a 12-string you were playing there?

Yes, and it was the Vox, which was a dreadful instrument. In fact, I sold mine to a collector that wanted it. They wanted that electric twanging sound and it had just come out so they were pretty knocked out by the sound of it and wanted it on there. You listen to it now and it sounds old-fashioned, but it was a different sound then that sounded fresh.

When I interviewed Tony Hicks of the Hollies we talked about that instrument because he played it so prominently on "Look Out any Window" and he told me how difficult it was to play.

It was so cumbersome and the action was dreadful and I never took the time to set it up properly. It was a demanding instrument and it shows in the playing of it. It was hard work, like chopping wood! [Laughs]

You were also on the A Hard Day's Night *soundtrack playing on "Ringo's Theme (This Boy)" where your sound comes clearly across in the film. Did you know George Martin at that point?*

Oh yeah, I had worked with George quite a bit at EMI. He wanted to get that low guitar sound and I was the guy in London who was sort of known for that, so he specifically asked for me and I did just that one title and the orchestra was there. I played my part, packed up my guitar and then I went off to the next session.

What models of guitars have you preferred over the years?

It's mostly been the Fender Stratocasters. I've got a few of those and sold one on that show *Pawn Stars,* which I'm sure you know about. I never really got on with Gibsons, although I really like this Gibson L7-C, which is a very nice acoustic guitar. I love to play that one and of course the guitar I did the Bond stuff on. At the end of 1961, Fender gave me a Stratocaster because they were giving them away for advertising. Then in 1962, when were about to do the Bond theme, my Strat was stolen from a gig, so I had to use this Clifford Essex Paragon guitar for the theme and then I got another '61 Fender Strat afterwards in the fall of '61. Or was it '62? Trying to remember back to 1962 is a little hazy. The older you get, you know…

I can't remember where I put my keys each day so it's all right by me.

I also had a Les Paul for a few years, but it was always Fenders for me for the most part.

And now we come to the "James Bond Theme." You had already worked with John Barry for a while at that point.

Yes, I began playing with him in 1958.

So this was the first adaptation of any of the Ian Fleming spy novels, this being Dr. No *the first of the James Bond films in 1962.*

Yes, that's right and funnily enough at the time of the session they were down to their last couple of pennies and they couldn't get distribution lined up and they didn't have much money. They felt that Americans might not even care about the film because there were already enough spy films in America, so why did they need to see another one? You know, that was the thinking for a bit.

There was a certain aura about doing the theme though because John Barry did such a great arrangement and I gave it all I could and it turned out to be quite the momentous recording, which I couldn't have really thought back then, especially fifty-plus years later. People are still talking about it now and that's incredible.

The piece stands on its own separate from the film.

It does. You've only got to hear it and you know it's got that spy film sound.

There's a sense of menace and intrigue to it.

Yes, that's exactly what it has.

It's hard to believe you got that sound from your guitar but you sure did.

Plus the fact that it was recorded in Cine-Tele Sound, which was CTS Studios in London and the way they did it with a few open mics and other things gave it an atmosphere more so than this closed in recording that they do now where everything is quantized.

I don't think you could even attempt to recapture that sound no matter what tricky retro devices you could come up with today.

No, a lot have tried and many have failed. In fact I got a call from the engineer who was doing the music for the film where Eric Clapton and I played. It was Michael Kamen and *License to Kill* was the film.

Yes, with Timothy Dalton from 1989.

Right. And Michael Kamen called and said, "Bring everything you used when you did the old James Bond films." The amplifier had deteriorated and in fact I've still got it; it's a Fender Vibrolux. They couldn't get the sound. I mean, they got a good sound after some work, but it wasn't that sound that they were looking for from the early '60s. That was really a one-off. A particular combination of studio, arrangements, and musicians that all worked out fantastic.

And that is why it cannot be replicated. You also did an album of Bond music on your own a while back.

Yes, that was *James Bond Now*.

It came out rather well, especially your playing.

I thank you Peter. The CD has done pretty well.

Now what was Shirley Bassey like to work with? Of course you played with her on "Goldfinger" which couldn't be any more of a classic.

She was very explosive and she made an impression. I did a few albums with her. She had a bit of Tom Jones in her way of singing. Her one fault was that if something went wrong, it was always someone else to blame, but at the same time she was very good. A story I must tell is when we were doing "Goldfinger" and she comes to that last note she was running out of breath and John Barry and others in the studio were saying to her, "C'mon, you've got to finish this off right, this has to be the take."

I heard some rustling about and then all of a sudden her bra came over the isolation sound booth and she called out, "Let's do it now, all right?" Off we went and she hit that last note, so there's the story on "Goldfinger." [Laughs]

Boobs are always a key to good music. [Laughs]

There are other stories like that, but I sometimes forget the details. Engelbert Humperdinck was another one I liked working with. Of course he was really known as Gerry Dorsey. I worked quite a bit with him on recordings and concerts. His manager Gordon Mills visited him when he was ill and gave him this new name and "The Last Waltz" was a really big hit; do you remember that one?

Not my cup of tea, but yes I do.

These days I have to chase and keep track of all the sampling being done. From the film *Beat Girl,* John Barry did the music and I'm playing on it. When Fatboy Slim did "Rockefeller Skank" my playing is on there and nobody asks and nobody pays and there's a website called www.whosampled.com and that's sometimes how I find out where my playing is and I have to fill out all this annoying paperwork to get my money.

So you have to chase these residuals?

Yes, and every time that song is played there's pennies and such for each play, but it does add up and while you want to get paid, filing the claim takes a long time and there's so many issues it's a pain. The suits always score.

Just look at the disgraceful payouts from Spotify.

An artist can get 16,000 plays and make $80 or something; it's ludicrous.

The music industry wasn't ready for the internet.

I know, I know.

You are also on the Serge Gainsbourg/Jane Birkin classic "Je t'aime...moi non plus." Please tell me you and the other musicians were playing by candlelight as they got in on in the studio—ha ha.

Yes, yes I am on that, but they were not there together in the studio! Serge was but Jane, who was married to John Barry...by the way, did you know that?

I did not!

That's another story. Anyway, at Phillips Studios Serge was there whistling something and there was no actual tune until a bit later, and a few weeks after that Jane put in all the ooohs and ahhs, so we missed out on all that! [Laughs]

Her ooohs and ahhs were very well done! It sounds like they were really sexing it up! [Laughs]

It does indeed, but no; no lovemaking on the floor or anything like that I'm afraid.

I got to know Jane quite well because John Barry did music for a film called *Deadfall* and what it was, was a guitar concerto with timpani and percussion every now and then, and it was being performed in a concert hall. John flew me from London to Spain where they had this island house and it turned out that I scored my guitar part and Jane and John had me there for dinner. They were breaking up around that time and dinner could get a bit uncomfortable. Jane later went off with Serge and she was a good person. Serge passed away too. Oh goodness, there's another one gone; are you still there, Peter? [Laughs]

Barely, but yes, I'm still kicking. [Laughs] *Did you have much interaction with Jimmy Page when he was just starting out?*

Oh yes. When he first started in sessions he really didn't know what was happening, and "Big" Jim Sullivan and I had to help him learn to read the charts and such. He was an interesting player coming up with all these great solos and riffs. Sometimes we had to tell him when to stop and when to start again. He was a very nice guy and he didn't really know what to do with his money as he was so young. I'm pleased with his success, but I tried to get in touch with him for my book and wasn't able to do so.

And how did the book do?

It did pretty well. A little slow at first, but it picked up, and since the *Pawn Stars* appearance in 2013, sales have picked up further—which is nice to see.

Recommended solo: "James Bond Theme" from the *Dr. No* soundtrack
with John Barry Orchestra (1962)
Further info: www.guitarman.com
Photo credit: from Vic Flick's personal collection

CHAPTER 16

Richie Furay

(Born Paul Richard Furay, May 9, 1944, Yellow Springs, OH)

One of the Godfathers of country rock, Richie Furay has had an amazing career that is still intact in what is now its sixth decade. Richie's talents are best recognized for his astute skills as a writer, singer, and performer but what doesn't get talked about as much are his skills as a rhythm guitar player and writer of guitar-based songs, as well as his 6- and 12-string playing on both acoustic and electric guitars. Of course, with the bands Richie has been in, it's understandable why that aspect of his career has been overlooked because he has been surrounded by some absolutely astonishing guitarists.

Richie had played in a group in New York called the Au Go Go Singers with Stephen Stills in the early/mid 1960s and went with Stills to California when Stephen was informed by record producer Barry Friedman that significant opportunities were possible if he relocated there. Stills did so, and brought Furay with him.

Neil Young and bass player Bruce Palmer left Canada in early 1966 as their band the Mynah Birds fell apart when their singer Ricky James Matthews (that's Rick James to you) was arrested after being tracked down by the US Navy for having been AWOL. Young and Palmer headed to LA in search of Stills and couldn't find him until they encountered Stills and Furay on Sunset Boulevard who had recognized Neil's ass-ugly Pontiac hearse. They finally connected, added drummer Dewey Martin and formed Buffalo Springfield right then and there in March 1966.

By April, the band was playing the Troubadour and then the Whiskey a Go Go, and after a bit of a bidding war, the band signed with Atlantic Records and released *Buffalo Springfield* on Atco Records (a subsidiary of Atlantic with many great acts) in December 1966. Regarded as an all-time classic, the album is dominated by the writing of Stills and Young, though Furay sings a number of Neil's songs as Neil's voice was deemed strange by the clueless producers who the band would be at odds with. Since we're focusing on Richie, let's mention the songs he sings, such as "Do I Have to Come Right Out and Say It," "Nowadays Clancy Can't Even Sing," and "Flying on the Ground Is Wrong." Here we get to hear the excellent, unique voice of Richie and, throughout the album, he provides solid rhythm guitar. The album would only reach #80 on the charts, but everything changed with the non-album protest single "For What It's Worth (Stop, Hey What's That Sound)" quickly written and recorded in late 1966 and soon to become a Top 10 million-selling classic in early 1967. The album was then reissued to include the single and another cut was removed.

Problems developed in a major way with Palmer getting busted for marijuana possession and Young disappearing at times and battling with Stills. Neil didn't even appear with the band at the Monterrey Pop Festival in June 1967, the band playing with Doug Hastings on guitar and David Crosby of the Byrds on guitar and vocals. Young would return and the sophomore album *Buffalo Springfield Again* was somehow pretty damn close to brilliant despite the inner workings of the band becoming a shambles. The album narrowly missed the US Top 40 and featured a litany of classics like "Mr. Soul," "Bluebird" (which hit #58 on the singles charts), "Rock & Roll Woman" (this hit #44), and "Broken Arrow." Furay finally got a chance to prove his mettle as a writer and came up with "A Child's Claim to Fame," the moving "Sad Memory," and the bawdy, horn-charged R&B raunch of "Good Time Boy" sung by Martin.

A big tour with the Beach Boys followed, but Palmer was deported in early 1968 for another drug issue and Jim Messina replaced him. The band completed a third album, but it was scattershot and uneven with the members rarely interacting. *Last Time Around* was still able to come up with some nuggets including Furay's winsome "Merry Go Round" and his excellent, heartfelt "Kind Woman." Richie was also part of a strange "partnership" on "The Hour of Not Quite Rain" that was a song where the music was put to a poem submitted by a fan named Micki Callen. This came about from a promotion by a Los Angeles radio station where the winner would have their poem put to music by Buffalo Springfield and said winner would also receive $1,000 and publishing royalties. No word on whether a lifetime of Jack in the Box coupons for hamburgers was included. By the time the album was released, the band had folded, playing their last gig on May 5, 1968.

Young, of course, became an enormously successful and daring solo artist and Stills became part of Crosby, Stills & Nash (which Neil would join/unjoin many times to this day as CSN&Y). Furay, Messina, and brilliant pedal steel guitarist Rusty Young (also on banjo, guitar, dobro, mandolin, and vocals) formed Poco in late 1968 with George Grantham on drums and Randy Meisner on bass and vocals. Poco was truly the first genuine country rock band and starting with their debut album *Pickin' Up the Pieces* in 1969 on Epic Records made some of the most groundbreaking rock ever.

The album spawned classics like the title cut, "Consequently So Long" and "Oh Yeah." Richie's writing prowess saw him involved in the writing of twelve of the thirteen album cuts, and six of those he wrote by himself. Though the album only peaked at #63 in the US, its influence has lived on for years. Even better was 1970s *Poco* which hit #58 and is one of the best albums of the '70s by any act regardless of musical genre. The album saw the debut of bassist/vocalist Timothy B. Schmit, as Meisner had bitterly left after the debut album.

Poco features the minor hit "You Better Think Twice," which is a fantastic song, but there's "Anyway Bye Bye" written solely by Furay and sporting some amazing vocal harmonies and killer guitar work marrying country and rock in a way few had dared before. If there is any doubt about that statement, try "Nobody's Fool/El Tonto de Nadie, Regresa," which essentially invented progressive country rock. This eighteen-and-one-half-minute opus is an astounding work that somehow avoids be coming pretentious and dull and instead is totally captivating. The changes, chord structures, solos, vocal arrangements, lyrics, and percussive playing are all so imaginative it was quite something to hear five musicians so sure of what they were doing, despite the chances they were taking. And, it all sounds so natural.

The live album *Deliverin'* climbed all the way into the Top 30 and produced a hit with the animated rocker "C'mon" that featured some crafty rhythm and writing by Furay and, as always, marvelous lead work from Messina and Young. Messina had departed by the time of the album's release and Paul Cotton joined on guitar and vocals from the similarly styled Illinois Speed Press. *From the Inside* was issued in 1971 reaching #52 as Poco took another step backwards sales-wise. While this wasn't Poco's best, any album with "Bad Weather" (written by Cotton), the title song (from Schmit) and Furay songs like "What Am I Gonna Do" and "Just for Me and You" is good enough.

With Jack Richardson producing, *A Good Feelin' to Know* (1972) should have been the album to make Poco a household name. Yet, it was not to be. Furay's title track is a charming gem that many Poco fans adore. How it wasn't a smash remains a mystery, though it did score some US airplay. It is as spirited and vibrant as any song could be and those guitars and vocals go together like Snoopy and Woodstock (I'm guessing you didn't expect *that* analogy). Furay's mini-epic "Sweet Lovin'" is another highlight as is his "And Settlin' Down" and others on the record. The single failed to chart and the album stalled at #69. Disheartened, Furay announced his intentions to depart the band.

Furay's last album with the band was *Crazy Eyes* in 1973. Ironically, this album returned the band (briefly) to the US Top 40. One of the band's masterpieces is included in "Crazy Eyes" written by Furay about the late Gram Parsons. This nine-and-one-half-minute work of genius shows Furay's undeniable skills as a songwriter and guitar player. To compose something like this takes some serious knowledge on guitar whether you're a guitar wizard or not. The orchestral treatments and the mix of dark guitars, sweet passages laced in vocal harmonies and Young's excellent banjo and pedal steel work all add a cinematic quality to the song. The jarring electric guitar stabs and the meaty instrumental sections once again lead to a Progressive style. Richie's "Let's Dance Tonight" and songs like a cover of J. J. Cale's "Magnolia" and the Parsons song "Brass Buttons" sung by Furay assure this was no half-hearted farewell from Richie.

So what was next for Furay? The country rock supergroup Souther-Hillman-Furay Band that paired Richie with Chris Hillman (ex-Byrds, Flying Burrito Brothers, and Manassas) and J. D. Souther who had written songs for the likes of the Eagles, James Taylor, and Linda Ronstadt, along with troubled ex-Traffic and Derek & the Dominos drummer Jim Gordon, keyboardist Paul Harris, and percussionist Joe Lala. Signed to Asylum Records, the band's self-titled debut album went Gold in 1974 (narrowly missing the US Top 10) and spawned a Top 30 hit with Richie's catchy "Fallin' in Love." The rest of the album was decent enough but perhaps a bit disappointing considering the talent. "Fallin' in Love" is vintage Furay, however, and his voice and the dirty guitars and catchy melodies work perfectly with a joyful chorus to boot. In 1975, *Trouble in Paradise* squeaked into the Top 40 but failed to build upon the debut album. On top of that, everyone was pulling in different directions musically and personally, so the group would disband.

Furay's solo career began with *I've Got a Reason* in 1976 on Asylum Records and, though the album certainly dealt with Furay's newfound faith, it was anything but preachy. More of a pop rock/AOR-sounding album, musically it had far less country rock than one would expect. The title track was an especially pleasant song. *Dance a Little Light* followed in 1978 and the title rock was a tight rocker with horns and quality guitar riffs and solos. The title song from 1979's *I Still Have Dreams* was a surprise Top 30 single, but Richie was never promoted by Asylum and he left for an independent release *Seasons of Change* in 1982. Richie would soon focus on family and faith, but he never left music behind and thankfully, has been very active once more since the mid 2000s.

Richie did return to the rock world in 1989, however—in a successful, surprising, and brief reunion of the classic Poco lineup of Furay, Young, Messina, Meisner, and Grantham. Signed to RCA Records, the band issued *Legacy,* which was a Top 40 Gold album producing two major hits in "Call it Love" (complete with a cheesy video MTV and VH1 aired to death but one that Richie was displeased with), which climbed to #18 on the charts and "Nothin' to Hide" that made the Top 40. "Nature of Love" and the poignant "What do People Know" were also radio hits. A track Richie cowrote called "When it All Began" strongly opens the album. A tour followed with keyboardist Dave Vanacore added to the lineup, but Richie left in 1990 and others would follow, though Poco are still together today.

Richie teamed up with John Macy for an album called *The Heartbeat of Love* in 2006, which returned him to the country rock sound. The Richie Furay Band began touring with regular dates by 2007 with an excellent double-live CD titled *Alive* that same year spanning Furay's lengthy career. Richie has guested with Poco on numerous occasions and a live CD/DVD *Keeping the Legend Alive* from 2004 saw Furay join Young, Cotton, Grantham, and bass player Jack Sundrud for what turned out to be an album any Poco fan had to be pleased with. Richie continued guesting with Poco in 2008 and 2009 and still does to this day.

A new Richie Furay solo album *Hand in Hand* was released in the spring of 2015 to very warm reviews as his excellent band with Scott Sellen on guitar and his son Aaron on bass, Richie's daughter Jesse Furay Lynch (vocals), Jack Jeckot (keyboards), and Alan Lemke (drums) make for a fine band sympathetic to Richie's classic days while adding a modern feel to those wonderful songs. *Hand in Hand* has among its best cuts, "We Were the Dreamers" detailing his days in Poco and his musical travels, "Don't Tread on Me" and an update of "Kind Woman" with Neil Young and Kenny Loggins.

And as for Buffalo Springfield? Well, it was beyond shocking to see Furay, Stills, and Young reunite for Neil's Bridge School benefit shows in late 2010, but even more so to see the band back on the road for seven shows in summer 2011, including an appearance at the infamous *Bonnaroo Music & Arts Festival* in Tennessee. Joe Vitale handled drums with Rick Rosas on bass. The shows were rough, raw, and rockin' but, even though a full tour was announced for 2012, Neil decided…maybe not.

Because he's Neil Young, and what Neil wants to do, Neil will do, and what Neil doesn't want to do, Neil won't do. It's that simple. So, we shall see if that tour ever pans out or not. The band went into the Rock and Roll Hall of Fame in 2007 and we all know Buffalo Springfield achieved more in their two-and-one-half-year existence than most acts could dream.

Richie Furay has played a role in some of the most important rock of the '60s and '70s, and he's still got a great voice, rhythm on guitar, and spirit to his music and life today. His writing, singing, and guitar playing are why he's in this book and I was thrilled to be a part of an enjoyable chat with the man in April 2015.

Hey, Richie, how are you sir?

Hey, I'm good, how are ya man? Aren't you off on an adventure with this book you're writing?

Yes, it has been an adventure. It's been almost a year now I've been writing it.

Well, I am beyond humbled that I would even be considered for such a book. [Laughs]

And why not? [Laughs] I've always been a rhythm player and not a great lead player and I listen for all kinds of things when I hear the guitar being played. Even if a player is not flashy, if it's a 6- or 12-string, acoustic, or electric, there's an art that's there. Add the writing and singing aspects— and there it is. You have also been surrounded by some terrific lead players over the years.

There's no doubt about that! [Laughs]

And with your excellent new solo album, this is perfect timing to speak with you.

That's so sweet man, thank you!

Who were some of your musical influences?

Some people may look at me like, "really?" but Ricky Nelson was a big one. I saw him when I was eight years old and he really got me interested. James Burton was another one, too. I loved rockabilly players like Eddie Cochran, Gene Vincent, and Buddy Holly. I moved onto folk music like the Kingston Trio and Peter, Paul, and Mary. I was always into the commercial artists and Dion DiMucci was a big influence.

Most of those make sense to me, although Dion catches me by surprise.

Well, I loved those harmonies of Dion & the Belmonts. And when I took my little folk group from college to New York, we soaked up all that Doo-Wop music and started singing it in the subways. I had a great opportunity about ten years ago to go to Israel and Dion was on that trip with me and I got to tell him that he was one of my idols. Next thing I know he had an album out with a song called "Put Away Your Idols," so I don't know if I had anything to do with that! [Laughs] There were also obvious influences like the Beatles and the Beach Boys, but really on it was that rockabilly stuff.

And what models of guitars have you used through the years?

I always seem to have a Gibson in my hands whether it was the 12-string I played in Buffalo Springfield or later on with Poco where I converted an ES-355 to an ES-335, because I am a rhythm guitar player and I didn't need it spread out in different ways like a stereo guitar might go, so I just had it converted to a 335 and that's what I mainly play today as an electric guitar.

Acoustically, at the time everybody wanted to be a folk singer, including me, they were all playing Martin D-28 guitars, so I had traded in a Gibson ES-295 for a Martin D-28 in Springfield, Ohio, when I left for New York City and that became the instrument that I played for the longest amount of time. Today, I have a fantastic Petros guitar, and I don't know if you know of those.

No, I'm not familiar with them.

Bruce Petros and his son make these outside of Appleton, Wisconsin, and I really like them. I'm also not afraid to try new things and I play a J-200 Gibson today and a D'Angelico I just got in New York last week, and those are really nice guitars. John D'Angelico had worked on my Martin D-28 when I had moved to New York out of college and shaved the braces and gave it a wonderful sound, but I don't travel much with that guitar anymore.

And then we have Buffalo Springfield...

Oh yeah! [Laughs]

I've heard different stories as to how you all came together in 1966, but when you did get together, did you know that all of your different backgrounds and influences were going to click?

I don't know that we ever actually did. Stephen and I had already known each other and played in New York and we both had been in and out with Neil. I really appreciated Stephen as both a singer and player and the way he phrased things, and we just became close in that regard. He (Stephen) and Neil were friends and we all just came together. And then there's the famous story of how we all met up and formed the band, and that is absolutely true.

I was going to ask how much of that tale about driving past one another on the road was true.

It is true. It was well before the days of cell phones and emails and Neil had come down to Los Angeles to find Stephen whom he'd met several months earlier as Stephen was working his way across Canada to get to California. Neil was coming down from Canada with Bruce Palmer and he had been down there in Los Angeles looking for us for about two weeks. We didn't go out much and the one time that we did go out was a significant time.

Stephen and myself and Barry Friedman were driving in my car heading east on Sunset Boulevard near where the Whisky was and Neil and Bruce were heading west heading for the 405 to go to San Francisco. They had given up on finding us and also on LA and were heading to the Bay Area, but there was a traffic jam and we happened to see this '53 hearse that Neil drove and we saw the Ontario plates on it and knew for sure it was him and waved him down and went into the parking lot and talked.

Neil had taught me "Nowadays Clancy Can't Even Sing" back in New York when he had come down to peddle some songs in the city, so I knew that one. Neil then came to the little apartment that we had been maintaining and I taught that to Stephen and we learned Stephen's new songs that ended up on the first Buffalo Springfield album and rearranged "Clancy," and when Neil heard our vocal arrangement, that sold him. That was the story and exactly how it happened.

And the name really came from a steamroller?

Yeah, it was on Fountain Avenue and I guess it was outside of our little apartment and the steamroller was working outside of our place and we came back with one of the tin signs off the truck—now, don't tell anybody. Shhhhh! [Laughs]

Your secret is safe with me. [Laughs]

We thought it was a good name for a group and sat the sign on top of the fireplace. How cool it was, because a few years later we got a note from the Buffalo Springfield Steamroller Company saying how happy they were that the name was back out in the public eye again for using the name. They were happy we were using the name.

I can assure that wouldn't happen today with how litigious we are now.

No, it wouldn't, but it also didn't happen back then as well because we were Pogo before we were Poco and Walt Kelly [creator of the comic strip Pogo] did not like it at all. We got a nice stack of legal letters from him basically saying, "Get out of my tree, this is mine"! It actually turned out to be the best thing for the group because just that little dropping of the "g" made it Poco and much truer to who we were.

I agree, Poco is where I envision a horse and a country setting, but with Pogo I see a bunch of loud children bouncing up and down on pogo sticks.

[Laughs] There ya go man, it was a better change!

Around the spring or summer of 1966 the band had landed a residency at the Whiskey, and then came the deal with Atco Records and the debut album. There were a few songs on there like "Do I Have to Come Right Out and Say It," "Nowadays Clancy Can't Even Sing," and "Flying on the Ground Is Wrong" that were all Neil songs that you sang.

I did indeed sing those three songs and I play them now live as a medley.

That's great! Did Neil or the label think you were better suited to sing those songs?

I can't remember quite what happened. It was me and Stephen singing for a while before we met up with Neil and we had a pretty good thing worked out with unison lead vocals and harmonies, and I think Neil was a little intimidated with his voice and I don't think he was getting a whole lot of support from the management at the time, so I ended up singing some of his songs.

And then on Buffalo Springfield Again *you had "A Child's Claim to Fame" and "Sad Memory," which was such a great song. Were those among your first writing contributions?*

They were certainly the first amongst my writing contributions to Buffalo Springfield at getting recorded anyway and "Sad Memory" was the first one and it was an accident. I was just waiting for the rest of the band to come in to record a song and I don't remember which one but I was out there fiddling around on acoustic guitar and then when Neil came in, he hit the talkback in the control booth and said, "Richie, we've got to record that song." Basically what he had heard had already just been recorded and then he added some guitar later on but that was basically it. That opened the door for me, and with "A Child's Claim to Fame" and another song I wrote for Dewey Martin to sing "Good Time Boy," I had more songs recorded.

"Good Time Boy" is a total 360 musically!

I know! I had so much variety in those three little songs! You've got this thing where Dewey wanted to sing like Wilson Pickett with "Good Time Boy," and then the country/bluegrass sound of "A Child's Claim to Fame," and then I guess what you'd maybe call a folk ballad in "Sad Memory."

I know on the Last Time Around *album in 1968 there was some sort of contest where someone could send in poetry and the band would write music to it and make it a song?*

You write the lyrics and Buffalo Springfield will write the music! [Laughs] Bruce picked the lyrics and Stephen and Neil weren't into it, so, tell you the truth, I don't know how much I was into it at the time, but we agreed to it. KHJ-AM was the radio station that sponsored it and we were getting some AM radio play out there at the time so we agreed. And these lyrics came in and nobody really wanted to do the music, so there I was again stuck in no man's land and I had to come up with some music and melody for that track, so there it was with "The Hour of Not Quite Rain."

I really liked the song "Merry Go Round" you had on that album.

Oh golly, that one I don't remember all that well. I think I was still learning and growing at that time. There was something that inspired me to write that, Pete, but what it was I don't remember!

That's okay! Neil didn't play Monterey Pop with the band correct?

That's right; that was one of those times where Neil was mysteriously vacant.

It's amazing the band lasted for those two-and-one-half years considering all that was going on in and out of the band the whole time.

There were nine people in and out of the band because of those two Canadians; one because of immigration problems and the other one deciding whether he wanted to be in a band or not.

And weren't you guys on an episode of Mannix *on TV?*

Yeah, I remember *Mannix* very well because I was not feeling well at all that day and I forget if we were playing live or singing over top of a track and lip-synching, but we did it. I could barely get up that day, but I do remember doing that.

Well, you've earned cool stripes for being on an episode of Mannix!

[Laughs] Absolutely!

"For What It's Worth" became a big hit as a non-album single and then ended up on a reissue of the debut album in 1967. Was that just a single to you at the time or was there a feeling of it being special?

It went way over my head and I'll tell you why. I was more into "Bluebird" and "Rock & Roll Woman" and those types of songs, and here's the story behind the song, Pete; the first record did not get the success that Atco and Atlantic was hoping it would. And Ahmet Ertegun came out to hear some new songs that we had written. And, me, Stephen, and Neil played some of the new songs we had and at the last minute Stephen said, "Oh, I have another one, for what it's worth."

How about that!

And when I heard it, it went over my head and I was thinking, "Well, that's a nice little folk song, Stephen, but man I'm way more into something else right now." However, Ahmet Ertegun said, "That is a hit." And when Ahmet said something was a hit, you had to go with it and we went right into the studio and recorded it and they took a song off of the album called "Baby Don't Scold Me" and it was re-released with "For What It's Worth."

In 1969, back then country rock, or whatever it was called back then, was not what you guys were doing. The intricate guitar parts and the vocal harmonies it appealed to me right away the first time I heard the band, which was much later on as a youth. It still sounds revolutionary to me today. Was Epic Records behind the album and the band or did they just throw the album out there as kind of just another signing?

I think initially they were behind it, Pete, but we had established a really strong following at the Troubadour, which was a big hangout in Los Angeles at the time. I think when we were signed they were willing to step out there. Of course it was new. Everything I've done musically has been part of a pioneering of a sound and this was certainly something new. The Byrds and the Flying Burrito Brothers had been mixing country and rock already, but we were bringing something different, and Epic was really excited about it and they were looking forward to putting the album out.

Something happened and who knows what goes on behind the scenes and for whatever reason Clive Davis soured on it, and if Clive Davis sours on something, you're not gonna get a lot of help. If it wasn't for David Geffen, we never would've recorded that second album.

Is that right?

Oh yeah. In fact, we were blocked out of the recording studio by Clive Davis. And David was a booking agent at the time and I was in his office when he made the phone call to Clive; and I never heard anybody talk like that before and next thing you know we were back in the studio a week later to work on the second record.

Oh, how I love that second album, which is my favorite Poco record!

Ah! How cool is that!

Well, look at what you had on there with "Anyway Bye Bye," the eighteen-minute song "Nobody's Fool." I mean, I have to label that as progressive country rock because, in my mind, that's what it was. Who in the world was doing that at the time?

Well, there was no one. And we were. It was Progressive, you're right. The Flying Burrito Brothers were more attached to the traditional country music, but for us, with Rusty Young being such an innovator on the steel guitar, it allowed us to branch out and do things that weren't typical. Of course we did "Honky Tonk Downstairs" on that particular record, but then we turned around and did something like "Anyway Bye Bye." There were a lot of experimental things that we were trying to do at that time.

And then there's the rhythm section that includes you of course. The drums and bass were very prominent in Poco, and it would've been very easy to just have those instruments sitting there doing very little, but that was not what Poco was all about. And you were a part of that with a sometimes chugging rhythm. Did you feel that the three of you made a nice rhythm section?

Absolutely. We played good together and Jimmy had a creative style on guitar and when we sat down to work on a song everybody was able to find their place. Nobody really stepped on anyone's toes and we were a three-guitar band just like Buffalo Springfield was. That was kind of unique and creative. As we talked about earlier, I was fortunate to have been around so many amazing guitar players that I was more focused on my songwriting than I was on competing as a lead guitarist. I can write a lead, but if someone was to say, "Richie, you take this one" I'd be more likely to have it come out as jazz! [Laughs]

I just don't do that, but what I can do is write a lot of hooky riffs that are on a lot of my songs and on my new album *Hand in Hand* there's a lot of riffs and I like that. Sometimes it's what you don't play as much as it is what you do play.

Exactly why I'm talking to you today!

[Laughs] Well, okay!

On that eighteen-minute track "Nobody's Fool" there's really not a lot of overly busy parts. It builds and also has a lot of open spaces and George's drumming is so good, and he was really underrated.

Oh yeah, for sure he was.

Rusty Young was such a dazzling player and it felt like, even though you had three guitar players, it was almost as though he was filling the role of what a keyboard player might bring.

Absolutely he was! When people heard him play through that Leslie speaker cabinet, people were like where is that Leslie sound coming from, there's no organ player?

And I remember the album was supposedly not a huge hit although it did reach #58, which to me is no crime, but I suppose it was wanted to be a monster hit or something. Then came Deliverin' *which was a Top 40 album and contained a minor hit with "C'mon," which you wrote. And, talking about riffs, "C'mon" sure has a great one! It seemed at that point you were finally on the rise.*

And then we hit a roadblock somewhere.

I recall reading that you guys were less than thrilled with how From the Inside *came out sounding, but I don't know how true that is.*

Yeah, during that time I was going through some troubling times in my life, spending so much time on the road. And Steve Cropper is a wonderful, wonderful guy and whether we picked the wrong producer or not I don't know, but you can't help but think we picked the right guy because he understood what we were trying to do and he could relate to us. I don't know if that's a public stance that came out later or what because I really appreciate what Steve did. He pretty much left us alone to work and I don't know that he really directed anything. Steve got a bad rap, because he didn't produce anything that was inferior sounding at all.

I don't think so in the least. That album had the title song and "Bad Weather" and your song "Just for Me and You."

There ya go.

Sometimes it's easier for critics to find a fall guy when there really wasn't one.

Sometimes it is and that makes me mad when that happens. Steve didn't get his due.

Then we reach A Good Feelin' to Know *and the title track is a fantastic song and yet the album didn't connect and should have done so much better.*

That's what drove me out of Poco. There was a certain thing that had to happen which was, you needed AM radio in order to move up to the next echelon and we were certain on this one. I went to a guy by the name of Richie Podolor, if you know him.

Yeah, he produced Steppenwolf and Three Dog Night among others.

Yeah, that was him. We were obviously looking for that producer who could give us that edge to get on AM radio. We took "C'mon," which you mentioned earlier, and a song called "A Man Like Me" and we went into the studio with Richie and recorded those songs and turned them in to CBS in New York and they were turned down. I was amazed and stunned, and I don't think Poco ever sounded as alive as we did on those two songs recorded with Richie. When they turned it down we went on another search for a producer and that's when we found Jack Richardson another wonderful guy who had success with the Guess Who, and we thought when we heard "A Good Feelin' to Know," that was it; there wasn't a person in that studio who didn't think we finally would crack that market.

Next thing I know we were traveling to the East Coast, because we played so many gigs and we had the radio on and I hear, "Running down the road, tryin' to loosen my load…" [he is singing "Take it Easy" by the Eagles here] and my heart sank and that's when I basically said it's not gonna happen for us. I went to David Geffen and that's when he put me together with J. D. and Chris.

So was the Poco album Crazy Eyes *already in the can or was that you sticking it out for one more album?*

That was me sticking it out for one more. Obviously I only had two songs on there as I was thinking ahead of other projects. We actually recorded "Believe Me," which Souther-Hillman-Furay ended up recording as well. I owed them another record so I followed through on my commitment. "Crazy Eyes" the song was a really cool thing and Poco never played it live, but my band today has worked that song out and we play it quite frequently live now.

Wow, that is a very tricky piece of music to tackle live.

It is. I want to tell you that with my band playing it, there's myself on guitar and the other guitarist Scott Sellen and his son on bass and a drummer. It was Scott who came to me and said, "We can do this"! And it was possible at that particular time with Scott playing keyboards, banjo, guitar, and lap steel on that song and it was quite a production and people were amazed that we could do it live and simply because of Scott's musical talent, although we have since added a keyboard player.

And again, there's that progressive country rock!

[Laughs] Yep!

And see, this is why you can sit there and tell me, well I'm not really a lead player, but to compose a song such as "Crazy Eyes" tells me of the talent you have on guitar. That's enough for me to say I want to know more about the guy who wrote that.

Well, I thank you.

Was Souther-Hillman-Furay considered a "supergroup" back then?

Well, that's what David Geffen told me. He said, "You know what? We'll just get you together with Chris and J. D. and we'll just put together another supergroup like Crosby, Stills & Nash." I just thought, "Really"? [Laughs] So that's what they were going for.

The first album did quite well. It just missed the Top 10 and went Gold.

It did and I had Richie Podolor producing that album. And it did quite well.

"Falling in Love" was a great song and a Top 30 hit.

Yeah, "Falling in Love" was a hit.

And then the troubled second record had a lot of problems around it.

Again, I wasn't really there for that second record and my life was falling apart at the seams at that time. Here we are working with Tom Dowd producing and anybody would've given anything to be recording with him, but my heart and my mind were just not in it then because my family was on the verge of collapse at that point. What can I say?

Priorities are what they are.

Yes they are.

And then emerges the solo career. There was I've Got a Reason, Dance a Little Light *and* I Still Have Dreams *in the late '70s.*

I had little support from Asylum, and David had left the label, but after the demise of SHF I owed them some more albums. I really liked some of those albums and *I've Got a Reason* was on the charts, but I couldn't get the support. I was listening to "Bittersweet Love" the other day, and I don't know why, but I think that could've been a country hit back in 1978 or whenever it was.

You got the year right! Most artists don't.

[Laughs] I got that one right at least.

And you were just inducted into the Colorado Music Hall of Fame.

Yes, Poco was put in this year. It was in January.

That's awesome to hear.

Thank you very much.

And you're in the Rock and Roll Hall of Fame with Buffalo Springfield as well. There was that Buffalo Springfield reunion tour in 2011; how did you feel about those shows?

I really enjoyed them and had a lot of fun. It came out of the blue and was a total surprise when Neil called and said, "Hey you know, I've been thinking it might be about time for Buffalo Springfield to do the Bridge School concerts. What do you think about that?" And I said, "I'd love to do that. I've been wanting to do those shows for years with my own band!"

We did try once in the mid-1980s at a reunion and it was a train wreck, it was just awful. So when we got together this time, we got together and for whatever reason, it was prime and ready and so easy. I don't want to make it sound like it wasn't any challenge for us to play, but when we started working on the songs they just came together.

I can't imagine there was much discussion about writing again, but perhaps about playing more than just those seven dates in 2011. I kind of remember hearing about a tour in 2012.

Well, I got hung out to dry. I was told, "You tell the world that we're going to do thirty more shows." We had started with the Bridge School shows in 2010 and then did those seven shows in summer 2011. There were two in Oakland, two in Santa Barbara and two in Los Angeles and then we played *Bonnaroo* in Tennessee. That was it and there was really not much more of a discussion and then we were done.

I'd already told the world we're doing these thirty more shows the following year but Neil just decided to go off and do something else and that's okay as I've never had a problem with Neil. But, just tell me! It cost me a lot of money and time with my own band. Everyone set things aside. I know Stephen did and he was disappointed at what happened and our drummer Joe Vitale also had to turn down gigs thinking that we were going to do these thirty shows. At this stage of our lives all I ask is, just tell me so that I can plan around it and do it right. I had to set my band aside for almost two years as we navigated through that thing.

I'll tell ya what did happen, was the inspiration for my new album *Hand in Hand*. I was looking to do some songs with Stephen and Neil thinking that we may do a Buffalo Springfield record and I had these little guitar riffs you can hear about four or five of them on *Hand in Hand* from "We Were the Dreamers" to "Love at First Sight." Those riffs turned into songs that I put on this album, which is actually getting a little bit of traction, which is amazing to me at age seventy!

It is getting nice reviews from fans and critics. I have many friends who are fans of yours and are very fond of the album. Your voice has really held up quite well. The first thing that gets criticized as an artist ages is the voice.

It's doing well and I'm pleased. I have my moments though; we just did ten shows in a row and we're not exactly traveling on Lear jets. We're packing up the Sprinter, unpacking, packin' up again and hitting the road. We did ten shows in a row playing from ninety minutes to two hours and I was worried about how my voice would hold up, but by the time we hit Daryl's House as the last gig it was in as good a form as it was the first gig. All I can say is it's God's grace I guess because I don't do anything to help it along. I do try to take care of my voice, but I've been very blessed to be able to sing at this point as well as I am.

In 1989, there was the Poco reunion album Legacy *and a tour. The album became one of your best sellers and you left in 1990, but you have continued to guest on shows and live albums with the guys.*

They are very dear friends of mine. Rusty and Paul are great guys. And we will still do things together, it's just that I'm not rejoining Poco or I will be a member of Poco, but I will certainly do a guest spot if the schedules work.

I'm very glad I got to speak with you and have the chance to feature you in this book.

Again, I'm very honored that I would even be considered for this because with rhythm guitar you never know who's listening. Now I feel I can drive a band with my guitar, where years ago I didn't know that I could, but I can now today. I can really drive the band.

Hey, you wrote "Crazy Eyes" with guitar and pen, so much respect is due. And "C'mon" has those choppy rhythm riffs and such, so you know, there's my reasoning!

Again, thanks for thinking of me! It's a very cool approach to a book and thanks for thinking of my name.

Recommended solo: "Crazy Eyes" from *Crazy Eyes* with Poco (1973)
Further info: www.richiefuray.com
Photo credit: Mike Kendall

CHAPTER 17

Eric Gales
(Born October 29, 1974, Memphis, TN)

Some dudes were born to play the guitar.

Eric Gales was just four years old when he began playing guitar and became a child prodigy. Gales's older brothers were musicians, so he was surrounded by musical talent and encouragement right away. Blues and hard rock were what appealed to Gales the most and showed in his playing whether it be Jimi Hendrix or Albert King.

Strangely, though Gales is not left-handed, he plays the instrument as such and also does the whole "right-handed guitar played upside-down" thing a la Jimi. This just seemed natural to Eric and things quickly took off as his bass playing brother Eugene taught him lessons and the natural ability did the rest.

As Gales began tearing up the club circuit, word of mouth spread about his talents and a deal was offered from major label Elektra Records in 1990. The Eric Gales Band featured Eric, Eugene, and drummer Hubert Crawford. The debut album *Eric Gales Band* came out in 1991 and produced a Top 10 rock radio hit in "Sign of the Storm" that also got a bit of MTV play. It is a true mystery why the album didn't sell better, but released at the beginning of the grunge era—perhaps it was all timing.

Songs like "Resurrection," "Piece of My Soul," and "No One Else" were so damn good. Gales had a combination of soul, power, and funkiness in his playing and was also a gifted vocalist. The sophomore album *Picture of A Thousand Faces* followed in 1993 and contained a minor radio hit in "Paralyzed." With "Guilty of the Innocence," that combo of soul and power stands strong and Gales' guitar solos have a tone that Hendrix himself would have been envious of. "God Only Knows" is another great track with a blistering wah-wah-laced solo at the end. Picking up on the version that guitar great Eddie Hazell (late of P-Funk) did of the Beatles' "I Want You/She's So Heavy," Gales and his band concocted a hair-raising rendition with those amazing solos and sounds that only Gales can wrench from his guitar. By the five-minute mark, you should be texting a friend and saying, "How the hell did I not know of this guy? Damn, you must check this out!"

In August 1994, Gales came on stage and jammed with Santana at Woodstock '94, which was a special highlight. In 1996, he teamed with both of his brothers to release *Left Hand Brand* as the Gales Brothers. A new deal with MCA Records led to the first album in five years: *That's What I Am*. With *Crystal Vision* in 2006, Gales released his most focused effort in years opening with the powerful "Retribution" where Gales' tone is on full display. It is truly criminal that Eric Gales isn't a superstar, but it is a gift that we get the chance to hear him record and play live gigs, so that part is what matters most.

Since 2007, Gales has been extremely prolific issuing albums almost every year and *The Story of My Life* in 2008 was a melting pot of blues rock in the vein of greats like Stevie Ray Vaughan and Cream. In 2011, *Transformation* was another winner, but the stakes were raised with the *Pinnick Gales Pridgin* album in 2013 that paired Eric with King's X bassist/vocalist Doug Pinnick and ex-Mars Volta drummer Thomas Pridgen.

The *Pinnick Gales Pridgin* album melts the speakers with vibrancy that any power trio would be proud of. "Collateral Damage" is a punishing beast and "Lascivious" and "Hate Crime" burn with fire, while a wicked twist on Cream's "Sunshine of Your Love" is creative and explosive. This is one hell of an album and considering the talent involved that's no surprise. Jimi Hendrix and Phil Lynott are smiling up in the heavens, trust me. And how about that ten-and-one-half-minute epic blues romp "Been So High (The Only Place to Go Is Down)" or the intro to "The Greatest Love"? Eric Gales is just the real deal folks—no truer words can be spoken.

So, could *PGP 2* released in 2014 top the debut? It sure as hell could come close. "Down to the Bone," "Watchman," "The Past Is the Past," "Every Step of the Way"—they're all frickin' great. There's no point to naming more songs because they're all so damn good.

And Eric hasn't forgotten his solo career either as *Good for Sumthin* was released later in 2014 with guest appearances from Zakk Wylde and Eric Johnson! Hearing Eric and Zakk tear it up on "Steep Climb" is a treat. Each note from both players pours out emotion and Eric's vocals remain so, so strong and perfect for the music he plays. A clever rearrangement of the Rolling Stones classic "Miss You" is top notch as well. "E2 (Note For Note)" is a pretty piece that sees the two Erics (Gales and Johnson) craft magnificent feel and melody before unleashing a torrent of trade-off solos that is beautiful chaos. To say the least, Gales did it again—another fantastic album.

Why Eric Gales hasn't achieved massive sales, I will never have an understanding of, but then again I didn't understand the awful movie *Vanilla Sky* or algebra either. The reason I love the guitar so much is because of what men like Eric Gales can do with it. There's a connection there between Gales and the instrument that is an absolute honor to listen to. That's as real as it is.

In January 2015, while looking at the one-and-a-half- inches of snow on the ground from the projected fifteen to twenty-four we were supposed to get according to the "experts," I was able to briefly chat with Eric.

Who were some of the main influences as guitarists for you?

A lot of different styles and genres were what I was listening to. Like Eric Johnson, Robin Trower, Albert King, Muddy Waters, and Hendrix and other styles as well.

What have been the types of guitars you've preferred through the years?

Mainly, it's been Strats.

What led to the decision to play the guitar "upside down"? Was it a Hendrix-Albert King thing, or just something you fell into as a natural comfort zone?

I just fell into it naturally. I also have two older brothers that played that way as well.

You have one of the purest tones I've ever heard—it's like liquid heaven. Did it take a while to achieve your sound and how did it fall into place?

Of course, it took lots of work. I was always workin' tirelessly at it, and then it just began to start falling into place.

You and the band did a cover of the Beatles' "I Want You/She's So Heavy" that is one of the greatest Beatles covers I have ever heard. The guitar playing is just phenomenal. Do you remember arranging this one?

Yes, my brother and I and Hubert Crawford did that together.

What can you recall about playing with Santana at Woodstock '94? I thought it was so awesome to see you up there in such a big festival.

It was one of the highlights of my entire life.

The last few albums of your career have been among the best you've recorded in my opinion. The new album Good for Sumthin *is fantastic. The collaborations with Zakk Wylde and Eric Johnson are amazing. How did those come about and how did you feel about the end results?*

I am very pleased with the outcome. This came about because they are friends of mine and having played with them before in the past had already set up a great relationship.

Another example of how great your latest albums have been is the two Pinnick Gales Pridgin *albums. I can't even begin to describe how much I play those albums. The version of "Sunshine of Your Love" is awesome. The original material is stellar. The three of you are a natural fit. Did it come together as smoothly as it sounds?*

Actually it did. We just went in and totally were ourselves in the studio.

You are one of the top players I've seen in regards to passion, feel, and spirit, and I've got some of those players in this book. There really seems to be a connection between you and the guitar that seems genuine. Is that accurate to say or a little too corny?

It's very accurate.

A final goofy question that my cats ask most players: if you could rename one of your songs or albums with a cat theme what would you come up with? My cats are curious—ha ha.

Ha ha. *Purr for Sumthin.*

Recommended solo: "I Want You/She's So Heavy"
from *Picture of a Thousand Faces* with the Eric Gales Band (1993)
Further info: www.ericgalesband.com
Photo credit: Michael Edmonds

CHAPTER 18

Frank Gambale

(Born December 22, 1958, Canberra, Australia)

Yikes. I could leave it at that as far as describing Frank Gambale's guitar skills. An Australian native, Frank came to the US in the '80s and graduated from the Guitar Institute of Technology in Hollywood, California, and graduated as Student of the Year. Let's just say he deserved it.

Through Legato Records he issued his first album *Brave New Guitar* in 1985, and right from the start this was something special and innovative. There was some blues on here, but it was the intense jazz fusion that made it stand out along with Frank's then unheard of sweep picking techniques. He played with the legendary violinist Jean-Luc Ponty for a while and then joined another legend with Grammy winning jazz pianist/keyboardist Chick Corea in the Chick Corea Elektric Band in 1987. His first album with this highly successful fusion act was 1987's *Light Years* that featured himself, Corea on keyboards, the incomparable Dave Weckl on drums, John Patitucci on bass, and Eric Marienthal on sax. The album won a Grammy.

The lighter, more acoustic-based *Eye of the Beholder* followed in 1988 and featured some great pieces in the title song, "Eternal Child" (with Frank playing some serious Flamenco guitar) and "Trance Dance." Next album *Inside Out* was an uneven mix of styles, but the title song and the four-part suite "Tale of Daring" and "Kicker" were very strong compositions. The album made the Top 10 on the jazz charts. In 1991, *Beneath the Mask* (a #2 album on the jazz charts) finally saw a return to the fusion sounds and "Free Step" and "Jammin E. Cricket" were quite hot. The band came to an end soon after.

During this period, Frank remained very busy releasing the groundbreaking, influential *Monster Licks & Speed Picking* instructional video (1988) to great acclaim and sales. His solo album *Thunder from Down Under* (1989) was released but had one hell of a horrid album cover! Don't let the cover fool you though, Frank's playing and writing was seriously great fusion.

Frank then became part of the Mark Varney-organized Mark Varney Project along with other awesome guitarists in Allan Holdsworth, Shawn Lane, and Brett Garsed. The albums *Truth in Shredding* (1990) and *Centrifugal Funk* (1991) were released at the same time Gambale was working at the Los Angeles Music Academy as head of the guitar department. Gambale's '90s albums were pretty special with 1994's *Passages* of note especially for the song "Little Charmer" and a cover of Cream's "White Room." "Little Charmer" is a must hear—simply astonishing.

In 2000, through Steve Vai's label Favoured Nations he issued *Coming to Your Senses* and formed his own label Wombat Records and has done some remarkable collaborations with classical guitarist Maurizio Colonna including *Imagery Suite* (2000) and *Bon Voyage* (2007).

On top of all that, Frank has also been a part of the jazz fusion act Vital Information (formed by ex-Journey drumming great Steve Smith) since the late '80s and has appeared on nine of their albums, both studio and live. His most recent solo works include *Natural High* (2010) and *Soulmine* (2012). The *Soulmine* album is quite different for Frank and features female singer Boca. It is a mix of soul/jazz/funk/pop and R&B without sacrificing the musical chops. Gambale would also reunite with the Chick Corea Elektric Band in 2004 and also has recorded three albums with GHS, which is a collaboration with Smith on drums and bassist extraordinaire Stuart Hamm. These albums are fantastic for any jazz fan.

And, how about Frank joining legendary jazz fusion band Return to Forever for a world tour in 2011? Unbelievable performances night after night from Gambale, bass wizard Stanley Clarke, drummer Lenny White, violinist Jean-Luc Ponty, and band leader/founder Chick Corea on keyboards. A live album *The Mothership Returns* was thankfully issued in 2012 capturing all of the brilliance. Frank's solo on "Senor Mouse" is one of those "was that for real?" moments and was worth the price of admission alone. The tour was a huge success and provided smiles for everyone including the band.

His signature model guitar the Carvin FG1 was released in 2011 and is simply gorgeous—one of the nicest thin hollow-body instruments you will see.

The 1988 home video release *Monster Licks & Speed Picking* should be in the Rock and Roll Hall of Fame for its influence on guitar playing alone. Although some had attempted ideas like this before, it was Frank Gambale who basically created, crafted, perfected, and introduced it to the world. Many have copied the style since, but there's nobody out there who does it like the man who invented it.

In October of 2014, I was thrilled to be able to talk to Frank and we had a really great conversation. With my charm, how could it not have been great? Well, here's how it went down:

This is quite a thrill, I must be honest.

Thank you. So what is the premise of the book?

Simply to give more exposure in a book format to players I have always admired from various genres that get nowhere near the press or attention, largely due to laziness by the media and a general lack of knowledge.

Well, that's such a great cause. The premise is good and you're finding a niche market. You don't want to do what's already been well tread already. It can be a popularity contest and it's not just rock musicians who play guitar.

Well said. Who were those that inspired you to begin playing?

It's usually chronological as I've been playing for about forty-five years. The guy who really made me want to play was Jimi Hendrix. I wanted to transcribe and learn what he was playing; that was really fun as a kid learning such great guitar music as "Little Wing." They were great parts to learn. I had two older brothers who were into guitar players, so as a seven year old, I was exposed to English blues acts such as John Mayall and his guitar players in the Bluesbreakers, but it was his voice and composition that I liked. Eric Clapton and Mick Taylor were guys I really liked as I was heavily into the blues as well.

And then I branched out into guitar and vocal harmony bands such as Crosby, Stills & Nash and the Eagles and country bands like the Dillards. And who didn't love the Beatles? I was really exposed to a lot of music in Australia and I was even into a band called Lindisfarne if you know them.

Oh yeah—part of the British folk explosion in the '70s; they were a wonderful band and talented players.

I found them unique in their own way. By the time I was thirteen, I found I was listening to more complex acts like Steely Dan and I liked Yes a lot. I also listened to George Duke's music and the Brecker Brothers because I was focusing on saxophone solos, and Chick Corea who I ended up working with for many years. I liked Frank Zappa's music and Jean-Luc Ponty was a major influence as I was really into composition. When a Steely Dan record would get released nobody would see me for weeks as I felt I had to transcribe every song and it was like being a kid in a candy store just learning all the chords, and the horn charts and the melodies and the bass lines.

That's interesting because their guitar players were unbelievable, even if they were just for one song or even one part of a song. Larry Carlton's solo on "Don't Take Me Alive" still gives me chills.

That's an outstanding solo, an outstanding solo. And their albums like *Katy Lied*, that record had something like ten songs with ten guitar players so that was the cream of the crop on there from LA and it was such a challenge to try to learn all those different parts from different players. There was so much richness in guitar on their albums, especially the early ones where they were still a band. "Skunk" Baxter and Denny Dias were melodic and very interesting players.

That was really opening my mind up but my sweep picking technique, which I developed was largely due to listening to other instruments like the solos by Chick Corea on piano and Michael Brecker on saxophone. So once I started transcribing sax and piano on guitar there was no precedent. It was up to me to find a way to play those notes; it was just processing information. And some of the lines were so hard to play and didn't fall in well at all that it forced me to find a technique that would enable me to play the thing that I was hearing. It was so foreign to the guitar, that it created a monster technique which is now part of the guitar lexicon, really.

How old were you when you began the technique?

Hard to say, but I think my early teens. It just struck me as being incredibly logical. You've got four adjacent strings for example, with one note on each string. It made no sense to me to do an alternate picking technique across those 4 strings. It makes perfect sense to drag the pick in one direction right across the string and go down or up and separate the notes. It seemed so obvious.

Not obvious to me! I love your humility, but I can't even wrap my head around the things that you do with the guitar. I was very fortunate to have seen you with the Chick Corea Elektric Band in Philly in 1988, and I had never seen or heard playing like that before.

That was still relatively new, people weren't sweeping back then. I developed something that was a diamond in the rough and I had to polish it. I wrote a book and did a video on the subject. The publisher of both didn't want me to use the term "sweep picking" and wanted to use the term "speed picking" because they felt people could relate to speed and not sweeping.

I'm working on an online school right now and I've just finished a very lengthy ten- to twelve-hours blues course that is very cool. And I also just filmed a complete update to sweep picking called *The Definitive Sweep Picking Course*. This will incorporate a lot of new developments since then, as I haven't really filmed anything on the subject since the '80s. It will be a sweep picking feast for anyone into that. Whenever I see anything on the technique of sweep picking, it is derivative of my first efforts. I've not seen anything that presents stuff I hadn't already covered. That's why I lay claim to it. There are people who did a little bit before and the idea was maybe starting to formulate, but I woke up a sleeping giant.

I agree 100%. I don't see anyone else who can lay claim to it. Just look at the timeframe.

Nobody will argue that Eddie Van Halen was the finger-tapping guy, or the one that formulized it as a technique. Yes, there were some who tapped before, such as Larry Carlton, but nobody will argue that Eddie was the guy who perfected it and made it what it has become. That created the monster that it is now, and kids have come up with ideas that have expounded upon it further, but in the '70s I was watching him and saying, "What the heck is he doing"?

When I saw you guys in 1988, seeing that Elektric Band, especially with Dave Weckl on drums, I was enthralled just watching all the players bouncing off of one another. When I was early in high school I started listening to a lot of jazz fusion, such as Return to Forever, Billy Cobham, Weather Report, and those Jeff Beck albums among others, and seeing the Chick Corea Elektric Band was a thrill with Herbie Hancock also on the bill. And that leads me to my next question: what was it like recently joining Return To Forever? How awesome a gig for you on big stages!

I had the time of my life. It was the greatest tour I'd ever done. I skipped a generation somehow because there were all my heroes. I needed little rehearsal time—I knew that stuff already! I grew up on all that stuff—all the Chick Corea and Stanley Clarke records. I was a heavy fan already, and talk about a special bonus with Jean-Luc Ponty on board! I had to pinch myself; it was incredible. It started in Australia and we filled the Sydney Opera House, so for a kid from Australia to play that venue with my family in the tenth row it was very special, a real magic carpet ride.

You had a really neat solo piece on an album called "Fe Fi Fo Funk."

That title is from *Jack and the Beanstalk* and I've always loved funk. I was a big fan of Earth, Wind & Fire. I got into funk-styled playing when I was at G.I.T. and I learned that rhythm guitar playing on one string and learning how to play for the groove. And without keyboards I started getting into layering guitars to play different voices like keyboards and that was one of the songs back then I wrote with that jangly sound.

How did playing with Allan Holdsworth come about? Was that Mark Varney that put that together?

Yeah, Mike gave me my first chance to record. He heard a demo tape and offered me a small deal. I was in fact his first signing. Now this was Mark, not Mike his brother who has Shrapnel Records. He had a well-mannered attitude and was more into jazz fusion as opposed to metal and that's why he was a lot less successful than his brother [laughs]. He asked if I would play with Holdsworth and just said, here's the budget and you can write, produce, and oversee it. In the contract it stated that each guitar solo had to be 3 minutes long!

[Laughs] That's too good a deal for any guitarist to turn down!

Yeah! And it didn't matter if it was good or not—just make it a long solo! I had to time the songs and make sure the solos were long enough. Allan cut his part separately as he was on tour. So I recorded live with the band and we gave the tapes to Allan to lay down his solos and we mixed the album together. There's an anecdote for you! I had nothing to do with the title *The Truth In Shredding,* which is embarrassing to me. When I hear shredding I think of metal and that's not me or Allan. I think Mark was trying to cross over with the title, but *The Truth In Sharing* would've been nicer!

How happy were you with the way the signature guitar the Carvin F1 turned out?

I'm utterly delighted with that instrument. Not only do I love the Carvin guitars, I love the people. To me when you do an endorsement not only do you want to do it for an instrument you love to play, but also for the people you are working with. Most of my endorsements have been long-term and I really get involved. Carvin is brilliant, I think they are awesome and make some of the finest guitars in the world in my opinion. Their quality is flawless and consistent.

They are one of the fastest-growing guitar companies out there and that's not even all they do, as they are involved in PA systems and amplifiers, etc. They do everything in-house and sell direct to the public, and because of that, they are able to keep everything at incredibly low prices for what you get. My guitar is made from the five finest woods. It's fantastic and everyone's guitar is unique because they can pick their own color, wood combination, pickups, inlay, curve radius on the fret board and more.

One final stupid question: if you could rename one of your songs or albums after a cat what would you come up with? My cats want to know!

Ooooohhh...I do love cats. I prefer them to dogs, but my wife is a dog person.

(No kidding people, but at this exact moment my cat Krimpet meowed, perhaps in disgust over Frank's wife being a dog lover—I have the tape to prove it!)

Let me think about this for a second. I had an album called *Thunder from Down Under* and there was a song on there called "Robo Roo." *Robocop* was big at the time and I am sitting on a robot kangaroo on the cover, so how about "Robot Cat"?

Works for me!

You caught me off guard with that one, but I appreciate humor and odd comedy especially.

That's me—trust me. I hope if you ever come to Philly I will be able to attend.

I need to play more gigs in the US, but it's a guaranteed money loser. When I book a gig in Europe, they pay part of the transportation and provide a hotel and the fees are higher, but when you add up the money for a US show, it doesn't work at all. I am willing to lose a little bit and do a tour here though because I want to play for the American fans.

I suppose it is a nice feeling to make those US fans happy, even if it's a smaller number of them.

Yes, it's not always about the money, is it? I always quote the classic, cliché joke: How do you get a jazz millionaire? Start him at $2 million!

[Laughs] Hey, that's pretty damn funny! That's not yours, is it?

No, I can't take credit for that one, but it is sadly appropriate.

CHAPTER 19

Gary Green

(Born Gary William Green, November 20, 1950, Stroud Green, North London, UK)

Gentle Giant were (and will always be) one of the most challenging of all the progressive rock bands. Unusual vocal arrangements, thought-provoking lyrics, complex time signatures, and ever-shifting styles utilizing a multitude of instruments (and most members played at least three or four different instruments) made for some heady and at times unnerving listening.

The Shulman brothers (Derek, Phil, and Ray) had already achieved some notice and success with Simon Dupree and the Big Sound in the late '60s but folded that outfit and formed Gentle Giant in 1970 with Gary Green on guitar, Kerry Minnear on keyboards, and Martin Smith on drums. From the outset, everyone would play different instruments, including recorder, violin, cello, xylophone, marimbas, sax, mandolin, trumpet, ukulele, and platypus (well, maybe not platypus, but I wouldn't be surprised to find someone actually played one on an album).

The interesting thing about Green was that he was really a blues-based player and not some sort of virtuoso or classically influenced guitarist as was typical of this genre. This makes him all the more intriguing. He somehow fit in and adapted perfectly and was with the band their entire career.

The self-titled debut album was an iffy affair, but songs such as "Alucard" and "Giant" informed the listener that this was no pop affair. *Acquiring the Taste* followed, the band more or less acknowledging with the title that yeah, they were out there. The blues and soul styles that appeared on the debut were gone, as evidenced by "Pantagruel's Nativity" (very cool stuff laid down by Gary here), "Wreck," and "Plain Truth."

With the concept album *Three Friends* (and new drummer Malcolm Mortimore), the band started to expand their fanbase. The album was unique and daring and pretty captivating. All the instrumentation was superb, but Green got a chance to wail on "Peel the Paint," playing through an echoplex and simply crushing his notes. "Mister Class and Quality" also allows Green space to showcase his chops and it's something! In 1972, Mortimore left and John Weathers joined.

In December 1972, *Octopus* swam out to record stores and was an ingenious effort with a harder edge. Opening track "The Advent of Panurge" has some strafing leads by Green showing his blues influences, and "A Cry for Everyone" has a very cool riff. The prog meets free jazz meets classical meets baroque of "Knots" is out there, but seriously intense, especially with those vocal arrangements. Sadly, after the *Octopus* tour that included dates opening for Black Sabbath, Phil left the band to spend more time with his family, which nearly ended the band. Thankfully, the other five members bonded together and opted to carry on.

Yet, Columbia Records were so disenchanted with the band they decided not to release *In a Glass House* in the US in 1973. A stupid move, of course, as works like "The Runaway," the title track, and "Way of Life" (which had some really zipping guitar lines) expanded the mix and sound even further. When he had the space to inject some guitars, Green did it with some of his best tones yet.

Many fans agree that 1974's *The Power and the Glory* was Gentle Giant's finest moment (and their first on Capitol Records) and it's hard to argue. One criticism of Gentle Giant's music was that it was too dissonant and was incommunicable. This was actually true to some extent and this album was only slightly different in some respects. But there was a slight move towards more accessible songs on here and the album became their biggest seller, even reaching #78 on the US charts. "So Sincere," "Playing the Game," "Proclamation," and "The Face" are highlights, and Green lays down a blistering solo on "The Face." This album is perhaps the most consistent in the Gentle Giant canon.

Free Hand saw the group in the US Top 50, and the LP had some Renaissance-era and jazz fusion flavors to it. The title cut is plain nuts as it grooves along, jumps and breaks down in all crazy ways. Live it is a fearsome beast as seen on the BBC *Sight and Sound* concert from 1978, and Green proves his brilliance amidst all the chaos—his playing is so, so right. And Gary's solo on the aquatic tale "His Last Voyage" is a delight.

Although 1976's *Interview* album was a bit of a slip, the astonishing live album *Playing the Fool: The Official Live* showed that this band could somehow nail down all this complexity, not to mention the fact that they would run around switching instruments with one another mid-song and also execute all those haunting medieval vocal harmonies and counterpoint harmonies. The album would reach #89 in the US and remains a serious fan favorite.

The Missing Piece was an interesting combo of prog and some more pop-oriented tracks and even nods to hard rock in their own weird way. "Two Weeks in Spain" just leaps out at the listener with those rhythms and oh, that guitar! "Betcha Thought We Couldn't Do It" kicks arse and teaches the punk rockers a thing or two as well. Even though the band did acquiesce on this album and more so on *Giant for a Day* (1978) and *Civilian* (1980), so damn what? These albums are a fine listen, if not quite the level of the classic records and showed their adaptability. Catchy songs like "Words from the Wise" from the former and the crunching hard rock of "All Through the Night" from the latter album prove that Gentle Giant were willing to move forward with their music and adapt to the marketplace.

Alas, sales, internal conflicts, and changing tastes dictated the band would close up shop in late 1980. Not only are Gentle Giant not forgotten, loads of music fans are discovering this band each year via Spotify, YouTube, and other sources—just read all the loving comments from old fans and newer ones. Sure, they are never going to be everyone's cup of tea, but for those willing to explore and broaden their horizons this is one band that will not disappoint.

After the breakup of the band, Gary played with Eddie Jobson for a while as well as the band Mother Tongue. In the 2000s he connected with former Yes member Billy Sherwood on the prog all-star Pink Floyd tribute albums for both *The Dark Side of the Moon* and *The Wall*, alongside members of Yes, Toto, Asia, King Crimson, Styx, and more.

Gary is now in Three Friends, a band that largely plays Gentle Giant material and includes two other former members of Gentle Giant. They still play live gigs as of 2015. Any hope of a Gentle Giant reunion is very dim, but this band keeps the music alive in a faithful way. Gary Green is such a fine player and is so deserving of more recognition (plus, he loves cats!).

I was able to speak with Gary in December 2014 and it was a total pleasure.

To start with, even though it's a stock question, I ask—who were some of the guys you listened to growing up that led to your interest in guitar?

Well, that's always the one first isn't it? And it's an important question. There's usually someone you look up to and start to emulate. Initially it was kind of my brother—my older brother Jeff—who is a guitar player. There was a guitar lying around all the time and he would play with his friends in the front room of our house, and I became interested in that and I wanted to do it, too. Then I started listening to the Shadows, an instrumental group popular in Britain with Hank Marvin on guitar. I guess you know who they were?

Oh yeah, many players have cited Hank Marvin as an influence, and although I don't know much of their music, I do know some of their songs and what Marvin was doing back then was pretty impressive.

Yeah, it was! And of course, we had the Beatles, and then it was the blues for me. I hung with this guy in high school and he was into the blues and it was through him I discovered Clapton, Beck, and Peter Green, who was the one I really loved. Eric (Clapton) was great though, and I must've seen Cream about thirty times, including some tiny little dives.

Really? Thirty times? Damn!

Oh yes! I saw Blind Faith at Hyde Park and Cream's farewell concert, as well as one of their first-ever gigs. And, when you start to hear things on the records you can copy the solos and the playing and start to get a feel for what these players were doing. the Shadows were a big one for me as well though, and Bruce Welch was a fabulous rhythm player for them who had a very deft touch.

It's interesting you mention rhythm because that's something I've noticed about your playing. It's very rhythmic, almost like you are in tandem with the percussion and bass. Is that something that makes sense?

Yes, absolutely. That's something that just falls naturally to me. I think I'm more of a rhythm player than a melody player. I'm not really a very good musician to tell you the truth. I don't read music and I don't write the proper way. I can figure things out, which is a strength I guess, but I couldn't tell you what the third note is in an A Major scale or any of that. I don't know that stuff. My love of it is the rhythm—that's what turned me on to music.

My Dad would play a lot of jazz like Benny Goodman, Duke Ellington, and he played Sinatra—all kinds of stuff—and me and my two brothers would hear it all. My oldest brother Mike played drums—he's gone now and I still have his drums. Him, me, and Jeff would hear all this music from our Dad. It all filtered down to me. Rhythm is just very important to me. I love drums, I play drums, and I'd like to think I'm a pretty good drummer, although I am sure there are those who would disagree! [Laughs] But I play rhythmically and, in time and for me, that's the way it should be. Rhythm is a key—I am an ensemble player.

To me, without rhythm, there truly can't be real music. Yes, you can noodle around in crazy time signatures, but rhythm should be central. A great rhythm player can only be appreciated if he's not there—it's a thankless job, but so vital.

Absolutely! As I've gotten older I have truly learned you cannot teach a sense of rhythm. You can expose people to it and hope it sinks in and they get it one day, but it's not easy. There are loads of famous players who have no sense of rhythm and it dismays me so much. It's frustrating because rhythm is everything!

You can only get by on guitar histrionics for so long.

Those histrionics drive me up a wall. I have only such a level of tolerance.

There is a time and a place for some of that playing, I can't lie and say I don't enjoy some of that, but all the time and endlessly? Nope.

Well, of course. It can exist in small doses. But what happens is, those players don't speak to me and leave no impression. Yet, I can hear two notes from B. B. King and be very happy. It stays with you forever.

And those rhythm/lead type players such as Chuck Berry, Pete Townshend, Keith Richards, Tony Hicks; they get it.

I'm with you 100% on all that. Pete Townshend is wonderful. Tony Hicks is splendid—all of these players understood the import of rhythm.

With Gentle Giant—and, let's face it, with all those unusual arrangements and songs you had—did you find it odd, or were you surprised that you had such a significant following? I mean, you were never as big as Yes, Jethro Tull, ELP, etc., but you drew good-sized crowds and sold a decent amount of records.

Yeah, we had an audience somehow! We weren't huge like you say, but were we surprised? No, I would say but not because we went into it with a sort of fearsome righteousness. Success and fame was secondary to us, because we were just trying to play what pleased us. Plus, we were very lucky in that the previous band the Schulmans had been in Simon Dupree and the Big Sound had made several good connections in the past with their manager who was Gerry Bron.

Ah yes, the Uriah Heep manager/producer who owned Bronze Records.

And Derek and the Schulmans knew Gerry very well and the upshot was that Gerry sponsored the first year Gentle Giant was together on a matter of trust of knowing the three brothers, and he financed our first seven or eight months together allowing us to rehearse. That was very freeing and allowed us to concentrate on the music. We didn't worry about selling well or popularity, which was kind of bold.

It certainly was and Gentle Giant was also on some strange bills back then like opening for Black Sabbath… [my dumb-ass dog begins barking…]

I hear you've got a dog barking over there!

Yes, and I'm not sure what he's trying to ask you.

[Laughs] Probably nothing important! We have two dogs actually…anyway, yes the Black Sabbath tour was an odd bill, and after we were with Gerry for a while, he had us play with Uriah Heep and Colosseum, who we did half a tour with. Once we moved from Gerry we signed with WWA and they had Sabbath so we toured with them in the States. And although it seemed odd musically, back then there were many strange bills all the time. It sort of worked, and the Sabbath guys were very down to earth, normal guys, which was quite a surprise. They were lovely blokes. It helped us with our stage show and we used our heavier material opening for Sabbath and it ended up going very well with their audience.

When Octopus *came out, (which is one of my favorite albums of yours) with songs like "Dog's Life" and "Boys in the Band" how did you feel about that album? Was that the one that started to open things up?*

I think so. We were starting to find our own identity. At the end of *Acquiring the Taste* I think we felt that we liked it, but for general acceptance it was perhaps too far out there. Then we did *Three Friends*, which was a narrow move towards the mainstream and with *Octopus* we were really jelling and writing to everyone's strengths. It was a really good album as far as the material goes. I think we felt it was a coalescence of the band and really stamped our identity.

My friend in high school had the Octopus *album and I borrowed it. He steered me away from the earlier albums but also lent me* The Power and the Glory *that seems to be the one that fans hold in the highest regard. Steven Wilson, of course, did the surround mix of the album in 5.1 this year and it got a very good reaction. Have you had the chance to hear it?*

I have it but haven't heard the 5.1 mix yet because I don't have a system to play it on! The remaster/remix of the CD is impeccable, however, you must hear it.

Neither do I! I don't get into the whole surround mix thing, but I've heard this was a good mix by Steven; he's the best. The mix of the standard CD itself is astonishing, I agree. Gentle Giant has never sounded like this.

I'm sure it's fine (the 5.1 surround mix), I mean, I know what the album is like! [Laughs] I've read a lot of opinions on it and the good things. This is one that the fans cite as being the favorite but there's always debate about the best of the catalog and such. They're all favorites of mine in a way.

And with Free Hand you narrowly missed the US Top 40, so things kept improving.

Yeah, and at that point we were now a five-piece band and we got a bit harder and drifted towards more compositional stuff. It was a really good period for the band.

Even though you eschewed typical guitar solos on most songs, you certainly came up with some good ones when you did. Songs like "The Face" and "His Last Voyage" are seriously good solo spotlights where you did let loose a little bit.

Absolutely! I really like the one on "His Last Voyage" too. I'm not a big ego-driven guy so it was more about playing for the good of the band which was Gentle Giant's main thrust anyway. We all felt the same thing—leave the egos aside and serve the music as it shall need. We didn't lay things down and say, "this solo will go right here" or anything of the sort.

The last few albums took a more commercial turn, but again there were some seriously good songs being crafted on those records. I still enjoy those albums.

Well, *Giant for a Day* I like parts of but less overall, but I do like *Civilian*.

I was just going to mention Civilian. *Genesis, Yes, Jethro Tull were all streamlining and making excellent albums despite the cries of treason from the old guard. With* Civilian *you were tossing in elements of new wave and even hard rock. For example, "All Through the Night" has a great, crunchy hard rockin' riff.*

Great song—Kerry wrote that one.

I thought continuing in that direction was quite possible, but unlikely everyone would have been on board.

It could've continued that way, it really could've. I truly don't think they (the Schulmans) had their hearts in it. I believe they really lay where *Free Hand* and *Power and the Glory* were, and they were free to be whimsical about what they were doing as opposed to something more commercial, which let's face it is what those last two albums were all about.

Oh, that's quite true. I'd imagine there had to be some sacrificing of what they held true musically.

It just wasn't where our best talents lay.

And it might've led to unhappiness.

Yes, you truly have to love what you're doing or it becomes very difficult. I believe that's true—if you do what you love, you will do the best that you can, and especially if you can make a living at it.

And there's the thing—this is why so many people are not happy—ya gotta pay the bills somehow.

Well there it is. If you can though, be true to yourself and try to find that happiness in what you do.

And that leads me to what you're currently doing now. Which is...?

Which is not much! [Laughs]

Ha ha. Now wait a minute, you still have Three Friends going, correct?

Yes, with Malcolm Mortimer and that's great and I would like it lead to more stuff.

And, can I ask the cliché question? Is there any hope at all of a Gentle Giant reunion?

No, is the answer to that question! [Laughs] It just won't happen. We're too far apart now. I do see Kerry every year and Malcolm, of course. John too, but now he has health problems and it's very sad. We just won't have any kind of reunion, and that's fine. The projects will continue with the catalog.

And what guitars have you enjoyed playing over the years?

I mostly play Strats and I used one on the first album and then the Les Paul after that on every album, and a Telecaster. Those would be the three in the Gentle Giant years. I used a Yamaha for the acoustic bits as well as a Hagstrom 12-string that was lovely. I'm pretty much a plug-in-and-play guy and don't worry about manipulating pedals. It gets in the way. And I should mention that Django Reinhardt was my favorite guitar player of all time. And he didn't even need all his fingers—it shows you what can be done.

You were on The Wall *tribute album in 2005 called* Back Against the Wall *that was organized by former Yes member Billy Sherwood. There were some very big names on it. How did you get involved with that project playing the Pink Floyd material?*

He just called me up. He's into all sorts of music and he invited me to come out and play. I didn't meet anybody on the album, but it turned out very well. It had me and Alan White and Edgar Winter...

And Steve Howe, Steve Lukather, Ian Anderson, John Wetton...

Yeah and Adrian Belew and so on! I suppose one could ask why bother doing such an album? Then again, why not bother? It was an interesting project and I really like David Gilmour's playing. I tried to doff my hat to him and yet do it in his style while adding my own parts—not an easy thing to do. Like with Three Friends we are free to some extent, yet we are playing a part and need to be true to the original music. We must be mindful that people want to hear those old songs again, and very much the way they remember them. We did that prog rock cruise with a lot of big name acts and it went well and we will be doing it again next year (2015).

Very nice to hear that! Now, a final, stupid question...

Now, now—there are no stupid questions.

Well, this one is. [Laughs]

[Laughs] All right then, let's hear it!

Okay, if you can rename a song or album after a cat that you played on with Gentle Giant what would it be? My cats are a curious type.

Oh my. Well, how about *Herding Cats Playing Gentle Giant Music?*

No, that stinks!

[Laughs] Well, I struck out there!

Perhaps something like the word purr or purring is in a title of yours?

So maybe *The Purry and the Glory?*

I will accept that, there we go.

I think you were helping me along and took pity.

Yes, that's exactly what I did!

[Laughs] Fair enough—I had such little time to think about it! I can be whimsical, I know I can! What's the interest with cats by the way?

Well, a combination of my warped sense of humor and my wife and I had five cats who we loved to death. We were not the crazy cat people though!

We love them too. We have had as many as thirty-two in the house! A lot were animal rescue cats; they are now in homes and we still have nine.

I am such a believer in animal rights and helping out all critters. Ours were all from outside or no-kill shelters.

Oh yes, us as well. And we have so many dogs, including old English sheepdogs. I believe there's a direct correlation between people who care for animals and their outlook on humanity as well. There's a quote from *Seinfeld* my friends like to use: "People? They're the worst!"

My philosophy: Animals rule, humans drool!

[Update: about three weeks later, Gary emailed me with an album title using a cat…Octopussy! He's an even better guitarist for it now I'm sure.]

Recommended solo: "His Last Voyage" from *Free Hand* by Gentle Giant (1975)
Further info: www.blazemonger.com/GG/Gentle_Giant_Home_Page
Photo credit: from Gary Green's personal collection

CHAPTER 20

Steve Hackett

(Born Stephen Richard Hackett, February 12, 1950, Pimlico, London, UK)

In December 1970, Steve Hackett joined progressive rock outfit Genesis. Drummer/vocalist Phil Collins had just joined as well, along with founding members Peter Gabriel (vocals/flute), Tony Banks (keyboards), and Mike Rutherford (bass/guitar). These five musicians would craft some of the most complex, beautifully played rock of not just the 1970s, but of all time.

Hackett had played in a band called Quiet World who had released an album in 1970 to little notice. But in the British magazine *Melody Maker*, he spotted an ad that caught his eye and decided to audition for the band in that ad: Genesis. *Nursery Cryme* was the first album by this lineup issued in 1971. The album was a mix of epics such as "The Musical Box," "The Return of the Giant Hogweed," and "The Fountain of Salmacis," along with shorter, quirkier songs with a distinctively British lilt such as "Harlequin" and "For Absent Friends." The lengthy pieces were tricky compositions that were daring, imaginative, definitely eccentric, and even bizarre, and the stories told within were downright nuts, especially "The Musical Box." The music, however, was spellbinding and Hackett's guitar work was revolutionary as he was truly one of the first (if not *the* first) to utilize finger-tapping and legato technique. It's all there for anyone to hear as proof.

The year 1972 saw *Foxtrot* released, an album that was even more daring (and hitting UK #12) thanks to the twenty-three-minute track "Supper's Ready," a song that cannot be described accurately in mere words. What is it even about? Who knows, although much speculation has occurred through the years. Hackett's guitar playing, especially in the emotional finale segment is without equal. His classical guitar piece "Horizons" has lived in infamy and ranks right up there with Steve Howe's "Clap" and "Mood for a Day" from Yes. It is a beloved 1:39 of baroque guitar work that is wonderful. The chilling opener "Watcher of the Skies" very well could be the most important seven-and-a-half minutes in prog rock history. All five members make this song of an alien's impressions of Earth truly remarkable right from the chilling Mellotron-laced introduction. Steve's familiar "weeping" guitar sound adds emotion to the powerful finale. If one was to seek what progressive rock was all about in the 1970s…send them right here and right to this song and then they will understand.

The concert album *Genesis Live* proved the band could carry all this off in a concert setting (not to mention the fact Gabriel was now donning outlandish costumes on stage, and various lights and slides were being used to brilliant effect).

With *Selling England by the Pound*, the group hit new heights and even scored a hit single in the weird, yet catchy "I Know What I Like (In Your Wardrobe)." It's hard to imagine writing epics such as "The Cinema Show," "Firth of Fifth," and "Dancing with the Moonlit Knight" from scratch, but somehow these guys got it done. The songs were richly detailed and beautifully executed and Steve's solo on "Firth of Fifth" is one of the very best guitar solos in rock history hands down. Each time, to this day, he performs the piece live, and the excitement builds in the audience as the solo approaches. "Dancing with the Moonlit Knight" has some wild finger-tapping proving that Steve was doing this long before Eddie Van Halen who has acknowledged Hackett's work in the past. This isn't even to mention the incredible playing by the other members.

Selling made it to #3 in the UK and #70 in the US where they would now tour regularly for the first time. The double-concept album *The Lamb Lies Down on Broadway* followed in 1974 and was as baffling as it was astonishing. *The Lamb* was lengthy, surreal, intense, harrowing, disturbing, confusing, and frickin' out there. It also was another UK Top 10 and just missed the US Top 40 as their popularity continued to build. The title cut and "The Carpet Crawlers" proved to be the best-known cuts, and the latter features weeping guitar from Hackett accenting the song's feel. Explosive songs like "In the Cage" and "The Colony of Slippermen" saw the band stretch out and the heavy angst of "Fly on a Windshield" saw Hackett expanding his sounds. The album was performed in its entirety on the exhaustive '74–'75 tour.

Tensions during the making of the album saw Gabriel leave the band and critics predicted the end. Wrong! The remaining four carried on and Collins doubled up on drums and vocals when auditions led to nothing. *A Trick of the Tail* was issued in 1976 and proved that not only could Genesis survive without Gabriel, they could thrive. The album's opening cut was a defiant statement: "Dance on a Volcano," an eruption of fusion and prog rock in odd time allowing Hackett to wail like never before while Collins, Banks, and Rutherford added intense colors to the palette. The heart-wrenching epic "Ripples" featured nothing short of some of the most aching, poignant, and sad lyrics ever, and Hackett's weeping guitar in the lengthy mid-section could not be any more appropriately placed. This whole album is masterful ("Squonk," the acoustic-based "Entangled" and the instrumental "Los Endos" all confirm this fact) and was an enormous success.

In 1977, *Wind & Wuthering* was a very romantically themed album and again featured some real gems like the ten minutes of "One for the Vine," "The Eleventh Earl of Mar," the whimsical "All in a Mouse's Night," "Blood on the Rooftops," and the fabulous "Afterglow." "Blood on the Rooftops" featured an impressive classical intro by Steve, and he also got to lay down a harsh, metallic sound on "In That Quiet Earth...." Chester Thompson (ex-Frank Zappa and Weather Report became the new live drummer on this tour). Despite the huge success now being enjoyed by the band, Hackett was not comfortable with not getting enough of his ideas through and left the band during the mixing of the double-live album *Seconds Out* in 1977.

Steve had already released a successful solo album in 1975 titled *Voyage of the Acolyte* and continued on with a series of excellent albums including *Please Don't Touch* (1978), *Spectral Mornings* (1979), *Defector* (1980), *Cured* (1981), and *Highly Strung* (1983) with the latter four albums all reaching the UK Top 25 (*Defector* even making the Top 10). All the albums charted in the US. The title track on *Spectral Mornings* is one of Steve's best compositions.

After a few more solo albums and a minor hit single ("Cell 151"), Hackett joined forces with ex-Yes and Asia guitarist Steve Howe, former Nightwing singer Max Bacon, bassist Phil Spalding, and ex-Marillion drummer Jonathan Mover as GTR in 1985. Hackett had actually produced a version of "Cell 151" by Nightwing, which is where he met Bacon.

A self-titled album from GTR came out in 1986 and did very well going Gold and reaching #11 in the US, producing two fantastic hits in "When the Heart Rules the Mind" and "The Hunter." Steve also had a darkly heavy, ripping instrumental cheekily titled "Hackett to Bits" on the album and played brilliantly throughout with other winning songs such as "Imagining," "Toe the Line," and "Jeckyll and Hyde" also standouts.

The GTR tour in 1986 was a very good one and the band added keyboardist Matt Clifford. Performances saw most of the album played, along with a great new song

"Prizefighters," alongside solo material from both Howe and Hackett and a few Yes and Genesis songs.

Not entirely happy being part of a band again and having issues with business strategies, Hackett left GTR in 1987 and has maintained his solo career ever since issuing albums of prog rock, acoustic, and classical music. Hackett has a very loyal following worldwide, proved strong by the wild success of his Genesis Revisited tours (the albums in this series have been *Watcher of the Skies: Genesis Revisited* [1996], *Genesis Revisited II* [2012], and two live albums from 2013 and 2014) from 2012–2014 with most dates completely sold out all around the world proving the undying love fans have for this music.

In 2014, Steve Hackett perhaps has somehow gotten even better in his playing. His *Genesis Revisited* shows of this particular leg of the tour were absolute knockouts with Steve proving he is one of the world's very best. Just hearing Steve and his band tackle all twenty-three minutes of "Supper's Ready," along with "The Musical Box," "Squonk," "Watcher of the Skies," "Fly on a Windshield," and "Firth of Fifth" among others was a total pleasure for the fans, but his guitar playing is simply at another level now. Hackett hasn't lost a step and looks great. More important is the fact that he just might be an even better player now, which is hard to fathom considering how brilliant he was in the '70s and beyond.

Steve is a member of the Rock and Roll Hall of Fame as Genesis was finally inducted in 2010. We didn't need that to know that this man was a gift to all guitar lovers. A new studio album called *Wolflight* in 2015 sees Steve doing anything but rehashing old ideas. His dazzling classical playing on the intro to "Love Song for a Vampire" gives way to an appropriately Gothic sound of mid-tempo rock and features a perfectly placed electric guitar solo. Steve also sings quite well. Another standout is "Black Thunder." If there's any question about which former Genesis member is still putting out the best music in 2015, it's Steve Hackett.

A massive fourteen CD box set titled *Premonitions* celebrating Steve's biggest selling albums from 1975–1983 on Charisma Records, with the first four albums newly remixed in 5.1 surround sound by Steven Wilson was released in the fall of 2015 paying further respect to a musician who totally deserves it.

Just days before seeing Steve live for my third time (!) on this latest *Genesis Revisited* tour on November 22, 2014, in Collingswood, New Jersey, minutes from my house, I was able to interview Steve.

Who were some of the players that were important to you in your early years and may have served as influences?

Brian Jones, Peter Green, and Jimi Hendrix were all inspiring. For classical guitar it would be Andrés Segvoia.

What are your preferred guitars of choice?

My preferred guitars are Fernandes and Gibson Les Paul for rock, and Yairi for classical.

Can you take me through the solo on "Firth of Fifth" and how that was composed or came to be? I can listen to that again and again and still be taken away by the beauty and grace of the piece.

It was originally a melody by Tony Banks. I then adapted it for electric guitar. I still enjoy playing that beautiful piece to this day.

Is it true that "Horizons" was a happy accident? I've heard different tales over the years. It is a piece that is every bit as recognized as any other song from those Genesis years by fans and goes down unbelievably well live still.

No, I actually wrote "Horizons" over the course of a year. I put a lot of thought and time into it, even though it's a short piece.

I am a big fan of your work on songs like "Dance on a Volcano" (which sounds like a bit of a nod to fusion to me) and "Blood on the Rooftops." I feel the first few Phil-era albums were excellent and some of your best playing, even if you weren't entirely happy then. The decision to leave Genesis must have come with a heavy heart I assume.

Yes, I enjoyed working on all the albums, including *Wind & Wuthering*, which I actually contributed more to, but it was hard for me because I needed autonomy as well and I was only able to have that if I left the band.

I was one of those who enjoyed the GTR album, which was obviously a more commercial enterprise. "Hackett to Bits" is damn good fun and I've seen you do this live solo. Do you have any good memories of that time?

Yes, I enjoyed recording the material and the shows were fun too. We were thrilled it took off so well in the States.

Spectral Mornings was a real benchmark in your solo career and the title track is stunning. Was this an especially important album for you?

Yes it was. I felt I was coming into my own as a solo artist then. Behind it was the idea that life goes on...every day took off for me as did *Spectral Mornings* and I still love to play those numbers.

The infamous "Six of the Best Show" in 1982 to date has been the only reunion gig for the Classic 5 lineup of Genesis with Peter. Do you have any recollections of that show and is there any hope at all of a reunion, perhaps even if it was just several shows (and provided Phil is able to play)?

Yes, I enjoyed being a part of that show. A reunion seems unlikely at this time, but anything is possible down the line.

The ongoing Genesis Revisited tour (which I've seen three times) has been a smashing success. Did this take you by surprise? The shows have been above and beyond what I was expecting—numerous standing ovations too, especially after "Supper's Ready." What a challenge that must be to play every night.

Yes, it did take me by surprise that it was such a success. I'm thrilled by all the response we're still getting.

Can you explain The Lamb Lies Down on Broadway *because I still don't get it!*

The story line is Pete's. The rest of us concentrated on the music. It's a modern tale of redemption and personal discovery.

Final silly question I ask every guitarist: if you could rename a Genesis song or album (or two) after a breed of cat, what would it be? My cats are curious.

I would rename "Fly on a Windshield"... "The Persian."

Recommended solo: "Firth of Fifth" from *Selling England by the Pound*
with Genesis (1973)
Further info: www.hackettsongs.com
Photo Credit: Lesley Wood

CHAPTER 21

Paul Hammond

(Born Paul Edwin Hammond, October 31, 1965, Bridgeport, PA)

As a guitarist for the world's finest and most authentic-sounding Led Zeppelin tribute band Get the Led Out (they really are the best), Paul Hammond brings the goods each and every night, as does the amazing six-piece band he is in based out of the Philadelphia area.

Yes, I said six-piece band. One may ask, why would a Zeppelin tribute band be a six-piece and not a quartet?

I'll tell you why. It's because down to every minute detail based on all those amazing recordings Jimmy Page produced and arranged, Get the Led Out perform the songs of Led Zeppelin as heard on the original albums.

So, where Led Zeppelin had problems re-creating the sound on detailed, layered recordings live such as "Achilles Last Stand," "Ten Years Gone," "The Ocean," or "Over the Hills and Far Away," Get the Led Out can play these songs as they sounded by utilizing a setup of Hammond on lead guitar, mandolin, and acoustic guitar; Paul Sinclair on vocals and harmonica; Andrew Lipke on keyboards, mandolin, lead guitar, acoustic guitar, and backing vocals; Billy Childs (formerly of hair metal band Britny Fox) on bass and backing vocals; lead guitarist Jimmy Marchiano also on backing vocals and acoustic guitar; and powerhouse beast Adam Ferraioli on drums.

These musicians are able to create an aural experience *any* Led Zeppelin fan would appreciate, and the guys have been at it since 2003. It took several years to find all the right pieces, but it is this lineup that has seen the band rise to very high levels.

Get the Led Out is no mere tribute act either. That term isn't a bad one, but it does sound a little on the cheesy side of things. First off, GTLO (as their fans have nicknamed them) don't impersonate the members of Led Zeppelin, so they do not wear the same clothes and say the same things on stage. They are who they are and there is no pretense. At a typical GTLO gig fans will hear anything from the overplayed radio classics such as "Black Dog," "Whole Lotta Love," "Babe, I'm Gonna Leave You," "Rock And Roll," and of course "Stairway to Heaven" to classic album cuts such as "No Quarter," "The Song Remains the Same," "Nobody's Fault but Mine," "When the Levee Breaks," and "Celebration Day" to deeper tracks like "Achilles Last Stand," "Down by the Seaside," "Hot Dog," "Hots on for Nowhere," and "In the Light."

Simply put, Get the Led Out is far more than what the term tribute act implies. In reality, they are bringing forth the albums in a live setting and thus are more of an aural authentication act.

The concerts GTLO put on are memorable and as faithful a representation of Led Zeppelin's music in a concert setting as could be. Are they better than Led Zeppelin? Of course not, but they are indeed fantastic to see and enjoy. Hammond's guitar playing is very, very faithful to that of Jimmy Page and that's no easy feat, especially in the way GTLO members are dedicating themselves to the studio craft of Page. Jimmy Marchiano is no slouch either, as his solo on "The Ocean" is always amazing. But it's Hammond and his spotlight segment on "Dazed and Confused" that is really mind-blowing and where Paul gets to inject some of his own playing. And yes, he does indeed break out the violin bow! The solos are divided up amongst Hammond, Marchiano, and Lipke as well, who also gets a few solos to do.

Paul also plays stunningly on songs such as "Nobody's Fault but Mine," "Fool in the Rain," "Achilles Last Stand," and so many more. Paul also was in an original band of hard rock quality in the early '90s called Sinclair fronted by GTLO lead singer Paul Sinclair, and their debut album from 1992 is very good material. Hammond also has an extensive background behind the scenes in mastering, consulting, writing, and playing for commercials, editing, building custom guitars, and more, and some of these jobs were for big name projects.

To show how big Get the Led Out now is, the band headlined a concert at the legendary Red Rocks Amphitheatre in Morrison, Colorado, just outside Denver, in 2014, and absolutely owned the place as shown on PBS television. In 2015, Phil D'Agostino took over on bass and the band received yet another excellent musician.

The amount of work that has gone into Get the Led Out is very evident on stage and the results are the endless smiles on the faces of Led Zeppelin fans of all ages, many of whom never got to see the band perform live and now have the opportunity to hear the songs as they were meticulously crafted in the studio all those decades ago just as meticulously worked on for live performance. And after all, all the guys in Get the Led Out are as big a fan of Led Zeppelin's music as any of the people paying to see them perform. No wonder it works so damn well.

In May of 2015, Paul and I had a very long, detailed, fascinating, and humorous chat that was an absolute blast.

Have you been made aware of the book and the concept?

I am aware, and I am very appreciative of you wanting to include me. It's definitely a great project and I agree with you wholeheartedly that there is too much out there about the usual suspects, and it's nice to see that the other musicians out there can get some respect. I know Steve Hackett is in your book, and I think he is one of the greatest players of all-time.

I think he may be even better now. His playing is extraordinary and those Genesis Revisited tours he's done have been magical.

I have wanted to see a show from that tour so bad but we're always playing on the road when he's around. We do a lot of shows through BRE Entertainment and they promised to get me into one, but I'm never here when he plays the area! In fact, the first concert I ever saw was Genesis at the Spectrum here in Philly.

I'm a Genesis nut and though I saw them a few times, I was too young back then.

Yeah, it was around 1978 on the …*And Then There Were Three*…tour. I went with my parents when I was around twelve years old and it blew me away. They were still doing all that great material like "Dance on a Volcano" and "Squonk."

Well, I was going to ask who some of your musical influences were. Was he one?

He kind of would be, but not so much that I played like him, because progressive rock playing was beyond me at that time, so it was more the common guys like Cream with Eric Clapton, Jimi Hendrix, Jimmy Page, Jeff Beck, because they were in the mainstream so much and really were the greats. Later when I got more into that textural, more complicated stuff like Hackett played that I could start to figure out, is when a guy like him became more of an influence.

I also was influenced by blues players such as Albert King and Freddie King and especially Johnny Winter, who I loved. And with hard rock and heavy metal, it was Eddie Van Halen and Randy Rhoads with all that classic Ozzy stuff. Another guy would be Brad Gillis of Night Ranger, who I saw play with Ozzy in 1982, shortly after Randy had passed away, and really impressed me. There's also Jake E. Lee who followed Gillis and was a great player.

I assume Gibson and Martin are two of your favorite guitar models?

They are, but only since Get the Led Out. I was never a big Les Paul player. For me it was always Stratocasters and Telecasters, with Gibsons being a secondary choice for me. But, being that Get the Led Out is based on note-for-note and sound-for-sound replication of Led Zeppelin albums, I had to find the closest I could to an original 1959 Sunburst Les Paul standard.

Initially I was playing the Jimmy Page No. 1 Les Paul that they reissued in 2006. I got one of the first fifty, not one of the fifty signed models, but one of the first fifty. So I played that for a while, and then I got a 2011 Custom Historic SG Standard VOS. I went to a good friend's house named George Alessandro, who is from the area and you've probably heard of him as he works with a lot of the top guitarists such as David Gilmour, and we compared three of my Sunburst Les Pauls.

I have a 1999 Historic, the Jimmy Page from 2006, and the VOS from 2011, and we compared them to three real Sunburst and goldtops from 1958 and 1959 and of all the guitars—if you were blindfolded you wouldn't be able to tell the difference with my 2011, so that's the one I tour with now. Of course Page used Fenders, too. More than people realize. On a lot of the records you can hear that trebly sound and it's much thinner than the Gibsons. If you listen to the *Presence* album, he uses a lot of Fenders.

It certainly sounds like a Strat on "Achilles Last Stand" and "Nobody's Fault but Mine."

Absolutely he is using Fenders on there. And on "For Your Life" he's gotta be using a Strat as you can hear the tremolo bar.

I know on In Through the Out Door *he's using a Strat on "In the Evening."*

Yeah, I think he's using a 1964 rosewood board Strat that was Lake Placid blue. The closest I could get to that tone is an Eric Johnson model Strat right off the shelf and nothing had to be done to it at all. I didn't have to do anything to it. I did not have to worry about modifications like changing the bridge, the electronics, the tuners, and all that stuff we had to do back in the '70s. Now, Fender are making guitars that don't need any of those modifications right off the shelf and are as good as what they made in the '50s.

My first professional guitar was a 1976 Fender Stratocaster Hardtail with no vibrato system and I ended up losing it. This isn't quite like the Peter Frampton story with the fire and all that, but I actually lost it to a friend who I had lent it to. He refused to give it back after we had a falling out. So I gave up on it. This was around 1997. My daughter was very young at the time and we moved and my life changed, so I just moved on from it.

I was on eBay one day, and very rarely do I do a search qualifier closest to my zip code, but you never know what you will find sometimes. So, I entered a search within a fifty-mile radius. Well, don't I see my guitar on there that my friend had refused to give back to me. It was the Fender Strat and I recognized it immediately because I had converted it from a 3 bolt to a 4 bolt and I had this big brass plate on it, and I had replaced the neck back in '81 or '82. It was at a pawn shop in Reading, Pennsylvania, so I guess my friend had pawned it up there and I emailed the guy who owned the shop and said that I had pictures of me with this guitar when I was a teenager on my front lawn and the guy knew of Get the Led Out and had seen us live, so he knew I was legit. I had to buy it back, of course, but involving the police and court and all this nonsense was not worth it to me, so I paid $350 for it and it was worth every penny.

That was a wonderful story with a great ending. I want to shed a tear.

[Laughs] It is great and I still use the guitar now. I guard it now!

Can I assume you're not lending that out again?

Nooooo! [Laughs]

Since you have an extensive background in mastering and sound, did that help you achieve the sound that you wanted on stage? Knowing how these albums were recorded/mixed/engineered/produced, it sure seems to me that your knowledge has played a major role in shaping what the fans are hearing up on stage.

Absolutely. It helped more than most people realize. Even some guitar players go, "Why do they need three players up there? It was just Jimmy Page."

Ah, but I know why.

You do know why. And serious guitarheads know why, but a lot of people don't even understand the concept of overdubbing in the studio, which Les Paul had invented way back when and he was a genius with that. So, knowing the concepts of multi-tracking and overdubbing has helped. I own some pretty incredible vintage studio recording equipment and gear.

I have an original Ampex 16-track 2-inch multi-track recorder from the Record Plant.

The Record Plant? That's quite something.

Yeah, and an RCA Records New York 16-track, 2-inch machine and a Studer 24-track A827 that came from Pharrell Williams's studio in Virginia Beach. So, utilizing all that equipment and studying Led Zeppelin's recordings, Paul Sinclair the singer and I can do this together. We hear the music and we can say, "That sounds like a Fender electric guitar that has a 300 millisecond delay on it and a pre-delayed reverb." Conversely, we can also hear a vocal and say, "Well, that vocal has a phase on it and we're not exactly sure what was used there, but we can emulate that by getting the front-house mixer to put that on the vocal."

Also, the intro on "Nobody's Fault but Mine" was heavily tape-flanged with echo and it backs off by the time the vocals come in, so they obviously did it by using the soundboard with a fader and I will emulate that live with the Fractal Audio Axe-Fx effects system. I only use that for effect, although you can use it for modeling, but what I actually do is write the effects into it and I use that for the intro and then I use an expression pedal for the depth of the flange. As the vocal comes in I can back it off and use it to where it's barely noticeable just like on the record.

So yes, the technical expertise I learned all those years and years has absolutely applied to Get the Led Out in every aspect of the live performance—the keyboard sounds, the vocals, the acoustic and electric guitars, mandolins, all of it.

And it shows. I'm a Led Zep nut and I have tons of boots and Jimmy had plenty of off nights for various reasons, but when he was on, man, he was one of the absolute best. But even so, with the way he crafted their sound in the studio, it was always a little empty in the backing, no matter how much Bonham and Jones did due to the overdubbing. When I see Get the Led Out, I now hear in a live setting what those songs sounded like in front of an audience, as they were recorded in the studio—which is no small feat.

I actually do not even label you as a tribute band and I love the idea that you do not dress like them or impersonate them in any way. I consider you more of an authentic dedication band if that makes even a lick of sense.

That's a very good way to put it. We've called ourselves many different things over the years. We're basically like a live classic rock orchestra. We compare ourselves in some ways to Bach or Beethoven in the sense that we try to take what was created, written and performed, and do it in the same way and with the same precision as a classical orchestra. It's been a very interesting and successful project. Even if people don't know the reason that they're hearing what they hear, it's because we play the songs like they've been used to hearing this music the last thirty or forty years.

Most casual people don't know the bootlegs or the live stuff other than maybe *The Song Remains the Same*. I am a huge Zeppelin fan and for the live material I wouldn't even play *The Song Remains the Same*. I'd go to the Royal Albert Hall show from 1970 or the *How the West Was Won* album, which the casual fan probably doesn't know. You cast the widest net by playing the music the way that people remember it. People ask if it's limiting and I say absolutely not because it takes way more effort and mental power to do it the way people have heard it on the albums. The tones, the multiple tunings, and such are a challenge, and we change the set every night so we always have to go back and brush up on something if we haven't played it in two or three months. This has also enabled me to do a lot of other things in life that I normally would not be able to do if I was working a typical nine-to-five or working for a studio. It's a very liberating thing to be involved with creatively.

Of course you have recorded original music in the band Sinclair. Is it considered sacrilege to place one of your tunes in the set? I'd love to hear it.

We do get asked that and we have put one in there a few times. The reaction was good and the original album *Sinclair* we did back around 1992 or 1993 sold out after our concerts, and we may repress the album on CD. In fact, I am working on an album entirely of instrumental guitar music, although I may get a vocal on one or two of them. Andrew Lipke also does original music that is inspired by classical and his music is available after our shows as well. So there is cross-pollination and it lets people know we have original music.

When I was first told about you guys by my friends I wasn't sure about going, but they swore up and down that I should go as a Zep fanatic and guitar fan. They told me that it was a six-piece band that did not impersonate Led Zeppelin, so that perked my interest and I enjoyed the hell out of the gig in Ocean City, New Jersey, and that was around 2012.

The fact it was at such a cool venue right on the boardwalk, next to the ocean, made it a memorable show and I've seen you there since. I've now seen you six times total, so I guess I liked the band. [Laughs] I've never once been disappointed, and even though I know it's coming every show, I consider "Dazed and Confused" to be a real pinnacle of the night because of your fantastic solo spotlight. What are some of your favorites to play, whether they are more obscure choices or ones that are played every show?

That's a good question and I always come back to the same ones. There's "The Rover," which I love to play. We usually play that one by request because it's a little off the beaten path.

I've not seen you play that one—damn! (Update! I can now say I've seen them play "The Rover" at their Philly show in December 2015!)

We do play it, just not often. I really get into that one, and maybe it's because it reminds me so much of my youth. Page's styling on that one, and his solo, are so good. I play that one really well and I love that solo. And "Since I've Been Loving You" is the most amazing C Minor blues song, and his work in that is so brilliant. The feel is so strong that it almost drips out of the speakers when you listen to it, and playing it live is an amazing thing.

I consider that the greatest solo ever if there is such a thing. The emotion and as you say, the feel are stunning.

That is a special moment. There's also "Black Dog." We don't say this as a cliché, but we play these songs as if we wrote them. What we put into them, and the feel of that one in particular, is where it all comes out. We adopt the spirit of the song. You can't help but feel like a rock star when you are playing "Black Dog" in front of a packed house. So that's one because of the energy.

And that is rhythmically tricky.

It is tricky, but that riff is something else in the way that it charges up and then rests. It's not non-stop and that is an aspect of Zep; that light and shade. The call and response of that song is a great part with the audience. And then there's the one all-time standard that everyone goes to… "Stairway to Heaven."

I've played that song over 1,000 times and I still enjoy doing it because of the feel and the musicality of it and the technique it takes to do it properly, and I'm not tired of it, which is a good thing I guess.

It does come across that you play it with conviction, because I'm sick of it, and the way it's performed by the band is the way it should be. And once the guitar solo comes in, the place is illuminated in joy. As for the albums, have you heard the new remasters? They're very good sonically.

I have heard them. And I like them as well as the extra tracks like "The Battle of Evermore" without vocals and the alternate guitar mix of "Over the Hills and Far Away." That stuff to me is the most fascinating; it lets us know even more about the songs and enables us to play even closer.

The alternate take on "Since I've Been Loving You" was great to hear.

That was great to hear. I loved that. It's like a peek into something you weren't supposed to see. I have many Zeppelin recordings of outtakes and live shows over the years. People just hand me CDs of this stuff, which is great, and I also had a lot of it anyway from collecting as a fan, and it all helps with my job listening to the different variations each night.

I wanted your opinion on the 2007 reunion gig at the O2 Arena in London. I was thrilled with it and what they were able to achieve after the previous reunion gigs had been train wrecks.

Well, I was fortunate enough to have been able to attend that gig.

You did? I envy you so much!

I did and I was at the soundcheck too. I am close to a guy named Joe Warren who works with the same charity that Jimmy Page's wife does, and before the Zep reunion happened, we had built a custom Martin acoustic guitar for them to auction off for the charity. I actually got to speak with Jimmy Page at this time via cellphone and I met his wife and kids at his house and, as a result of that, when the 2007 reunion show happened, fortunately I was in with Graeme Hutchinson who was one of the administrators of the trust and I was in the inner circle of people of Jimmy Page's camp and I was able to attend and sat in the A-100 area with people like Brian May of Queen, who I talked to for hours. It was a rock and roll dream, it really was.

I was in the inner circle of the biggest rock stars of all-time in England and it was unbelievable. Jeff Beck sat five rows down from me. People from Def Leppard, David Gilmour, Brian May, I mentioned already—and he was also part of that charity—they were all near me. I saw the soundcheck with Dave Lewis.

Ah yes, the Led Zeppelin history writer. I like a lot of what he has done for them and find most of it detailed and fascinating.

He knows more about Led Zeppelin than anybody in the world, although Graeme Hutchinson is up there too. Anyway, I tell ya what, if there's any time whether you could find enough electricity in the air to run a house off of, this was it. It was such an anticipated event and a momentous occasion, you could feel it building. There was only a finite amount of tickets available sadly, but what an event. To me it was special because of so many factors—it was for Ahmet Ertegun who had passed away, it was for the fund to support education and keep music alive in schools, it was with Jason Bonham on drums—just so much to appreciate.

It was also great that they pulled it off from start to finish and, from a performance perspective, you couldn't compare it to anything because you were seeing Led Zeppelin now and not in the '70s. It was better than a lot of those shows soundwise, and Robert Plant couldn't hit all those notes of old, so he did it his own way and it was fine in that sense. In fact, it was better that way. The fact that they released it on CD and DVD as *Celebration Day* after all those years, in 2012, was great, and I even went to the movie theatre so I could see it on the big screen, made it all fantastic.

I don't think they should do a tour. There was a lot of conjecture back and forth at that time and, from what I saw when I was there, those guys are on separate islands in life. They are not all on the same page, no pun intended!

Too late! That was an awful pun, and I applaud it.

Yeah, I know. [Laughs] But I know Jimmy wanted to tour and he wasn't happy. I mean, Led Zeppelin is his baby.

You can see that Jimmy is wounded. I never thought a tour would happen due to Robert Plant. Robert knew, in my opinion anyway, that he could not do those types of shows three or four nights a week and wanted to leave it with this one great moment that summed it all up.

He doesn't want to do it anymore. There's also a lot to Zeppelin that wasn't good to him and I can understand that being in a band. Seeing everything he'd have to deal with, plus a lot of the bad memories of things that happened in the latter portion of their career makes him reluctant. It's easy to say, oh, it's the biggest band in the world and they could make a billion dollars, but that doesn't matter if the quality of life and the things that happen in and around that aren't good for you. Another thing is that John Bonham was the guy who was it for their musical style, and it is so difficult to replace that, which is why they decided to break up in 1980. There's not many like him, but there are just a few. We are actually fortunate enough to have a similar guy in Adam Ferraioli.

I was going to say that you have a pretty damn close thing to Bonham yourselves.

Adam is one of the few and drums are everything to a powerhouse rock band. Jason Bonham is more straightforward then John was, who had that syncopated jazz and swing thing going along with the power. But Jason is damn, damn good at what he did with Zeppelin.

I've seen Jason play with Foreigner, UFO, his own band Bonham, and even Virginia Wolf when they opened for the Firm in 1986, and he is one of the best and most powerful out there. That being said, he's not the drummer his dad was and so few are.

I wanted to ask you about the experience of playing at Red Rocks in Denver last year for PBS television. The online clip of "Immigrant Song" gave me chills on the website.

That was basically another pinnacle moment for me, like being at the Led Zep reunion show. I had to pinch myself. It's such a nice venue. PBS in Colorado was looking for a tribute act because they do a fundraiser every year and they also used a Beatles act for a few years called 1964 and one of the Pink Floyd ones that I think may have been the Australian Pink Floyd.

Out of all the Led Zeppelin tribute bands they chose us because they saw our video we had out there and they knew what we were capable of. All that time and effort was sort of validated by this because they saw just how much went into our presentation of the music. It bumped us up to the next level and that's what you always want to see—and not just in music but in life. You should always want to get better and reach for that next level no matter what you do. Once you start to think you're the best at whatever it is you do and you don't need to work as hard anymore, that's where the decline settles in. We thought it was a one-and-done kind of thing, but once they saw how much work and effort we put into each concert they hired us back, so we go back in September of this year. [They did, indeed, play again at Red Rocks on September 24, 2015.]

It would be great for the fans to have a DVD of that show, but I'm guessing that it's cost prohibitive.

Yeah, you can't really release something like a DVD of our show because for commercial sale there's synchronization rights involved that push it per song to something like six figures each song. We'd never sell enough copies to justify that, so it would have to be for demo purposes only where you can promote on the site and not for commercial sale. I have a copy of the whole thing but just for myself, although we're not really worried about that kind of thing. Next time, there will be more cameras and more individual roaming cameras, so it will look so much better than what I have.

Did Paul have troubles with his voice in the altitude?

He did a little bit, and there were some slight pitch issues, but nothing anybody but us would've noticed. It's physics, so of course the further up you go in the altitude it's different air levels and oxygen levels. One time we played at the Air Force Academy in Colorado Springs and I got that "Rocky Mountain High" where I was slightly disoriented and light-headed.

That's why it's so tough to beat the Broncos there in football at Sports Authority Field or whatever they call it now and the balls fly out of Coors Field when the Rockies play baseball. The altitude is real.

It is, trust me. It is actually healthier air. We were told by the EMTs we were the only act at that time who didn't need oxygen to play at the Air Force Academy.

There's your new tagline for the website: Get the Led Out, the only band who didn't need oxygen to play at the Air Force Academy and still rocked the house!

[Laughs] Exactly, that's a funny tagline to use!

Two songs I wanted to ask about that I've never seen you play are "Ten Years Gone" or "Wearing and Tearing." "Ten Years Gone" is my favorite Zeppelin tune and has what I feel to be Page's best guitar work all-around on a song.

We do "Ten Years Gone" and fairly often. As many times as you've seen us I'm surprised you haven't seen that one. We really nail it. It's not typical of Page to play Major 7th chords and he does that a lot on that song. That is one of my all-time favorites too. [Update! I finally saw them play this in July 2015 in Ocean City, New Jersey!]

The emotions of that song and Page's guitar themes are breathtaking. I feel every ounce of expression in that song with the guitars and the vocals and lyrics.

That actually is very emotional to play and it gives me chills when we do it.

I know "Wearing and Tearing" is one you might lose people on, but that is a barnstormer all the way designed for the stage. Zeppelin was trying to get it out as a non-album single in time for Knebworth in 1979, but it didn't happen and they didn't play it and never did. To my knowledge the only time it's ever been played was in 1990 at Knebworth by Page and Plant with Robert's band, which was an obvious nod to the 1979 show.

I think you're probably correct on that fact. We do feel like we might lose people on that one. When we do "Achilles Last Stand" we lose people as well. I think we would do "Wearing and Tearing" at some point because we don't shy away from anything. The next challenge is "For Your Life" from *Presence*. We just added it in the last year or two but only a few times.

Have you played anything off Coda?

We do "Hey, Hey (What Can I Do)," which was added to *Coda* later on in the box set. I'd like to do "Darlene." I like "Ozone Baby" as well. In the band Sinclair, back in the day, we did "We're Gonna Groove." Paul knows the exact numbers of the songs that we've played in the catalog, but I think we've only not done ten or eleven songs. We'd like to tackle "The Crunge" and "Carouselambra" someday. We've reached such a level now, that we might do some of the solo material.

Really? That's a fantastic idea. I was going to ask that, but thought that it might be a silly question.

Not at all! We have been discussing doing something from *Pictures at Eleven*.

I love that album.

I love that album too. I really love the early Plant albums.

As do I. In fact, Pictures at Eleven *and* The Principle of Moments, *which Plant more or less disowns are the two best he ever did.*

I agree, and he had Robbie Blunt on guitar.

I have him on my list for this book but I could not find him anywhere on the Internet, which is a shame. Talk about an underrated guitar player.

Blunt was fantastic and you were right reaching out to him, because he's a perfect choice.

I did a bio of him, but hopefully I can get in touch with him. There were so many excellent songs on those two albums that always remind me of summer because that's when they were released in 1982 and 1983 when I was just starting high school. "Slow Dancer" is very much like "Kashmir" and Cozy Powell is on drums and Phil Collins was on all but two cuts, including "Burning Down One Side," which was the first single and is a great, modern-sounding song for that time.

That is such a great song! Paul Sinclair loves that tune and wants us to do that one live if we were to do this. "Far Post" is another great song.

Oh yeah, very sophisticated and much like "Burning Down One Side," I have no idea what the hell it's about. "Big Log" and "Moonlight in Samosa" are incredible songs with lots of textures.

And what about that solo on "In the Mood"? That's ridiculous! You can't fake that, it's gorgeous. Playing "Sea of Love" the way the Honeydrippers did with Page and Plant would be hilarious to do and it would be appreciated. I'd like to get some songs by the Firm in there too.

There's great material there to play live such as "Fortune Hunter," "Closer," "Radioactive," "Live in Peace," and especially "All the King's Horses." Then there's "Wasting My Time" from the Outrider album, which is as Zep as it gets and the Coverdale/Page record that had so many great riffs and solos and some of Jimmy's most inspired playing.

I saw Jimmy's solo tour in 1988 and I saw the Firm on both tours. Paul Rodgers—what a voice. When I was at that Led Zeppelin reunion show, Rodgers did a few songs and I was next to Brian May and I kept saying how great Paul Rodgers still is, and he nodded in agreement and then I remembered that Paul sang with Queen, so it's a good thing I didn't say anything bad about him! Not that I would have, of course, because he's brilliant.

He's my favorite singer. He still has it 100%. He's one of the few vocalists who can still sing like gold. I saw him with Bad Company last year and he was spot on.

I also very much liked the Page/Plant album *Walking into Clarksdale*.

That had a muddy sound, but a wonderful album with some really subtle songs.

We don't think it would take away from what we do if we add these kinds of things and most other bands don't do it.

It's a great, great idea. This was a total pleasure and you are a very knowledgeable musical guy, so it was great speaking with you. A final question: if you had to change a Led Zeppelin album or song named with a cat theme, what would you come up with?

Hey, that's hilarious, I love it! Do you have cats?

My wife and I had five cats.

Who do I hear meowing?

That's Krimpet.

What kind of cat is she? We love cats.

I don't know. She's just a krimpet [Laughs].

[Laughs] Good enough! Let me think… *"Stairway to the Big Bed"*?

That's pretty weak! C'mon, something like "Since I've Been Loving Mew"?

[Laughs] Ha, okay, okay, I will get one. Hmmm…from *Physical Graffiti*, how about "In the Mouse's Time of Dying"?

That's good enough! I'm glad we solved this critical musical question.

Good luck with the book, and thanks so much for including me. I know it will do well. The guitar players involved will promote it for sure. My dad will love it because he's such a guitar aficionado.
    And now his son will be in a book of underrated guitarists.

Recommended solo: "Dazed and Confused" (live with Get the Led Out)
Further info: www.gtlorocks.com
Photo credit: from Paul Hammond's personal collection

CHAPTER 22
Michael Hampton
(Born Michael Hampton, November 15, 1956, Cleveland, OH)

Not too many high school kids get to an after show party at a concert by a major band, get the chance to jam a little bit, and end up in the actual band shortly thereafter, but that's exactly what happened to "Kidd Funkadelic" himself Michael Hampton.

Hampton nailed the gig with Funkadelic in 1974 by playing an incredible take on the legendary song "Maggot Brain" for George Clinton himself, which has one of the greatest guitar solos ever laid down by the late Eddie Hazell. Clinton was so impressed that Hampton was offered the gig right then and there to join the band on tour filling for Hazell who was going through a variety of issues.

Hampton's parents had to sign off on a legal letter allowing him to tour as he was only seventeen at the time. Michael's first album with the band was 1975's *Let's Take It to the Stage* where he shared guitar duties with Hazell (who would be in and out of the band for a number of years) and Gary Shider. The album features "Get off Your Ass and Jam" that sports a mind-blowing lead guitar and a funky beat that has been sampled by everyone from Public Enemy to Tupac Shakur. With lyrics such as, "Shit! God damn! Get off your ass and jam!" what more do you need to know? The guitar solo actually wasn't played by any of the three players in the band according to Clinton, who said it was actually some white guy who showed up and needed the cash and asked to play. Paul Warren was his name. Seriously.

A compilation of outtakes entitled *Tales of Kidd Funkadelic* was released in 1976, and the eerie, synth-dominated thirteen-minute title cut freak-out fuses classical with funk, jazz, and horror movie music with Bernie Worrell's keyboard wizardry on full display. Hampton is on this album in parts and in late 1975 was also on Parliament's *Mothership Connection* album, which was a Top 20 US album that garnered Platinum status and contained the infamous "Give Up the Funk (Tear the Roof off the Sucker)" as well as "Unfunky U.F.O."

Hampton also played with Parliament on the album *The Clones of Dr. Funkenstein* in 1976, which went Top 20 Gold and featured "Dr. Funkenstein," "Do That Stuff," and "Funkin' for Fun." As with the last few albums, Hampton shared guitar duties with Shider and Glen Goins.

The next Funkadelic album *Hardcore Jollies* surfaced in 1976 and contains "Cosmic Slop," which is a live version of a song that had appeared a few years earlier. This version contains some of the most mind-melting guitar soloing any music lover could possibly hear. The solo is an amalgam of searing notes with perfect liquid tones and a sense of drive and attack that is downright phenomenal. The song itself has a downbeat mix of funk, rock, and fusion that never gets fancy. Hampton's solo on this version of "Cosmic Slop" is one of those moments where, as a music lover, you can just shake your head and say, "*That* is why I feel something when I hear music!"

In 1977, the Parliament album *Funkentelechy vs. The Placebo Syndrome* was another funk/rock assault that went Platinum and contained the #1 R&B smash "Flash Light," as well as "Funkentelechy," which got down with a sleazy groove and boundless energy as most Parliament tunes had; and who cared that it was eleven minutes long? The next album from Parliament was a Gold album titled *Motor Booty Affair* in 1978 that contained the nine-minute Funkfest "Deep," which Prince certainly must've listened to a few times as well as "Liquid Sunshine." This album saw Goins no longer on guitar with Hampton and Shider sharing guitar chores with J. S. Theracon and Phelps "Catfish" Collins. *Gloryhallastoopid (Or Pin the Tail on the Funky)* followed in 1979 accenting funk and R&B, like the last few albums that veered further away from rock but were still very entertaining listens with great female vocal and horn arrangements.

Funkadelic achieved excellence with 1978's *One Nation Under a Groove* that went Platinum and made the US Top 20 by far the biggest success for Funkadelic. The title cut was a Top 40 single and remains a funk classic. "Who Says a Funk Band Can't Play Rock?!" saw Hampton as a co-writer, also wielding his axe and squeezing sounds that were aligned with the vocals and led to blistering solos throughout. To say the least, this was a song that heavily influenced the Red Hot Chili Peppers. Hampton's guitar playing throughout the album is fantastic and a bonus EP included a wild take on "Maggot Brain" when Hampton goes for the throat at full throttle and takes one of the greatest solos anyone could imagine from Eddie Hazell and somehow carves out his own slice in rock history.

In 1979, *Uncle Jam Wants You* was next up with the classic "(Not Just) Knee Deep" a fifteen-minute workout that sports an ultra-fat dance/funk groove and was a big influence on many rap and hip-hop artists. Though it takes seven minutes to get there, Hampton's solo is another prime example of his knack for slicing and dicing leads that duck and dive throughout the nearly three minutes he's given to blaze away with some outlandishly speedy runs and ear-piercing individual notes. In 1980, *Trombipulation* was uneven and was the end of the band's glory days, although "Let's Play House" ended up being sampled by Digital Underground for the 1990 novelty nugget "The Humpty Dance," so there were some shining moments even if those moments were ultimately responsible for "The Humpty Dance"!

The Electric Spanking of War Babies was a Funkadelic album intended to be a double album, but the relationship between George Clinton and Warner Bros. Records was not good at this time, so that did not happen and this album faded quickly. Sly Stone was one of many involved with the album. Some of the songs recorded at the same time ended up on Clinton's solo album *Computer Games,* including the classic hit "Atomic Dog," and also on later P-Funk releases that cobbled together songs from various sessions. Soon, both P-Funk and Funkadelic were gone, replaced by a combination outfit still intact today called P-Funk All-Stars. For most of the 1984–1993 era, there was no activity, but with so many rap stars sampling P-Funk and Funkadelic songs through the years, Clinton put the All-Stars back together in 1993, and they played the *Lollapalooza Festival* in 1994.

And in 1999, Clinton toured as George Clinton and the P-Funk All-Stars appearing at *Woodstock '99* with classic members Bootsy Collins, "Catfish" Collins, and Bernie Worrell. Clinton still has the All-Stars going and Hampton is still on board, always making each show memorable thanks to his solo on "Maggot Brain" (never played the same on any night) and his scintillating work throughout every song. Michael issued a solo album in 1998 *Heavy Metal Funkason* that showed another side to his playing and he unleashes wicked work on cuts such as "Time to Get Up" and "Sloppy Metal (Unsung Love Song)." Hopefully, we will get another solo record out of the man that has some better production, but the playing was not an issue here.

Among the other acts Hampton has played with are Fred Wesley & the JB's, Bootsy Collins, Bernie Worrell, 420 Funk Mob (on the album *Live on the off Days* from 2004), and The Brides of Funkenstein with whom he got to lay down a now-infamous guitar solo that went through a Korg synthesizer creating an unusual sound on the song "Never Buy Texas From a Cowboy" from the 1979 album of the same name that did rather well. The song is over fifteen minutes long, but that was nothing new to Michael.

As of 2015, the man is still gettin' it done with his brand new Kidd Funkadelic Band, embarking on the *New Funk 'N' Roll Tour* of 2015-2016 showing the same skills as before as one of the finest players you'll ever get to see play. And, he's also a member of the Rock and Roll Hall of Fame inducted with both Parliament and Funkadelic back in 1997.

In late May 2015, Michael was kind enough to go into great detail about his amazing experiences and career in a conversation I had with him that went like this:

Hey, Michael, how are you?

I'm ready to go man, I've got my notes and everything! [Laughs]

[Laughs] *Okay, let's rock! Who were some of the main influences for you as you started playing guitar?*

Ah, Wes Montgomery was a big one, Leroy "Sugarfoot" Bonner from the Ohio Players was one, and there was B. B. King, Albert King, Brian May of Queen, Ritchie Blackmore from Deep Purple, Jimmy Page, of course, Jimi Hendrix, and Eddie Hazell—there were just so many guitar players who I listened to. Steve Cropper of Booker T. & the M.G.'s was another one, David Gilmour of Pink Floyd was too and so was the guy that did "Scorpio," Dennis Coffey.

I interviewed Dennis Coffey for this book!

Ha! Well, there ya go. I listened to lots and lots of guys before I even picked up the guitar. I would listen to rock, pop, R&B, jazz. I don't want to forget Chuck Berry and the guy who did the solo on Dr. John's "Right Place, Wrong Time." [*That would be David Spinozza*] I also liked Roy Clark from the show *Hee Haw* who was really good and Jeff Beck.

You sure had a lot of influences to say the least from a variety of genres.

Yeah, well, we really only had one good radio station, but I would buy albums and listen to all this stuff. If there was a guitar on a song, I'd listen to it.

Was Frank Zappa an influence?

Oh yeah! See? I forgot someone. He was out there and he was a great, great player.

As for how I got hired for Funkadelic and the whole Cleveland story, there was a party thrown by this guy Ed Sparks. And my cousin Lige Curry and I went over to his house after a Funkadelic gig. We were just going there to maybe jam or something. I was trying to put together something for some of the people who were there hanging out and I taught what I could to some of them. I had taught my cousin to play bass and we were able to do some things but nothing intricate, so I figured if we brought our instruments, we could get through a jam or something and we brought our equipment there to this party after the Funkadelic show.

Back in those days, you could literally walk backstage after a gig and maybe meet some of the band that was playing and we walked in sometimes into soundchecks or after gigs and that was what led us to this after show party.

And this was in Cleveland right?

Yeah, it was. Bloodstone was on the bill with Funkadelic. I remember that Bloodstone had all these Orange amps everywhere and Funkadelic were the headliners. The stuff was still set up at the house after the show at the party so we went to go play a little bit.

Some of the guys from the band were there but not everybody. I didn't look around a lot because I was trying to stay focused on what I had to do and that was to play the lines right.

We had to do something people knew, so I played the solo on "Maggot Brain," which I knew very well and, later on, about two weeks after the party, Tiki Fullwood, who played drums for both Parliament and Funkadelic, called me and they were playing a sold-out show in Landover, Maryland, and he had a ticket for me. I cleared it with my parents and they let me go to the concert. My cousin drove me to the airport and I went and saw the show.

There was a guitar player from Michigan who had a bad acid trip or something and [*note-this seems to have actually been Eddie Hazell who was arrested for assaulting an airline stewardess and air marshal on a flight while on PCP, which is usually a bad idea. It led to a one-year jail sentence*] that coupled with Eddie Hazell leaving the band led to me getting the call. They may have had somebody else in mind, I don't know, but they remember me playing at the party.

And you would have been just seventeen years old or so at the time.

Yeah, that's right. And now I think the Capital Centre is a shopping mall in DC or something, but that's the arena I saw the band at that night when I was invited! [Laughs]

[Laughs] *A lot of bands played there, and quite a few shows were filmed by the in-house cameras and the Capitals played hockey there and the Bullets (now Wizards) played basketball there, too.*

I'm kind of jumping around but Landover, Maryland, was the first time I realized, hey I might be good at this because in school I wasn't so great at sports like football and basketball. So that was the first place where it really hit me that I could play guitar more seriously. I started messing around with different ideas and the weird thing is, I went home after seeing the band and started practicing a lot and then once I joined the band, my first show was also in Landover!

Obviously, one of the pinnacle moments of a Funkadelic show was the build-up to the solo on "Maggot Brain" and I know Eddie was in and out of the band in the mid to late '70s for various reasons. The solo was never played the same each night and it seemed like improvising was the key as opposed to being instructed what to play.

Yes, I was never instructed what to play. When I first did the solos as I was playing for my friends I would play exactly what was on the record, but live it became different. The studio version of the original "Maggot Brain" had a lot of parts on it and I tried to remember all that. When I would start the solo live, if it was just me playing, I'd wait, start it, and then keep going until I got a cue to reach the end. With Eddie, I let him start it. He wouldn't play it like the record—maybe a few bars at the top, but then he would go to the stratosphere.

So, it seems like it was just those first few notes and then a lot of improvisation.

That's right more or less. When I would come in, I would start it from the top and then go along like the record according to how much time we had. So, I did remain true to the original, but I also did my thing. I never really traded licks with Eddie. I'd play along in his style and try very hard to be a complement and give him that respect. It didn't make any sense to me to just trade solos for twenty minutes so I tried to blend in with him.

UNSTRUNG HEROES

It seemed like Eddie was in and out of the band an awful lot.

Yeah, he just kinda showed up when he wanted to. It was just like that. He was also doing a lot of sessions at the time and doing other things musically. I never really talked to him about it.

You're the guy laying down that solo on the version of "Cosmic Slop" on the Hardcore Jollies *album, which is one of the best guitar solos I've ever frickin' heard. Can you take me through that solo?*

Ron Bykowski was one of the first guys who wore that Kiss-styled makeup and he played the original solo on "Cosmic Slop." He played the licks and the feedback and he was really precise. I would play along with the original version and practice and I came up with something that I felt worked live. I felt like I was maybe expounding upon it and it was based on his original solo. I did the scratch-down, or whatever they call it. And we recorded it in an airplane hangar where the stage was being put together with the mothership and all that, and our gear was set up so we were doing a run-through and the equipment was all set up.

So this was a live take with no audience.

That's right, other than who was there. We went over it a few times and we got it while it was still fresh. The solo and this version were still based on the original, but we were going for a groove and we got it.

The One Nation Under a Groove *album had "Who Says A Funk Band Can't Play Rock?" and that solo has an interesting sound. Clearly, this song influenced bands like the Red Hot Chili Peppers, Fishbone, and others. How did you arrive at that combo of solos and riffs?*

We recorded that in Detroit and "Junie" Morrison came down from the Ohio Players and did some things on there with vocals and the chord changes and the solo I did before the vocals were laid down. I plugged the guitar straight into the amp and that was pretty much it. I don't think I even used a wah-wah pedal on there.

Did you ever cross paths with Kiss, being on the same label (Casablanca Records)?

We did cross paths a little bit at parties and stuff, but I was never formally introduced to them. I do remember those wild platform shoes though.

And what has it been like working with such a character like George Clinton?

Well, as much as I like cartoons…

[Laughs] *Let's move on!*

Yeah, I'm just not sure where to go with that right now.

You also laid down a very unusual and lengthy solo on "Never Buy Texas From a Cowboy" with the Brides of Funkenstein.

Yeah, that was recorded in Detroit, too. They brought this mini-Korg synthesizer and they had a mini-guitar rigged into it and whatever pickup they had made that sound where it blended the synths and the guitars.

That does have an odd sound.

Yeah, but it was tracking pretty well and the bends I did came out really good. There was also a version that's on tape somewhere of me playing through all of "(Not Just) Knee Deep." I don't know where that it is, but I know I did it.

You had a solo album called Heavy Metal Funkason *back in 1998.*

My cousin talked me into doing it. I didn't want to put that album out. I brought a drummer in and it was not even supposed to be called that. They released it without me having a say in the final mix. I just basically put it together to see what they were gonna do, and they pretty much did what I thought they were gonna do!

It's almost embarrassing actually. I haven't given up on the idea of doing some of those songs again and playing some live, but as far as what they did to it in the studio, I was not happy, but what are you gonna do?

Well, now that you said it, the mix isn't very good, the drums sound like a demo at best, but there are some monster riffs and solos on there and songs worth working over again.

Definitely! It doesn't sound good at all! I will try and get back at it and make it work again.

Over the years, what have been your primary guitar models you've preferred?

I always had the Gibson SGs back in the day. I really like Flying Vs and always have, and I've got that Jimmy Page double neck Gibson 1275. The SG and Les Pauls I was always into and I played Strats as well. Mostly I like those Flying Vs though. There's just something about those that I really like. I liked those guitars like those Bluesmasters guitars, but I could never afford one! And I did like Gretsch guitars, too. But I do love those Flying Vs.

And what is this latest project you have going here in 2015?

I've got the Kidd Funkadelic Band and there are a lot of good players in it. Kelton Cooper who did work with Kool & the Gang is on guitars and vocals, and there's two keyboard players in Lenny Underwood and Devone Allison, and Darryl Dixon who played the original sax solo on "Flashlight" with P-Funk and I'm really excited about that. I mean, that was Maceo Parker on that song, but that's Darryl doin' that legendary solo! When we rehearsed it, I said, "This is all I want! This is what it is!" We also have Billy Grant on bass and Scott Jordan on drums. The singer is Michael Angelo, who can really sing a lot of styles.

I just really wanted a lineup of good musicians to get back out on the road as quickly as I can and play. I hope it works out and we should be able to do a good job.

That sounds like a really good ensemble.

This is kinda where I am right now and I gotta stick to it. I haven't been in this situation since before I joined Funkadelic, Peter! So, I need to stay focused on what I'm doing and it will be different, but I am diplomatic and I will not be dictating to any of the players. It will be a collective effort and they have my back.

I thank you so much for this interview and I wish you all the luck in the world with your new musical venture. Life is always an adventure and not always fun, so best of luck, man.

I appreciate it man; we'll all be all right whatever faces us. If you're happy, I'm happy, and I wish you luck with this book!

Recommended solo: "Cosmic Slop" from *Hardcore Jollies* with Funkadelic (1976)
Further info: www.michaelwhampton.com
Photo credit: Patti Heck

CHAPTER 23

Tony Hicks

(Born Anthony Christopher Hicks, December 16, 1945, Nelson, Lancashire, UK)

As guitarist for the Hollies, Anthony "Tony" Hicks has played on over thirty hit singles from this most legendary of groups, who rivaled the success of the Beatles, the Rolling Stones, the Who, and the Kinks, among others.

An early interest in Skiffle music and a subsequent stint with Ricky Shaw and the Dolphins eventually led to an offer from the Hollies to replace their original guitarist Vic Steele, who had left the band in early 1963. Hicks was initially unsure about joining but wisely did so.

The Hollies first classic lineup featured Hicks, singer Allan Clarke, guitarist/singer Graham Nash, drummer Bobby Elliot, and bass player Eric Haydock (a few others had passed through in the early days, but this lineup was the first to enjoy success and did so into mid-1966).

Early hits accented the band's amazing three-part harmonies (of which Hicks was a part). From 1964's "Stay" through 1967's "Carrie Anne," they scored twelve Top 10 hits out of their next thirteen singles in their native UK, with "I'm Alive" reaching #1 and "Just One Look," "I Can't Let Go," and "Stop Stop Stop" all hitting #2. Success was now happening in the US, with "Bus Stop" their biggest hit achieving a #5 showing there. The brilliant "Look Out Any Window" was their first Top 40 single in America and featured Hicks playing a challenging riff on a Vox 12-string guitar, which wasn't exactly commonplace, nor easy to do.

"Stop Stop Stop" in fact featured a significant banjo part by Hicks, which showed his versatility and uniqueness. With new bass player Bernie Calvert, the band pushed ahead with some odd departures in both singles and albums all to great results musically, though not all of their audience appreciated the changes.

The 1967 album *Evolution* took quite a few chances, but it was the 1968 album *Butterfly* that had a psychedelic feel where they really surprised people. The album was a Top 10 seller in the UK and narrowly missed the US Top 40. Hits continued during this era with such ingenious tunes as "King Midas in Reverse" and "Dear Eloise." The title cut on *Butterfly* was also a work of psychedelic pop rock art.

A division within the band about musical direction saw Nash leave prior to the *Hollies Sing Dylan* album, which surfaced in 1969 and featured his replacement Terry Sylvester. Though the album was harshly viewed by Nash and some critics and fans, just as many people enjoyed it and the album hit #3 in the UK. Nash of course, became part of a little outfit you may have heard of called Crosby, Stills & Nash.

The civil rights-era anthem "He Ain't Heavy, He's My Brother" was a monster hit in 1969 hitting #3 in the UK and #7 in the US. A fella by the name of Elton John played piano as a little-known session man on that track and also played on their Top 10 hit "I Can't Tell the Bottom from the Top" in 1970. Hits continued throughout the world, but Clarke departed in 1971 showing frustration as Nash had. Yet, a final album with him called *Distant Light* was rather good and would enjoy huge success after the fact.

Swedish singer Mikael Rickfors was hired and the band scored a hit with the dramatic "The Baby." Although Rickfors was an odd choice and had an accent, he was an excellent singer. Bizarrely, a single was then lifted from *Distant Light* called "Long Cool Woman (In a Black Dress)," which has a swamp rock feel and was quite open sounding and raunchy. It skyrocketed to #2 in the US. Yet another US hit came from that album in the engaging "Long Dark Road."

Then the current lineup with Rickfors issued *Romany*, which was a very good album giving the band a US hit in the feel-good "Magic Woman Touch." By 1973, after another album, Rickfors departed when Clarke returned. Another swamp rock-styled song "The Day that Curly Billy Shot Down Crazy Sam McGee" was a UK hit, but in 1974 came *that* song—"The Air That I Breathe" from the album *Hollies*.

A haunting but beautiful song, this single would soar to #6 in the US and #2 in the UK. Here, Hicks displays his knack for the ultimate in taste with an airy sound, with brief but dreamy solos in both the intro and the mid-section. Clarke's vocals are phenomenal and it's no wonder this previously obscure song by Phil Everly (written by Albert Hammond and Mike Hazelwood) became the huge hit that it was. The song has been covered at least twenty times, but no version touches this one. The guitar solo is one of my personal favorites of all-time and Eric Clapton was quoted as saying he wished he'd played the intro solo and that it was the "most soulful" one he had ever heard. Rather nice, eh?

Another Night was a solid album and spawned the excellent title cut, a minor US hit that has a somewhat dark feel and some biting guitar work, along with a moody synth riff. Check out the solos Hicks lays down here; it's dynamite stuff.

By 1976, the band was no longer scoring new hits in the US and UK but certainly were elsewhere around the world. And, in the UK, there was a resurgence based on the band's history as the concert set *Hollies Live Hits* shot to #4 in the UK and a hits package *20 Golden Greats* went to #2 in 1978. So, the love was still there for the band.

Some fine albums were ignored during this timeframe, including *Russian Roulette* and *Five Three One-Double Seven O Four*. In 1980, a minor hit occurred with the dramatic, orchestrated "Soldier's Song" and that same year saw an album of Buddy Holly covers called… *Buddy Holly* (zero points for creativity there). By 1981, Sylvester and Calvert left, but a reunion with Nash and the addition of bassist Steve Stroud led to a new album *What Goes Around* in 1983 and a US Top 30 hit covering the Supremes' "Stop! In the Name of Love." A tour followed, but Nash would return to CSN right after.

Clarke retired in 2000 and was replaced by former Move singer Carl Wayne, but he sadly passed away in 2004. Peter Howarth then took over and guitarist Steve Lauri joined as well. Ray Stiles has been on bass since 1986 and Ian Parker on keyboards since 1991. The band still tours each and every year worldwide and always enjoy strong-selling compilation albums. Studio albums have included *Staying Power* (2006) and *Then, Now, Always* (2009) and a new song "Skylarks" appeared on the 3 CD collection *50 At Fifty* in 2014.

Tony Hicks is a most skilled guitarist and truly deserves recognition for being so. He also plays banjo, sitar, mandolin, bass, and keyboards, and writes and sings. He's a member of the Rock and Roll Hall of Fame as the Hollies were finally inducted in 2010. Remember him when you're arguing with a friend about who some of the best guitarists are.

On a bitterly cold late November day in 2014, I was able to talk to Tony about a variety of topics, and he was a total gentleman as I expected.

Who were some of the guitar players that inspired you to begin playing?

You'd have to go all the way back to the early Elvis Presley records and Scotty Moore who did things with very little equipment, which was quite remarkable. James Burton stood out, too.

And how old were you when you began playing?

I was thirteen when I did my first TV appearance with a Skiffle group in Britain. I had to get time off from school to travel from the North of England to London for a show called *Carroll Levis Discoveries,* which was kind of the forerunner to *Opportunity Knocks.* You're really talking about the early day versions of the stuff Simon Cowell does now. Are you familiar with Skiffle?

Yes and I was going to ask if that was any part of what you played and heard when you were young. I know how huge it was in the UK at that time.

Yeah, it was just what you sort of did at the time. It wasn't a case of how well you played if you got in a group, as long as you had a guitar!

With the early Hollies records, the one thing that impressed me the most was that even though you were known as a vocal group, just how much musicality was involved especially from a guitar standpoint.

At the time, amongst the likes of the Stones, the Who and the Beatles, the Hollies were known as a "group's group." As far as my personal contribution then it's no different than it is today. I've always tried to work around the vocals as tastefully as I can. That's all I've ever attempted to do because, as far as the Hollies are concerned, the vocals are the main drive. There was no way to make it all convoluted—that's a simple fact.

"Look Through Any Window" sounds so chiming, so beautiful and so perfect, and I assume that's a 12-string you were playing. How did you come up with that arrangement? That was not typical fare in 1965.

Yeah, that was a 12-string Vox guitar. And this may sound silly, but I don't really know how I came up with it. I just did it. We were on the road seven days a week and we picked up the song and I fiddled around until I got something that worked. As you say, that was a 12-string and it was a Vox and it was quite difficult to play. It wasn't all that smooth to play. I went through a Vox amplifier in Abbey Road Studios. There may have been some tremolo on there. It's all fairly simple sounding, but I suppose it did jump out when it came on the radio, and keeping it simple is all I've ever really tried to do.

When the Hollies started evolving in the late '60s with albums like Butterfly...

And there's the contradiction. We were getting hits every time we made a single and the albums didn't have much to do with that material and that's what confused a lot of people. It also had to with where we were at that time. We'd been coming to America and doing the Greyhound bus trips and hearing all these different sounds on American radio. Going into Greenwich Village and meeting the Lovin' Spoonful before they even recorded—we met up with them and heard all this material that ended up on their first album. And then on the West Coast we got friendly with the Mamas and the Papas and it did influence us.

You might want to mention that the banjo on "Stop Stop Stop" came about from being taken by our record label to a place in New York called the Round Table, which was a Turkish belly-dancing club and the lyrics came from that. So I got a banjo and played the best that I could of what I came up with that I was hearing in my head.

And now you were starting to introduce a multitude of instruments into the sound.

Yeah, I also bought a lovely autoharp, which I'd seen John Sebastian play in the Lovin' Spoonful. I played autoharp on a few songs, including a song called "Pay It Back with Interest" if you know that one.

Yes I do—wonderful song.

So whatever countries we were in, we used any influences we picked up. As you know on "Carrie Anne" we used the steel drums. As we had so many singles, we were desperate to make sure that the albums didn't sound the same. Whether it be the contents of the song or the instruments being used.

I can see what you're saying about the public perhaps not being so sure about your styles on the albums as opposed to the singles, although even some singles were stretching things such as "King Midas in Reverse."

Hmmm…an interesting song? Yeah. And it goes down well when we play it live still. But that was never one of the main Hollies singles, true. It did reach the Top 10, but was far from a #1, #2 or #3 hit that we had so many of.

And the Hollies Sing Dylan *album in 1969. Now that was something I enjoyed, but did that create a sort of divide within the band?*

[Laughs] Well, not at the time, there wasn't! I mean, I've read Graham Nash wasn't too into it, because by then he was really into America and wanted to be there, but he was leaving as we started that album anyway. It just seemed that those Bob Dylan songs were around and we took them a stage further with some different chord arrangements and it was very successful for us. Graham and I are still friends and he just came around the house about six weeks ago promoting his book and we had a lovely dinner with him and his son, but yes going back to your question, I think he didn't understand why we were doing it.

I'd imagine not having everyone on board was tough.

By then he'd met the likes of Stephen Stills and David Crosby and he probably thought it was a mistake to do it. It wasn't a mistake though—just a matter of opinion.

I actually was a very big fan of the '70s era Hollies. You had some dynamite songs like "Magic Woman Touch" and "Long Dark Road," which you co-wrote among many others. Do you have a fondness for that period? I think that era contains some of your best stuff.

Very much so; I think the songs were very worthy. Unfortunately, it did turn that although Mikael Rickfors had a great voice and he looked the part, he wasn't as fluent with English as we would've liked. When we recorded at Abbey Road our recordings were pretty instant as we knew what we wanted to do when we got in there—most of our records were actually first, second, third takes. When Mikael came along it wasn't like that anymore. We didn't realize that the slightest inflection in the English language would make us have to go back and do it again. But I do have very fond memories of him and that period because without it I don't know where we'd have been.

And then during that time, out of nowhere "Long Cool Woman (In A Black Dress)" is released and hits #2 over here, but Allan had left by that point and you had Mikael now, but Allan would return and Mikael would leave about a year and a half later, if I've got that right?

[Laughs] Yes indeed! We have America to thank for that major hit record. Ron Richards our longtime producer, who was actually quite good, just hadn't spotted the potential in that one. That actually was interesting, and brought a lot of good our way. What happened was I was in New York and the head of A&R at CBS said, "I know you haven't used that track anywhere, but we think we have a shot at a hit with that here." We always let various countries have a go if they thought they could do well by a song.

As you say, it was a smash and in America the beauty was we left it very bare when we recorded it because if anyone saw something special in it, they would've had us add vocal harmonies on and try and build the track and do too much. So it was a blessing in disguise in many ways. It was just a simple, chugging riff with three guitars and some guitar harmonies with bass and drums and nothing else.

It is a very open recording and it does lend itself to that "swamp rock" feel. I've read there was a big CCR influence in the track over the years, but I don't really hear too much of that.

It is not true in the least. Not at all. There were no inhibitions or pre-conceived ideas. Just going in and getting it done really. It wasn't even issued as single in the UK until it hit in the States. It is the last song we play in the set now, and it hadn't been for a long time really. We had been closing with the more melodic numbers such as "He Ain't Heavy…" and "The Air That I Breathe" but we've switched it up, and it's a bit wild really to close with it.

It began a stretch of excellent albums including Distant Light *and* Romany.

I also really liked *Distant Light*—that was a good one, that was good fun, and there are some really good songs on there.

The Rickfors era had some great songs too on Romany *and* Out on the Road *that never even got released in the US or UK I believe.*

Well, we realized that we were going down the wrong track with Mikael. He never wanted to be the center-stage performer. He would've been just as happy playing guitar by the drums and he had no real desire to be up front, which for a front man presents a problem.

I guess that's why it's a front man and not a by-the-drumsman.

Yes, right! [Laughs]

As much as "The Air That I Breathe" still gets played here on the radio, I never tire of it. It still sounds fresh and is just rich with emotion. I know Phil Everly had recorded it first.

That was one that Allan brought in to Abbey Road and I must say that when Ron Richards heard our demo of it he said, "Record that and you'll have a #1." He was right.

The guitar solos—the intro and the middle one—are just eloquent and note perfect. It floats in and just has so much in so little an amount of notes. I had read that Eric Clapton said that was one of his favorite guitar solos by anybody. Do you remember crafting that solo?

Yeah. I was in Studio 2 in Abbey Road and I was pushed down the steps and told to add an intro on it! [Laughs] So that's what I did. If I recall, there was no overdrive on that to give it sustain; it was just going through a Leslie speaker. It gave it that sustain sound on the intro. It's overlaid, of course, but the solo itself, there's no overlay there. I did that and then I went home.

It's one of my favorite songs by anybody period and the solos just add to it.

I had heard that Eric had said something before, so that's nice. Good 'ol Eric! [Laughs]

And there's also "Another Night," a bit of a dark one with some excellent guitar work. It was a minor hit in the States but never appears on any of your compilations!

I know what you mean, I like that one, too. I guess that's one that crept underneath the net as it were. We did have a period of doing it live and I enjoyed that, but it's not one that people have been shouting out for.

Well, I'll shout out from all the way over here!

We'll do it then!

Thank you.

You're very welcome [laughs].

You've had some cool guests over the years as well, like Rod Argent and Gary Brooker of Procol Harum…

Yes, we did and there was good 'ol Sir Elton John.

Yes, of course he played piano on "He Ain't Heavy, He's My Brother."

He also played Hammond organ on "Perfect Lady Housewife."

Elton was just a session man at that time in 1969—did you know him well?

We did. We were being published by Dick James and he was a staff writer there at the time and we saw him quite a lot. In fact, our publishing company had about twenty to twenty-five Elton songs but most won't see the light of day.

In the '90s you guys did a cover of Prince's "Purple Rain" that was not only a shock, but I thought it was a wonderful arrangement with some excellent guitar work. Who brought that in?

Well, I'm not so sure he brought it in, but my son who is also a musician is probably Prince's biggest fan. He still sees him live whenever he gets a chance and he was introduced to him through Dhani Harrison (George's son) who he does a lot of work with; so I suppose that answers your question.

And who is doing the guitar harmonies on that with you?

That would be Alan Coates, our other guitarist.

I thought it was great.

Yeah, I enjoyed doing it, but it wasn't everybody's cup of tea, and some thought we shouldn't have been doing it.

Yeah, but I'm never with the majority, so I don't care what they thought!

I remember doing a gig in Germany with a lot of Americans in the audience who let it be known we should not be covering Prince!

And what are the types of guitars you prefer?

My collection these days is mainly Paul Reed Smith. I was one of the first in England to use those—I've got quite a decent collection of them, including some very rare ones like a PRS Metal, which you couldn't even give away back then, and it's very valuable. They do what I need them to do, those guitars. I also use a banjo called a Nechville and I use an electric sitar because we still do "The Baby," which was a hit in the Rickfors-era you like and it's a very well-liked number.

If I play acoustics I use an Irish-made guitar called a Lowden. I also have a number of Gibsons and Fenders mainly for recording, and I also like Parkers.

Were you pleased with the new song "Skylarks"?

Yeah, we put it together and I put a lot of guitars on there and it came out well. These days you can just piece things together wherever we are all over on our own and I had time to work on it.

Recommended solo: "The Air That I Breathe" from *Hollies* with the Hollies (1974)
Further info: www.hollies.co.uk
Photo Credit: Rob Haywood

CHAPTER 24

Joel Hoekstra

(Born Joel David Hoekstra, December 13, 1970, Iowa City, IA)

A gifted, inventive player and down to earth guy, Joel Hoekstra has escalated in the guitar world over the last decade or so and with damn good reason.

With an arsenal of licks, riffs, and solos, as well as a gift for composing, Hoekstra was born in Iowa City but raised in Chicago where he was able to soak up all kinds of musical influences. He began as a youth playing both piano and cello and gravitated towards guitar in his early teens. The background in classical and playing both piano and cello very much allowed him to build an interesting combination in his guitar playing involving everything from hard rock, heavy metal, jazz fusion, classical and AOR.

Joel's name began getting serious attention in the rock world when he joined Night Ranger in 2008. It was no easy gig, as he was replacing beloved original guitarist Jeff Watson, who had departed. However, Hoekstra took the opportunity and ran with it and built an incredible chemistry between he and the band's other original guitarist, Brad Gillis. All the harmonies and solos were now at another level of intensity and the shows as energetic and fun as always.

Extensive touring would follow and the band wouldn't get to release a studio album again until 2011's *Somewhere in California*. This album was the best thing Night Ranger had recorded since the '80s and restored the band's classic sound but with a modern edge. Just listen to the guitar playing on the track "Lay it on Me." The opening riff is filled with legato runs and

©Mark Lavern

tapping that is highly creative without being flashy. The whole album has a great vibe as typified by the explosive feel-good vibe of "Growin' Up in California." The guitars simply sound great and Hoekstra and Gillis make it all seem so effortless. The album was the first Night Ranger album to reach the charts in over twenty years, and a tour with Journey and Foreigner followed that also saw Joel somehow playing both with Night Ranger *and* Foreigner for about a month as Foreigner leader/guitarist Mick Jones had taken ill with a heart problem. Now that's having skill and talent and being prepared with little warning!

That's hardly all Joel was up to at that time as he had been playing in the Broadway musical *Rock of Ages* since 2009. He also had an appearance in the film as well that was released in 2012.

In addition to all of that work, Joel has been a part of the Christmas spectacular Trans-Siberian Orchestra as a touring member since 2010 and he has numerous musical highlights, particularly his emotional solo in "Oh Come All Ye Faithful/O Holy Night" that is a beautiful, beautiful exhibition of emotion and a feel of the Christmas spirit in his guitar playing. He simply gets it. So much talent!

Joel has also issued three solo albums of differing styles with *13 Acoustic Songs*, *The Moon is Falling*, and *Undefined*.

With Night Ranger, a new album called *High Road* was issued in 2014 with some outstanding songs in "High Road" that shows a bit of a country rock sound, "St. Bartholomew," "I'm Coming Home" (complete with stunning guitar harmonies), and "L.A. No Name" a sparkling acoustic instrumental with dazzling guitar work from Hoekstra and Gillis. What a way to finish the album—absolutely terrific guitar work and composition.

And so, in 2014, Joel embarked on a tour with Night Ranger and then another tour with Trans-Siberian Orchestra, all the while recording a new studio album with the legendary band he was named guitarist of around mid-year, Whitesnake!

In fact, just before this book was completed Whitesnake released their album *The Purple Album*, which is all Deep Purple songs from the Coverdale years and is Hoekstra's first with the band. A tour is accompanying the album in the spring of 2015. Yeah, I'd say this guy is in demand and insanely busy, but he's as genuine as they come and we were able to chat a few weeks before Christmas while he was on tour with Trans-Siberian Orchestra.

Who were some of your influences growing up as you started to play and even after you started realizing you had a career in music?

My parents are classical musicians and had me playing cello/piano at a very young age and growing up with so much music in the house was a huge influence. I started playing guitar because of AC/DC and was very much into hard rock and metal early on…Iron Maiden, Black Sabbath, Ozzy, Dio. Then as the years went by, I learned to appreciate more melodic bands like Foreigner, Journey, Boston. I'm also into classic bands like Pink Floyd, Led Zeppelin, the Doors, and progressive bands like Rush and Yes. Then of course the technically proficient players like Steve Vai, Joe Satriani, Yngwie Malmsteen, and Steve Morse.

What are your most preferred guitars?

I primarily use Gibson Les Pauls and Taylor acoustic guitars. I really love Fender Strats/ Teles as well, and for Floyd Rose style guitars I love my Jackson PC-1 and my EVH striped series guitars. I also have a few guitars from a small company called Atomic that I really like.

It seemed like you and Brad Gillis really clicked in Night Ranger. There are some dynamite guitar harmonies in their songs and great solos. Was that a special gig? They seem to have a blast every time they play a show. And, is there a cooler guitar song to play then "Don't Tell Me You Love Me"?

Ha Ha! Yes, Brad is a great guy/player and a great friend. I had an absolute blast in my seven years in Night Ranger. *Lots* of special moments.

The albums that you did with Night Ranger really got them back to what they did best. Could you describe the opening riff and solo to "Lay It On Me" from the Somewhere In California *album? It's awesome.*

Thanks! There is a YouTube video of me teaching the opening lick. The solo just involves some bending, tapping, legato runs, and a nice harmony ending with Brad. It's kind of hard to describe, but really it's just a lot of my fallback licks.

Trans-Siberian Orchestra is a phenomenon and deservedly so. I first saw them in 2000 in at the Tower Theater in Philly with my wife and pleaded with people to see the show, and another couple went with us but nobody else. A few years later, all the people who didn't want to go with me were telling me to see this amazing band (Yeah, thanks for the tip you boobs!). Now that you have been a part of this extravaganza since 2010, have you grasped the whole thing and see the joy that you bring people every night during the Christmas season?

Thanks! Yes, it's been an honor for me to be a part of. Paul O'Neill really cares about the fans so much. He'll stop at nothing to deliver them a unique/special experience.

Can you take me through how you approach the solo on "Oh Come All Ye Faithful/O Holy Night"? I'm not kidding when I say I get chills at your tone and feel on that piece—it's so, so beautiful.

Thanks again! I always try to keep things pretty close to the records because, as a fan, that's often what I like to hear players do. I basically learned Al Pitrelli's interpretation and put my flourishes/touches in here and there and put some 8-fingertapping in the break at the end.

Was your experience with the Rock Of Ages *musical a challenge playing in such a different type of environment?*

Not really. I moved to NYC to do a show called *Love, Janis* that was about Janis Joplin. I did that for two years solid in NYC (about 700 shows) and then performed it in regional theaters for another couple years. I also traveled with a show called *It Ain't Nothin but the Blues* and subbed in the pit for shows like *The Boy from Oz, La Cage Aux Folles,* and *Tarzan,* so I had a good amount of theater experience coming into *Rock of Ages.*

Congrats on getting the Whitesnake gig. Talk about a band of legendary players (and I interviewed Bernie Marsden for this book, too). I know you've just done the new album for 2015; how will you approach the 'Snake classics live on the tour?

Thanks yet again! I'll try to be as faithful to the classic solos as possible because I think that's how fans like to hear it and put in my touches here and there.

Final silly question I ask most players for my cats: If you could rename a Night Ranger, Whitesnake, or even Trans-Siberian Orchestra song or album after a type of cat what would you come up with? I've gotten some hilarious answers.

Hmmm…I suppose renaming "Sister Christian" "Brother Joel" would get me some residuals…? Let's go with that.

I thank you again for participating and allowing me to feature you in this book!

Thanks for including me. I really appreciate it.

I was hoping so much to see the show in Philly Dec. 23 [2015]. Did you know you were playing on Festivus that day?

Sweet! A Festivus for the Rest of Us!

Recommended solo: "Lay it on Me" from *Somewhere in California* with Night Ranger (2011)
Further info: www.joelhoekstra.com and www.whitesnake.com
Photo credit: Mark Laverman

CHAPTER 25
Randy Jackson
(Born February 28, 1955, New Orleans, LA)

Randy Jackson is a versatile guitarist/vocalist/songwriter originally from New Orleans and is best known for his years with progressive/hard rock band Zebra, whom he still plays with to this day.

Zebra was a trio formed in New Orleans in 1975 with Randy Jackson, Felix Hanneman (bass/keys/vocals), and Guy Gelso (drums). Influenced by Led Zeppelin, Rush, and the Beatles, they developed a loyal following in the Bayou but could not secure record label interest and thus relocated to Long Island, New York, around 1978. It was not until 1982 that a deal was signed with Atlantic Records.

In 1983, the debut album *Zebra* was issued and quickly went Gold, reaching the US Top 30. There simply was no other act like Zebra around at the time, and the MTV/rock radio hits "Who's Behind the Door?" and "Tell Me What You Want" found favor with hard rock audiences. Jackson's unique vocals (very high-pitched like Rush's Geddy Lee at times, and beautifully understated at others) made the band stand out. Randy's guitar playing was of particular notice however. His use of 6- and 12-string acoustic guitars and electric guitars definitely had a nod to Jimmy Page but Jackson's style and deft playing skills were leagues above many of his influences. The complex solos on tracks, like "As I Said Before," "The La La Song," and the seven-minute epic "Take Your Fingers from My Hair" were exemplary. There wasn't a bad song to be found on the whole album.

The year 1984 saw the release of *No Tellin' Lies*. The album failed to match the sales of the debut, only peaking at #84. Despite this, as a whole, this was still a solid album with great songs. The hard-hitting "Wait Until the Summer's Gone" had a vicious solo and the Top 20 rock radio/MTV hit "Bears" was an amusing anti-hunting song that proved very popular. Randy's guitar work on the Prog-styled title cut and "But No More" continued to show his excellence. "No Tellin' Lies" had some interesting changes in it and "Lullaby" was a ballad with a heavy Beatles influence.

In 1986, *3.V* was arguably the band's finest moment but failed to chart. Atlantic was no longer behind the band, and the album was lost. "Time" showcased amazing guitar work and writing, and "Better Not Call" had a scorching solo, while throughout the album Randy continued to craft his guitar playing to suit the band's developing sound. The late '80s saw little Zebra activity and Randy joined the re-formed Jefferson Airplane for a tour in 1989.

After the fantastic *Zebra Live* in 1990 (including a devastating rendition of "The La La Song" and a crackling take on Led Zeppelin's "The Ocean"), the band focused on gigs in their two home bases of Long Island and New Orleans. Randy pursued a solo project called China Rain and released an album several years later. Zebra would continue to gig semi-regularly and finally issued *Zebra IV* in 2003, which was an impressive piece of work featuring more stunning guitar playing on tracks like "Why" and "Arabian Knights."

The year 2010 saw the band inducted into the Louisiana Music Hall of Fame and the same accolades occurred on Long Island in 2012. *Zebra the DVD* was issued in 2008 mixing in live footage from both New Orleans and Long Island showing the band still at 100% and Jackson's guitar work hasn't lost one iota.

Randy remains very busy aside from Zebra, playing solo acoustic gigs and live shows with an orchestra doing the music of Led Zeppelin, the Doors, and the Beatles. *Empathy for the Walrus* is a solo acoustic album Jackson released in 2014 performing lesser-covered Beatles songs showcasing just how wonderfully talented and creative this man is and that he will always be not only as a guitarist but an arranger and vocalist.

I was honored to speak with Randy in May 2014, and here's how that went:

Do you recall how you came up with the solo on "As I Said Before"? I love that song, and the solo and riffs are special in that one. Was that a song from your club days? There's so much going in that tune.

Yeah, I really don't remember as it was so long ago, how I approached the solo. I added some things in the bridge to keep it bright and then it gets rather heavy. That was a song we had done for years and the original version was a bit longer and Jack Douglas (the producer) rearranged it and I think he made it better. He tightened up some of the parts. It didn't change anything but did reduce the amount of times we did things.

What would you say are some of the most memorable solos that you have recorded on the Zebra albums?

I think my favorites are the solos in "Time" and the one in "Why" from *Zebra IV*. I really like that one.

And for me the one in "Take Your Fingers from My Hair" truly stands out.

Yeah, you know it's funny, because the ones on the first record I had played for so long and so many years that they don't get thrown into the mix that I remember as well, but that one does stand out.

Is that because you lived with them for so long before getting signed to Atlantic?

Before we put the record out, yes. Even looking back on the first record, I really liked the solo on "The La La Song." I thought that was really cool.

Do you remember what happened with 3.V in 1986? Did Atlantic even promote it at all? I found out it was released by accident and I did see the video for "Can't Live Without" on MTV a couple of times, but that was it.

They did give it a little itty-bitty push in the beginning and then we got out on the road, it was funny because that was when Bon Jovi's *Slippery When Wet* had come out and it seemed like we got lost in the sauce with that whole thing. We'd go out and do interviews and one of the first questions they'd ask is, "What do you think about this whole Bon Jovi phenomenon"? It was just bad timing. It was sad because I thought the record was really good. It was a whole album that was cohesive and there weren't any parts that didn't fit. It was a very disappointing thing, but trying to point fingers at people or putting the blame somewhere; I think it's really all timing.

Who are some of the players that were an influence on you? I can certainly hear Jimmy Page and George Harrison in there.

Obviously Jimmy Page, and I love the Beatles. When I started out learning to play lead guitar I listened to a lot of the Allman Brothers Band and Grand Funk Railroad, actually with

Mark Farner on guitar. I think it was because in general it was heavier than the Beatles and it was playable. Hendrix was around the same time and I would play a little Hendrix, but I wasn't quite there yet, so when Grand Funk came out, it was more attainable for me as it was more song oriented and not as complicated whereas Hendrix was still way out there for me.

I know you've used guitar harmonies in the studio with yourself and I was wondering if any of the great guitar harmony bands, like my favorite band Thin Lizzy, as well as the Allman Brothers Band who you mentioned and Wishbone Ash, were acts that you admired.

Absolutely, I think when you listen to any of the guitar harmonies that Zebra did, certainly those bands were a big influence, and if you listen to the Allman Brothers Band and Steely Dan too; it's there like you said.

Even to this day where are you at in your head before you hit the stage? Are you ready to go or is there a process?

I usually warm up my voice for a while before a Zebra show, but with the acoustic shows I do, I usually do so in the first four or five songs. It really depends on what type of show it is.

Your new solo album Empathy for the Walrus *is very interesting because there are a lot of Beatles songs here I don't recall artists even trying that way.*

Thanks man! I got asked to do it by the label. They knew I've done it live for years and asked me if I'd like to do a whole album of it. I said, "Sounds awesome!" and we picked the songs in about five minutes.

It was very interesting to hear you cover "Free as a Bird," which was a "new" Beatles song in 1995.

Yes, I love that song! I don't know how many others, if any, have tried it, but I was certainly going to give it a shot.

Not common knowledge here...but you were in the Jefferson Airplane on the reunion tour in 1989. How did that come about? And what was the experience like?

Well, they were rehearsing for their tour in 1989 and I guess in the middle of their rehearsal they decided they really needed one more person to cover guitars and some keyboards, and Kenny Aronoff [the drummer best known for his years with John Mellencamp and John Fogerty], who I knew, put my name forward and they flew me out to San Francisco and I was on the road with them right after that and it was awesome.

    I was getting to play with a band that I had grown up learning to play their songs and at the same time getting to visit some of the venues I'd only heard about but never played. I got to meet Bill Graham at the Fillmore West and we did like five or six shows there. They did it just like they did back in the '60s—they had the projector with greased lights and people moving it with their hands projecting it to the back and it was all real authentic when we did those gigs, and it was quite an experience, and the whole band was just awesome.

Did you guys relocate Zebra from New Orleans to New York in hopes of getting a better shot at a deal?

Yeah, because even though some bands had gotten signed out of New Orleans the labels weren't really looking for anything in rock down there and most of the bands that did get signed were usually forgotten about. So it was either New York or LA and we knew some people in New York and moved up there.

Is it true one of your songs was on a local sampler album and an executive from Atlantic heard it and signed Zebra?

Well, he was directed to it. There was a radio station called WBAB-FM and the program director had started playing our demos in regular rotation and we started to become one of the most requested bands at the station. And a guy from Atlantic who was just starting out named Jason Flom went to the station and was trying to get them to play some new artists on Atlantic and the program director told him he had to check out this band Zebra he had been playing and gave him the whole story. That's really how it kinda happened.

And that first album became the fastest-selling debut album in Atlantic's history!

Yeah, there ya go! We were doing really well at that time [laughs].

I mean, "Who's Behind the Door?" you could not escape that from radio and MTV.

You know, funny enough the initial sales were what gave us that title (of fastest-selling act on Atlantic) and the only people who ever heard of the band were the people who had been coming to see us in the clubs for years. So in a way we were the biggest club band ever! It took another three months before we saw another surge thanks to MTV.

I remember from No Tellin' Lies *that "Wait Until the Summer's Gone" was getting a lot of MTV play as well and, I could be wrong, but I swear that was a Playboy Playmate named Marianne Gravette naked in the zebra paint. Am I wrong?*

Yeah, that's who it was!

I have her embedded in my brain because when I was around twelve or so, I used to find Playboy *magazines my dad would hide and she was in one of the issues!*

Blame your dad for that! [Laughs]

No, I thank him for that! Thanks for the video though.

You're welcome! Marty Callner did that video and he had some great ideas. He was great to work with.

"Bears" got a lot of MTV play as well and was amusing. The bear beats the hunter.

Yes, that was a favorite of ours.

Final question: what guitars are your preferred choices these days?

I really like the D'Angelico. They made a 6-string for me that's really, really awesome. It's not too heavy and the sound is just phenomenal. It stays in tune and it's called a New Yorker. I still do play the B. C. Rich; I still have the double-neck.

Recommended solo: "Take Your Fingers from My Hair" from *Zebra* with Zebra (1983)
Further info: www.thedoor.com/randy.html
Photo credit: Bob Geiger

CHAPTER 26
Danny Johnson
(Born Daniel Johnson, June 14, 1955, Shreveport, LA)

Danny Johnson is a serious talent (as well as a damn fine singer/writer), who has played with quite a few people over the years and yet is one of many in this book who deserve far more attention. Sure, like any of these guys and gals he's been in magazines and whatnot, but here is a true axeman that more folks should be aware of.

Danny really played, wrote, and sang his ass off in the '70s with some seriously great bands in Derringer and Axis. These were two fine examples of the classy, no-frills hard rock acts that were around in the US on major labels who opened for major acts and had a modicum of success but have unfairly been cast aside in rock history.

Derringer was a cracking, good band with its namesake Rick Derringer on guitar and vocals, drummer Vinny Appice (later in Black Sabbath and Dio), and bassist Kenny Aaronson (later with Billy Squier). The album *Derringer* was issued in 1976 on Epic Records and was a great album that sported the minor hit "Let Me In" along with cool tunes like the galloping riffs of "Sailor," which was sung and written by Johnson and the amazing slow-builder "Loosen Up Your Grip." "Sailor" is so outrageously good, it was awesome to see a guy like Rick Derringer allow Danny a chance to show how great he was as a player, singer, and writer. This song is explosive, and check out the end of the solo where the leads harmonize with the bass! The material was of supreme quality and the band was a very tight unit.

Sweet Evil and *Derringer Live,* both from 1977, were excellent albums, and cuts like "One Eyed Jack," "Drivin' Sideways," "Sittin' by the Pool," and the title cut were most impressive. This was 1970s hard rock with some funky elements and it was a musician's band but never got too stuffy. *Sweet Evil* is an American hard rock gem of an album and it's such a shame Derringer couldn't keep it together as a band. Every Derringer album should've been a smash but alas, it didn't happen.

Derringer only peaked at #154 in 1976, but still holds up as one of the best examples of hard rock from an American band anyone could enjoy. *Sweet Evil* hit #169 and *Derringer Live* would rise to #123. Maybe that next studio album could've been the big breakthrough, but who knows.

Average sales didn't keep the band going and Johnson soon merged with Appice and bassist/vocalist Jay Davis as Axis. This band seriously rocked, and their 1978 LP *It's A Circus World* was a well-produced power trio dedicated to hard rock making it an album to die for. "Armageddon," "Cats in the Alley," "The Juggler," and "Brown Eyes" are furious, cleverly written slices of music. Label and management issues betrayed the band, but Johnson's guitar work smokes in this environment. Though they did numerous live gigs, there was no promotion for the record and the band dissolved quickly with Appice later joining Black Sabbath in 1980.

Danny then had a major opportunity, linking up with Aerosmith for a week of rehearsals in 1979 and nearly got the gig, but it didn't work out because his haircut was too short (more on this in our interview that follows!). A stint with Alice Cooper followed and saw Johnson playing on the album *Special Forces* in 1981 that briefly charted, though this was a rough time for Alice commercially and personally due to heavy drinking and drugging in an era he barely remembers.

Danny then joined Rod Stewart's band later that year (joining his former band mate Vinny Appice's revered drumming brother Carmine Appice) appearing on the *Tonight I'm Yours* album, which produced smash hits in "Young Turks" and "Tonight I'm Yours (Don't Hurt Me)" and included the Johnson co-penned radio hit "Jealous." Danny was also on board for a world tour where Rod's band rocked like never before. A pro-shot concert from Japan shows how smokin' this lineup was, especially on the rendition of "I Know (I'm Losing You)," the Temptations tune that the Faces had done so well. Rod would never rock like this again sadly. Danny would depart in 1982 and went on to play with Phil Seymour and Billy Burnette as well.

In 1986, Danny surprisingly earned the guitar spot in Alacatrazz where Yngwie Malmsteen and Steve Vai had preceded him. The album *Dangerous Games* sold poorly, but Danny did a nice job in a supremely tough spot replacing two over-the-top guitar virtuosos and fit into the scheme as a team player very well. *Dangerous Games* had a few highlights, including a cover of the Animals' classic "It's My Life" and odd songs like "Blue Boar" and "The Witchwood."

After the tour, Alcatrazz disbanded in 1987 and Danny became part of Private Life, an AOR band who released two albums of commercial, melodic rock in the late '80s and '90s featuring female singer Kelly Breznik. Despite production by Eddie Van Halen and opening for VH, the band didn't sell.

Danny remained busy in the '90s and also produced (as well as wrote songs for and played guitar on) former Rainbow, MSG, and Alcatrazz vocalist Graham Bonnet's fine solo album *Underground* in 1995. By 1996, Johnson had joined legendary hard classic rockers Steppenwolf, and has been there ever since, side by side with infamous Steppenwolf leader John Kay. Danny couldn't have fit in any better and is a damn good reason to see this band live.

His axework is everything it's always been about: a sense of place, pacing, class, and never playing above the song or what is required, always adding his signature tone and style mixing in blues and rock and avoiding pretentious flash. Hearing Danny play "The Pusher" is a highlight of each and every Steppenwolf show and worth the price of admission in itself. It's really a perfect fit and proves this is no nostalgia act, but a vital live force with Danny for close to twenty years now.

Johnson also remains devoted to his solo career as well as producing, writing, teaching, and doing sessions as well. His solo effort *Love Sweat and Blood* was issued in 2012 and there's no doubt that Danny is playing and singing as well as ever.

Danny and I had a long, productive conversation for a few hours on a fall afternoon in October 2014. What follows are some of the highlights of the great tales he told.

Hey man, we finally speak!

Sorry I've been such a pain in the ass to get a hold of lately. I've been putting this thing together with Carmine Appice, Kenny Aaronson, and Jimmy Crespo—now there's a great player for ya: Jimmy Crespo. He's soooo good. You remember him?

Sure, from Aerosmith. Always thought highly of that album he was on:
Rock in a Hard Place.

Ya know I auditioned with them for about ten days in 1979 when Joe Perry left.

Aerosmith?

Yes, and I thought it went very well and I became really close with Brad Whitford. Brad invited me to his house and I would stay there. Steven was very nice to me when we worked but we didn't hang a lot.

When disco and new wave came out, rock 'n' roll became out of place for a while. I was in a music store around that time and a guy was bad-mouthing me. I had my hair cut short, so not too many people recognized me. Anyway, he was telling a guy that worked there that "He was horrible man! I saw him at the Troubadour and he didn't have his Marshalls and his hair was cut short, and it was terrible"! So, that's kind of what things were like back then for rock musicians.

Anyway, it went on for about seven days and I was having a ball because it was all paid for and I flew out to New York from California. My lifestyle at the time, however, did not mesh with theirs. I'm sittin' there having played with Derringer and Axis and tasted a little success, but basically I was an out-of-work musician and now I'm auditioning and hanging with Aerosmith! When I got the call, Brad asked if I would mind coming out to jam a little because they were having problems with Joe Perry, and would I mind flying out if everything was paid for. I said where and when! Are you kidding me? It sounded like they were wondering if I'd be okay with it. Hell yeah, I was okay with it.

I did my bit and I thought I was well-rehearsed and tight and I knew the songs really well. I was prepared. They were all having a rough time back then and I was not into any of that partying stuff at that point and it was a tough thing to see. Some of the guys weren't getting along well and it was difficult to be in the middle of it. After my audition I was pretty pleased with the guitar playing. I knew the songs, and I'm not a great harmony singer, but I did that aspect well enough regarding backing vocals. I don't know exactly what happened, but Joey Kramer really missed Joe Perry and I wasn't sure how it would go. Brad and Tom were pulling for me. I was playing the songs like the record, but I was told I was playing too tight. Not uptight, but tight.

Is there such a thing as too tight? Was I playing the songs correctly, and that was a bad thing? I thought I was in the pocket and I know how to groove, but it seemed to be going well until that comment. They didn't eat until midnight most days and it was like living with vampires. It was a great experience looking back though, playing with such legends, but just not a good time for the band at all.

That sounds healthy, eating at midnight!

It was the '70s you know, and I didn't want to rock the boat—I just wanted to play. After the bar, the New York scene and a friend's place every day, we'd get back to the hotel and people would be coming back from night shifts and we were just getting ready to eat and finally play around midnight. There was never any sunlight!

After about ten days I needed to know if there was any word as to me getting the gig and Brad called Steven Tyler and without even hearing the call I knew it was over because of my hair and not partying. And to be honest, to hear an Aerosmith without Joe Perry is like Jagger without the Stones in my opinion, so it would've been tough. It's even in the book *Walk This Way* where they say I was the best guy, but Steven didn't like my haircut.

You also were in Alcatrazz, which was to me a strange fit even though I really liked what you did with them. It was just an odd situation as they went from Yngwie Malmsteen to Steve Vai to you.

You're really hitting on something there, because I am not that kind of guitar player at all. You obviously know and understand my career, and I really want to thank you for thinking of me by the way, but I am not an "Eruption" type player. I won't blow your mind, I am a "band" guy—I play for the song and not the solo. Guys like Yngwie and Steve Vai. I chose early on that I wanted to be good but not too good.

Well, that's why I like your playing so much. It's of such quality and you lay back until the time is right for the solo, but you also have the appropriate chops in the verses and other sections of a song.

Graham Bonnet was one of my favorite singers—a real powerhouse. As far as Alcatrazz goes and all those complicated scales and such, I knew whole tones, major, minor, and sevenths, and all that, but back in the Derringer days there was this guy who taught the more complex scales such as Arabic, Phrygian, and other scales I'd never heard of. I started feeling insecure and I got to know this stuff through him. I have since forgotten it because I didn't need it. I mean, why the hell do I need to know Egyptian music if I'm playing rock and roll?

I'd say that's a valid point [Laughs].

Yeah, you feel me here, brother! [Laughs] At that time, Rick asked what happened to my playing right before the second Derringer album. I asked what he meant and he said nothing sounds right. And I said, "Well, now I know more with all these scales I just learned." Rick then looked at me and said, "Do me a favor; forget those scales!" He told me the way I was playing originally was what he wanted all along and that I should never have gotten caught up trying to be something I wasn't. I went from tasty and bluesy to artsy and complex. I learned so much from Rick who I think is one of the best guitar players on the planet. It was a good lesson for me, not to be that kind of player and focus on what I do best.

Anyway, Steve Vai had made a deal with Alcatrazz when he left the band that he would help me out to get ready for the gig. They owned a studio with him and he wanted the studio for himself. He offered to buy them out and help me learn some of his tricks and how to get ready for a show with Alcatrazz. They were like, okay, our new guy (me) is good enough to learn most of that stuff, so we aren't going to just sign off on the studio for that. Then he offered the band a chance to do demos for the new album at the studio and to help me as well. And he really did help me for a few months, which was cool of him to do.

When you did the Dangerous Games album with Alcatrazz, that album was already a major departure for them, but when it came time to tour, how were you able to be yourself playing all that complex material?

You're talking about the *Dangerous Games* tour?

Yes, the one in 1986–1987.

Well, that's a very good question. Obviously, they wanted me to be able to pull off as much Vai and Yngwie material as possible. Some of those signature songs like "Hiroshima Mon Amour" and "God Blessed Video" had to be played recognizably and that just wasn't my bag. I don't even know how I got the job because I was not the right man for it.

Graham was a great singer and you had Jimmy Waldo on keyboards, Gary Shea on bass, and Jan Uvena on drums. These were really good musicians and they were tired of guys using them as a platform to jump off of and become bigger than Alcatrazz, so they were ready for something simpler and more song-oriented. I consider myself a player who wants to be in a band and not a showboat. In other words, I play what I think the music needs, even if that means me not even playing a guitar solo in a song. I think that's why I'm still around; I know how to stay out of the way of a good vocal and a good song. George Harrison didn't always do a lot in terms of solos and such and do we even need to go into how brilliant he was?

No we don't. George was above and beyond being a great player in part, because of what he knew not to do! When I heard you had joined Alcatrazz, even though I was a fan of your playing through Derringer and Axis, I was scratching my head a bit thinking, how does he fit in here?

I'm sure the album was a disappointment to a lot of people. Wendy Dio was managing the band and I got Richie Podolor to produce the album. He had done Three Dog Night, Iron Butterfly, and Steppenwolf, and maybe that wasn't the best way to go as he'd done a lot of pop albums around that time, too. He hadn't worked in a while and I knew him well and really thought he was a good producer and he had enjoyed a lot of success, but he did not know how to produce a heavy metal band.

There was an overload of keyboard and drum programming as well; a lot of clattery stuff.

Yeah, there was, but Jimmy Waldo, the keyboard player, was happy with it and Alcatrazz was ready for something different, but the audience was not happy with it at all. It was a little guitar shy. I went along with it because I knew Richie would get Graham a lot of vocal spots and I thought Graham really delivered on that album. I wasn't worried about replacing Yngwie and Vai, but I also felt that the guitars were really absent.

It certainly felt like a more cohesive album—very group oriented—but it fell prey to then-current trends.

I can't even listen to it now. It just didn't come off like I had hoped. I do play "Dangerous Games" in my solo shows still. It's a far heavier version of the song though, without that lame "d-d-d-dangerous games" part. A lot of pop bands in the '80s liked to enunciate the letter d! [Laughs]

As far as the audience, Richie had no idea what a heavy metal band was supposed to sound like and the fans wanted that sound and this album had nothing to do with that and they hated it. He didn't realize that what he thought was cool was going to destroy us. That first show I did with Alcatrazz in '86 the fans were less than thrilled. I did my best impersonating Steve Vai, and whether you like Steve Vai or not, he is great at what he does. Yngwie is great at what he does. That is not what Danny Johnson does, however. The guys in the band were okay with it though, they wanted a simplified sound and it was too late for the fans for that change. Without Yngwie or Steve, a new guy had to be a real burner and that wasn't me.

You're anything but a "shredder."

I'm not a shredder, I'm not a virtuoso, and I'm just me. I can play a little, ya know? But I lean more on the blues as opposed to noodling. More legato than staccato—I'm not into typewriter playing on the guitar. But ya know...Yngwie was very nice when I met him. He was playing a Bach piece with one hand while drinking a Heineknen with the other hand when I saw him live and he was incredible. I told him that speed aside, he had really nice vibrato and he can play the blues, and he was very appreciative that I said that. I asked him if he could do a little more of that and he said he couldn't because the fans wouldn't want that.

Now, you were with Rod Stewart for the Tonight I'm Yours *album in 1981 is that right?*

Man, it's funny you mention that, because right now we are rehearsing for a tour of China as the Rod Stewart Experience. It's me and other former members of Rod's band doing material from 1976–1982. Obviously we don't have Rod, but the guy we have sings so much like Rod and looks like him—his name is Rick St. James and he's phenomenal. It was organized by Carmine Appice, the drummer. We also have Jimmy Crespo on guitar, Phillip Chen on bass, and Alan St. John on keyboards who is the only non-member playing with us. It's a great lineup.

My wife and I decided that we could just rehearse here at our place. We have a lot of space, and we have like 200–300 acres of land, but Jimmy has bad allergies and we have a bunch of animals so we had to work around that and the rehearsals went very well after we figured things out. It's a good show and the stage looks nice. It's all in white, and it really looks like Rod's old stage setup, and we have some road crew members who worked with Rod. In my opinion, the album you mentioned is one of Rod's worst albums.

That album had some big hits like "Young Turks" and "Tonight I'm Yours (Don't Hurt Me)," though that I liked.

Yeah, but it sounded weak. I know it was 1981 and all that, so I'm perhaps being a bit harsh. The way we play those songs now is more aggressive, and you'd be amazed how good "Young Turks" can sound without those crappy synthesizers replaced with guitars. I didn't want to do it, but when we took the cheese out, it worked pretty well.

Was Rod good to work with?

He was nice to me, and he was going through some stuff back then, so there were highs and lows. It was the '80s and it wasn't always about the music. It took us a while to get going each day, and it wasn't until three or four in the afternoon when we started being productive. And then it was tea time. And after tea time, well...the butler would bring in so much alcohol that we wouldn't be able to finish the tracks we had finally gotten started on.

And then we'd go next door to the club and eat and drink, and there were pretty girls and not much inspiration for getting back to work. Then we'd go back to the studio with everyone hung over with Rod saying "This is great," or "This sucks." So, there wasn't much in the way of musical commentary. He had a great ear though, and he knew when something was good and there were good musicians and great engineers, so it worked eventually. Whatever else was going on, I didn't participate; I just was all about the music.

The album was just marginal to me and my guitar was removed off of a lot of the tracks. We had three guitar players, which was too many. It's a shame because I had a good sound going. Between me, Jay Davis (bass), and Carmine we had a killer three-piece going, like the Jeff Beck Group, but there were other musicians there and it wasn't permitted to reach that level. That's the way it goes sometimes, but Rod was leaning on me about arrangements and some musical help because I wanted the band to rock, but there were too many voices. I think he leaned on me because I played the clubs and I knew what was real.

And then there's the Steppenwolf gig, which has led to eighteen years and counting. What a great ride that has been for you professionally and personally.

At this stage of my life I just want to surround myself with good, positive people and I have had that with Steppenwolf. I'm not the original guitarist, but I've been there twice as long as any other guitar player. To me, Steppenwolf *is* John Kay. We do so well for each gig and where we stay in each city in terms of hotels and accommodations. I get treated like a king and it's wonderful. To be almost sixty and playing in a band like this and enjoying it so much is great.

I saw a pro-shot clip from around 2008 of the band playing "The Pusher" and your guitar solo was just perfect. It was like the song was just building to that moment and the fans were waiting for it.

John likes that about me. John does not want a guitar warlord or shredder, so I was a good fit. I wanted this gig for a long time, and they had called me a few times before but I was under contract the first time with Eddie Van Halen when I was in Private Life in the late '80s and that band just never worked out. Eventually, the third time they asked is when I was available and they found me at the right time. I had just produced a Graham Bonnet album *Undercover* in 1995 that I was pleased with. John said to me "You come highly recommended and I want you in this band."

Other people had told John about me anyway and that I was a guy who could play hard rock and the blues with a touch of psychedelic music. To me John is one of the last living rock legends of the '60s and he still looks good and sings well. It's an honor to be playing guitar next to him and I know how great this is as a gig.

It is a great gig. I'm sure there are a lot of people who don't realize how many hits Steppenwolf had.

I sometimes think I'm pullin' something over on someone to have such an awesome gig. Back to the Rod Stewart thing for a minute…we had to replace Phillip Chen with Kenny Aaronson, who used to play in Billy Squier's band, so we've still got a great lineup, and with Jimmy Crespo there…I tell ya, he's a damn good player from his time with Rod as well as Aerosmith and Bonnie Bramlett. He's just really good and nobody knows about him.

He is solid and I liked what he did with Aerosmith for sure. You've had a great run in your career yourself!

Listen buddy, it's been great talking to you. I can tell you're gonna do well with this book because you know your stuff and sound like a hell of a guy and I thank you again for thinking of me.

Recommended solo: "Sailor" from *Derringer* with Derringer (1976) and "The Pusher" (live) from *Live in Louisville* with Steppenwolf (2004)
Further info: www.dannyjohnsondj.com
Photo credit: from Danny Johnson's personal collection

CHAPTER 27
Davey Johnstone
(Born David William Logan Johnstone, May 6, 1951, Edinburgh, Scotland)

One of those guitar players who many musicians respect, admire, and know, but the bulk of the public doesn't know enough about, Davey Johnstone has been Elton John's guitarist for the better part of forty years or so.

Davey's career began with lots of sessions in the late '60s, which led to a stint with folk rock act Magna Carta and the albums *Seasons* (1970) and *Songs from Wasties Orchard* (1971). The producer of these albums, Gus Dudgeon, was enthralled with Johnstone's skills on electric and acoustic guitar, mandolin, banjo, and sitar, among other instruments and had him play on songwriter Bernie Taupin's self-titled album in 1970.

Bernie of course had just begun a songwriting partnership with Elton John and it was then that Elton met Johnstone and had him play on some cuts on Elton's album *Madman Across the Water* in 1971, including the outstanding title song and a little song called "Tiny Dancer" (are there many songs better than this, especially the middle eight section?). Johnstone was then asked to join the Elton John Band and did so in 1972, forming an alliance with Elton, drummer Nigel Olsson, and bassist Dee Murray.

Honkey Chateau would become Elton's first US #1 album in 1972 and contained the smash hits "Honkey Cat"

MELANIE ESCOMBE

and "Rocket Man" as well as the truly mesmerizing "Mona Lisas and Mad Hatters." "Rocket Man" featured Davey on electric, acoustic, and that sweet slide guitar that seems to send that rocket man right out into space. "Have Mercy on the Criminal" was a blues-oriented song with impeccable playing and arranging that was a real departure for Davey, Elton, and the band, and allowed Davey to show some more styles and sounds people may not have expected.

Don't Shoot Me, I'm Only the Piano Player topped the charts in 1973 and featured the annoying #1 hit "Crocodile Rock" and the gorgeous #2 hit "Daniel." Deeper into this album one can find such nuggets as the horn-laced "Elderberry Wine" and the Stonesy swagger of "Midnight Creeper" where Davey gets to lay down some crunching solos.

The year 1973 also saw Davey issue a solo album, *Smiling Face*. Elton was on an unbelievable creative run that continued with one of the greatest albums ever molded to wax in *Goodbye Yellow Brick Road*. This double-album not only was another #1 LP in America but has sold a crazy 30 million worldwide. The title track (which hit #2 in the US) takes the listener through a stream of visuals with unusual lyrics and a stunning vocal delivery from Elton. Davey Johnstone's guitars subtly dance around the numerous (and I mean numerous!) chord changes, adding a floating feel that accents the cinematic feel of the song. Is this one of the greatest songs ever written? Why yes, it is. I'm glad you asked.

The barnburner "Saturday Night's Alright for Fighting" narrowly missed the Top 10 and allowed Johnstone to rock out with blazing power chords in one of the '70s finest guitar intros. The glam rock-styled "Bennie and the Jets" was another US #1 and in the UK the Marilyn Monroe tribute "Candle in the Wind" became a big hit and saw Johnstone adding some sympathetic touches, including guitar harmonies counterpointing Elton's own vocal harmonies creating a beautiful, layered sound.

And there's so much more here! What about the soaring "Grey Seal"? Davey picks his spaces, sometimes leaving the song devoid of guitars but his wah-wah flavorings add so much, especially in those short interludes after the driving chorus where it almost sounds like a happy, quacking duck (or seal as it were). Oh yeah, there's also the opening eleven-minute gargantuan "Funeral for a Friend/Love Lies Bleeding," which is full-on '70s prog rock. The appropriately morose intro features layers of ghoulish synthesizers playing in tandem with blowing wind effects and then comes more instrumental work for a band that is on fire.

Johnstone's guitar work is exceptional here with great rhythm work and those memorable riffs during the chorus, including those choppy, funky chords that then give way to those biting open notes. The way Davey lets his guitar chords ring throughout the song adds extra juice to the arrangement. Throw in a wicked guitar solo with some slashing scales and we've got all we could ask from the man. And what about "All the Girls Love Alice"? Here, Davey creates some wild guitar tones on this harrowing tale lyrically but gritty rocker musically.

In 1974, Elton's one-off cover of the Beatles' "Lucy in the Sky with Diamonds" went straight to #1 and was a wholly original take on the track, and Johnstone added wonderful guitar parts with some interesting tones.

The next album *Caribou* was hastily recorded in less than ten days but went to #1 nonetheless and contained the rollicking "The Bitch is Back," which opens with another one of those crucial Johnstone guitar riffs showcasing his gift for rhythm and textures. The song went Top 5 in the US but probably would've hit #1 if it didn't dare to include that word bitch. Those heathens! "Don't Let the Sun Go Down on Me" was another Top 10 hit and a truly beautiful one. Album tracks that shone included the chilling "Ticking" and "I've Seen the Saucers."

The year 1975 saw Elton score another #1 hit with "Philadelphia Freedom," one of his very best songs and the only single credited to the Elton John Band. Though the song has a classic Philly soul sound and many thought it was written about the upcoming Bicentennial celebration in Philly in 1976, the song was actually written about Billie Jean King's pro tennis team the Philadelphia Freedoms. Bjorn Borg anyone? No? Anyway, here, the spirit of Philadelphia is captured even if it was accidental, and Davey's guitars play a key role in the chorus and outro chorus.

The year 1975 also saw *Captain Fantastic and the Brown Dirt Cowboy* debut at #1 in the US charts, the first album to ever do so. This album was very risky as the songs were detailed and long and only one single was issued in the dramatic, personal "Someone Saved My Life Tonight," which made the Top 5 despite being nearly seven minutes long. The album was autobiographical, detailing the early struggles of John and Taupin. The title song had country influences but also veered into rock, and Johnstone's guitar detail was amazing. "Tower of Babel," "Tell Me When the Wind Blows" (snarling guitar on this song), and "Bitter Fingers" were among the finest on this stupendous non-commercial album. Johnstone really played a critical role in the sound of this album.

Then Elton made changes to the band, letting Murray and Olsson go and adding bassist Kenny Passarelli while bringing back early members Caleb Quaye (guitar) and Roger Pope (drums). James Newton-Howard also came on board on keyboards. Davey and Ray Cooper were maintained. *Rock of the Westies*, yet another #1 album included the #1 single "Island Girl" as well as the funky rocker "Dan Dare (Pilot of the Future)" complete with talk box guitar and the oddball rock/funk-based album opener "Medley (Yell Help/Wednesday Night/Ugly)" that featured some awesome guitar from Johnstone and some seriously funked-up clavinet by Newton-Howard with Labelle on backing vocals. "Grow Some Funk of Your Own" was a carefree rocker cowritten by Johnstone that was a Top 15 single and became a great live number. Some fans were not thrilled with the album and noted the personnel changes.

In 1976, came the infamous pairing with Kiki Dee (after Dusty Springfield was too ill to sing) "Don't Go Breaking My Heart," which topped the charts worldwide. Let's face it, this is cheese on rye but so what? It's a damn good pop song and has a Motown feel with excellent string arrangements and Elton and Kiki sound great together. Listen to the guitar parts from Johnstone: very soulful and punchy and there's those great little lead fills after the brief breakdown following the choruses where the strings build back up. It's all about the subtlety and knowledge of what goes where, even if it's just for three or four seconds.

Another double-album *Blue Moves* surfaced in 1976 and received a mixed reaction though it is now rightfully regarded as one of Elton's best. "Sorry Seems to Be the Hardest Word" was a Top 10 hit and the album sports breathtaking highs like the vibrant, cinematic-sounding "One Horse Town" where the guitars are sheer power at times; the eight-minute pained, orchestrated, gut-wrenching epic "Tonight," the explosive neo-prog rock/jazz fusion of "Out of the Blue" (here we get some crackling good guitar work including harmonies between Johnstone and Quaye, and this song could pass for Return to Forever or Yes), the dazzling "Crazy Water" and the pretty acoustic song "Cage the Songbird" written about Edith Piaf and featuring David Crosby & Graham Nash on backing vocals. "Cage the Songbird" was one of five tracks Johnstone co-wrote on the album, which went Platinum reaching #3 in America but was viewed as a disappointment sales wise. *Blue Moves* is a seriously involved work and an album all involved with should remain proud of.

Elton then announced he was retiring from live performing in 1977, and did so right on stage stunning everyone including the band. Elton would then release a series of poorly conceived albums each lacking his classic band.

Johnstone went back into sessions and also joined Alice Cooper's band playing on *From the Inside* in 1978, which included the huge hit "How You Gonna See Me Now" which Taupin co-wrote. Davey also played on 1980's *Flush the Fashion,* which sported the new wavey Top 40 hit "Clones (We're All)" and he co-wrote more than half of the album. Johnstone played with Meat Loaf on the *Dead Ringer* album in 1981. Davey also played on the 1981 solo debut by Fleetwood Mac's Stevie Nicks *Bella Donna.*

The year 1977 also saw Davey form a band called China with some of Elton's band (Roger Pope on drums, James Newton-Howard on keyboards, and Davey on lead guitar and vocals, with Cooker LoPresti on bass). The album China put out was self-titled and had some amazing material, none more so than "One Way Ticket," which rocks hard with some cool chord changes and aggressiveness. This band (minus Pope) would tour with Elton in 1977 when he announced his retirement.

In 1982, the classic Elton John Band was back touring behind Elton's album *Jump Up!* that sold well and produced some hits including the moving John Lennon tribute "Empty Garden (Hey, Hey Johnny)." In 1983, *Two Low for Zero* produced a string of hits, including the engaging "I Guess That's Why They Call it the Blues," which Johnstone co-wrote and features Stevie Wonder on harmonica. The other hits were the upbeat pop rock of "I'm Still Standing" that had a sweet lead solo by Davey and "Kiss the Bride." The melancholy "Cold as Christmas (In the Middle of the Year)" was another highlight on yet another Platinum album.

For the rest of the '80s Elton would remain a hit king with such tunes as "Sad Songs (Say So Much)," "Nikita," a live version of "Candle in the Wind" and "I Don't Wanna Go on with You Like That" among others. Davey played on 'em all. In 1989, *Sleeping with the Past* was Elton's best of the decade sporting the hits "Healing Hands," "Club at the End of the Street," and the tearful but elegant "Sacrifice," which went to #1 in the UK—Elton's first song to do so there. "Sacrifice" is a sorrowful tale lyrically but a sparsely arranged song musically and Davey adds tiny little fills that slide in and out beautifully. It really makes a difference.

The One was a fine album released in 1992 procuring hits in the moving title track, "Simple Life" and "The Last Song." Of course, in 1994, Davey also played with Elton on *The Lion King* soundtrack making everyone weep to "Can You Feel the Love Tonight" and "Circle of Life." *Made in England* was an excellent album as well in 1995 containing hits in the title song, "Blessed," "Believe," and "Please," which is bathed in Davey's chiming '60s-sounding guitars.

Throughout the 2000s, Elton has released some very strong albums to lesser sales in this musical world of piracy and short attention spans, but *Songs from the West Coast* (2001), *Peachtree Road* (2004), and the brilliant *The Captain and the Kid* (2006) are all excellent works and Davey continues to be a key element in the music.

Davey's work on *The Captain and the Kid* is very creative as he plays acoustic and electric guitar, mandolin, banjo, and even harmonica. The wistful, country and western inflected title cut is special and Davey is all over this song with licks and accents that would leave the song empty were they not there. "Just Like Noah's Ark" is a raunchy rocker and allows Davey the space to rip out a Duane Allman-styled solo that is money. For Elton to have created such a wonderful album this deep into his career was certainly impressive. The album made the UK Top 10 and US Top 20.

Davey also formed a band called Warpipes and issued an album called *Holes in the Heavens* in 1991, and he also teamed up with fellow guitarist John Jorgenson for an acoustic instrumental album titled *Crop Circles* in 1998 well worth hearing that shows another side of his playing. Johnstone also played on a few cuts on Stevie Nicks' album *24 Karat Gold: Songs from the Vault* in 2014. Davey has also worked with Belinda Carlisle, Lenny Kravitz, Rod Stewart, and Eric Carmen, among others. Even cooler than all that was the fact that Davey also did music for an episode of Fox-TV's *King of the Hill* in 1997.

Elton John has continued to make albums to this day and remains a hot-selling ticket live. With Davey Johnstone by his side, Elton can continue to rock, even if it's like a crocodile in a sequined Donald Duck outfit.

In March 2015, as I stared at close to a foot of snow outside, I was honored to speak with Davey while on tour with Elton John and we had a seriously great conversation.

Hello Davey, how are you doing?

I'm good; let me just turn down the soccer.

Which match?

It's replay of Aston Villa and West Brom. I'm really laying back and just watching sports all day.

I think you're entitled. So you're aware of the book and what it is about?

Cool! Yeah, I do and I think it's great and good luck on the project.

We know why all the greats are talked about, but it's time to let the other guitarists get some attention.

Oh, they are all great players and guys but yes, the same ones tend to get mentioned. Some of them are good friends of mine. There should be no animosity between players because that's just stupid. I am friends with some wonderful players like Joe Walsh, Kenny Wayne Shepperd, Jimmy Page, Eric Clapton. I admire what they all bring to the table. I think what you're doing is a really good thing because there are too many guys who get a little neglected.

Thanks. I think it's a cool idea, but perhaps not the biggest selling idea.

The reason this tickled my fancy when I heard about your book—and forget about me—is that there are too many excellent players who will never get the attention and these are some ultra, ultra-good players, and I find that a drag. Although a lot of the time that can tend to be because those players don't really want to get that attention. The decisions you make also play a huge role and how you play on those tracks, what you bring to the music, and what you don't do as well; that all makes a difference in whether people notice what you do or not.

Quite frankly, I've had such a long career and I couldn't give a shit either way because I love to do what I do. It still works. We've just done the new Elton album and it was absolutely natural. The way that Elton and I work together in the studio, usually the first or second take is the one. That shows that I'm still on the right track.

And after all this time, it's still usually just one or two takes?

Yeah, just so easy and it's great, it really is.

And this is the new studio album in progress?

Yeah, we just cut ten tracks and with the current state of the business—if there is such a thing as a music business anymore—we have to do bonus tracks. I wish they'd just release albums with ten songs like the old days. Now it's about pleasing the distributors and suppliers so we have to record these extra "exclusive" tracks.

Less is more and I've always believed that; quality over quantity. [This new album is called *Wonderful Crazy Night* and is out in February 2016 with another tour.]

I loved the thirty-five- to forty-minute albums. They'd be done and you'd be blown away that there was such brevity in such a short amount of time.

Yes! And you'd want to put it on straight away again. You can bore the shit out of audiences by having too many songs and too much filler. Anyway, we're gonna go back in and for the hell of it cut a few more around the end of April, but the album itself is done as far as we're concerned. It's just real natural, it rocks, it's optimistic and up-tempo and it's the best kind of stuff that he's done in my mind for the last fifteen to twenty years.

Elton has been on a pretty good roll the last few years, especially with The Captain and the Kid *in 2006, which also has some really fine playing by you. Of course there were no hit singles, but there* are *no hit singles for veteran acts anymore because labels won't even bother.*

The problem with that album and *Peachtree Road* was that the label said we will not be promoting these albums. So, when you aren't getting help from your company to get radio play, people don't hear about it and that's the bottom line. It's a shame because those were really good albums as you say. As I say, if you don't have that camaraderie between your record company and the people who are supposed to be working your music, you're fucked and that's basically what happened with those records in my mind.

It's a shame, and it put Elton off of making those kinds of records, which is what he does most naturally with the band we have now with me, Nigel (Olsson), Matt Bissonette, Kim Bullard, and John Mahon.

Ah, Matt Bissonette. I remember him from David Lee Roth and Joe Satriani.

Yeah, I've known him and his brother Gregg for years. When Bob Birch passed away, Matt was the first guy I thought of, and some of the band had him over, and he had no clue about what we do. He's had a very good gig with Rick Springfield for like twelve, thirteen years that was comfortable.

I told him we travel at a ridiculous rate and we play very long sets each night, and if you're up for gigging five nights a week, the job is yours. And he told me turning down a gig with Elton John and the band wasn't a very good idea, so he joined and he's been here ever since.

Who were some of the musicians who influenced you when you were getting started?

I had many influences. When I was young it was Elvis Presley and Buddy Holly. I had two sisters who were like ten and twelve years older than me, so I would hear them playing this music and I was like, "Wow!" I loved it, and Scotty Moore who was Elvis's guitar player was big to me. I knew I was always going to do this. Music was in me and I always thought it was something I should do.

I played violin for a few years as a youth and that really prepared me for getting my fingers used to the guitar right away. Hank Marvin of the Shadows was another big influence for me. He was my first main player that I loved. The Beatles and the Rolling Stones, of course, were very big. I still think the world of George Harrison. George always played the right thing. Instinctively he played what was right for the song. He took a long time to get his parts together and he was amazing, as was Keith Richards. To get to meet those guys later on was quite a trip.

Then I got into acoustic guitar because I really wanted to get into the meat and potatoes of guitar and finger picking and open tuning. There was a Scottish folk singer/guitarist named Archie Fisher who was a wonderful player who really influenced me. He was contemporary as well as traditional. I was always into music that was good, whether it was guitar, banjo, or mandolin. That in turn made me a different kind of guitar player. Players like Bert Jansch, John Renbourn, and John Martyn—all these guys were very different players. Getting to see these guys play and then play with them was such a thrill for me.

There was also a guy named Barney McKenna who was in the Dubliners, and he unfortunately passed away about four years ago. Barney was just a batshit banjo player—truly unbelievable—and he was a huge influence on me. His banjo was tuned like a fiddle and it was tuned an octave down, but the spacing was still the same; it was tuned in fifths. It was very different from the guitar and made me learn a different form of music and playing. I mean, that whole Gaelic thing is in my blood anyway. I got to jam with him a few times, and it was right around that time that I was asked to do a session with Elton in 1971.

And you had done a few albums with Magna Carta by that point, correct?

Yeah, I had been with Magna Carta for a few years. We had a lot of fun playing all these esoteric songs with banjo, mandolin, acoustic guitars, and such. I was actually using a violin bow on electric guitar not knowing that Jimmy Page had been doing that, and this was 1969. It wasn't like it was something I was copying; I was doing this on my own.

Anyway, when I got the call from Elton, it was just to do an acoustic guitar part. They had tried Mike Chapman and Mick Ronson and others and they hadn't gotten it yet, so I got the call and this was mainly to play on the title track of the *Madman on the Water* album. Gus Dudgeon [*the producer, who had also worked with Magna Carta*] knew me and put my name forth and brought me into the studio. I heard the song and asked, "What am I supposed to do on this?" So, I just played what came into my head and they said, "That's what we were looking for." We proceeded to do "Tiny Dancer" and "Holiday Inn" where I played mandolin and that was that. Then I got the call asking if I'd like to be part of the touring band with Nigel Olsson and Dee Murray. Elton really wanted a rock 'n' roll band and didn't want to do just lushly orchestrated things and ballads, so I made the band a trio behind Elton and this was in January 1972 and it was the beginning of the whole thing.

I was kind of mystified why Elton wanted somebody like me in his band. He was an up-and-coming rock star and that was quite obvious to anyone and I thought he'd want to go with someone more established, but he saw something in me I wasn't aware of. He's a very shrewd guy. Everyone was asking him, "What are you doing getting this Scottish folkie in your band"? He kept saying, "You just wait and see" and he was absolutely right.

The album Don't Shoot Me, I'm Only the Piano Player *has some songs on there with great guitar playing that don't get a lot of attention like "Elderberry Wine" and "Midnight Creeper," which has a nice Stones sound to it.*

Yeah, I love that album. I've pretty much loved every Elton John album I've played on, but "Midnight Creeper" was a lot of fun. I was going for fun riffs that nobody else was really doing at that time and "Elderberry Wine" was great. It was like, "Let's double track this rhythm guitar part and we'll make it really funky and vari-speed it."

That became a trick we would use a lot in the future. I had a lot of fun in those days. "Mercy and the Criminal" was a major track for us as well. It was basically a blues song and the guitar solo on that song was on the live take, which was the second take overall. I double tracked the solo because we all loved it so much since it was off the wall. And then I put an octave below the following week, when we got back to London. Paul Buckmaster wrote a string part around my guitar solo, which was kinda cool. It gave me a lot of confidence to carry on with what I was doing because everybody seemed to like what I was playing.

One of the things I've admired about your playing so much through the years is your ideas. Different arrangements and, like you say, different octaves were in there and double tracking where you wouldn't expect it. For example, there's an odd harmony on "Candle in the Wind" where you add a guitar harmony along with the vocal.

The original version, correct?

Yeah, from Goodbye Yellow Brick Road*.*

Elton wanted some acoustic parts and then he wanted some electric parts and he had a riff in mind and I thought, "Oh, that's the cheesiest thing I've ever heard." Then I played it and it worked and I said, "Oh shit, he's right." And since that day I've listened to him. He loves guitar. He can't play it to save his life, but he comes up with some great guitar ideas. He loves the fact that he can suggest a riff to me and that I understand what he means. There's an excitement in that. He really enjoys that I can pick up on what he's talking about and then make it come to life. It's really a lot of fun.

The song "Goodbye Yellow Brick Road" is one of my favorites. My band used to cover that, and not all that well, but there are so many chord changes in that damn song!

There are so many chord changes in all the songs that Elton writes!

The writing is baffling at times in terms of the complexities.

Like you say, there's the song "Goodbye Yellow Brick Road." I defy most guitar players to have any idea what we are really doing on that song. It's really absurd. That's because Elton is such a great piano player and that writing comes to him naturally. My job is to make all that work and that's why I used a Leslie cabinet to get different tones and qualities to work in conjunction with the piano. I used to take the piss out of him and say, "Can't you just write a damn song in A or E for Christ's sake"?

For example, he wrote "Candle in the Wind" in E because I had been berating him so much about writing songs in B flat and A flat and D flat. I'd say, "Fuck man, I'm a guitar player. Can't you play in a regular key?" In retrospect it made me a more rounded player and I had to work harder, so his writing really made me have a different idea about open tuning like on "Rocket Man." That song was in B flat and we decided to tune the acoustic guitars to an open B flat chord and the result was just phenomenal. When the guitars come in on the chorus, it's like holy shit! They just sparkle, you know? I'm a big fan of that idea.

I guess I understood what Keith Richards was doing with the Rolling Stones on "Brown Sugar" with that open G tuning. I've used that a lot like on "The Bitch is Back" with that open G tuning. The difference is, on that I also used two low G's where Keith uses one G and clips the bottom string off.

I was going to ask about "The Bitch is Back" because it sounds like there are several guitars doing different things on there and it's just an amazing arrangement.

Yeah, there were two direct tracks right into the console and there were two dirty tracks and a monster filthy track and Dee played his bass through my Pignose and we added the phasing and, voila, there you go!

"Funeral for a Friend/Love Lies Bleeding" is just an epic gargantuan and I cannot get enough of that piece no matter how many times it gets played on FM rock radio or anywhere else.

We still open with it. We actually dropped it for several years, but we've brought it back for the last few tours and it's so much fun to play. As soon as people hear the wind and the bells they start freaking out and you also get chills on the stage where it's dark with the dry ice and smoke. People tend to love it.

Your guitar playing on that is outrageously good.

Oh, thank you!

No, thank you! It's just something else. That song is what truly made me an Elton John fan as a young kid because even though I loved songs such as "Daniel" and "Your Song" and "Rocket Man" here was something colossal and progressive I could sink my teeth into and absorb. It was pure progressive rock with touches of fusion and a side of the band few knew of.
On top of that, the chemistry of the Elton John Band with you, Dee, and Nigel, and the way the instruments were mixed, made it outstanding. The chemistry was fantastic.

We did all the overdubs. We were a true quartet, and I did all the guitar overdubs whether it was acoustic, electric, slide, lead, rhythm, mandolin, banjo, etc. Elton loves playing mellotron, so we had some of that and organ, which he didn't really like playing, and he played synthesizers for a while as well.

It's funny what you were saying about the prog rock aspect. I was really into that because I loved John McLaughlin and the Mahavishnu Orchestra, and on *Honkey Chateau* I suggested getting Jean-Luc Ponty, and he came to the studio and we had a blast. We were able to bring in our own influences and that's the side of me that came out in our band.

I think one of the problems with guitar per se is that guitarists frequently copy licks and styles of other guitarists. For me I did not want to do that because I felt it had been done already, so why not do my own shit? An innocent coincidence was on "Have Mercy on the Criminal" where the intro sounded like "Layla" by Derek and the Dominoes with Eric Clapton. It's ironic because I hadn't heard "Layla" yet. It's a different tempo and vibe, so it's not the same, but it was amusing.

As for my playing, I was so determined not to copy anyone else. I just wanted to play my way, in my style, in order to give the band a different identity.

It's not an easy thing to accomplish as far as your own style. There are the same notes and strings and chords and to create one's own identity with the instrument is quite an achievement.

I've been very fortunate. When there's a song as great as "Candle in the Wind" you've got a great starting point. Elton writes really fast and he's sitting there with Bernie's lyrics at the piano and I have my guitar and we can get a song done in fifteen minutes, maybe even five or ten minutes. It's ludicrous the way we work, how quickly it happens. That's mainly because Bernie Taupin is a brilliant lyricist and then Elton is a brilliant piano player and it's just a magical thing really. I guess Elton, I, Dee, and Nigel was one of those things that was meant to happen.

John Lennon was hanging around our band in 1974 and I was very fortunate to hang with him at that time, and he said, "As far as I'm concerned what you guys are doing is the best stuff since our band." It was like, "Fuck, this is John Lennon saying this"! He started coming to gigs and playing with us. He hadn't been playing live very much and he was very intrigued by the way we were playing. The guy was tremendous and we played about six or seven songs with him at Madison Square Garden, which was really fun. To get that kind of admiration and recognition from someone you admire like that and from your peers or people you idolize, that inspires a lot of confidence obviously.

It's almost all you need really, you know?

The danger there is to sit back and say, "I'm fucking great." That's when it all ends. The trick is to basically go with and say thank you very much and move on to the next thing, which is what we've done. We've been writing and creating all these years through different styles and lineups and albums and I don't regret any of it. Some of it was shit obviously, but I don't regret it at all. This new record remarkably reminds me of what we did in the mid-'70s. I know Elton is thrilled with it. It's what he should've been doing all along in my opinion.

About a year ago he said to me, "I'm not going to write any more pop songs, that's not me anymore." And I said, "Well, why would you do that? You're a major pop star and a rock legend so why would you do that and turn your back on that style that's made you a household name?" He told me, "I'm too old." And I said, "Fuck that; you still play as well as anybody."

You know he is still one of the greatest piano players out there and I have worked with some of the best, like Chick Corea and Herbie Hancock and David Paich and Steve Porcaro of Toto and James Newton-Howard, and they are all great players, but they are all in awe of Elton because he brings it in such a way that is natural and not contrived at all. Nobody knows how he does it.

Being here so close to Philadelphia, it shouldn't be a surprise that "Philadelphia Freedom" is one of my very treasured Elton John songs. I find it interesting that it is the only song credited to the Elton John Band.

Yeah, that kinda happened because we were such a good band and had a vibe, but we gave a little credence that is was the Elton John Band. The cool thing about it was that it was a nod to Philadelphia and a nod to his good friend Billie Jean King, who is also my dear friend. Her tennis team was called the Philadelphia Freedoms, so he asked Bernie to write the song based off of that.

It's amazing too, because the song is so misinterpreted as a song for the Bicentennial of 1976, which was a major event in Philly, but the song was a #1 hit in 1975!

Many times Elton has been unfairly criticized for jumping on the bandwagon when in fact he's created something new. It gets my goat sometimes because he is so pure in his love of what he does. Someone will hand him a set of lyrics from Bernie, sit down at the piano, and, as I said earlier, he will have a song done in ten minutes. It's very much a soulful thing that has been misinterpreted over the years.

Critics would say, oh he's going to do glam rock now, or this, or that, or musical theatre, which is hilarious because when we did *The Lion King* soundtrack in 1994, all of a sudden everyone wanted a song in a film like that. Later on, when we started the Las Vegas shows, which were a massive success, everyone else hopped on board yet again and started copying Elton.

And, on "Philadelphia Freedom," some people said it was Elton doing Philly soul, which I never agreed with as once again the arrangements are so wonderful and truly Elton and not someone else. The strings and that jangly guitar going through the chorus are also great, just like on "Don't Go Breaking My Heart" where these little guitar fills come out of each chorus leading the song back to the verses, and it is those musical moments that stick in my head so much. Most people hear a great pop song and I do too, but there's just so much going on there in all the detail that it is anything but a simple pop song.

It's funny because a lot of people that say the phrase "a simple pop song" don't get it. Do you know how fucking hard it is to write a hit song?

Very hard!

If it was that easy, everyone would be doing it. A lot of bands maybe stick to one method if they've had one hit and we've never done that.

Not even close!

"Crocodile Rock" for example way back when, that was our tribute to rock music from the '60s and it was totally misinterpreted! I think Pat Boone might've even fucking sued us for "Speedy Gonzalez" or something. Anyway, the licks were a bit of Duane Eddy and there was some Scotty Moore. We were just paying tribute to some of our favorite music and people were like they've sold out. Okay, whatever. I think sometimes that can be the hardest part to ignore that criticism.

In a way we've had the last laugh because we enjoy it all and appreciate it so much more now. We're all reasonably together; I stopped using alcohol about five-and-a-half years ago and Elton's been sober for twenty years, so it's better. We realized if we carried on the way we were going it was going to be really dangerous. So, we just thought if we're gonna do this 'til we drop, we better be able to handle it. Our shows are long, since we play around two-and-a-half hours or 2 hours, 45 minutes, so you have to be healthy now.

One of the best albums you guys did was Blue Moves *in 1976. The guitar playing was tremendous on songs like "Crazy Water," "One Horse Town," and the fusion of "Out of the Blue."*

Oh yeah, that was a lot of fun! At that point Caleb Quaye was back in the band on guitar and we had such a good time. We called ourselves the "tapestry session" because it was our job to make things shine and sparkle. It's always great to have another guitar player to bounce off of and Caleb and I are great friends as well. John Jorgenson is another good example of that. He is a monster player. I also get to hear all my parts live that way whether they were double tracked or layered a certain way or another instrument was on there like mandolin. *Blue Moves* was a lot of fun, man.

The album got criticized at the time but the musicianship was stellar. There was only one hit, but so what?

That's right, what was the hit?

"Sorry Seems to be the Hardest Word."

Okay, yeah and that was really only a hit in France. In fact, the first time we played it there, they threw vegetables at us.

Which begs the question: Who the hell brings vegetables to a rock concert?

Angry French people who don't want to hear ballads! [Laughs] An album usually isn't about the hit singles. If you remember *Captain Fantastic and the Brown Dirt Cowboy*, that really only had one hit, which was "Someone Saved My Life Tonight" and what an unlikely hit that was.

Yeah, it's almost seven minutes long!

It was very long and it's not overworked. It's also a very deep, emotional song. That album was great. You can clearly hear the other instrumentation behind the piano and vocals. The backgrounds on that album and *Goodbye Yellow Brick Road* were really, really great.

And, around 1977, you formed a band called China and put out a really cool album. A song called "One Way Ticket" was awesome on that album. I assume why it disappeared was the fact that Elton put the band back together for a tour (his last for some time as it turned out) and there was no way or no time to promote it properly?

That's exactly what happened! It was me and James Newton-Howard, and James remains one of my best friends to this day and I've done a lot of playing on some of his movie scores. He realized back then I'm done with the whole touring thing and life on the road, so the fact that the band was songs by me and him and he didn't want to do it anymore, that was pretty much it. We didn't set out to do anything commercial obviously. As a matter of fact, it was us pretty much saying, "I defy you to buy this record"! [Laughs]. Elton co-produced the album and he loved that James and I were doing a record together. But yeah, the commitments we had and James not wanting to tour led to a quick end there.

And then in 1978 you joined Alice Cooper for a while.

I did indeed. Two years, and we had a blast. Oh man, did we have all kinds of fun!

I can only imagine! [Laughs]

It was great to play all those classic songs on stage.

Your guitar playing blended in very well with those songs and the albums you were on. No doubt Alice went through horrible times but he's come out of it a total champion.

Alice is doing great and what an intelligent man. He's a super funny guy. I don't believe rock 'n' roll is brain surgery. You gotta have fun. I don't wanna be pulling my hair over something complex. It's not worth it to me.

You've also gotten in on the writing on a number of songs with Elton through the years including one of his all-time classics from the '80s "I Guess That's Why They Call It the Blues." Do you have any recollections of how that song came to be?

I had actually seen the lyric in advance. I flew from Monserrat to Los Angeles and that's quite a long trip with several plane flights and we got drunk and missed our connection, so we had down time and I saw the lyrics from Bernie for the album (*Too Low for Zero*), which didn't happen all that often, and I saw that song and went, "Oh, man that is such a great lyric." When it came to recording that song Elton said, "I think we should actually write this one for guitar." So I said, "Sure." And the two of us wrote in twenty minutes in the studio and started recording it straight away. I came up with a couple of the hook lines that come in there and it was like, "Wow, this is great." Amazingly to me, it was like the third single from the album and even though there were some other great songs and one big one I can't remember just now…

"I'm Still Standing"?

Right, "I'm Still Standing." I always thought of this one as a great song and a big hit, which it finally became. Live I think it should be gentler. We tend to make it too heavy-handed live. Maybe one day we will play a small venue and get it the way I envision it. If you listen to the song, it's quite beautiful and gentle. There's some nice production and guitars in there. It's not a Gospel song; it's a cool little track. Over the years, we've written about fifteen to twenty songs together.

In 1989, the Sleeping with the Past *album had a stunning song called "Sacrifice" on it.*

Oh, what a great song.

Do you still play it live?

Only in Europe and the UK, but not here in the States.

It was a big single here making the Top 20, so it's not obscure or anything.

No, it's not but it was much bigger there. Elton has this thing where he will say, "We will only play 'Skyline Pigeon' in South America and we will only play 'Sacrifice' in Europe." "Sacrifice" was his only #1 in the UK, which is hard to believe. In fact, for decades, Elton was much bigger in the US than in Britain.

I always found that odd.

We did too. I think maybe there was backlash from the Brits because we were from there and we made it bigtime in the States. Now it's great though. It's wonderful over there and has been for at least twenty years or more.

I'll tell you something about "Sacrifice" that's quite funny…we did it in Denmark in the midst of winter, which in Denmark is pretty brutal. I was fast asleep and it was around 2:00 a.m. I was woken up by one of the roadies who said, "Elton needs you in the studio. He really wants you in there now." I'm half out of it, and I threw a parka and snow boots on and trudged over to the studio and Elton is waiting for me and says, "Sit down and put the headphones on." He had a keyboard set up by Freddie Mandel with some cool sounds and Guy Babylon had just joined the band, so we had some really cool things for that period of time sound wise.

The '80s were not my favorite time for production with bombastic sounds and such, but when I heard "Sacrifice" for the first time that night at two in the morning, I was just like, wow that's just an amazing song.

And there are those beautiful little guitar fills on there. It's you just knowing where to fill in the spaces and leave other spaces open.

Thank you! That was a Hank Marvin thing, if you know who he was.

Absolutely, from the Shadows. Many have cited him as an influence in this book already.

That was my tribute to Hank. If I'm going to do a tribute to a player I admire, it will crop up somewhere and people like yourself who know guitar players will pick up on it. I actually initially had parts that were more than what ended up there and we chopped it in half. It made more sense and more laid back and that was the producer Chris Thomas and Elton that did that. They said, "We love it all, but if we play just the first part, we don't need any more notes than that." And it worked out very well; you learn something new every day.

Well, I thank you very much for your music and this conversation. It was a real pleasure.

I hope you have success with this venture. I think this is a very worthwhile thing you are doing and it's always great when somebody gets a bit of space in a book or whatever that lets people know a little bit more about them.

I'm actually finishing up a documentary on Elton that I did with my son Tam. It's about the early days of Elton until his retirement in 1977. It has a lot of rare, unseen concert footage and interviews and such. Hopefully it will be done in about a year and we have a test screening coming up.

Now that sounds excellent because that is Elton's golden era.

Then this will be right up your alley.

And what guitars have you preferred through the years?

I love my Les Pauls; mainly my three pickup Deluxe custom model from 1972. Also, I have a Fender Telecaster which almost plays itself! There's also my old faithful Yamaha FG-140 I bought in London in 1969 and it sounds better than ever, thanks to the guys at the Yamaha Custom Shop fixing it up for me.

Recommended solo: "Funeral for a Friend/Love Lies Bleeding" from *Goodbye Yellow Brick Road* with Elton John (1973)
Further info: www.daveyjohnstone.com and www.eltonjohn.com
Photo credit: Melanie Escombe

CHAPTER 28

Terry Kath

(Born Terry Alan Kath, January 31, 1946, Chicago, IL; died January 23, 1978)

Mere words do not do the legacy of Terry Kath justice. I will try, however. In fact, Terry is actually the inspiration for me even doing this book.

Chicago was a septet of truly innovative, brilliant, creative musicians who feared nothing musically. Every band member was integral, but none could equal what Kath brought to the table, with not only his guitar playing but his soulful singing and excellent writing. Terry played in several bands in the '60s leading up to Chicago, including a cover band called the Missing Links, which included several future members of Chicago.

By 1967, the band that became Chicago formed as the Big Thing and then became Chicago Transit Authority in 1968, moving to Los Angeles under the guidance of fellow musician and producer James William Guercio. They would then sign with Columbia Records. The band featured Kath, Robert Lamm (keyboards, vocals), Danny Seraphine (drums), Peter Cetera (bass, vocals), Walt Parazadier (sax, flute), James Pankow (trombone), and Lee Loughnane (trumpet).

Chicago Transit Authority was the band's debut album released in April 1969. A double album, it was an explosion of jazz, rock, hard rock, pop, R&B and freeform music. Initially a slow seller, the album would eventually sell over 2 million in the US. The classic hits were the acoustic pop of "Beginnings," the jazz/pop of "Does Anybody Really Know What Time It Is?" (these were both Top 10 singles but not until several years later), the blistering cover of the Spencer Davis Group's "I'm a Man," and the infectious "Questions 67 and 68."

To prove how much indifference there was to CTA at first, "Beginnings" didn't even chart and "Questions 67 and 68" only hit #71 in 1969, and few people believed a band like CTA could actually reach the mass marketplace. Those knuckleheads in the industry would be proven wrong to the tune of over 100 million albums sold to date.

While all these singles on the album are genius, things reach new heights on the gritty hard rock of "South California Purples," the opening six-and-one-half-minute instrumental "Introduction" and the fourteen minutes of closer "Liberation." Every player shines throughout, but to absorb Kath's playing on these cuts is to truly understand the connection one man can have with his guitar. If that sounds corny, that's fine.

Then there's "Poem 58," perhaps the greatest eight minutes and thirty-five seconds of guitar playing one is likely to ever hear. Each note is ripped away with passion, conviction, and a feel that are undeniable. Just when one thinks it's over, Terry goes for more, and never does this sound like it's for show. No, this is exactly what Kath would do for an audience, his bandmates, his friends, and family. His playing was from within and not for any other reason than to express himself and his passion. It was frightening how good he was, and this was just the debut album!

Oh, and if you want to hear him even further in touch with his instrument, how about "Free Form Guitar" where he annihilates any pretense. Sure, this may sound like a bludgeoning of a guitar with loads of feedback, but closer inspection reveals this to be more of a classical piece in some ways. Kath is using expressionism and testing the limits of the guitar and the listener, but doing so in a musical way that sounds non-musical. It was also done in just one take. To me, *Chicago Transit Authority* just might have the best guitar playing of any album I've ever heard, and this was just the start.

Chicago (commonly referred to as *Chicago II*) was issued in 1970 and was another double album. A Top 5 multi-million seller, it produced a pair of Top 10 hits including the infamous "25 or 6 to 4." Here Kath wails like no tomorrow, laying down one of the most famous guitar solos on a pop hit of all-time, though this was no mere pop song. It goes without saying that this went down tremendously live (and still does), and Kath would always extend the solo. The way the guitars and the horns blend is magnificent and, in fact, Kath had a way of making his guitar at times almost sound like it was the fourth horn in the band as he was that musical.

The seven part, seven song suite "Ballet for a Girl in Buchannon," written by Pankow, was quite an accomplishment and from the suite there were two major hits in the uplifting "Make Me Smile" and the dreary ballad "Colour My World" both sung soulfully and passionately by Kath and "Make Me Smile" has a ripping jazzy solo that showcases more stylistic shifts from Terry. Elsewhere we have "The Road" and "In the Country" to enjoy Terry's playing on and his nine-minute piece "Memories of Love" that shows the man's soul and also goes a very long way to show how diverse his musical tastes and influences were as this is a very mellow, languid piece of music.

In 1971, *Chicago III* was yet another double album with more musical experimentation and extended suites and jams like the first two. It is mind-boggling that any band could create the breadth of material here on the first three albums, essentially six albums of music. "Sing a Mean Tune, Kid" sees Terry in funk, rock, and blues modes with uncanny soloing, and "I Don't Want Your Money" is Terry grasping each note as if it was his last. The album hit #2 and produced hits in "Free" and "Lowdown."

With *Chicago V*, the band shifted towards a more radio-friendly sound, but despite naysayers claiming the band "sold out," nothing could've been further from the truth. True, "Saturday in the Park" was a monster hit, but this album still had daring cuts such as "A Hit by Varese," "State of the Union," and the protest song "Dialogue (Part I & II)," with the latter song a Top 40 single. This was also the first of five straight #1 albums (and *Chicago V* topped the charts for a whopping nine weeks). *Chicago VI* was a mellow affair, but featured such wonderful songs as the haunting "Something in this City Changes People," "Critics Choice," the Kath-sung "Jenny" (about one of his beautiful doggies—woof, woof), the sly funk of "Hollywood" with some great guitar and the spirited, defiant Top 10 hit "Feelin' Stronger Every Day" along with the jazzy ballad "Just You N' Me" (another Top 10 hit). *Chicago VI* is still an album of understated, moody grace.

Percussionist Laudir de Oliveira would now make the band an octet, and 1974's *Chicago VII* returned them to the form of old in some ways, while keeping the current pop gems in focus. The album initially was conceived as a jazz effort, but turned into a mix of the new pop-oriented songs and some seriously involved pieces that ventured towards fusion such as "Aire," "Devil's Sweet," and "Prelude to Aire." Three major hits were accrued with "(I've Been) Searchin' So Long," "Call on Me," and the dreamy acoustic number "Wishing You Were Here" with some of the Beach Boys on backing vocals (Terry played bass and sang incredibly well on this cut, and all the singles went Top 10 except the latter which just missed at #11). Terry's cut "Byblos" was a diversion for the band and shows his creativity and sense of song. Terry also wrote "Song of the Evergreens," which is a mesmerizing cut that seduces the listener into a meditative state before Terry unleashes a furious, fiery solo for several minutes at the end that makes one appreciate his genius all the more (trumpeter Loughnane actually sings this cut, not Terry). This was yet another #1 album.

In 1975, *Chicago VIII* was to be the next chart-topper and produced two more big hits in the nostalgic, humorous almost Randy Newman-sounding "Harry Truman" and the infectious look back at growing up "Old Days." "Old Days" was an effective pop tune, ushered in by Terry's menacing power chords that then give way to the sweeping pop feel of the song, which made the Top 5, cheesy lyrics aside.

This underrated, wonderful album also had rockers such as "Anyway You Want" and the surprising hard rock heaviness of "Hideaway" where we get to hear Terry in yet another setting in which he excels throughout. "Hideaway" is aggressive hard rock and Terry comes up with creative licks and solos, including in the key change. "Ain't it Blue?" allows Kath to sing and lay down some wonderful blues solos in a pop rock/R&B scenario, and then there's "Oh, Thank You Great Spirit" where we hear Terry pay homage in word, voice, and guitar to the late Jimi Hendrix. This seven-minute epic shows the spiritual connection between Terry and his guitar and Hendrix as well. The guitar playing is straight from the soul and cannot be equaled. *Chicago VIII* has some of Kath's very best playing hands down.

Chicago IX was yet another #1 selling over 5 million and it was just a greatest hits album! Then, in 1976, came *Chicago X*. This album caused a divide amongst diehard fans because of "If You Leave Me Now." This orchestrated, string-drenched ballad became a #1 single and won two Grammys. However, it would see the band start to be labeled as soft rock or worse, wimp rock. It's actually a great song, but some in the band, including Kath, weren't thrilled with it. There were two other minor hits, but Terry's opening rocker "Once or Twice" and his eloquent "Hope for Love" are true highlights and proof that the album wasn't all ballads ("Skin Tight" and "Scrapbook" are also winners).

In concert, the band still tore it up on tour as evidenced by their appearance on German TV's popular *Rockpalast* show from February 1977. Terry's playing was as passionate and fiery as ever. *Chicago XI* continued the run of Top 10 Platinum albums and garnered another huge hit with a beautiful song in "Baby, What a Big Surprise." "Little One" was also a minor hit, featuring a soulful, emotional vocal from Terry, which in retrospect, is a tough one to hear each time due to the loss of Terry on January 23, 1978. Even though *Chicago XI* was a patchy effort it wasn't Terry's fault.

The ripping "Takin' It on Uptown" features searing guitar work and some delectable funk riffs (and Terry's killer vocals), while "Mississippi Delta City Blues" opens the album in awesome fashion and Terry's vocals and guitars are from another world. This tune had been played live through the years, and this was the studio debut of it. Perhaps an appropriate closer to the album is "Little One," an orchestrated ballad where Kath uses the depths of his voice almost as though he was saying goodbye, making it a tough one to listen to.

After Terry suddenly passed from an accidental gunshot wound, the rock world was never the same. Chicago is still going strong and has had many phases since, and I remain a fan. The band has also had some incredible guitarists pass through over the years. None, however, could come close to Terry Kath. This man defines soul, passion, and talent, and every day I listen to his music is a much better day.

There are many musicians I admire, way too many to list, but there are so very few who have touched me as emotionally as Terry Kath. A forthcoming documentary about his life by his daughter Michelle was due in 2015 and has been in the works for years [As far as an update, it is hoped to be issued in 2016 and is now complete, but whether it surfaces, I can't say. It is titled: *The Terry Kath Experience: A Documentary*.] Hopefully that film and maybe even this entry here in this book are ways more people can discover and cherish this man's musical legacy. I'd like to think Terry would be pretty damn happy with that.

Recommended solo: "Poem 58" from *Chicago Transit Authority* with Chicago (1969)
Further info: www.terrykath.com
Photo credit: David Dionne
Update: Terry and Chicago were FINALLY inducted into the Rock and Roll Hall of Fame for the class of 2016.

CHAPTER 29

Mark Kendall

(Born April 29, 1957, Loma Linda, CA)

A founding member of Great White, guitarist Mark Kendall established himself as one of the most tasteful players in all of hard rock/heavy metal in the 1980s.

Kendall never gave way to shredding or effects-laden solos during Great White's biggest years and has remained a classy player to this day.

Great White started life in the late '70s in the Los Angeles, California, area as Dante Fox, a name they would thankfully ditch by the early '80s. After releasing an EP in 1983, the band signed to EMI and released their self-titled debut album in 1984 and hit the road opening for Whitesnake and then Judas Priest.

In 1986, *Shot in the Dark* featured a cover of Angel City's "Face the Day" that got some MTV airplay, but it was 1987's *Once Bitten* that saw the band emerge as a successful act both musically and commercially as the album went Platinum. "Rock Me" became a hit single and was all over MTV. This song is where Kendall laid down one of the finest guitar solos of the decade.

A slow burning, seven-minute song (there was also a single edit and a radio edit), there is a quiet intro barely above a whisper with slight touches of crystal-clear blues fills with harmonica and hi-hat leading to the seductive verses driven largely by a throbbing bass line and Jack Russell's vocals. The chorus kicks things up before it drops back down again and, when it comes, that incredibly tasteful solo steeped in the blues, it's a master class in tone, texture, and taste. Each note is perfect, and the solo is very lyrical. This was not typical guitar playing in the late '80s. Clearly, this is a player who understands playing for the song matters most. "Save Your Love" was also a hit from the album.

In 1989, the album *...Twice Shy* went Double Platinum thanks to the Top 5 smash "Once Bitten, Twice Shy," a cover of an Ian Hunter tune that was a simple groove-based boogie rocker. A Grammy nomination followed as did other hits in "The Angel Song" (which made the Top 30) and the aching blues of "The House of Broken Love" featuring a really sweet set of solos by Kendall, especially the lengthy intro.

Hooked was a Gold album in 1991 and contained the hits "Call It Rock n' Roll" and "Desert Moon" with the latter featuring a strong solo. There's also "Congo Square" a Led Zep-styled seven-minute epic with some bluesy acoustic work and organ and a clean-sounding blues solo where each note speaks, then the next solo is a subtle wah-wah heavy one, and then the third one features more of Mark's usual sounds and ripping solos. Great White had so many rock radio hits because the songs sounded so damn good on the radio. Hooks, riffs, solos at the right place, a full mix and a great rock singer in Jack Russell; it all worked.

Although grunge started taking over and album sales declined beginning with *Psycho City* in 1992, they still scored two more radio faves in "Big Goodbye" and "Old

Rose Motel" which is seven-and-a-half minutes of sophisticated quality mixing blues and rock to perfection. The soloing here is divine and makes this a hotel well worth checking into (I am ashamed at that pun). Add in the pretty piano touches from longtime member/producer Michael Lardie and it's as good as it gets. Just listen to the outro solo—it could go on for hours and still be worthy. The eight minutes of "Love Is a Lie" has some seriously emotional guitar work as well. Despite the grunge-friendly '90s now developing, Great White remained true to their sound: blues-based hard rock all about the guitars and vocals.

The band took a huge departure with 1994's *Sail Away* album, a largely mellow, acoustic affair producing a Top 10 rock radio hit with the title cut and also had "Gone With the Wind" a tune that featured Clarence Clemons of the E. Street band on saxophone. But the tides were changing and 1996's *Let It Rock* came and went but was a solid return to hard rock. In 1999, *Can't Get There from Here* deserved more attention but did feature another Top 10 radio hit in the crunchy "Rollin' Stoned."

The group disbanded in 2000 due to ongoing conflicts and a mess followed with Russell using the band name for solo gigs in clubs, and a tragic fire occurred due to pyrotechnics being foolishly utilized at a club gig in Providence, Rhode Island, on February 20, 2003. Guitarist Ty Longley perished as did over 100 people. Great White had nothing to do with this, but leave it to the media to get the facts wrong; it was a Russell solo show not the real band.

The real Great White re-formed in 2006 and toured heavily before issuing *Rising* in 2009. Russell's combative attitude, health, and substance issues led to his absence in 2010. Several name fill-in singers were used until Terry Ilous (formerly of XYZ) took over for good. *Elation* was issued in 2012 and went for a slightly more blues-oriented approach and a new album is slated for 2015 as Great White continue to survive in sometimes murky waters, but often swim above other acts of their time. This is largely due to the excellence of guitarist Mark Kendall, a fine player indeed.

Speaking of which, he's also a fine dude. In fact, one of the nicest, down-to-earth guys you could meet. We spoke in November 2014 and had a blast.

Who were some of the guys that were an influence in terms of guitar playing?

When I first started playing guitar I was just interested in music in general. It was always around our house because my Mom was a singer and my Dad played trumpet, so that tuned my ear. I used to hum along with tunes and what made me want to play originally was this band in a garage I used to watch through my side window. My dad then got me a guitar and I was able to learn my way around the neck very quickly.

I was able to pick things up really well—don't ask me how. The Yardbirds was the first band I learned a song by, which was "For Your Love." And as far as players go, once I started picking out actual players in my early teenage years, my dad got me three albums that solidified it: Cream's *Disraeli Gears,* the Jimi Hendrix Experience *Are You Experienced?* and the Doors' *Strange Days.* I would sit there and hum along and figure out the melodies, which I had done even with older albums my parents had, and songs like "The Girl from Ipanema" and Elvis tunes. I was always focused on melodies at first—not players.

So you were more melody and song based rather than emulating some guitar hero or something.

Yeah, it was much more the melody for me and even vocal lines. The first guitar player who I wigged out over was Carlos Santana. He was the guy who I watched and said there's nobody better anywhere than this guy, ya know? Seeing the way he squeezed notes made me form my first band and all we did was Santana songs. Johnny Winter completely floored me, too. He really made me want to play and at age fifteen. Billy Gibbons of ZZ Top captivated me because he played with tons of feel, and it wasn't coming from paper. My dad forced me to read music and I ended up relying on my ear far more, although I did learn to read.

Yeah, I just think in any situation, if you have a monster ear, which I do think I have thanks to my family, if I was a monster sight-reader as well, the opportunities would be endless. I started discovering more and more players though and I started to pick things out and figure out what they were doing and their styles.

I blame my music teacher and it was the only formal lesson I ever had. He was teaching me things like "Tom Dooley" and I hated it, so I decided not to be a theory guy and turned to Cream and Hendrix and not "Tom Dooley!" So, that pushed me in that direction that I chose. Even when I was in 4th grade, I wheeled my amp with a friend of mine and we played "Wipeout," "Pipeline," "Secret Agent Man," and "Gloria," and I actually had picked up those songs by hearing them at that young age.

I can tell because the solo on "Rock Me" is so tasteful from the clean start, the eruption in the mid-section and the tasty fills and use of dynamics throughout; it sounds every bit as good today as 1987. Did you feel that was a special one then?

Actually, I did feel really good about that one because I've always been into dynamics. For instance, those guys that play 64th notes, that's really the only look that they give you and that's never done much for me. They leave themselves with nowhere to go. I feel that fast flurry of notes should only be used as a surprise. If that's all you do, yes, the person listening might go, wow that was intense. But four minutes later, it's like what else are you going to do—just this all night?

I've always been fascinated by a beautiful melody and there's no rule that says you can't do that as opposed to speed and flash. I hate to use this as an example because it's so overplayed, but listen to "Stairway to Heaven." It does live forever because it has so much melody attached to it. If it's Speedy Joe flailing away super-fast, that's not going to be remembered in twenty years—maybe not even twenty weeks. To each his own, I mean, some of those speedy guys are so much better than me, but it's not my thing.

I'd rather hear guys like Terry Kath, Billy Gibbons, Paul Kossoff, Rory Gallagher—it was all so very real and from the depths of their souls.

Rory Gallagher. Oh man, I saw that cat live. He was a monster!

He's the first act I ever saw in concert. I was blown away and I was just thirteen years old.

I met Stevie Ray Vaughan just after he had gotten sober and I saw a video from when he had just gotten sober around 1989 and watching him sweat and leave it all out there, it just doesn't get any more real than that. He's playing things because that's what's inside of him at that moment. When someone has that amount of feel in their playing I just wanna cry. There was one part where he was talking about his sobriety and his words and the way he delivered them…it was a breakdown moment underneath all of it where he said, "I don't want to preach to anybody but those drugs and booze will do nothing but take you down," and there was just as much feel in his voice on that topic as his playing that night—that's as real as it gets, man.

I really do believe it comes from within with these people. I sat down and had a heart-to-heart with Billy Gibbons of ZZ Top and the way the man speaks, you can just tell he has this gift of feel.

That passion is so obvious in that playing, not that a flashy fast guy doesn't have passion either. It's just that I prefer the guy who pours it all out in a way that translates to the common guy rather than the fancier one. All styles are worthy though with that being said. I mean, your solo in "House of Broken Love" is quite emotional and real, you know?

It truly is to each his own in terms of taste and style. I always try to play for the song and not my ego. I ask what can I do for the song and make it work and save the ego for a solo album [laughs].

Another reason I dig your playing and Great White is because you are far more of a hard rock band than a metal act despite being played all the time on Headbanger's Ball.

Yeah, we are a hard rock band with blues overtones in it. I think it's been easy to lump us in with hair metal and things like that were the fashion. If you just listen to the music and put the look aside, I think you will hear our influences: blues, hard rock. Michael Lardie our keyboard player is influenced by Elton John and Billy Joel and our drummer loves metal, and I love Johnny Winter, Alvin Lee, and Billy Gibbons. And when that all gets put together and you hear us play in a room you're gonna go, "Well, I hear some blues, some rock, some hard rock, some piano"—there it all is.

And you guys had nothing to do at all with hair metal.

I always tried to tell journalists when they want to lump us in with hair metal, like Poison or whatever, I'm just like, "Well, we do have long hair and the same guy that made clothes for Nikki Sixx made my clothes, but my hair never wrote a song." And, what is all the '70s hard rock called? Bell bottom rock? And is the '60s bead rock or bong hair rock? You know what I mean?

That's just an easy way out of not learning the music and needing a clichéd label, that's all. It's short-mindedness and nothing more.

Yeah, it is an easy escape. I can see why they would call some of the stuff that everybody was writing at that time musically and talk about the music in one way, but to call all of it from 1980–1990 hair metal is weak.

When you scored that massive hit with Ian Hunter's "Once Bitten, Twice Shy" was that intended as a single, or recorded as filler, or maybe a b-side?

Totally by accident! What happened was we had the album *Once Bitten*…which of course had "Rock Me," and when it came time for the next album we decided to call it …*Twice Shy*. Everything was good; we had all the songs and we were recording it and Izzy Stradlin' from Guns N' Roses, who our manager Alan Niven also managed then came to Alan with that song and said, "Hey, these guys should do this Ian Hunter song."
It was not a Mott the Hoople song as a lot of people think, but an Ian Hunter solo tune that got in the charts in the UK [*It actually got to #14 there in 1975*]. It was an unknown song here in the States and Alan dug it, and we thought it was a good rock 'n' roll tune so we did it and put it on the record. When it was all done, Capitol insisted it was the first single. We didn't feel bad about it because we also had "Lady Red Light" and all those other good songs to back it up, but we had no idea it would take off.
That song is kind of a blessing though as we made it our own and we didn't sing it the same way in the chorus and we gave it a little different look. I think he was happy, because, at that time, he really wasn't doing anything and I knew his sound man and we had borrowed his drum riser back when we opened for Judas Priest, so that all was kind of a coincidence. So we met him and went out to dinner with him back then, around 1984, and now a few years later in 1989 we do his song and he made so much money that he got a band together and was back on MTV and recording and touring again and he told Alan that at his shows he said people were coming up to him asking why he was playing that Great White song! [Laughs]

Well, understandably. You really made it your own boogie rock classic.

It was out of the blue, but every band has a story like that—you just never know how the stars will line up. Some guy says you should do this song and there ya go.

To be honest, with the shades and wild blond hair I used to think you LOOKED like Ian Hunter!

[Laughs] Ha ha ha—ya got me there!

How much of a role did MTV play in your success in the '80s?

You were basically getting a free commercial every time. They were playing us so much, and when you get that kind of attention…I mean our fans were just glued to MTV and the MTV Unplugged thing, that was just kinda out of the blue, too. We weren't really playing any Zeppelin songs in our set, but Jack was very good at mimicking things and he really nailed Robert Plant very well.

The night before the show, our manager called and told me to learn "Babe, I'm Gonna Leave You," and I told him this isn't just some simple song—there's lots of intricate picking and a significant solo and a few different changes and stuff.

This was the night before the taping?

Yeah! And I asked if we were going to get a chance to rehearse it, and he said, "Just play it in the dressing room or something." I was like, "You have to be kidding me!" So we pulled it off and I was pretty nervous going through all the changes in my head, and I was glad to get it over with. And, of course, MTV put that video of "Babe, I'm Gonna Leave You" in massive rotation! Then we started getting tortured by fans to do more Zeppelin songs, so the one year we went in and recorded a bunch of Zeppelin songs, including ones we'd never even played growing up, like "In the Light" and others that even Zeppelin didn't play live. And we didn't put it out until about six or seven years later as *Great Zeppelin: A Tribute to Led Zeppelin*. We tried to re-create the songs exactly as they would do it and it came out great.

On the Sail Away *album you had Clarence Clemons from Bruce Springsteen's E. Street band on there. How cool was that?*

Right, our manager at the time was also Clarence's manager and he was around the studio and put a sax solo on a song for that album and he played live with us once. Talk about feel, that guy could squeeze notes out of that sax better than anyone. I couldn't believe how incredible he was.

I didn't know he had also played live with you guys, that's awesome.

Yeah, it actually was the night that my son was born—my second boy—I went straight to the gig afterwards and he played with us on a few songs that night. That was a real treat.

With the current lineup and the new album Elation, *how are you feeling these days about everything?*

It's been about five years now with Terry Ilous (formerly with XYZ) and we love the guy. He was filling in for a while, and when Jack couldn't return, we stayed with it and now that we have a better feel for him, we are writing the next album in a different way. He melds into my guitar really well and has some great blues chops. If I had to compare him, I'd say he has a mix of Glenn Hughes and Paul Rodgers in there—very bluesy. When we play those blues-rock riffs, that's where he really shines. We've been writing a lot of songs and we will have a new album at the beginning of the New Year.

And what are the guitars you still play after all these years?

I'm still fond of the Fenders; I like the Stratocasters and Telecasters. What I'm playing right now is a Les Paul I use low-output vintage pickups. Over the years I get everything I need from my volume knobs on my guitar. I don't have a trillion stomp-boxes anymore. I just rely on my fingers and use that for the dynamics. I want the guitars to sound musical when I roll off the volume and get the natural sustain when I crank it up.

It feels and sounds more natural, rather than going through the pedals. It's just where I'm at now. I do have some old Marshall amps that have that true tube saturation as opposed to the pre-amp thing where it's too buzzy. I keep trying to improve my sound and experiment. I was at this vault in Reno checking things out and the guy told me Billy Gibbons had been there for four hours just working on pedals to find that sound, and it's so inspirational to know this master player in his sixties is still willing to keep searching for that perfect sound and hasn't just settled.

Do you still have that shark guitar?

Yes! I have it right here with me. It needs a little work as far as the way it plays, but it's a cool novelty guitar and fun.

Who made that for you?

That was Ed Roman, who passed away a few years ago. A guy named Michael Risinger built that for me, and just before Ed died, he was going to have a reality show and I was going to be on the first episode about that guitar. The fans always ask me where that guitar is and I have to tell the story over and over again how I had given it to Dick Clark years ago for his Hard Rock Café in Los Angeles and it's been moved around to Reno and Hawaii and all over. When a guy like that asks you if you could donate your guitar, you say yes—I mean, that's Dick Clark you know?

I hope you've never seen the film Great White, *which is a laughable piece of crap that was such a blatant ripoff of Jaws that it was pulled from theaters after just one week in 1982. It's wretched and the effects look like they cost less than a can of Chef Boyardee ravioli!*

No way, I've never seen it!

And Vic Morrow is even in it doing a horrible Robert Shaw impression.

Vic Morrow? Oh no!

You need to see it man.

Well I certainly will now, because everyone used to think my dad was Vic Morrow. When I was little we went to this Italian restaurant and got the food free because they thought he was Vic Morrow!

How ironic is that then?

Very ironic! In *Jaws* of course, they had so many problems with the mechanical shark because it kept breaking down in the salt water.

Yeah, Spielberg said he hated his life because it was such an ordeal getting the shark to work and look convincing and they had so many problems filming on the ocean with sailboats getting in certain shots in the background and such. The movie remains a masterpiece though and I've seen it over 100 times.

One of the reasons it works so well is what you don't see, as opposed to what you would've if the shark operated better. It worked out even more that way and ended up like a Hitchcock film on the sea.

Just like Halloween and John Carpenter's direction.

Another great example because it follows him around with the camera and his face is rarely in full vision the first hour.

Exactly! I insist you endure Great White *because it is a pile of shark droppings that will provide serious laughs—trust me.*

I will, I will!

This has been great, I appreciate you talking to me—I am sure we will hang out in the future.

We will definitely hook up brother, I will get a hold of you if/when we hit the Philly area, my pleasure, and I enjoyed it!

Oh yeah, one final stupid question: if you could rename a Great White song or album after a cat, what would you come up with?

Oh man. How about "Felix Is Coming"? That's the best I've got.

That works because I have a cat named Felix!

CHAPTER 30

Dave Kilminster

(Born David Kilminster, January 25, 1962, England)

British guitarist Dave Kilminster played both piano and guitar as a youth and became proficient at both. Fast forward to 1991 and he was named Guitarist of the Year by *Guitarist Magazine* and he went into teaching at various academies.

Kilminster is known for his skills as both a left-handed and right-handed guitarist. A natural lefty, he badly hurt his wrist go-carting (!) and then began playing right-handed. His success teaching and doing sessions, as well as instructional videos, started getting him some much-deserved attention.

In 1999, Kilminster became part of the short-lived band Qango, which also included John Wetton (bass/vocals), Carl Palmer (drums) of Asia, and keyboardist John Young. A few live dates and the concert recording *Live in the Hood* occurred in 2000 (Wetton and Palmer would eventually reunite in Asia). The few who attended these gigs quickly spread the word about the outstanding, largely unknown guitarist in the band.

By 2002, Kilminster joined Emerson, Lake & Palmer keyboards legend Keith Emerson in his band playing complex guitar patterns on ELP songs in concert that were largely guitar-free in their original form. Kilminster lived up to the task and won recognition for his achievements. He continued playing with Keith until 2006. Not only that, but he guested on guitar for the rare reunion shows of Emerson's legendary progressive rock/neo-classical pre-ELP band the Nice in 2002 and appears on their live album *Vivacitas* from 2003. Kilminster also toured as a member of ex-Uriah Heep and Blackfoot keyboardist Ken Hensley's band in 2003.

In 2006, Dave got a chance to audition for ex-Pink Floyd bassist/vocalist Roger Waters's band. He got the gig and has been with Roger ever since. The 2006-2007 tour saw Pink Floyd's legendary album *Dark Side of the Moon* performed in its entirety, and Dave has been with Roger ever since, alongside fellow guitarists Snowy White and G. E. Smith.

It is on this massive stage where Dave got to let the world at large know what they'd been missing all these years. The *Dark Side* tour was one thing, but the now-infamous tour presenting Floyd's *The Wall* album was quite another. This monstrous undertaking of a tour began in 2010 and concluded in 2013 (yeah, that's a fairly long tour!). The tour cost around $60 million to stage, but seeing as it grossed a paltry $458.6 million, I'd say Roger and the guys did okay.

The show was nothing short of stunning as was the musicianship. The ultimate moment each night, of course, was "Comfortably Numb" where Kilminster would be perched at the top of "the wall" and had the difficult spotlight (and it was very bright and white!) cast upon him whilst performing what is arguably the most famous guitar solo in rock history. The fact that he aced it night after night and somehow remained true to the original, yet added his own inflections, speaks volumes about the man and his gift.

And, to get a taste of Dave's solo career, his albums *Scarlet* (2007) and *...THE TRUTH will set you free...* (2014) are a further example of the outrageous talent and virtuosity on display, not to mention diversity on both acoustic and electric. Oh yeah, he's also a dynamite singer.

He has been teaching, transcribing, and lecturing for years and I can assure you I would fail any of his classes because I would totally be in awe. Dave is also a part of Porcupine Tree leader Steven Wilson's band and was on the road with him again in 2015.

Dave is also a funny, wonderful guy and provided some great quotes in an interview I did with him in September 2014.

Who were some of your influences regarding why you picked up the guitar and your desire to play?

To be honest, there weren't any! I actually come from a long line of pianists, and the sole reason I started playing the guitar was because we didn't have a piano at home... so I would play piano at school, and at my Grandmother's house...but it drove me nuts that when I was at home I had nothing to make music on.... So the guitar was (initially) just a stopgap until I could get a piano!

Of course, later on I discovered Eddie Van Halen, Brian May, Jeff Beck, Pat Travers, etc., and realized that the guitar could be cool too!

What was it like switching from left-handed playing to right-handed? Was it difficult or beneficial?

Initially it was a total pain in the ass! Hahaha.... But in retrospect, I think it's probably a good thing to have the strongest hand (i.e., my left hand) on the fretboard doing all the hard work!

What is your guitar of choice? Is it that lovely "Rose" Suhr guitar?

It depends on what I'm doing I guess.... I have a Tom Anderson drop T with cream P90s that I tend to play a lot at home...and I really got into playing my '88 Les Paul custom in the studio recently! But yeah, "Rose" is the most versatile and musical sounding guitar I have...

You are one of the most intelligent and thoughtful players I've heard and seen. Does your extensive background in teaching and guitar knowledge help in that respect?

Thank you! I guess all the transcriptions and lessons that I've written over the years have sort of help.... But I'm self-taught, so I think I've always had that drive and commitment for knowledge, and to be the best guitarist that I can be.

How did you approach how to play the "Comfortably Numb" solo for The Wall *tour if 2010–2013? That is arguably the most famous guitar solo in rock history. I thought you handled it very well, and it was a highlight of the show. Was it a challenge, and what was your thinking?*

I guess my main consideration was not to try and replicate the solo heard on the record as closely as possible with the same notes, bends, inflections, nuances, etc., but to play it with my own soul and spirit. For a solo like that, it has to come completely from the heart...and you really can't fake that!

To be honest, the main challenge for me was actually the physical act of balancing on a wobbly platform forty feet up in the air with no safety harness...while 50,000+ people look on, with huge expectations and video phones! The pressure was pretty intense...although a lot of it was self-imposed I guess, because I really wanted to perform it as well as possible every night....

Your solo tune "Static" rocks! It's a mix of funk/fusion/hard rock to my ears. Would you like to do more solo projects if you have the time?

I've actually JUST finished my new album! It's called *...and THE TRUTH will set you free...*It'll be on iTunes, of course, and will also be available from Amazon.com and direct from Cherry Red Records. It features the same guys who played on my first solo rock album *Scarlet—The Director's Cut*; Pete Riley on drums and Phil Williams on bass...we all played in the Keith Emerson band together, and they're a totally incredible rhythm section! I think on this new album you'll hear some of my early influences in there too like Led Zeppelin and definitely some Queen as well, as I had a lot of fun tracking up vocal harmonies.

Could you describe your time a little with both John Wetton and Keith Emerson?

Well, I guess John gave me my first break, so I'll always be thankful to him for that... and it was very cool to be able to play hit singles (Asia), technically challenging pieces (UK) and prog epics (King Crimson) all during the same gig! Not to mention singing harmony vocals, which I love doing.

And through playing with John and Carl Palmer (in a band called Qango) I got to meet one of my musical heroes, Keith Emerson! That was such an amazing time... playing music that I grew up listening to!

I managed to talk Keith into doing the whole of "Tarkus" as well, all thirty minutes of it! And to play those pieces live—listening to Keith just wailing on the Moog, or the Hammond...along with my favorite rhythm section ever! It was just heaven.

On a goofy note...if you could rename a Pink Floyd song or album after a cat, what would you choose?

Is this for the special Pink Floyd/cat compilation album *A Saucerful of Milk*?!

Hahaha...okay, ummm "Get Your Filthy Hands off My Tiddles." "Don't Leave Meow." "Careful With That Catnip, Eugene." "Hey Mew." "See Emily's Cat Play." "Waiting for the Worming Tablets." "Outside the Caterwaul." "Bring the Paws Back Home."

Hahaha...okay, they're getting worse....Sorry, that was "The Final Cat."

Thanks for your time, and your playing all these years! I'd have to add a Floyd/cat song in "Not Meow John"!

Ha ha ha, it was absolutely my pleasure!!!

CHAPTER 31

Bruce Kulick
(Born Bruce Howard Kulick, December 12, 1953, Brooklyn, NY)

Bruce first came to attention as a guitar player in Meat Loaf's band supporting the *Bat out of Hell* album in 1977. If that wasn't cool enough, Bruce's brother Bob was also a guitarist in the band (and had been an early associate of KISS).

After that, Bruce became a founding member of Blackjack, a cool AOR band that released two albums with only the first achieving moderate success and the minor hit "Love Me Tonight," which is a near-perfect pop rock song. The lead singer of Blackjack was one Michael Bolotin, who would later become a huge success as Michael Bolton, making lots of housewife and dentist office music to nauseate the soul. That aside, Bolotin was a really good rock singer at this time.

Bruce then played on Billy Squier's solo debut *The Tale of the Tape* in 1980 (including the classics "You Should Be High, Love" and "The Big Beat") but didn't end up a part of Billy's band, thus he joined the Good Rats for a stint that saw him on the album *Great American Music* in 1981. With Bolton a solo artist now and still doing hard rock, Bruce joined his band for Bolton's self-titled debut album in 1983 that produced a minor hit in "Fool's Game." It was commercial pop metal, but it was well done.

Then, in 1984, Bruce joined KISS, but initially as a fill-in guitarist. Guitarist Mark St. John had an arthritic condition that prevented him from touring and Kulick was tapped to fill in for St. John on the tour supporting the successful *Animalize* album in late 1984. St. John played only two partial shows and one full show before KISS decided that Kulick was the proper fit after all, and it was definitely the right choice by founding members Gene Simmons and Paul Stanley (along with drummer Eric Carr). Bruce's first official show as a member was December 8 in Detroit, Michigan, before a packed house. It was aired as an MTV Saturday Night Concert and released on home video.

In 1985, *Asylum* was issued and was Bruce's first album with the band although he had done some work on *Animalize*. *Asylum* was a dreadful album but did contain the hit "Tears are Falling" that features one of the finest solos in the history of KISS. This is a great, great song from a poor, poor album. The solo is very tricky and has loads of melodic touches but speedy parts as well.

In 1987, the Platinum selling *Crazy Nights* was issued with a very glossy, overly slick sound that was in at the time. There were a few hits including the cornball anthem "Crazy, Crazy Nights" that had an excellent solo and the power ballad "Reason to Live," another fine solo included that fit the song perfectly.

Hot in the Shade followed in 1989 and contained a Top 10 smash in "Forever," which was co-written with Michael Bolton (remember the connection?). Bruce's beautiful acoustic solo adds to the somber, subtle style of the song. The 1990 tour saw the band in top form playing their best in years and with a set featuring lots of '70s classics.

Tragically, in November 1991, Carr passed away from cancer and was replaced by Eric Singer, formerly with Black Sabbath, Badlands, and Alice Cooper. *Revenge* was an appropriately angry album in 1992 and featured some of Bruce's best work with the band, not to mention heaviest. Songs like "Unholy," "Domino," "Paralyzed," and "Heart of Chrome" were downright filthy. The solos Bruce came up with here are exemplary and "Unholy" sports some sinister playing. *Alive III* followed in 1993 reaching the Top 10 (as *Revenge* had done) and captured the band in damn good form. A KISS tribute album *Kiss My Ass* surfaced in 1994 and there was a brief tour including South American dates that were among the best of the band's career.

In 1995, the group organized KISS Konventions at which fans could trade, buy, and see various memorabilia, and watch the band play impromptu acoustic gigs. MTV caught wind of this and requested the band appear on the popular *MTV Unplugged* series. It was highly suggested that original KISS guitarist Ace Frehley and drummer Peter Criss be part of the show as well. Taped in August and aired on Halloween night 1995 on MTV to huge ratings, the unplugged show was magnificent and breathed new life into these songs, allowing the numerous naysayers to see the incredible depth and quality of these KISS songs from both writing and playing standpoints. Bruce's blazing acoustic runs and leads on songs not really suited for acoustic guitar was beyond impressive.

KISS actually had a studio album started that year in *Carnival of Souls* that was finished in early 1996. The album was shelved when the original lineup embarked on the massively successful Alive Worldwide reunion tour of 1996–1997. Once the tour was completed, *Carnival of Souls* (already easily available as a bootleg on the Internet) was issued as something of an afterthought. Although it was clear KISS was modernizing their sound and perhaps going a bit grunge rock, there are some excellent nuggets here such as "Jungle" (a surprise Top 10 rock radio hit), "Hate," "Rain" and the lone song Kulick would sing in KISS, the excellent "I Walk Alone."

Although KISS kept both Kulick and Singer on board as fully paid members through 1996, Kulick officially split from KISS at year's end. Bruce became part of a new band called Union in 1997 that included ex-Motley Crue front man John Corabi. They would release two studio albums (*Union* in 1997 and *The Blue Room* in 2000) and a live album. This was a solid project and more rootsy playing from Bruce was prevalent.

Bruce accepted an offer to join the legendary Grand Funk Railroad and has been on board since joining in 2000. He has injected his own style in all those classic songs featuring the great guitar work of Mark Farner. Not an easy task at all, but he more than does it especially on a tune like "Inside Looking Out." Bruce has also issued three solo albums, the most recent being *BK3* in 2010, which has killer guest spots from Gene Simmons, Toto guitar god Steve Lukather, the late Doug Fieger of the Knack, and Eric Singer. *BK3* is a really good album and Bruce Kulick is a guitar great hands-down.

Bruce was kind enough to answer some questions I had in December 2014 and here are the results:

Who were some of the influences as you were starting to learn the instrument?

Well, the Beatles changed everything for me. I loved music, but their songs and performance changed my life. That continued with the British Invasion and guitarists like Jimi Hendrix. So Led Zep, Cream, the Who, and on and on, all shaped my world.

What are the guitars you've preferred over the years in the studio or in concert?

I have an amazing 1953 conversion Les Paul, that is just chock full of major Mojo! That has made many appearances. I have a few ESP's that have recorded very well, as well as Gibson SG's, my ESP Signature Models, Fender Custom shops and many more. Live, I use ESP's mainly Viper or Eclipse or Vintage Plus models.

What kind of experience was it touring with Meat Loaf behind the Bat out Of Hell *album? Especially being so young?*

Well, happily I did tour with a few other bands, to get the feel for being on the road. But taking Meat Loaf from clubs, to arena shows etc., was very exciting. Sometimes it was very stressful with a large band, and many personalities, including my brother Bob! But I had some serious Todd Rundgren guitar parts to perform, and the band was terrific.

I really thought Blackjack was a band of great players and had serious potential. Your minor hit "Love Me Tonight" was such a great song and I remember it on the radio when I was a little kid. Hell, you even had the song "Stay" sampled by Jay-Z! What were your thoughts on that and the band as, of course, Michael Bolotin who became Michael Bolton was a damn good rock singer.

I knew Michael was a star. Blackjack didn't take off like it should have, but all the players have had great careers and of course Michael became a household name! I recently had dinner with Michael and it was great catching up with him and all. I learned a lot from working with him; we were very close in those days.

When you first joined KISS in 1984 how awkward was it sharing those few shows with Mark St. John? A truly bizarre moment in rock history I'd say.

It was strange, but at least I know I won the gig fair and square! Remember, he was their contracted guitarist who got ill, and I was just filling in. But I fit better, with all respect to Mark.

Can you take me through the solo on the KISS hit "Tears are Falling"? That is an incredibly memorable solo and an excellent, melodic song I remain fond of, even if the album it came from was not a great one.

Paul and I worked on it. And what came out of that collaboration was very special indeed. I love my crazy wide high B and E string riff, that I kind of stole from Steve Howe, for that solo. Yes was a big influence along with the other obvious bands I mentioned to you.

Playing on Billy Squier's first album Tale of the Tape *in 1980 was a very cool gig. How did that come about and was that a good experience?*

My brother Bob knew him, and when Bob had a conflict doing the work for him, I got the call. I studied Billy; he was meticulous and smart. I am very proud of being on that album.

The MTV Unplugged *album has some more fantastic acoustic work by you and I still think the band never sounded better than right there, truly showing not only musicianship but just how great all these songs truly were written. A lot of those solos are not easy to play on acoustic and I especially love your work on "Domino," "Got to Choose," "Coming Home," and "I Still Love You." That must have been fun but also tricky with Peter and Ace involved.*

I agree it was a very excellent show and shot so beautifully. Paul sang so superbly, and we all played TIGHT. Playing them on Ovation guitars was a challenge. I had a bit of a trick with a Tech 21 pedal to kick in, to give me a little more boost and compression. But it was hard. The Peter & Ace part was awkward, but I am a "team player," so I was welcoming Ace and even had him hooked up with a pedal, too!

I assume there was no point where you would have donned KISS makeup, but what new character would you have come up with? (And I'm pretty sure a platypus wouldn't have gone down well, but that's my idea—ha ha).

That's a crazy road to go down! Once Peter made Gene and Paul call Eric, and Ace started to become a "wild card," so Tommy was always ready to suit up. It was obvious; it's the Catman and Spaceman forever. No more other creatures to be in KISS. Business wise, it was smart in my estimation. Those characters are iconic. And Tommy and Eric do well in them.

*The reunion era in 1996 must have been an awkward position to be in having an album sitting on the shelf (*Carnival of Souls, *which you got to sing lead on "I Walk Alone"). How difficult was that time, and was the writing on the wall about the reunion happening?*

I was confused what took so long for us to finally start. Well, once we did, it was the smart way to prove to Ace and Peter, KISS can carry on if they don't agree to the Reunion in a respectable manner. I wasn't aware of that at the time, but that's a fact. I was told when Ace and Peter signed, so we were about three-quarters through recording. I knew it was the end of me being in the band. Happily Gene and Paul paid me for an entire year, even though I did nothing.

Has the Grand Funk Railroad experience been a good one and have the fans responded? That's a tough role to fill with Mark Farner absent. You've been there well over a decade now and those are some dynamite guitar songs you get to play each night and add your personality to.

GFR is a terrific band with great songs. It's not over-the-top KISS performances, just straight ahead rock 'n' roll, and the fans respond wonderfully all the time—it's fourteen years now! Like Ace before me, I know how to take enough of the signature riffs from Mark Farner and do it justice in my own way. So the gig is a great match for me. I am blessed to have Don and Mel as the rhythm section on stage. And Max Carl and Tim Cashion are amazing singers and musicians rounding out the band. Excellent talent on the GFR stage!

CHAPTER 32

Dave Lambert

(Born David Lambert, March 8, 1949, Hounslow, Middlesex, England)

Dave Lambert is one of the great unsung guitar players, especially for his work with veteran prog/folk rockers Strawbs.

Lambert first came to attention on guitar and vocals with Fire, a British psychedelic pop/rock act who released a few singles in the late '60s including the truly awesome "Father's Name is Dad" and the silly (but fun) novelty tune "Round the Gum Tree." An album called *Magic Shoemaker* was issued in 1970 and remains a highly collectible obscurity that music fans have really taken to over the years. The original release of this album on Pye Records is one of the Top 100 collectible albums of all-time. It's a concept album about a shoe cobbler and his magic shoes that allow him to fly and become a hero. Why wouldn't you want to hear that?

Lambert then joined the King-Earl Boogie Band and played on the album *Trouble at Mill* in 1972. This was more or less a Skiffle act that was led by two ex-members of Mungo Jerry who here covered "Plastic Jesus" and had cool songs such as the chilling "Bad Storm Coming" where Lambert laid down some sweet solos on electric guitar. Ewan McColl's "Go Down You Murderers" is six minutes of seriously unique music as well. Perhaps Mumford and Sons own copies of this album. This was a neat little musical act lost in history but well worth inspecting. The album was produced by Dave Cousins of Strawbs, which led to Lambert joining Strawbs later that year.

Strawbs started life as a folk rock act in the late 1960s in the UK (after a short stint as a bluegrass act) and built up a loyal following that led to a signing to A&M Records. The group was led by vocalist/guitarist Dave Cousins and also featured drummer Richard Hudson, bassist/vocalist John Ford, and keyboardist Blue Weaver at the time Lambert joined in 1972. By that point Strawbs had established themselves as both a folk rock act and a progressive rock band and had released five albums: *Strawbs* (1969), *Dragonfly* (1970), *Just a Collection of Antiques and Curios* (1970), *From the Witchwood* (1971), and *Grave New World* (1972).

Classically trained keyboard virtuoso Rick Wakeman had joined the band in 1970 and left in 1971 to join Yes after the *From the Witchwood* album, and it was after this point that Strawbs started bringing in more of a hard rock edge and hints of pop and further experiments in prog and folk. With the addition of Lambert, Strawbs became recognized much more as a guitar-led rock band beginning with the excellent *Bursting at the Seams* album in 1973, which also became a huge seller, reaching #2 in the UK album charts.

Bursting at the Seams also produced two huge hits in the folkish sing-along "Part of the Union" (now oddly used as a sing-along anthem for Major League Soccer team the Philadelphia Union at their home matches) that would equal the album hitting #2 in the UK and the infectious driving rock of "Lay Down" that hit #12 and remains Strawbs' finest moment. "Lay Down" is one of those songs you can't get out of your head from the moment you hear it. Dave Cousins does a wonderful job vocally and Lambert's melodic guitar lines (including the opening solo) are sublime. Throughout, the song has undeniable spirit as it continues to build to those marvelous choruses. It's very difficult not to feel uplifted when hearing this song. Just prior to the bridge, Lambert lets out some ripping hard rock power chords (something he also does at the song's conclusion) adding to the excitement of this great example of '70s British rock writing. How this wasn't a hit on US radio (sounding like a more rocking version of the Beatles and ELO), I will remain baffled by.

It didn't stop with just the hits on this album. "Lady Fuschia" is a beautiful song awash in acoustic guitars and sitars with amazing vocal harmonies and biting lead guitar parts that break up the acoustics but add to the grace of the piece. "Down by the Sea" opens with menacing guitar parts that sound like the Outlaws used for "Green Grass, High Tides" and Metallica for "Welcome Home (Sanitarium)" (I'd bet on it actually!), then give way to acoustic guitars and organ and a Cat Stevens-folk vibe before heavy, grinding guitars slice through transporting the listener into what sounds like heavy Genesis and Jethro Tull. Orchestration also plays a major part here as the song builds to its finale. Writing like this is something to behold.

Unfortunately, this lineup crumbled after the tour for the album and Cousins and Lambert were then joined by Rod Coombes (drums), Chas Cronk (bass) and John Hawken (keyboards). Yet, the changes did not affect the band, and the amazing *Hero and Heroine* album followed in 1974 to great reviews and sales reaching the UK Top 40 and becoming their first album to crack the US Top 100. The song "Hero and Heroine" opens with a wall of crashing symphonic keyboards and guitars with thrusting drums that are then followed by a galloping, Southern rock-styled verse and a reprisal of the opening theme. The second verse is sung a capella and the themes repeat until the finale.

The Lambert-penned and sung "Just Love" is a raucous rocker that definitely involves some Southern rock and boogie rock that livens things. The lilting "Shine on Silver Sun" was a Top 40 UK single and "Midnight Sun," "Out in the Cold" (the acoustic guitars on this country rock song are crystal clear aided by some campfire harmonica, and the quaint lead guitar licks are perfect), and the creative eight-and-one-half-minute epic "Autumn" are all examples not only of how the new lineup jelled, but of the high quality and imagination of the writing and playing. "Autumn" is uncanny writing. The songs start with evil percolating synthesizers, a mid-tempo drumbeat, and then Mellotron that sounds like a King Crimson song joined by smartly arranged guitar parts (both acoustic and electric) with a Yes feel. The song has three distinct parts and everything ties together perfectly.

It was very hard to top the last two albums, but with 1975's *Ghosts*, Strawbs came close. The album opens with the eight-minute title song and Lambert shines with his creative guitar playing, especially during the dreamy first few minutes and the truly outstanding, rollicking guitar solo and is laid over some wild bass and drum fills. There also were key tracks such as "Grace Darling," a haunting song opening with a children's choir, "Lemon Pie," and another impressive epic "The Life Auction." *Ghosts* scared its way into the US Top 50, but the band would never return to the UK charts somehow.

Nomadness followed late that year and contained the lighthearted "Tokyo Rosie," which has some dynamite guitar fills and the delicate tale of "The Golden Salamander." The punchy "To Be Free" includes an outstanding solo with about three different sounds, all adding up to an example of Lambert's creativity. Songs like this also allow him to really find his space. "Little Sleepy" is a spicy rocker sung and written by Lambert that sounds like Eric Clapton, the Stones, and even early Aerosmith in spots. The riffs are hard edged and the chorus has some warm Chuck Berry-sounding chords while Dave's vocals are tailor made for this song.

With *Deep Cuts* in 1976, the band continued on with shorter songs as *Nomadness* had done. "I Only Want My Love to Grow in You" has all the elements of a smash single. Stunningly gorgeous melodies and guitar fills that sound like George Harrison and a warm sentiment. The guitars just melt at the heart and although the song is undoubtedly commercial, that does not make it any less of a special moment. The oddball rocker "My Friend Peter" had more of that tasty, riff-leaden rock that Lambert was so adept at. "The Soldier's Tale" is another song where Lambert shines, the man coming up with heavy-hitting riffs in a band with folk and prog leanings, putting him right there with Jethro Tull's Martin Barre.

Deep Cuts has some of Lambert's choicest guitar playing and sounds, courtesy of producer Rupert Holmes (yes, the "Escape-Pina Colada Song" guy) who did a good job here although there is some filler. "Beside the Rio Grande" is another highlight with Lambert supplying a variety of guitar sounds (including funky wah-wah) and this cinematic song does echo the Strawbs' glory days.

In 1977, *Burning for You* was the last Strawbs album to make the charts in the US. Although another commercial rock album, damn, this does have some of Dave Lambert's best solos. Check out the zany "Alexander the Great." Lambert's guitar work is on fire and his solo here ranks among his best. No doubt that he was more than pleased to be rocking out like this! "Cut Like a Diamond" has a jabbing, gritty riff that once again is pure hard rock as is "Heartbreaker," while "Barcarole (For the Death of Venice)" is spellbinding beauty with tranquil guitars and soothing vocal harmonies.

Deadlines was to be the final album in 1978 seeing new drummer Tony Fernandez and Robert Kirby and John Mealing remaining on keyboards as they had the previous album. *Deadlines* had more concise, mainstream material prominent. Despite that, the creepy "Deadly Nightshade" was a bombastic treat and "Words of Wisdom" was a strong song, but the band was now running on fumes and they soon disbanded (although another album was recorded and went unreleased until the '90s).

Strawbs would re-form in 1983, and did a small amount of recording, but Lambert would not be a part of the band again until 1998. There are two factions of Strawbs now: an acoustic act and a full band, with both Cousins and Lambert a part of each. A full-band album *Deja Fou* surfaced in 2004 with the lineup of Cousins, Lambert, Cronk, Hawken, and Coombes. The album was very strong and "On a Night Like This" and especially the sweeping epic "Under a Cloudless Sky" were excellent.

Lots of touring followed until 2008's *The Broken Hearted Bride*. Lambert's "Shadowland" is an uplifting track and has a guitar solo accented by colorful piano. "Through Aphrodite's Eyes" has some very emotional soloing in it and is also a standout. *Dancing to the Devil's Beat* quickly followed in 2009 and saw Rick Wakeman's son Oliver (now formerly of Yes like his dad) on keyboards. The acoustic number "Copenhagen" was positively lovely. Oliver was replaced in 2010 by John Young and then his own brother Adam Wakeman came on board in 2012 and has been there since (he's a busy man also a full member of Ozzy Osbourne's band since 2004 and as touring keyboardist for Black Sabbath since then, too).

Strawbs still play live as of 2015, and Dave Lambert is just one of those guys that this book is dedicated to. He is a key ingredient in one of the true unsung great acts of British rock and it's a thrilling catalog to take a trip through. Oh, and the guitar work will not disappoint.

In March of 2015, Dave was very kind to answer questions of mine in a chat with very detailed answers. I do believe you will find this very entertaining:

Who were the players you listened to that you could cite as an influence as far as guitar playing goes?

My early guitar influences were mostly drawn from the pop records of the late '50s/early '60s. That was because I have an older sister and she was buying the current hits. Hank Marvin was always on the turntable, either with the Shadows or Cliff Richard. Then there's Buddy Holly, Eddy Cochran, the Everly Brothers, Bill Haley, etc. I listened to them every day. All of these were to influence, and inspire, my playing. We didn't have much up-to-date music on UK radio in those days, but the BBC did often feature Les Paul and Wout Steenhuis and I think they both influenced me subconsciously. Both of those players used multi overdubbing and I started messing about with that, with the help of an old Elizabethan tape recorder, quite early on. I still get a kick from listening to Eddie Cochran and I consider him to be the Father of Rock, not rock 'n' roll but rock. He used techniques that all of today's great players employ to this day and his rhythm playing was exceptional.

Having said all this, I believe my main influences came from the classical music recordings that my mother used to play in our house on most days. Beethoven, Grieg, Holst, Elgar, etc. That music is never far from my thoughts.

However, the moment that changed my life was hearing "Hey Joe" on my car radio. Jimi Hendrix connected with everybody, almost immediately. The way he approached playing was a breath of fresh air; it was uninhibited and unrestrained and it gave us all a license to get out there and to play from the heart.

What have been the models of guitars you've preferred over the years, both studio and in concert?

My first choice for electric guitar has always been, since 1973 my 1969 Gibson Les Paul Custom, otherwise known as the Black Beauty. Of course I use other instruments in the studio; Stratocaster, Telecaster etc., when a different sound is required, but as soon as I pick the Gibson up again, it feels like settling back into your own comfy armchair. I love the warmth of the sound the Les Paul has and the dimensions of the neck suit my fairly large hands.

Early on I had a 1970 Les Paul Deluxe, the one with the slim pick-ups. That was a great guitar, but it didn't have the range of sounds the Custom has. The marriage of a Les Paul and a Marshall amp must have been formed in heaven.

We do a lot of shows these days with Acoustic Strawbs and I play a Dean Key Largo that was given to me by a friend in California. For live work the Dean is as good an acoustic guitar as I've ever used. As well as being a beautiful-looking stage instrument, it plays very smoothly and evenly and the pick-up and electrics are perfect for me. The advantage with the Dean is the deep body that gives a powerful bass end, essential for me because I play a lot of lines on the bass strings.

For many years I played a 1968 Fender Redondo, which is a small body acoustic with a very slim neck. Tony Zemaitis put a bridge pick-up on the Fender for me and it sounded great and played beautifully, the only drawback being that it didn't have a cutaway, so playing at the top end was sometimes difficult. I had the guitar fully restored in 2003, but I don't play it anymore. The most playable acoustic I have is the Washburn DL; the reason I don't use it on stage is that, because of the slim body, I can't get the bass response I need for live work.

When you joined the band for the Bursting at the Seams *album, the band became much more aggressive musically. "Down by the Sea" is a very heavy song and I swear that opening riff has been used by everyone from the Outlaws to Metallica!*
"Lay Down" is to me, one of the greatest songs of the '70s. The vocals are warm and spirited, but there's also a drive with the guitars and some memorable hard rocking riffs. Where did those riffs come from and was there any fear of alienating the older fan base?

I was brought into Strawbs in order to help provide a harder more aggressive sound and performance. I had come from a fairly heavy rock background, so, for me, it was just a case of playing in my natural style. "Lay Down" was one of the earliest tracks I recorded with the band, and it was the perfect piece for me to put my own stamp on. Dave Cousins wrote the song and chord sequence and what you hear on the record is my "rock" interpretation of the song. To this day it remains one of my favourite tracks. For the recording I played my sunburst Les Paul De Luxe through a 100w HH amp.

The riff for "Down by the Sea" was recorded with the same configuration, but we played around with the sound a bit for that one; first I put down the riff on guitar and then we played it back through a speaker placed under the grand piano while Blue Weaver doubled the riff on the piano with the loud pedal held down. I think it worked really well and, as you said, the riff has been imitated many times since.

Some of the original folk fan base was horrified when I was brought into the band; it was a bit like the Bob Dylan/Judas scenario. The decision was made in order to better the bands' chances of making an impact in the US and Canada and it proved to be the right one.

The album Hero and Heroine *is one of my favorite albums of Strawbs. Can you take me through the title track and your contribution to it? This is a very symphonic piece, but also rather forceful with that main theme. This album also had the epic "Autumn" that really reminds me of early King Crimson and then becomes a beautiful Strawbs piece in the end, and a song you wrote and sang "Just Love" that to me sounded like an Allman Brothers Band romp with some boogie and southern rock. Any fond memories of that album?*

The "Hero and Heroine" track started life as a "hoe-down" type of song which, in one day, turned into the symphonic piece on the recording. John Hawken, our keyboard player, and I worked for hours developing the riffs and when we'd got it Dave Cousins said good night; he'd realized he had to get home and re-write the lyrics immediately because the song had changed so drastically.

"Autumn" was one of the only tracks we put together on the road. We developed it over a few days while we were touring the US and the lyrics weren't even completed the first couple of times we performed it on stage, we were so keen to play the piece. We were touring constantly with King Crimson at that time so it's quite feasible there may be a bit of their influence, but I wasn't aware of it at the time. I enjoyed the whole of the *Hero and Heroine* period, the recording, in Denmark, and the live performances. I had changed my De Luxe for a 1969 Les Paul Custom Black Beauty and that guitar through a Twin Reverb or a Marshall 100 almost played itself. "Just Love" was a straightforward rock song and it was the type of song I'd been writing and performing before I joined Strawbs; it represented a kind of "past to present" for me at that time.

Your guitar playing on the song "Ghosts" is outstanding. The solo is especially lyrical. Was that a difficult solo to create? "Lemon Pie" is another beautiful example of your playing. I also feel your guitar sounds on all the albums Tom Allom (who went on to Def Leppard and Judas Priest) produced sounded amazing. Were you happy with the sounds you were getting in the studio at that time?

Also, the Ghosts *album nearly made the US Top 40 and represented a peak here in the States. Was the band aware that things were building here?*

We were on a UK package-tour a little while ago and at one show I heard a couple of the guys from Martin Turner's Wishbone Ash whistling a tune. The tune sounded familiar and I asked them what it was. It turned out they were whistling my solo from "Ghosts" which, of course, gave me a real kick. I used my Strat on that album for quite a few songs, including the "Ghosts" solo and "Lemon Pie." I remember John Peel reviewing "Lemon Pie" in the press and calling my guitar playing "sophisticated." I didn't understand what he meant then and I don't understand it now; good or bad? I have no idea, but I'm very happy with what I played on that track.

I used to enjoy working with Tom Allom at that time. Tom had a very varied musical background, including engineering the first two Black Sabbath albums, and he was always keen to experiment with new sounds. He also had a great ear for an interesting harmony part when I was over-dubbing. Some of the guitar chord sounds on the albums aren't quite what I would have preferred; I'd have liked them to have been thicker, but I'm pleased with most of the lead guitar sounds.

When Tom was producing my solos I rarely used an amp. He used to plug my Les Paul directly into the desk and overload the sound to achieve a controllable distortion, just enough to provide sustain. I don't think I'm over indulgent when I'm putting my guitar parts down but I like it to be relaxed and not hurried. I've been lucky with the producers we've had over the years; they've all been quite happy to let me work on until I, and they, are perfectly happy with it.

We were in Japan when *Ghosts* started to climb the US chart and we abandoned going on to Australia and flew straight back to the US and started the *Ghosts* tour.

Nomadness *saw the band writing shorter, more concise songs but some of my favorites are here like "The Golden Salamander" and the rocker "Little Sleepy," which you wrote that is a killer song. Did you enjoy the band rocking out on occasion?*

Nomadness was a completely different approach for us, an experiment if you like. For the first time we didn't have a regular keyboard player. After John Hawken left the band, we went into the studio and recorded tracks with guest players, Rick Wakeman, Tommy Eyre, and John Mealing. The benefit, for me anyway, was that a lot of the tracks were guitar led. I used an Ovation Breadwinner on quite a few tracks for that album. For a lot of the rhythm tracks we put a cardboard tube in front of a Pig Nose practice amp and a microphone at the end of the tube that turned out pretty well.

I played the Black Beauty on "Golden Salamander." I started off with an acoustic, but when we tried the Gibson it took on a better feel. The track is mainly my guitar with Dave C playing dulcimer. I like listening to "Little Sleepy." Again, it was one of my rockier songs and, yes, we always enjoyed "rocking out" whenever we got the chance, although Dave C never joined in.

The Deep Cuts *album had a brilliantly written song "I Only Want My Love to Grow in You." To this day I have no idea how that wasn't a smash hit here in the States. Your guitar playing on this track reminds me of George Harrison and could also have fit nicely on a song by America or Gerry Rafferty.*

Deep Cuts was produced by Jeffrey Lesser, who stayed with us for a time after that, and Rupert Holmes. They brought a fresh approach to our recordings and I think Jeffrey gave me the best guitar sounds I ever had on record. When I came to put the guitars on "I Only Want My Love…," it was me and Jeffrey in the room for most of the time. He gave my Gibson one of those sounds that make you want to play and play. I can see what you mean with the George Harrison comparison, but that was never intentional; maybe it was subliminal, but there again what isn't? We thought it was a sure-fire hit record and I think it should've been. On a lot of the tracks on *Deep Cuts*, "The Soldiers Tale" and "My Friend Peter," for instance, I used a Telecaster with a Bigsby tremolo.

Even though some fans and critics didn't like Burning for You, *I did. "Heartbreaker" and "Cut Like a Diamond" have some vicious riffs by you. How did you feel about this album and those songs?*

We recorded *Burning for You* in Holland and, for the most part, we had a relaxed, fun time. We had two keyboard players by that time; John Mealing and my dear friend Robert Kirby, who also did our orchestral arrangements. Once again Jeffrey Lesser was producing and I felt my guitar sounds were in safe hands. "Heartbreaker" is a track that features among my all-time favourites; of my own songs that is. The only regret I have is that awful synthesizer sound that doubles my guitar riffs, it must have sounded state of the art at the time, but it sounds like crap now. I really don't remember how the "Cut Like a Diamond" riffs came together, but it's a very powerful and biting track; once again Jeffrey came up with excellent guitar sounds for my Les Paul.

A final, silly question I ask most players: If you had to rename a Strawbs album or song using a cat theme what would you arrive at (i.e., Burning for Mew—*hey, that was pretty damn good!). My cats want to know—ha ha.*

Sadly I can't think of anything for that; *Purring for You* is about as much as I can offer. On a similar theme though; when we're on the road I always refer to *Ghosts* as *Goats*.

Recommended solo: "Ghosts" from *Ghosts* with Strawbs (1975)
Further info: www.strawbsweb.co.uk
Photo credit: Les Cotton

Andy LaRocque

(Born Anders Allhage, November 29, 1962, Gothenburg, Sweden)

The world of heavy metal could not be the same without the deviled ham that is King Diamond. And, King Diamond could not be the same without guitarist Andy LaRocque, who has been the King's right-hand man since King left the mighty Mercyful Fate to begin a solo career back in 1985.

LaRocque has added guitar textures and solos that have taken King Diamond's ideas into different worlds melodically by using a variety of scales and modes bringing a neo-classical feel. LaRocque is also a producer, arranger, and writer, and owns the successful recording studio Sonic Train Studios in Varberg, Sweden.

When the King left Mercyful Fate in 1985, he formed a band with LaRocque, drummer Mikkey Dee and ex-Mercyful Fate members Timi Hansen on bass and Michael Denner on guitar. The hilarious holiday single "No Presents for Christmas" was the first release and was followed by debut album *Fatal Portrait* in 1986. This album was different than a Mercyful Fate record as there was a light and shade that a Fate record would not have had. Another seasonal classic appears in "Halloween," and tracks such as "The Candle," "The Jonah," and "Charon" have a progressive rock side to them. The album sold well, but was followed by the even bigger *Abigail* in summer 1987, a concept record set in the 1700s–1800s dealing with demonic possession that remains one of the greatest heavy metal albums ever made.

The guitar playing on *Abigail* and the attention to detail is impeccable. The story is macabre and creepy and the music is a perfect accent. The production and sonic clarity still stands the test of time. One classic after another fills the album including "Arrival," "Abigail," "A Mansion in Darkness" (co-written by LaRocque), "The Family Ghost," and the album's closing masterpiece "The Dark Horsemen" with breathtaking leads by both LaRocque and Denner and harmonies to chill the spine. The album impressively sold close to 200,000 copies in the US with no radio support, though MTV spun the video for "The Family Ghost" a good amount.

In 1988, with new members in bassist Hal Patino and guitarist Pete Blakk the band released another concept album called *Them*. This album told the tale of the King and his sister Missy staying with their evil grandmother who has returned from a stay in a mental asylum. The grandmother and certain "invisible guests" drink a mysteriously red "tea," with the cups floating in the air. The whole thing does not end well for Missy, their mother, or the grandmother, and King is placed in an asylum as well. It's all campy horror film stuff and wonderful fun. The video for "Welcome Home" became an MTV smash with the King wheeling around his "grandmother," and the album sold over 200,000 cracking the US Top 100. The production and mix are a bit harsh, but the music and story are campy, evil fun. The creepy instrumental "Them" is an excellent opportunity to hear LaRocque's guitar playing in a different vein and "Tea," "The Invisible Guests," and "A Broken Spell" (another LaRocque co-write) are great.

A sequel was released in 1989 entitled *Conspiracy* featuring the hallowed "Sleepless Nights" with some incredible, speedy, fluid soloing and a killer main theme. The black and white video was as ghoulish as it could get. The solo on this track is so good and so richly detailed, it is a perfect piece of evidence as to the genius of Andy's playing. The nine-minute epic "At the Graves" and "A Visit from the Dead" are also among the best songs here. Dee left before the tour and was replaced by Snowy Shaw.

In 1990, *The Eye* was released and the story was set during the French Inquisition between the years of 1450–1670 and detailed some of the atrocities that took place including the burning of supposed witches at the stake. This remains one of the finest King Diamond albums, but the group's label Roadrunner Records and the band were not happy with one another and the album was underpromoted in the States, though sales were still respectable. "Eye of the Witch" and "Burn" have remained fan favorites and are outstanding songs, while "Into the Convent" and "1642 Imprisonment" are also highlights. As always, the guitar work was spellbinding, and the instrumental "Insanity" features that great light/shade mix LaRocque is so good at.

In 1993, Mercyful Fate reunited and, until they folded again in 2000, King somehow kept up a ridiculous pace of King Diamond and Mercyful Fate tours/albums. During some of the downtime, LaRocque joined vocalist Chuck Schuldiner in Death, recording the now-legendary (and much revered) album *Individual Thought Patterns* in 1993. Tracks such as "Leprosy," "The Philosopher," and "In Human Form" display the technical approach to this Death Metal classic, which is leagues above what most people thought the genre was capable of. It is one of the most influential and important heavy metal albums ever made and LaRocque's contributions are critical.

Also in the Death Metal realm, Andy played the brilliant guitar solo on the song "Cold" from the amazing At the Gates album *Slaughter of the Soul*. This guitar solo is truly one of those "you must hear" moments.

The first King Diamond album in five years, *The Spider's Lullaby,* came out in 1995 on Metal Blade Records (where the King has remained ever since), and was only a partial concept album. Many great songs appeared, including the hilarious "The Spider's Lullaby" (which, as a serious arachnophobic, I can very much relate to) as the character is going through madness due to his fears. "From the Other Side" and "The Poltergeist" show new melodic sensibilities in the band's music.

The year 1996 saw *The Graveyard* issued, a somewhat controversial album that was anti-child abuse. A rather long record, it contains some of LaRocque's best guitar work yet and with songs like "Heads on the Wall," "Black Hill Sanitarium," "Meet Me at Midnight," and "Trick or Treat" it is also a very detailed work. *The Graveyard* is one of King Diamond's most rewarding albums and raising awareness about child abuse and abduction was a very commendable thing to do.

In 1998, *Voodoo* was another intriguing effort (the title cut featured a guest appearance on guitar from the late Dimebag Darrell of Pantera) and told a frightening tale in the Bayou, while *House of God* from 2000 was a more fantasy-oriented yarn featuring the excellent track "Black Devil." Fans were very pleased with the long-anticipated sequel album *Abigail 2: The Revenge* in 2002. While the sequel wasn't quite as good as the original, it was an excellent album in and of itself with the story and music blending in very well, and LaRocque's skills on tracks such as "Mansion in Sorrow," "The Crypt," and "The Storm" left no doubt that he was still in command of his instrument.

The Puppetmaster was yet another winner in 2003, as the King's warped visions came to life and LaRocque co-wrote four songs on the album including "Darkness" and "Living Dead." The first official King Diamond live album *Deadly Lullabyes: Live* was released in 2004 and the re-creation of the King's vocals and the band's music as a whole in concert is something to behold. This is no throwaway live release and it documents the love between the King and his audience, who are singing every word.

After a lengthy absence, the band returned with *Give Me Your Soul...Please* in 2007, which received strong reviews and a Grammy nomination. There was no tour due to the King's back problems and then he suffered a heart attack leading to triple bypass surgery in 2010. Slowly, the King and band returned to live work for a few appearances in 2012, leading to a hugely successful and sold-out tour of North America in late 2014 accompanied by the two CD compilation *Dreams of Horror* where LaRocque and the King remastered the songs in amazing detail without sonic compression, making the songs sound even more awesome than before. A new studio album is planned for 2016.

The current lineup has the King, Andy, guitarist Mike Wead, and drummer Matt Thompson since 2000 and bassist Pontus Egberg since 2014. The dual leads between LaRocque and Wead are as sinister as the King would command.

LaRocque has made guest appearances on guitar with numerous acts such as Falconer, Witchery, Evergrey, Sandalinas, and more. Andy has also produced some of these bands and has also produced or had acts record in his studio, such as Eidolon, Dragonland, Sacramentum, and Dreamland. He has always played a major, major role in the King Diamond sound and production and engineering. Andy's use of minor scales, arpeggios, harmonies, and runs is part of his distinguished sound, and there isn't one solo with King Diamond that isn't worth hearing. And that most deviled of hams King Diamond, knows this very well.

In January 2015, Andy was kind enough to answer some of my questions and here are his words:

Who were some of the players that inspired you to begin playing guitar? Would any of those players surprise a fan, and I've always heard something of a classical influence in your playing and the scale runs you do and the arpeggios.

My first influences were back in the early/mid '70s with bands like T-Rex, Alice Cooper, Status Quo, Blue Oyster Cult and Black Sabbath, but also the melodic style of Slade and Sweet and later Thin Lizzy, AC/DC, followed by UFO (Schenker-era) and Ozzy with Randy Rhoads. Steve Vai with Alcatrazz was amazing!

What are the guitars of choice for you in studio and on stage?

I'm using Dean guitars for live and the studio, which I think sounds and plays very nice, all equipped with different Seymour Duncan pickups, which I have pretty much used on all my guitars since late '80s and some of the Deans have Floyd Rose trems.

How do you get your tone?

If you are asking for my equipment, I use Line 6 Spidervalve HD-100 mkII (100 watt all tube head), which is a great amp with lots of power and all the fx needed for live use. In addition to that, I have Marshall Vintage 30 cabs, which in my opinion, are really good live and in the studio.

Can you describe the solo on King Diamond's "The Black Horsemen"? It still gives me chills to this day, especially the outro solo and ending harmonies.

Well the outro solo is done by Michael Denner; my solo is in the middle of the song. I don't really know how to describe the solo. It is melodic with some fast passages and just a very good addition to what's going on in the background. Everything on that album was a little magic and I think we caught a really good spirit throughout the whole recording process of *Abigail*; that's probably why it's considered a classic today...

Another memorable solo of yours is from the At the Gates song "Cold." This is a brilliant solo—was it a quick process or a long time to compose that?

No, it didn't take very long to compose that, the studio sent me a cassette (yeah, cassette tape!) so I could practice and work something out before I went to the studio to record it. When I came to the studio, we recorded it pretty fast, since I already had all the parts worked out.

When were you aware of the impact the Death album Individual Thought Patterns *had? It is now regarded as one of the greatest metal albums ever?*

I wasn't really aware of how big the impact was going to be. At the time I started to talk to Chuck about it, around late 1992, we weren't doing anything with King Diamond and I thought it'd be a good period to try something different. After the session Chuck asked me if I wanted to join them for the tour, but we had been really busy with Diamond up until mid-1990, so I wasn't ready for that at the time, plus I was working with songs for another project that came out later called *Illwill* with Snowy Shaw and Sharlee D´Angelo.

Do you try to work a certain type of playing into the themes of the stories being told on the King Diamond albums?

Yes, depending on the feel of the song, some parts have to be expressed in a certain theatrical way and that you can adapt to the story/lyrics in a nice way if the lyrics are written at that time.

Were you guys aware of the impact MTV had on King Diamond in the US with the heavy play of the videos for "Family Ghost," "Sleepless Nights," and especially "Welcome Home"?

MTV had a great impact on metal in the '80s and I'm very grateful that MTV played us!

Recommended solo: "Sleepless Nights" from *Conspiracy* with King Diamond (1989)
Further info: www.sonictrainstudios.com and www.kingdiamondcoven.com
Photo credit: Hakon Grav

CHAPTER 34

Ronni le Tekro
(Born Rolf Agrim Tekro, October 5, 1963, Oslo, Norway)

Ronni le Tekro is truly one of the unsung virtuoso guitar players in the world. This Norwegian guitar genius has been in the band TNT since their inception in 1982.

TNT initially sang in their native language on their self-titled debut album. Once the band secured a deal with Mercury/Polygram, they were able to focus on the US and other territories. With insanely high-pitched American singer Tony Harnell joining in 1984, the band now had a stunning vocalist with high range that combined with bassist Morty Black (who had joined in 1983) and drummer Diesel Dahl.

Their English-language debut *Knights of the New Frontier* featured the MTV hit "Seven Seas" in 1985 (a year after the album had been issued worldwide). "Seven Seas" is a distinctively European-styled metal tune with deft melodic touches and an accent on heaviness that is influenced by Rainbow. Ronni's solo is classically influenced but uses a sound and style that shows a love of Ritchie Blackmore and is proof positive that there are other Scandinavian guitarists aside from Yngwie Malmsteen who could play like this. The beauty here is, it wasn't all just about flash and speed, though those attributes are here, too.

In 1987, *Tell No Tales* saw their US popularity increase thanks to the MTV hit "10,000 Lovers (In One)," an insanely catchy song that showcased Harnell's operatic vocal pipes and featured a brilliant, unusual, thoughtful guitar solo. The solo and riff are widely copied by guitar playing fans on YouTube, none of whom have the sound and skill of Ronni. TNT also opened dates for Great White, Twisted Sister, and others, while headlining club gigs.

In 1989, *Intuition* became the band's biggest seller in the States with a new drummer in Kenneth Odiin and contained two more MTV gems in the beautifully crafted "Intuition" and "Tonight I'm Falling." How these songs didn't reach US radio more is a mystery, but clearly TNT was never going to break out further in the US.

In 1992, with new drummer John Macaluso, a new deal was signed with Atlantic, but *Realized Fantasies* lost out in the grunge era and went nowhere. The juvenile album cover art didn't exactly help. The album was of high quality, however, and featured longer, more involved songs. After fading out for a number of years, the band returned with drummer Frode Lamoy and keyboardist Dag Stokke, but 1997's *Firefly* and 1999's *Transistor* were reactions to nu metal and grunge and not well-received reactions either.

Dahl returned in 2000 and, four years later, *My Religion* was a fine return to form and Le Tekro's playing was as beautiful and complex as ever, and the track "She Needs Me" was hard rock excellence—a mix of modern and classic TNT. Ronni's solo on this track was a real keeper. *All the Way to the Sun* was issued in 2005 and featured the melodic rocker "Driving" and a gorgeous Queen-like version of Louis Armstrong's "What a Wonderful World" that highlighted both Le Tekro and Harnell.

By 2006, Harnell departed and was replaced by ex-Shy front man Tony Mills. The first two albums were not well-received by the fan base, but 2011's *A Farewell to Arms* was a good attempt at the band's vintage style. Still, Mills had a tough go replacing Harnell and, in 2013, he departed. Bassist Victor Borge has been on board since 2005 and, sadly, Stokke passed away in 2011, with Roger Gilton replacing him.

In 2014, the lineup of Le Tekro, Harnell, Dahl, Borge, and Gilton reunited for a lengthy and successful world tour that, not surprisingly did not include the US. In 2015, Harnell left yet again, ending up joining Skid Row, and TNT began searching for their next singer.

Ronni continues to hone his craft every year either with TNT or his solo recordings (his latest album was released in 2014), and is at one with the guitar. In fact, Ronni and Bernie Hamburger developed the Quarterstepper guitar, which has double the frets of a normal guitar spread throughout the guitar's neck with quarter-tone intervals, something I would have no idea how to play.

In September 2014, I was fortunate enough to have the man let us know some surprising and amusing answers to some questions I had.

Who were/are some of your favorite players even if they aren't direct influences?

Ian Bairnson of Pilot, Bill Nelson of Bebop Deluxe, Robert Normann (a Norwegian technical wonder from the '50s), Tony Iommi, Ted Nugent, Frank Marino of Mahogany Rush.

What is your favorite guitar of choice?

ESP Strat and Fender Strat '72.

Where are you at in your head when you play the guitar? Do you forget about all your troubles and just escape into the instrument?

I do! I'm getting stoned like the others.

Can you explain how you get your tone?

I have the highest fret action on the planet, which explains it.

Can you take me through the solo on "Seven Seas"? I absolutely adore that song from the first time I heard it on the radio in 1985 when the album came out in the US and seeing the video on MTV.

The solo on "Seven Seas" was completely improvised, although it sounds composed—that's what fascinates me thirty years later.

How in the world did you compose "Sapphire"? I hear a distinct classical influence?

I have always been into classical music like Penderezki, Beethoven, Grieg, etc. "Sapphire" is a variation over classical fugues.

I hear some Ritchie Blackmore in your playing? Were Rainbow and Deep Purple an influence?

Always. That's the problem with hard rock today...there's no "Purple" in it. They all sound technical and rehearsed. They were the kings of music gone wild.

Our cats wanted to know if TNT renamed an album or song after a cat what would it be called?

TNT—"def Garfield!"

Could you mention a solo or composition that has really stuck with you through the years?

"Gymnopedia" by Eric Sate.

CHAPTER 35

Bernie Marsden

(Born Bernard John Marsden, May 7, 1951, Buckingham, Buckinghamshire, England)

Bernie Marsden played with a host of acts before deservedly hitting the big-time with Whitesnake. Marsden played with such acts as Wild Turkey, Babe Ruth, and Paice Ashton Lord (playing and writing on this band's one and only album *Malice in Wonderland* in 1977) with little notice but had briefly been with legendary British hard rockers UFO in 1973 touring and recording a few demos before moving on.

Joining the newly formed Whitesnake led by ex-Deep Purple front man David Coverdale in 1978 changed everything, and it was here where Marsden's undeniable writing and playing skills were able to be utilized. Each Whitesnake album during this time period saw the band building to superstar status in the UK, Europe, and Japan but largely unknown in the US, despite moderate chart action.

Bernie formed a guitar tandem with Micky Moody, another fine player who was an especially great slide player. But Bernie was a master at playing with delicacy, mixing in blues and rock in his playing. Every note counted in his solos, and each one was as memorable as the last—a true testament to his writing.

Whitesnake's style from 1978–1982 was a combination of blues, hard rock, and R&B. The band was able to avoid pretensions and came up with a simple, yet stellar formula. The classic 'Snake lineup of Coverdale, Marsden, Moody, bassist Neil Murray, and Coverdale's ex-bandmates from Deep Purple in keyboardist Jon Lord and drummer Ian Paice had chemistry that oozed into the songs and albums and biggest of all…the live performances. All six members had a job to do and did it with the greater good of the band in mind.

Beginning with the 1978 EP *Snakebite*, each album that followed showcased Bernie (and Micky's) well-respected blues styling mixed in with hard rock and the occasional element of jazz and boogie. They were as good and subtle a guitar tandem as exists in hard rock history. The debut album *Trouble* established the blueprint: tight rock 'n' roll, with blues and some boogie rock. The title song and the storming "Take Me with You" were excellent songs based in the blues but rocked up. *Lovehunter* followed and has a similar style with "Walking in the Shadow of the Blues" and "Love Hunter" instant classics.

The band's finest hour was *Ready an' Willing*, which was to become their first Top 10 album in the UK and also cracked the US Top 100. "Fool for Your Loving" became a Top 20 single in the UK and was a classy taste of what the band was all about. The song even hit #53 in the US despite no promotion for the band or touring there. Marsden co-wrote the song that was initially written for B. B. King, but they kept it for themselves. The title track was a groove-heavy cut that was also a UK hit single. Dramatic cuts such as "Carry Your Load" and "Blindman" showed sophistication as did the brilliant "Ain't Gonna Cry No More" that was half acoustic and echoed Led Zeppelin.

One of the finest live albums of the decade was next up with *Live…In the Heart of the City*, which is a firecracker from start to finish. If you ever need to prove to someone that Whitesnake was actually a blues band before all the hairspray of the late '80s, here's where you should start. This is a tremendous live album and the rendition of "Ain't No Love in the Heart of the City" is phenomenal and the crowd laps it up, giving Coverdale everything he is asking for. The guitars are a joy to hear. Whitesnake truly were one of the greatest dual lead guitar bands of all-time. Powerhouse versions of the Deep Purple classics "Mistreated" (here in eleven minutes of spine-tingling form soaked in sweat and emotion) and "Might Just take Your Life" (where Bernie sings some lead doing a damn fine Glenn Hughes impression) are a major highlight as well.

In 1981, *Come an' Get It* slithered its way to #2 in the UK and produced the stunning "Don't Break My Heart Again," a song of emotional depth that few critics thought Coverdale and the band capable of. The song hit the UK Top 20. "Child of Babylon" and the mid-tempo "Girl" were great songs and then there was "Lonely Days, Lonely Nights" that featured blissful guitar work and aching melancholy that make this song one of the greatest Whitesnake would ever record.

In 1982, *Saints & Sinners* was a letdown, yet it was another UK Top 10 album. Many of the songs were generic, didn't leave a lasting impression, and the inter-group dynamic was now suffering leading to Marsden, Murray, and Paice all leaving before the tour for the album. This album did spawn the now-legendary "Here I Go Again," which was a Top 40 UK single co-written by Coverdale and Marsden. Of course, when the song was re-recorded by the band for 1987's *Whitesnake* LP, which sold over 8 million in the US alone, it went to #1 on the US singles charts aided by a music video with Coverdale's fiancée Tawny Kitaen romping around in a smidgen of clothing. Also on *Saints & Sinners* was the crushing blues of "Crying in the Rain" a tour de force of power and conviction that would also be re-recorded for the 1987 album.

The guitar work on every Whitesnake album is amazing as Coverdale has always had incredible players such as Mel Galley, John Sykes, Adrian Vandenberg, Vivian Campbell, Steve Vai, Warren DeMartini, Steve Farris, Doug Aldrich, Reb Beach, and Joel Hoekstra. That's a serious set of names. Bernie is at the very top of this esteemed list.

After departing Whitesnake, Bernie formed Alaska, who released two albums of AOR-styled pop/rock with *Heart of the Storm* (1984) and *The Pack* (1985). He has issued numerous solo albums over the years, including a very fine effort called *Shine* in 2014. He has also been part of Company of Snakes playing both old 'Snake material and new songs and the Moody/Marsden Band with old axe foil Micky Moody.

Blues rock virtuoso Joe Bonamassa recorded one of Bernie's songs on his 2012 album *Driving Towards Daylight,* paying homage to one of his favorite players. Bernie has guested with Whitesnake in concert over the last several years, which has been a great thing to see. The man playing his 1959 Les Paul is a familiar sight to any fan and Bernie has his own custom PRS model as well.

Bernie has continued with his solo career issuing his new album *Shine* in 2014 and Bonamassa makes a guest appearance on the record. Bernie's guitars and his voice are really in fine form after all these years. *Shine* is an album that proves Bernie is not just a guitarist but a genuine and honest singer/songwriter as well, and he really has a wonderful singing voice.

It was also a true treat to hear from Bernie himself and here's what we were able to chat about in November of 2014:

Who were some of your main influences as far as guitar playing goes?

George Harrison, Peter Green, Eric Clapton, Duane Allman, Steve Lukather, I could go on and on!

What are your preferred guitars of choice live or in the studio? I'm assuming the '59 Les Paul is one of them? And how do you feel the signature guitar with PRS turned out?

I pretty much take the guitar I want at the time and I enjoy playing it that day. The Beast is an incredible guitar—ask Joe Bonamassa—the reissue was very, very good I have to say. The PRS sig is a proud moment for me, a best seller at this time and now in six versions!

How and why did you and Micky Moody work so well as a guitar tandem in Whitesnake and beyond? The two of you complemented each other incredibly well and within songs. Your trade-off solos with Micky on "Ain't No Love in the Heart of the City" in particular are so wonderful to listen to. And was there a favorite Whitesnake album you played on? To me, Ready an' Willing was the very best.

We always had an understanding; we knew we were good players, but neither of us were attention seekers as lead guitarists. It was always about the quality of the songs and how to make the guitars fit within the structure—we were very good at that—on stage, well that was different; we could play a bit! I like *Ready N' Willing* and the live album is close.

Is it true there was a chance of playing with Paul McCartney and Wings around 1978 or so? You would've fit in so well with that sound.

I had a call from their office via Howie Casey; we were going to have a play, not an audition. After a few weeks passed, I was looking for a gig, then I ran into David Coverdale—he thought I had joined Wings! He was in London to put a band together, we got along very well, and then I had to call the Macca office to ask them to un-consider me!

One of my favorite solos of yours (and Whitesnake songs) is "Don't Break My Heart Again." That solo showcases your taste and knowledge of what fits within a song and where flash is not needed. Could you describe your feeling on that solo and song?

That solo is down to producer Martin Birch; it was the run through. The first half of the song I was getting a sound, and by the time the solo arrived, I had it, and just played through; after the take Martin said, thank you, that's it. I was amazed, spent another hour on it, and then he went back to take one, no wonder he worked so well with Peter Green!

What were your thoughts on the hit reworkings of "Here I Go Again" (1987) and "Fool For Your Loving" (1989)? As a co-writer of those classics, were these versions interesting to you? Also, you have a solo acoustic version of "Here I Go Again" that is simply sublime on vocals and acoustic—is that how the tune was originally written on guitar?

"Here I Go Again" is a monster from many angles. The original song was a Top 10 record over here in the UK; I knew it was a good song, but I was no way prepared for the remake in 1987. I like the up-tempo version a lot, Dan Huff on guitar, but there is intensity on the slower version. The song is featured so much on TV and movie soundtracks, I guess it is my bit of rock immortality! The acoustic version is how the song began; I never tire of playing it live, and people's reaction is amazing and always different.

Was your tenure in UFO a good one? I know it didn't last, but you were the first guitar player to head them in the right direction.

My time in UFO is still vague! With hindsight, it was a great new experience that I didn't appreciate at the time. But it was all new at the time; musically I tried to inject some grit. The previous guitarists were pretty much space cadets and into freeform, I wasn't that type, even at twenty years of age. I even found them my replacement Michael Schenker. I apologize to Michael after all these years. He's a great player and was remarkable to watch and hear when I first met him.

What was it like being involved in those Shakespeare productions of Henry V *and* A Winter's Tale*? Quite interesting I'd imagine.*

I loved the discipline, totally different gig for a road musician. I was able to be creative within another whole group of very talented and creative people. Both times it was Shakespeare at the National Theatre in London with Sir Nicholas Hytner directing, so as a rookie I was in incredible company. I would love to do it again at some point, Broadway are you listening!

What has it been like to work with Joe Bonamassa? And on your new solo record Shine*?*

Knowing and working with JB is a joy. He is a great guitar player, has a wonderful band, and works his ass off! I loved his version of "A Place in My Heart." He did it his way and it worked beautifully. It was almost certain he would be on the *Shine* sessions, but I was conscious of letting him have a non-blues track; sure we can play blues all night, but on the record I had this Jack Bruce type vocal thing going and I wanted to hear that JB guitar sailing through, which it does. He played the Beast by the way.

Silly question I ask most guitar players for my cats: If you could rename a Whitesnake song or album after a cat, what would you come up with—ha ha?

"Live in the Heart of the Kitty." That is *so* bad!

Recommended solo: "Don't Break My Heart Again"
from *Come an' Get It* with Whitesnake (1981)
Further info: www.berniemarsden.co.uk
Photo credit: Olivia Marsden

Dave Meniketti

(Born David Meniketti, December 12, 1953, Oakland, CA)

Dave Meniketti has been slinging his guitar in Bay Area hard rockers Y&T since 1973 when the band was known as Yesterday and Today (after the Beatles album).

Y&T was a covers band but ditched that scene for being an original act by 1974, and the band's classic lineup was set with Meniketti (also an outstanding vocalist), rhythm guitarist Joey Alves, bassist Phil Kennemore, and drummer Leonard Haze. After two solid but unexciting albums on London Records went nowhere in the late '70s, they slimmed their name to Y&T and signed with A&M Records in 1980, soon unleashing *Earthshaker* in 1981, one of the greatest debut albums by an American rock act ever. If songs like "Hungry for Rock," "Hurricane," "Rescue Me," and the dramatic seven-minute finale to the album "I Believe in You" don't speak volumes as to how good this band was, then I'm not sure how to help you understand this band's greatness.

Sales were still slow, but on the rise. In 1982, *Black Tiger* was a mighty beast indeed. The crunch of the title cut, the power of "Open Fire," the high drama of "Forever," and the direct rocker "My Way or the Highway" were very strong songs. The album boasted a bold production by Max Norman, who worked on Ozzy Osbourne's legendary first two LPs. *Black Tiger* made the outskirts of the UK Top 50 and they put on a tremendous set at the Reading Festival there. The band's career was moving forward now.

The year 1983 saw *Mean Streak,* an even better album that featured the awesome title song, which became a Top 25 rock radio hit in the US—the band's first. With a snarling, insistent and highly memorable riff, "Mean Streak" boils over with excitement. Meniketti delivers an awesome vocal performance along with one of his finest solos. No wonder this track is so beloved and broke the band in their home country. "Hang 'Em High" is as heavily charged as the band ever got and "Straight through the Heart" equally punishing. Y&T's sense of balance remained in check though, and "Midnight in Tokyo" has all the right melodic touches.

With *In Rock We Trust,* in 1984 the band achieved new commercial heights as the album narrowly missed the US Top 40 and came close to Gold status. The richly melodic "Don't Stop Runnin'" became an MTV favorite with its ultra-corny video and received significant radio play. Though this album wasn't as heavy as the last few and saw some slicker material, it remains an enjoyable listen. Y&T also adopted an awkward mascot at this time in a robot named Rock who would join them on stage. The band was now playing bigger venues on their own and opening for Twisted Sister and Rush among others. A headlining show was filmed in San Francisco and aired as an MTV Saturday Night Concert event in 1985. In that show Meniketti had a guitar solo spotlight and dedicated it to Jimi Hendrix.

The live album *Open Fire* contained a new studio track, "Summertime Girls," which was an irresistible song despite being the slickest thing they'd ever done. The song hit #55 on the US singles charts and the video was a huge hit on MTV featuring lots o' scantily clothed babes on the beach...and that damn robot. Some headbangers griped, but what's wrong with a hit single? The track still sported a fine guitar solo and the band was having fun.

While Meniketti could play speedy, he often chose to rely on notes that had purpose and sincerity as opposed to "shredding," which is why he was/is so respected. The riffs had purpose and were often thematic, while the solos had crunch and tenacity. The band lost their way for the mid- to late-'80s, but so did many acts. In 1985, *Down for the Count* was appropriately titled and not representative of who they were.

A switch to Geffen Records saw 1987's *Contagious* fare respectably reaching #78 in the States (the title cut was a radio/MTV hit) but not to the levels expected. Jimmy DeGrasso was now in on drums. The song "Contagious" was a shouty, Bon Jovi-sounding anthem but got the job done. The album chased too many current trends, however, and the band was losing their vision. Even so, the aching blues of "I'll Cry for You" is chilling and remains a career highlight.

Alves was replaced by Stef Burns in 1989. After 1990's *Ten* (appropriately the album peaked at #110 on the charts) that featured the killer speed metal tune "Goin' Off the Deep End" and the minor hit power ballad "Don't Be Afraid of the Dark" the group split, re-forming in the mid-'90s for a few decent albums that were more focused and stripped back and a smattering of live shows. It wasn't until the early 2000s that the band resumed regular touring duties.

Still together to this day, the group delivered *Facemelter* in 2010, a triumphant return and a seriously heavy affair musically. An outstanding track called "On with the Show" ranks among their finest compositions and "Blind Patriot," "I'm Coming Home," and "Shine On" are all such strong tracks. *Facemelter* is one of the very best Y&T albums and was a joy for the fanbase.

Kennemore tragically passed away in 2011 after battling cancer, which was awful, but Brad Lang took over bass duties, joining drummer Mike Vanderhule, who had been on board since 2006, and John Nyman on guitar since 2001 when Burns left for Huey Lewis & the News. This is one of the strongest and proudest (and longest-running) lineups Y&T has ever had.

The familiar sight of Dave with either his Gibson Les Paul or Fender Strat is a vision of bliss to Y&T fans around the world. Meniketti also has serious respect from other musicians who have publicly stated their admiration for his playing including Joe Satriani, Steve Vai, and Ronnie James Dio among many others.

In June 2014, I was fortunate enough to spend some time talking to Dave about the guitar and his career (and cats).

Who were some of your influences as far as guitar playing goes and how did you get into guitar playing?

Well, it was a great time to be getting into guitar playing because Jimi Hendrix was coming on the scene and all of the British Invasion bands of the '60s and players like Jeff Beck and Clapton and so on and so forth. There were just so many different types of players coming on the scene in that ten-year period (1960–1970) that were inspirational to me, and definitely Hendrix was one of the first because of his style and the types of songs that he was writing and crafted.

For some reason I just turned into this guitar-playing freak, and I would just sit and listen to music all the time on the FM channels that, at the time, were playing all kinds of varied things. I sat there with my little reel-to-reel tape deck and, if something sounded good, I would tape it and try to find out who it was, and that was kind of my intro into rock music. A couple of years after I started playing the guitar I got into the bluesier side of things, and while not just blues, I loved the Allman Brothers Band and the playing of Dickey Betts and Duane Allman, and there were so many different avenues of playing hitting me all at the same time, and I really loved that stuff because to me they were playing more from the heart with all these extended jams, and then they would come into these great riffs and it didn't seem planned out—it was spontaneous.

Correct me if I'm wrong, but I hear some of the late Paul Kossoff of Free in your playing. You mentioned passion and playing from the heart and this guy, to me, was exactly that. He felt the blues and his vibrato was incredible.

Oh yeah, a great player and another guy to me—and probably you as well on the under-appreciated list—is Leslie West. Leslie has got tons of passion in his playing and always has, and I love his vibrato and the way he attacks his guitar playing. So that was another guy that influenced me early on as well.

As a child of the '80s who grew up on MTV, I was thrilled to death when you did what I believe was your first video for "Mean Streak" in 1983 and started getting video play. I also liked that you took a lighthearted approach to your videos with songs like "Don't Stop Runnin'" and "Summertime Girls," which got significant play. Were you aware of the impact MTV was having on your career? There was also the Saturday Night Concert Series show from 1985 that Y&T were featured on.

Yeah, I mean we knew that things were growing. We were just having a heck of a time just breaking into the US market because breaking the States is a tough one, as every state is like another country. At that time you could go from state to state and hear some different songs on the radio in certain markets, not like now where it's like one giant radio station with the same songs. Because of that variety, there were people in many states who just were not hearing our music because maybe a station didn't know who we were or a programmer just didn't want to take the chance and play us or whatever.

So we were aware that when the "Mean Streak" single and especially the video broke out, that was really our first chance to get any kind of action in the US. And when "Don't Stop Runnin'" ended up getting quite a bit of play on the radio in 1984, that I think was more of a turning point for us because we were getting asked to do some things amazingly like *American Bandstand*.

We were on tour with Twisted Sister on the East Coast and had a couple of days off and we were in our hotel in New York, actually at the Mayflower, and I remember our manager got off the phone with somebody and he comes over to us in the lobby and says, "We have to get on a plane tomorrow morning early because we're going to be on *American Bandstand*." We were like, "What? That is so bizarre!"

[Laughs] and we had to think about that, and so things started to happen around that time and that record started to go places and we were aware that things were moving, but to us it was still a very slow process. And we were getting good tours, too, so that helped.

It was 1984 when I saw you guys in Philly open up for Rush at the Spectrum. The next day, of course, every kid would wear their shirts proudly so everyone knew what show they'd been to. I showed up to school in my Y&T shirt and the kids were like "When did those guys play?" I said, "Last night," and they asked, "Wasn't Rush last night and aren't they your favorite band?" I said, "Yes, they are." So they said, "Why do you have a Y&T shirt then? Where's your Rush shirt?" My response was, "I already have a Rush shirt!" I actually got a few friends into your music because of that damn shirt!

[Laughs] I'm thinking you were in the minority there but I thank you!

I was also very happy to see the classic four albums from the '80s remastered finally and under your control.

Basically, we were granted the licensing rights by Universal for those and, of course, we had to fight long and hard for that and we had to bend a little bit, but we figured why not? It's worth it for us to spend way more than we should per CD just to get these damn things out there because for twenty-something years, every time I'd see a fan, they'd ask when are we gonna finally get *Black Tiger* and *Mean Streak* on CD, and *Earthshaker* and *In Rock We Trust*? And I'd think, gosh I'd love to and at that time we talked to Universal and they just said, "No, you can't have them." When my wife took over as our manager eleven years ago (2003) that was one of the first things she took care of with Universal and they finally let us do it.

I gotta ask about that riff and solo on "Mean Streak." Could you possibly tell me your memories of how you came up with those?

Yeah, "Mean Streak." Hmmmm…that's a tough one to remember, but I think I did it the way I always approach my solos: I approach them in the studio. When we wrote a song in our rehearsal studio, we would demo it down to a cassette or something like that and we'd remember the parts and everything, and I never worked my solos out. I was just never that kind of guy to do that. I would just spontaneously play whatever when the solos section came around. So when we recorded the actual tracks in the real recording studio, I would sit there and compose a solo. I would actually try ten goes at it and figure out if I got anywhere with it and listen back, and if I said God, this doesn't do or say anything or I got half of it, let me keep going—it was that kind of a thing. And that's how I would end up doing a solo on most of the Y&T albums. Certainly in the '80s, that is exactly how I would do it. I just played it until I thought that I nailed it.

And that's amazing to me, because that solo in particular sounds so composed because it is memorable and thematic. It belongs there and it has purpose. I hear each of those notes every time I hear "Mean Streak."

Yeah, and on the outside looking at me soloing as I'm standing over the recording console and the engineer and producer are in-between me, it was kind of a bizarre thing because I'm so into getting into what I am doing and at the end of every take I am panting and sweating and my fingers would be hurting like crazy because I'd be digging in so hard, and every once in a while you'd stop after a solo and feel good and the guys would go "Holy shit! That's it!"

And I'd listen back and go, "Nah, that ain't happening [laughs]!" That's the way I approach everything that I do, whether it's lead singing or lead guitar playing—it's all out of emotional value and nothing worked out in advance. Like I said, when all of a sudden I hear a part that I hit on and it sounds cool, I'll try to remember that and the next take that I do, I repeat that along with nailing the other part that I thought sucked!

Would you pretty much say Gibsons are your guitar of choice or would it be a Fender?

It's a cross between a bunch of different guitars now. *Mean Streak* era was pretty much all my Les Paul. There were occasional songs here and there where I took the Strat out, but I didn't really play a Strat too much in that era. My first guitar was a Strat because I was inspired by Hendrix, of course. And then I got into Les Pauls because of Jimmy Page, and I thought that's the guitar for me, and once I got one, I never looked back and I sold my Strat. In the mid-'80s or so I started picking up a Start once in a while for a certain part on a record or something like that.

Truth be told, about 1985 or so, a guy that was a really big fan worked for Kramer. He found out that Joey (Alves) was a really big fan of Kramers, and he said, "Dave, would you like to try one, too?" And I said, "Yeah, actually I like the one that Joey got." So they sent me one and I still have it and still play it. It's an old, white Kramer Baretta, and I've used that guitar for sixty to seventy percent of the solos I've played on every record from *Contagious* on.

I had no idea. The things you learn.

In fact, a lot of people don't realize that some of their favorite solos that I've played over the last twenty years were played on that Kramer. I love the feel of it and the attack and the way it acts when you hit it certain times, depending on the amplifier that you were using. It has a great feel for soloing. Nowadays, I keep it between three guitars. I still solo with the Kramer, I still solo with two of my Strats, and definitely with the Les Paul.

And my question from my cats is what album or song would you rename after a cat?

[Laughs] Well…speaking of cats, our guitar player John just got bit by a cat while visiting his family in Norway. We flew out to do the Sweden Rock Festival and he went there a week in advance of the festival. A cat bit him and scratched him so hard on his hand, that I guess one of his fangs went into his tendon. Basically, what happened was one of his hands swelled up like crazy and he was on antibiotics when we played Sweden Rock and then he got home and it was still bad even with a second antibiotic and he had to get it operated on. They had to open up his hand and cut it out!

He was in serious pain due to the infection and bacteria, which had really messed up his hand. In fact, he has to go back and get his tendon reconstructed because it actually disintegrated in one part of his hand.

Was this a feral cat that was outside?

You know what? It was somebody's cat like a cousin or something like that, and they were all freaking out because the cat was trying to get out of the house and they asked John to grab it and the cat went nuts on him and there ya have it. And since then, I can't tell you how many stories I keep hearing from all kinds of people in the medical profession and otherwise that say getting hospitalized for cat bites happens all the time. I was like, "Well, holy shit!"

Ah, I've got it then! Perhaps a remix album called Catagious?

[Laughs] *Catagious*, there it is! [Laughs again]

This is what happens when you're teaching elementary school kids—I apologize! And wasn't John the robot named "Rock" for you guys in the '80s?

Well, he was one of them. I'm trying to think back now. On that MTV concert you said you watched…

The show from 1984?

Yeah, that was the one. He was the robot then.

To be honest, I remember the robot being booed pretty profusely when you were opening for Rush in Philly.

[Laughs] Of course, of course! We knew we were taking a chance and we knew that playing to Rush fans, there was a decent possibility that Rush fans were just gonna hate us! We just said, we gotta do what we do and maybe by the end of the set we will win some of them over.

Oh you definitely won some over musically, but when the robot came out I remember going to my friends, "Oh no!"

Ha ha! Yeah I know. It was kinda cornball, but at the time it was a funny and fun thing to do. And it was for John and a couple of the other guys that got in the suit. And, of course, they hated it because it was so hot. John was great at using the stilts, because you had to use two-foot stilts since the costume was seven-and-one-half to eight feet tall.

Well, its stuff like the robot and the MTV videos that I gravitated to Y&T for because you looked like you were having fun and that you were genuinely good guys. No real horror stories or tales of debauchery.

That was to our benefit and to our detriment because people said maybe if you guys were bigger assholes and more debauched you would've been bigger! We were too normal and, if that's what it was, well, so be it. We truly loved what we were doing and we weren't pretentious fucks, you know?

There are quite a few positive comments about how damn good this band still is in concert. To be honest, the last album Facemelter *should not have been as good as it was considering your age, you know?*[Laughs]

[Laughs] This band live is just in another place right now. We are so proud of ourselves right now, and I don't want to just ring my bell, but honestly man, I've been doing this for like forty years and every time we go out and play a show, I can't tell you how high the percentage is at the meet and greets that tell us they've seen the band for twenty to twenty-five years and that this is the best they've ever seen the band. I mean, sure they could be kissing our asses, but you can really tell that they mean it. That just means a lot to me.

Recommended solo: "Mean Streak" from *Mean Streak* with Y&T (1983)
Further info: www.yandtrocks.com
Photo credit: Jill Meniketti

CHAPTER 37

Dario Mollo

(Born Dario Alberto Mollo, December 30, 1959, Genova, Italy)

Dario Mollo is a guitar virtuoso born in Italy who began his musical career with a metal band called Crossbones in 1981. The group had impressive players and, though it took a while, they did eventually record an album that saw release in the late '80s, though the group would disband as Mollo had musical visions that were much higher.

He would open up a recording studio (Damage, Inc.) in his native Italy and he continued to write, produce, and play with others all the while having his eye on recording another album.

Mollo would be introduced to ex-Black Sabbath singer Tony Martin, and they recorded a fantastic album as the Cage in 1999. The self-titled album allowed Mollo to showcase his breathtaking skills on cuts like "Cry Myself to Death," "Time To Kill," and "Infinity" along with a cover of Deep Purple's "Stormbringer." The album received very good notice amongst the metal community, and the meshing of Dario's guitars and Tony's voice was natural.

The *Cage 2* followed in 2002 and was equally as good with songs such as "Terra Toria," "Overload," and "Amore Silenzioso." A cover of Led Zeppelin's "Dazed and Confused" was tremendous. This is one of the best Led Zeppelin covers out there, seriously. Again, the

playing and songcraft here was really well conceived. Another album was released in 2012 entitled *The 3rd Cage*. The album lacked the magic of the first two, but still had some great songs, including "Violet Moon," "Cirque Du Freak," and "Wardance." The guitar work was as exciting as ever.

Linking up with another former Sabbath vocalist, Mollo and Glenn Hughes (also ex-Trapeze and Deep Purple) formed Voodoo Hill and two albums were a result: *Voodoo Hill* (2000) and *Wild Seed of Mother Earth* (2004). These albums allowed Dario to go some different places than the Cage albums and it was an opportunity to hear him flourish with yet another amazing vocal foil.

Besides running his state of the art studio, Mollo remains active with his playing, whether it's in a solo capacity or with Tony Martin once again in his band Headless Cross. Dario has produced or engineered such diverse acts as Anathema, Satan, Cradle of Filth, Lacuna Coil, and Skyclad and has earned much respect for his ear and knowhow in the studio as for his guitar excellence.

I was able to interview Dario in August of 2014 and ask some questions that he was more than happy to answer.

Who are some of the guitarists and bands that have inspired you to play the instrument?

I started to play guitar after listening to Deep Purple; my style is a mix of Ritchie Blackmore, Eddie Van Halen, and Tony Iommi.

Can you describe what it's been like to work with such incredible singers as Tony Martin and Glenn Hughes?

They are very different singers: Tony is a perfectionist and he takes quite a long time in writing/recording, Glenn is a genius and everything seems very easy for him—he takes no time to do a huge amount of work.

How do you get your tone?

I am experimenting all the time. I have my tone in my mind; I can replicate it also with an acoustic guitar.

What are your guitars of choice?

I prefer Stratocaster shape and Les Paul sound; basically they are starts with humbuckers and Floyd Rose.

It shows in your playing how much practice you have dedicated to the guitar. Just how many years did it take for you to get to where you felt you had achieved your own style and sound?

I learn something new every day, but I practice very little; I'm lucky to be able to play fast and clean very easily.

Can you describe the origin of the riff and solo on "Cry Myself to Death" with the Cage?

During the writing process of the album, Tony asked me for a new song at 3:00 p.m., at 5:00 p.m. of the same day the song was ready, sometimes it happens and these are the best songs.

Italy has always had a strong progressive rock scene; is there also a good hard rock/metal scene over there?

Not commercially but many people love this kind of music, unfortunately not the industry.

Silly question: if you could rename a song or album you've done based on cats what would you call it? My cats want to know—ha ha!

I have many cats here in my home and I love them a lot, I could dedicate an album to my favorite one, something like *Songs for Teo…*

CHAPTER 38
Vicki Peterson
(Born Victoria Anne Theresa Peterson, January 11, 1958, Northridge, CA)

Vicki Peterson has played on some of the biggest hit singles of the 1980s and made it sound like she was playing in the 1960s. Her jangly style has always been an appealing part of the sound of the Bangles, the band she formed with her sister Debbi (drums) and Susanna Hoffs (vocals/guitars) in 1981, Los Angeles, California. Bassist Annette Zilinskas completed the lineup.

The early style was a mish-mash of punk and pop and they were still known as the Bangs at this point (for legal reasons in 1982 they became Bangles). An EP was issued on Faulty Records in 1982, which saw them in a new wave/pop mode. The label soon went under, but I.R.S. signed the band and reissued it in 1983. A bit later, Zilinskas left and ex-Runaways bass player Michael Steele joined. A major label deal with Columbia followed and *All Over the Place* surfaced in 1984, reaching #80 in the US and producing a minor hit single in the UK with "Hero Takes a Fall." The album was enjoyable power pop/new wave and also featured "Going Down to Liverpool," a dreamy '60s pop song that was a cover of a tune by Katrina and the Waves. This is a great example of the sounds that Peterson was playing on guitar, and the video with the girls being driven around by a stoic Leonard Nimoy is genius.

© CHRIS SIKICH

After opening major arena shows for Huey Lewis & the News and Cyndi Lauper, the girls returned with *Different Light* in 1986 that became a massive hit album, selling over 3 million in the US and scoring enormous hits with the Prince-penned "Manic Monday" that hit #2, and the silly "Walk Like an Egyptian" that became a #1 hit. A cover of the Jules Shear song "If She Knew What She Wants" (#29) and "Walking down Your Street" (#11) continued the hit parade. All of these songs were concisely played, proving the band had serious musical talent. Peterson's guitar work was melodic and creative, especially on "If She Knew What She Wants" and a fantastic version of Big Star's "September Gurls" where she was sublime in her guitar playing with a detailed solo paying homage to that power pop classic.

Vicki had a chance to really rock out on a scorching cover of Simon & Garfunkel's "Hazy Shade of Winter" from the *Less Than Zero* soundtrack in late 1987, showing a heavier edge, and the song went all the way to #2. *Everything* was the band's next album going Platinum in 1988 and creating two Top 5 singles in the psychedelic-pop styled "In Your Room" and the #1 ballad "Eternal Flame," which Hoffs supposedly recorded while naked. Hey, whatever works. "Be With You" was also a Top 30 hit, but the end was near due to internal dissension and conflict and they split in 1989. She filled in for the Go-Go's on guitar in 1994-1995 for some live dates.

Vicki went on to play with the Continental Drifters for a spell. The band re-formed in 1999 and recorded the song "Get the Girl" for the soundtrack of *Austin Powers: The Spy Who Shagged Me,* directed by Jay Roach, who was the husband of Hoffs. The song was an sprightly pop rock song with some '60s flourishes, and it showed just how they were even better as musicians and singers a decade later. A reunion tour followed in 2000, and they sounded excellent and the shows did very well.

The reunion album *Doll Revolution* came out in 2003 and was unjustly ignored. This was such a strong album and a rollicking take on Elvis Costello's "Tear off Your Own Head (It's a Doll Revolution)" kicked some butt, while the pretty "Something You Said" became a minor radio hit. "Stealing Rosemary" (with a simple, yet perfectly executed solo) and "Single by Choice" (written solely by Vicki with some strong lyrics and reverbed guitars) were also examples of how good this album was.

In 2005, Steele left and Abby Travis took over until 2008 and she is now in the Go-Go's. In 2011, *Sweetheart of the Sun* was released and featured new bassist Derek Anderson and longtime keyboardist Greg "Harpo" Hilfman. This album contains rootsy '60s and '70s elements, including country rock and '70s AM-friendly pop rock. "Anna Lee (Sweetheart of the Sun)" is one of the very best songs the group has ever recorded, echoing both Neil Young and Big Star with a dose of R.E.M. Simply wonderful writing, singing, and playing, as Vicki's guitars chime and rock in all the right ways. "I Will Never Be Through With You" is sleepy country rock channeling CSN&Y, Poco, and the Byrds, and the acoustic number "Circles in the Sky" sounds like something Gram Parsons might have done, while "Ball n' Chain" rocks.

Most important to note is this is who the Bangles really are, and bravo to them for putting out such an album. Vicki Peterson proves throughout the record how diverse her tastes and sounds are. And how about the explosive, thoroughly authentic cover of the Nazz classic "Open My Eyes" from the '60s? This is table-set for the girls and they knock it out of the ballpark, and Vicki's biting guitar riffs are just as snarling as Todd Rundgren's on the original, and their vocals couldn't be any better. Vicki Peterson is a guitar player who deserves more recognition, and if the band continues to put out albums like the last few, she will receive more of the attention as a guitarist she truly has earned.

Vicki was yet another guitarist who made me happy by answering some of my queries in February 2015 and here are the words that followed:

Who were some of your main influences as far as when you were first playing guitar?

I first started playing guitar as an accompaniment to songwriting, really, so I was listening to the way Joni Mitchell and Paul Simon played to support their songs. Of course, I was a big Beatles fan, so I absorbed the way George Harrison played melodic lines again, I think, in support of the song, as opposed to a separate musical statement. I was never really interested in learning to play lightning-fast licks or how-many-notes-per-second-can-I-fit-into-a-beat kinds of solos. Later, I was hugely impressed with Bonnie Raitt and Nancy Wilson of Heart. They were the ones who probably reinforced the belief that a female guitar player was a beautiful thing.

What types of guitars have been your favorites through the years, live or studio?

I've played the same guitars live and in studio for the most part for years—a '73 Gibson Les Paul and a '67 Fender Stratocaster have been staples. But since we designed a Bangles model guitar with Daisy Rock Guitars a few years ago, I've been playing that instead of the Strat on the road—the old guitars have to stay home now. I also love the sound of my Gretsch Country Classic Junior.

There is a very distinct '60s sound to your playing. Is it fair to say acts like the Beatles, the Hollies, the Who, the Byrds, and such have played a role?

Why, yes—is it that obvious? I guess it's natural to reflect the sounds you first fall in love with, and for me that was '60s-era pop records. But I also think that playing clubs in the early '80s with punk bands and friends like the Dream Syndicate and the Three O' Clock influenced my playing, making my approach looser and less self-conscious.

How exactly did the Prince-written "Manic Monday" come about and how was it decided to approach that song?

The song came to us on a cassette recording. Prince had suggested we just sing over his tracks, but of course we tracked the song ourselves, using the cool harpsichord figure he'd written. Although it's very "Prince" in many ways, I always thought it fit us well—sounds like something we could have written—wish we'd written, actually!

The rendition of Simon and Garfunkel's "Hazy Shade of Winter" had a very aggressive, heavy edge to it. The guitars really had a lot of drive. Who came up with the arrangement?

We'd been playing that song in our set since the early clubs days and brought it out again for the *Less Than Zero* soundtrack. The rock edge to it just seemed to fit the time and temperature of the film. Rick Rubin, who'd been producing the track with us, hated the "time...time...time" intro we came up with so much he took his name off the recording.

"In Your Room" had a trippy, psychedelic vibe. How did you get the guitar sounds on that song?

Oh boy, now you're testing my memory! I think that was the song that I played David Lindley's mandocello on—for the main guitar figure. We wanted that drone sound, almost like an electric sitar (which I have played on subsequent songs, but I don't think on this one).

In 1994–1995, you toured as a member of the Go-Go's. Was that a good experience and how did you have to adapt your style to those songs?

It was a wonderful experience in many ways. I enjoyed the novel feeling of being a "side-guy" (or "side-chick" as Jane Wiedlin called me) and concentrating on playing. I had been playing more first position folk rock-type chords in the Continental Drifters at the time, so switching to Charlotte Caffey's style—all barre chords all the time—gave me a mild case of Carpal Tunnel Syndrome!

Doll Revolution was a strong reunion album and "Something You Said" should've been a smash here in the US, although it did become an adult contemporary hit. Sweetheart of the Sun is one of the best things you've ever done, and your playing on "Ana Lee (Sweetheart of the Sun)" is wonderful. The song reminds me of Tom Petty, the Byrds, Neil Young, and then you add yourselves in the mix. The cover of "Open My Eyes" by the Nazz is perfect and smokes! It was a choice that makes total sense. You must be proud of the way these albums came out going at it after all these years?

I am very, very proud of those recordings. We had to fit the actual hours in the studio into already busy lives, but we worked very well together and, for the most part, made the records we wanted. Brad Wood co-produced *Doll Revolution*, and he was generous, fun, and easy to work with.

By *Sweetheart of the Sun*, we were anxious to do it all in-house. Literally—it was recorded at Matthew Sweet's, Susanna's, and then my own home studios. I enjoyed being my own engineer and doing some of the final guitar parts in solitude. I am a serial band member and love interaction and brain storming, but on *Sweetheart* I learned to trust my instincts, too.

A final silly question I ask most players: If you could rename a Bangles song or album (or two) after a cat what would you come up with? My cats are curious—ha ha.

Tell your cats that they are being very kitty-centric and self-absorbed. But they're cats and won't care. (I do love cats). I can imagine two cats named "Crash and Burn"…

Recommended solo: "September Gurls" from *Different Light* with the Bangles (1986)
Further info: www.thebangles.com
Photo credit: Chris Sikich

David Rhodes

(Born May 2, 1956, London, UK)

One of the most original-sounding guitar players of the 1980s, David Rhodes was far more concerned about sound and atmosphere than he was doing elongated guitar solos or becoming a guitar god.

Rhodes started playing in his teens but didn't really become part of any serious musical projects until the band Random Hold, who were more on the artsy side of things and part of the burgeoning new wave scene. They came to the attention of ex-Genesis singer Peter Gabriel, who had them open for him on his 1980 tour of North America, which was an amazing opportunity. Shortly thereafter, Gabriel invited Rhodes into his band and he hasn't left.

Rhodes was able to play on some of Gabriel's groundbreaking third self-titled solo album in 1980 and then appeared on the 1982 masterpiece *Security,* which was an eerie, atmospheric album featuring a lineup of Gabriel, Rhodes, bassist/Chapman Stick player Tony Levin, drummer Jerry Marotta, and keyboardist Larry Fast, which, to this

author, is the best lineup Gabriel ever had. Aside from how successful the album was, it was the quality of the playing and the songs that were so stunning. The material was unorthodox and demanded the players to think outside the box, which they most definitely did.

Lengthy tracks, such as "The Family and the Fishing Net," the pulsating "Rhythm of the Heat" (recorded with the Burundi drummers of Africa), and longtime Gabriel favorite "San Jacinto" have something that is unconventional and artistic about them, yet totally intoxicating. Rarely will you hear Rhodes lay down common guitar licks as that's not his thing and not why he was hired. Of course, the album also spawned Gabriel's first US Top 40 single in "Shock the Monkey," which also had an award-winning video that was beyond demented and wonderfully so. The 1982–1983 tour featured the best performances of Peter's career and were thankfully captured on the double-live album *Plays Live* that captures highlights from several stellar performances on the North American tour. This was just before Peter hit the "big time" and was more or less the end of an era.

David also kept busy by playing with UK new wave/synth pop act Blancmange appearing on their albums *Happy Families* (1982), *Mange Tout* (1984), and *Believe You Me* (1985), two of which went Gold in the UK and produced a string of hit singles, some of which David appeared on. Rhodes also played for a bit with Art Rockers and fashion-heavy acts Japan in 1981, touring and playing on the live version of "The Art of Parties" which was a b-side to Japan's biggest single "Ghosts."

Adding to David's astounding resume was playing on Joan Armatrading's Top 20 UK album *Secret Secrets* in 1985, as well as being part of the studio-based project Vitamin Z, who enjoyed a hit with the song "Burning Flame" that same year. Also in 1985, he played guitar on some tracks on the album *Strange Animal* from Canadian progressive rock/pop singer/keyboardist Lawrence Gowan, simply known as Gowan. The album was a Top 5 seller in his native Canada and features the masterpiece "A Criminal Mind" that also made the Top 5 there. Gowan has been the singer/keyboardist in Styx since 1999.

The year 1985 also saw Gabriel do the score for the film *Birdy* that utilized some of the instrumental tracks of songs from *Security* and added new pieces. The score was moody, trancelike, and not surprisingly very atmospheric. The year 1986 saw the release of *So* and it was now official: Peter was a megastar.

So went to #2 on the US charts (#1 in the UK) and sold over 5 million copies. "Sledgehammer" not only became a #1 single but one of the most popular and influential music videos of all time. The song was a real departure for Peter with an accent on a Motown groove and a danceable feel. Rhodes' guitars had to be different on this track and he made it work seamlessly.

Another Top 10 hit was "Big Time," a supremely funky cut with punchy guitar stabs, while "In Your Eyes" became a much-beloved song with Rhodes adding color through his shimmery, jangly sounds dancing around Youssou N'Dour's glorious vocals. "Red Rain," "That Voice Again" (with those jangly guitars once more), and such were also tracks where David played his distinctive sound to positive effect. The '86–'87 tour lasted over a year and included dates on the Amnesty International tour in the summer of '86 dubbed *The Conspiracy of Hope*.

During this time, Rhodes played with Talk Talk, appearing on the marvelous album *The Colour of Spring* in 1986 that featured worldwide hits such as the phenomenal "Life's What You Make It" (slicing guitar parts here—just wonderfully done, and some of David's finest work), "Living in Another World" and "Give it Up" which happened to be the three songs David played on! The album was critically acclaimed and pushed Talk Talk to another level (and landed in the UK Top 10 and US Top 60). Rhodes also toured with the band when not with Gabriel and appears in a concert video from this tour with Talk Talk filmed before a massive crowd in Spain.

The year 1988 saw Rhodes playing on Peter Gabriel's astounding score for director Martin Scorsese's controversial film *The Last Temptation of Christ*, and this music, along with additional music not used in the film, became Gabriel's next album *Passion* in 1989, which won a Grammy and was haunting and involved some Middle Eastern music. There were few vocals and no lyrics, and Gabriel's band only appeared fleetingly amidst all the other musicians used. This is a very, very special piece of music.

In 1989, David laid down some e-bow guitar on Paul McCartney's engaging hit "My Brave Face" in a session that was just the one day, and he also played guitar on two cuts on the Pretenders album *Packed!* in 1990, including the excellent song "Criminal."

In 1992, *Us* was Peter Gabriel's next album, including the vengeful "Digging in the Dirt" when David had a chance to add some gritty guitar for a rare turn, the bouncy "Steam," the moving "Blood of Eden" with Sinead O'Connor, and "Secret World." The album was another huge hit and Gabriel toured the world and then some in 1993–1994, also bringing his WOMAD Festival to the US for the first time and headlining Woodstock '94.

Peter would not release another album proper until *Up* in 2002, but did release *Ovo*, a UK-only release for the Millenium Dome Project that featured other singers as well and the score for the film *Rabbit Proof Fence* in 2002 entitled *Long Walk Home*. All of these projects featured Rhodes, who also played a multitude of instruments on *Long Walk Home*. As for *Up*, it was a rather good album, but like *Us* was inconsistent. Nonetheless, it was great to have Gabriel back and hearing Rhodes's playing once more on some of the album's finest songs including the beautiful "Sky Blue," the harrowing "Darkness" (which echoed Peter's early '80s glory days), "No Way Out," and "More Than This." Peter put on yet another mind-blowing multi-media type tour for the album in '02–'03 and also did a few other tours, though as is his wont, he has yet to issue a proper follow-up album, instead opting to do saccharine orchestral albums of covers and his own songs.

In 2010, he formed the David Rhodes Band and released an album called *Bittersweet* with a truly excellent band, including Ged Lynch on drums, Charlie Jones on bass, and Dean Brodrick on keyboards. *Bittersweet* was a really good album, but in 2014, the self-titled *David Rhodes Band* bettered that album and had a stripped down trio of Rhodes, Jones, and Lynch. This album is so damn good! It will surprise people in that it is a dirty, gritty album of rock, art rock, R&B, alt rock, post-punk, and blues. Rhodes' voice has a shaky quality that works fantastic and even sounds a bit like his boss Mr. Gabriel. There is crafty material like the driving "If I Could Empty My Head" and "Waggle Dance," "My Blue Balloon," and "You Are the North Wind." This is high-quality music and Gabriel fans would dig it.

In 2012 and again in 2014, Rhodes was back with Gabriel's band for the *Back to Front* tour in which the *So* album was played straight through, along with other classics to rave reviews.

And, if all this wasn't enough (and it is!), David was a part of the lovely, talented, wonderfully bizarre Kate Bush's band for just the second-ever tour in her career (the other was in 1979) where she played shows from August 26 to October 1 of 2014 at the Hammersmith Apollo in London. Seeing as all tickets sold out in fifteen minutes, I'd say these shows were a big deal. The list of accomplishments is long for David Rhodes, but most importantly he has always been his own player, never trying to be something he wasn't. Maybe that's why he gets so much work.

I was able to have a chat in January 2015 on a variety of different topics and here is what David had to say:

Who were some of the players that inspired you to begin playing guitar and shape your sound?

Of course, I thought that Clapton in Cream was great, and Hendrix wondrous (which he still is whenever you hear him). The other players that caught my ear were John McLaughlin with Miles Davis as well as Lifetime and his solo album *Extrapolation*. There's Chris Spedding with Nucleus as well. Phil Manzanera of Roxy Music leant me his copy of *Anthem of the Sun* from the Grateful Dead—Jerry Garcia was wonderful. I also enjoyed the *Live Dead* album by them.

Ralph Towner's playing, which I first heard on the Weather Report album *I Sing the Body Electric* sent me looking for his other work. *Diary* is a beautiful record. I listened, but I fear I never had the wherewithal to play like any of them. I did play a tiny bit of rhythm guitar in a school band, and then stopped at about sixteen to do other stuff, some sport and some art. I ended up at art school in London, as punk was starting to take off. I was actually on the same course as Glen Matlock of the Sex Pistols for my first year. They had just started to rehearse at that time.

The punk ethos of attitude over musical competence seemed and still seems right to me. I've always felt that it's better to have convictions and ideas rather than be another competent but dull player. So I guess notes and the speed of their delivery never held much interest for me. Sound and mood are much more important.

What types of guitars have you preferred over the years?

I started out mainly playing a Jazzmaster, which was a lovely old instrument. I bought it when the band I was in landed our first and only record deal. I then bought a Strat after working for Gabriel for the first time. Strangely, now I'm more of a Gibson player. I like the chunk of them. I play a Les Paul Studio mostly and an SG. I'm actually not too fussed over the tools. I think given any instrument and any amp players figure out a way of sounding like themselves quite quickly.

You have been a mainstay of Peter Gabriel's band since 1980 or so. In my opinion, the albums from Peter Gabriel 3 through the Birdy soundtrack were the best. Your playing was perfect for those albums, which had a very eerie atmosphere and a unique sound that nobody has equaled since. Security in particular is a favorite album of mine. Do you have fond memories of that era and any songs that are among your favorites to play from then or beyond?

It was an exciting time. PG wanted to experiment and I think to get away from using heavyweight sessioneers and use people specifically for their character and what it would bring to his thing. I enjoyed playing quite minimally and making sounds that blended with the keyboards of PG and Larry Fast. PG wanted guitar in the band, but not someone who wanted to solo and have a wind machine blowing in their hair. I may have had some hair then but not a huge amount. A wind machine would have been redundant. Traditional soloing was really not an option. I've never done that. We played "Family and the Fishing Net" a lot on the recent *So, Back to Front Tour*. It's a tune that people wanting to hear the hits struggled with. I really enjoy playing it.

The Plays Live *album from 1983 captures one of Peter's very best lineups. Can you tell me what it was like playing with that band (also including Tony Levin, Larry Fast, and Jerry Marotta)?*

It was wonderful. It was a very idiosyncratic outfit. Tony was as ever brilliant, Jerry brutal, Larry so creative with his sounds. I felt quite naive in amongst the gang, but I held my ground. I was the least worldly, but we had a lot of good times and sounded good. I remember Larry talking about "Lay Your Hands on Me," which when performed, was always teetering on the edge of falling apart. He suggested that there was inbuilt entropy in that tune. He then went on to say that that feeling ran through all the performance. We were trying to cover a lot of sonic ground and also not play things too straight. It was an interesting take on what was going on.

You played a significant role on the Talk Talk album The Colour of Spring *(and also played live with them I believe), including all three hits on that album. In particular, your playing on the classic "Life's What You Make It" was fantastic. How did you come up with that sound and those memorable guitar parts?*

Yes, I recorded with Talk Talk, and then toured with them in Europe, which was the only touring they did. I missed a couple of weeks, because I chose to do the first Amnesty tour with Gabriel. I was asked to go in and do a session for them one evening. I arrived at the studio and started to play a little bit. Mark Hollis asked me if I knew the work of a trad jazz clarinetist, called Acker Bilk. Acker was a player that used to play on a lot of TV variety shows in the sixties and seventies. His big hit was "Stranger on the Shore." I said that of course I knew his style. Mark suggested that I should play like him. Again, I wasn't enough of a player to play like that, but I felt I understood the mood and louche quality that I think Mark and Tim Friese-Green (the producer) were after. I came up with the part. The sound was a combination of the pedals I used and a Mesa Boogie. I was paid £120 for my work.

You also did some work with Japan, which was a musical arrangement that made sense. Do you recall working with them (I know it was only briefly around 1981)?

I was asked to join them on their *Tin Drum* tour. It was a little strange, but I enjoyed it and learned from the experience. Playing "The Art of Parties" was always fun. Mick Karn was a lovely bloke and it's very sad that he died recently. I bumped into Richard Barbieri a few months ago, having not seen him for a long, long time. It was a pleasure.

I'd imagine doing the rare, recent tour with Kate Bush had to have been musically rewarding. Could you describe what those shows were like from your perspective?

Playing for Kate was brilliant. She's lovely, funny, challenging, and very sure of what she wants. The band was great, my friend John Giblin (PG 3-era) on bass, Omar Hakim on drums, Jon Carin (Floyd/Roger Waters) on keys, along with some other exceptional players. The rehearsal period was long and intense. Having said that, Kate was generally approving of the way I approached the music. I'd made sure I was well prepared and had worked on sounds before going to the first rehearsals.

A few days before the opening we were doing production rehearsals, and seeing what the whole thing was going to look like. It was adding up to be something mind-blowing. The band was the main part of the first section of the show. The second part we were mostly hidden. The third part we were very much part of the action.

Four days before the first night, Kate said to me that when I started a solo in the final tune of "Sky of Honey" that not only did all the band have to don bird masks, but that I had to get off of my riser and dance with her. My dancing has always been limited. After having said that, I am shameless, so I danced with her happily every night for a few weeks. With the movement and the bird mask I think my playing was enthusiastic but perhaps a little wayward!

Another act you played with quite a bit was Blancmange. It seemed you jelled really well with those guys. Was that a good experience, and were you able to have a decent amount of input in what you would play?

Neil of Blancmange is a good friend. I've recently worked on a new album for him. His overriding thing is that he wants things to groove. He's very much an electronic writer. The playing I did for the latest Blancmange record is metronomic and with no overt guitar expression. The album is due out in March here in 2015 [*Semi Detached* was indeed issued in 2015]. I think in the past I tried too hard to express too much of me within their material. I did have free rein. "Feel Me" is a very cool track that I really enjoyed playing, "Blind Vision," too.

I also know you played (as did Tony and Jerry) on the Gowan album Strange Animal, *which is a very strong record. "A Criminal Mind" is a chilling song and there are many good moments on there. What was that experience like?*

I came to that album later in the process. Actually the guitar player who started the project was Chris Jarrett. He had been the lead guitarist in the teen school band I was in; a strange coincidence. I went in and played along to what was there. I remember enjoying it and it being trouble free...always a good sign. I guess I fitted in well. The record was a big success for Larry.

The David Rhodes Band has put out two albums and the latest self-titled one is outstanding—not a bad cut on there and so many different styles. You must be very pleased with the results, because this is some seriously good music.

I am happy with the album. If more people would buy it and more people come to see us play, I'd be even happier! I'm lucky that Ged Lynch (Gabriel connection) and Charlie Jones (Page and Plant, Goldfrapp) are such great players, and that Chris Hughes (producer) is so good. Tchad Blake (maestro) mixed it. To have that caliber of cohort is cool indeed!

One final silly question I usually close with. If you could rename a Peter Gabriel song or album you've played on after a type of cat what would you come up with? My cats are curious—ha ha.

I'm afraid your cats will have to remain curious. I have been a cruel and heartless father who only permitted his children to have goldfish. I know nothing of the feline specie. Having said that, the second time I met Kate Bush was at her house and I was shocked to see the hugest cat I've ever seen; a Maine monster. I kept my distance.

Recommended solo: "Life's What You Make It"
from *The Colour of Spring* with Talk Talk (1986)
Further info: www.davidrhodes.org
Photo credit: Michael Palmer

CHAPTER 40

Wendell Richardson

(Born Wendell L. K. Richardson, January 15, 1948, All Saints Village, Antigua)

World music before there was such a thing, Osibisa was truly a musical act from all corners of the world with Africa playing a major part. The fact that they became successful and were accepted internationally is a very cool thing indeed.

Osibisa had an original lineup featuring Teddy Osei (sax/flute/vocals), Mac Tontoh (trumpet), Sol Amarfio (drums) Loughty Lassisi Amao (percussion/horns), Robert Bailey (keyboards), Spartacus R (bass), and Wendell Richardson (guitar/vocals). Osei, Tontoh, and Amarfio were from Ghana, while Amao was from Nigeria, Bailey from Trinidad, Spartacus from Grenada, and Richardson from Antigua in the West Indies.

The group had been formed by Osei in London, who had been there on a music scholarship from Ghana in 1962. By 1969, Osibisa came into being, and in 1971, they issued their splendid self-titled debut album *Osibisa* on Decca Records in the UK and MCA in the US. The album combined everything from West African music to pop, Latin, funk, R&B, soul, and jazz but was certainly a precursor to world music. The album had so many colorful sounds, it was a wonderful feeling to just listen and absorb it all. The production by Tony Visconti (who had worked with and would work with David Bowie, T. Rex, Thin Lizzy, among others) did a really nice job of capturing all the sounds and styles and keeping it cohesive.

Osibisa was a surprise hit rising all the way to #11 on the UK album charts and #55 in the US. The cover artwork and logo design by Roger Dean (of Yes, Asia, Uriah Heep fame) was as creative as the music and enhanced the overall package. The seven-minute pieces "Phallus C" and "The Dawn" featured brilliant guitar solos from Richardson that crept out of nowhere. Richardson's rhythm work is part of the overall framework of Osibisa and it's easy to miss it if you aren't paying attention due to all the percussion, voice, and bass parts.

One of the things to admire about Wendell's guitar playing is the fact that he is not playing in a band that spotlights the guitar and yet when he gets those moments to shine—does he ever. His jazzy, afro-pop, rock, and blues licks and fills will please any guitar fan and "Phallus C" sports an excellent one for sure. A catchy, funky song called "Oranges" is as tasty as the fruit ("orange" you glad I made that terrible analogy?).

The live shows of Osibisa captured the spirit of the album and then some and audiences were thrilled at the band's performances. A second album *Woyaya* was every bit as good as the debut and was again produced by Visconti, featuring another stunning Roger Dean design with the now-familiar Osibisa elephant with wings mascot. Among the highlights were the Richardson-penned "Move On," the title track, and "Beautiful Seven," which the band referred to themselves as. "Woyaya" would be covered by Art Garfunkel a few years later. Now, that's respect. The album hit #66 in the US.

Heads featured a truly unique and demented album cover (by Marti Klarwein who had designed covers for Santana, a band that Osibisa sounded like in many spots) and more excellent material in "Mentumi" that was a Richardson co-write and featured some very good acoustic playing from Wendell in a rare turn, as well as "Kokorokoo" and "Wango Wango" that Richardson composed alone. The album made it to #125 in the States and was produced by John Punter and the band. Richardson departed from Osibisa in 1972 and would end up in legendary blues rock act Free replacing the absolutely brilliant but absolutely troubled Paul Kossoff, who was having major drug issues that would sadly claim his life in 1976.

While it was a bit of a headscratcher on paper, the decision by Free to add Richardson was a very cool move, and Wendell acquitted himself quite well on a US tour in 1973, as the band supported the awesome *Heartbreaker* album. Paul Rodgers (vocals/guitar), Simon Kirke (drums), Tetsu Yamauchi (bass), and John "Rabbit" Bundrick (keyboards) made a bold move bringing in Richardson, who had little to do with Kossoff's style. A listen to a rare bootleg of a show in Fort Worth, Texas, offers proof that this was not a perfect musical marriage but neither was it a disaster. It went rather well considering the difficult and trying circumstances, and Free would soon disband with Rodgers and Kirke helping form the mega-successful Bad Company, Yamauchi joining the Faces and "Rabbit" going on to the Who.

Richardson would return to Osibisa in time for the high-quality release *Welcome Home* in 1974 produced by longtime Uriah Heep producer/manager Gerry Bron, and quite well. The joyous "Sunshine Day" became a hit single in many countries (and a minor hit in the US). "Welcome Home" was another song of great spirit and "Seaside-Meditation" had a blistering guitar solo. This would be Osibisa's last album to reach the US charts at #200, though they would still have a loyal live following in many territories.

With *Ojah Awake* in 1976, Osibisa crafted another strong album with the seriously great dance feel of "Dance the Body Music" and "Flying Bird (Anoma)," a beautiful track that Richardson co-wrote. Thankfully, we get to hear Osibisa in their prime in a major concert setting with *Black Magic Night: Live at the Royal Festival Hall,* a live double album from 1977 that allows the band to really stretch things out and the jamming is intense. Richardson's guitars really get going here and "Fire" sounds phenomenal. Richardson would depart shortly thereafter and Osibisa is still going today after a myriad of lineup shifts.

When Richardson first left Osibisa, he made a very good solo album titled *Pieces of a Jigsaw* in 1973 under the name Dell Richardson. The cover art was a fantastical design by familiar friend Roger Dean. The title song is a lovely little jazz/pop tune smothered in a mix of light percussion, piano, and breezy acoustic guitars while Wendell (or Dell) delivered a soulful, raspy vocal that Seal would be pleased with. It is a truly great song that you will want to play often, and Richardson offers a sweet mix of acoustic and electric solos on guitar.

Richardson also formed the Digital Interface Band and has played many years with that project and continues to record solo, as his album *Omowale Byter* came out in 2014, and Dell's voice and guitar are still instantly recognizable. I was truly excited when Dell got back to me and we were able to do an interview in April 2015.

Who were some of the guitarists who influenced you as you were beginning to play the instrument?

The guitarists who influenced me most were Chuck Berry, Albert King, and B. B. King, as well as Wes Montgomery, George Benson, Andres Segovia, John Williams, Jimi Hendrix, and Steve Winwood.

What models of guitars have you preferred to play through the years?

As for guitars I like to play, Fender Stratocaster, Gibson Les Paul, Martin acoustics, Taylor acoustics, Granados Luther series, and Nylon Classic.

From the beginning Osibisa was a truly unique band in that they combined everything from the music of West Africa with Latin, R&B, funk, pop, and rock sounds. The debut album Osibisa *remains my favorite of the catalog. I love the rhythms of the song "Oranges." Do you remember laying down the solos on "Phallus C" and "The Dawn"? Those are highly expressive solos and really jump out since only certain songs by the band allowed for guitar solos.*

The album *Osibisa* had "Oranges," which was easy because we were playing it before at live performances, "Phallus C" was most challenging; it was once my favorite of guitar solos, but now it's "Fire" and "Living Loving Feeling" from the live album *Black Magic Night: Live at the Royal Festival Hall* recorded at the Royal Festival Hall in London.

"Phallus C" was written by Roy Beadeu (Spartacus R.). Yes, that was in 9/8 time signature and very expressive. In Osibisa there were such imaginative players as Robert Bailey with Lasisi Amau on percussion using the sticks on the side of his congas; you had to play well, plus we were hungry to perform. "The Dawn" was expressive, no minor scale theory. The term then was "Let off, and take off"! And indeed there was not much guitar solos in the music of Osibisa with so much drums and chants and such.

Woyaya *and* Heads *were just as groundbreaking with songs such as "Beautiful Seven," "Move On" and the title song on* Woyaya, *as well as "Kokorokoo," "Mentumi," and "Wango Wango" on* Heads. *You also had a part in writing some of these wonderful songs.*

How easy or difficult was it to find the spaces you would play in with so much going on in all these songs musically? And how would you decide on an acoustic part or an electric part?

Also, Roger Dean designed some amazing album covers for Osibisa. It seemed to go perfectly with the spirit of the music, do you agree?

Woyaya, you will observe that the credits changed as this album was re-issued to CD. It was covered by Art Garfunkel, and also the 5th Dimension; a song of which Osibisa would have to perform at all performances. *Heads* with "Beautiful Seven," "Wango Wango," "Mentumi" and my part in compositions; a stressful time indeed.

We produced this album; Robert Bailey also did a beautiful song called "Do You Know." I long awaited the introduction of the acoustic guitar as they found it too soft among the chants and percussion, etc.

Roger Dean's artwork was the best of the Osibisa albums. His work was married to the music, He also did my first solo album *Pieces of a Jigsaw*.

Welcome Home *is when you returned to the band and that album produced the memorable hit single "Sunshine Day." The grooves, the rhythms, and the spirit of Osibisa's music were a key element to the sound. These albums were always well produced, and by this point, you had Gerry Bron of Uriah Heep working with the band.*

I assume it was important to get the music and the vocals sounding cohesive as a unit because the albums really sound great—even today. "Seaside-Meditation" also has one of my favorite guitar solos by you. Do you recall creating that one?

Welcome Home was a new era for Osibisa. They now accepted my acoustic guitar not only on "Welcome Home" but also on "Flying Bird" (Anoma)." They finally discovered the power of the acoustic guitar, and of course the power of my voice. "Sunshine Day" was quite a hit without promotion. Gerry Bron and Ashley Howe produced this album. "Seaside-Meditation," I was never satisfied with that instrumental. To me, I never played anything worthy until the very end of it. Keep on trying, I said. Playing rhythm and licks and fills; that was much better.

In 1973, you were asked to join legendary blues rock band Free (who I feel were one of the greatest bands ever), due to the sad drug problems of their brilliant guitar player Paul Kossoff. This must've been a very difficult time for everyone, but what little I have heard (there is a hard-to-find bootleg of a show in Fort Worth, Texas, from January 19, 1973), and I happen to think you did a really nice job under tough circumstances.

How did Free or their management contact you and what are your thoughts looking back on that tour?

Yes, back in 1973 I auditioned for Free at the Rainbow in Finsbury Park. I got there and we all plugged into 400 watts of amplification; that was goodbye Osibisa. With Free, after the second blues jam, they said, "He's in." Then I was told I would have to send my passport to Island Records and by the weekend we were on our way to do an American tour.

They gave me a stereo to study their music, but the more I played their music, I began to hear just how awesome a guitarist Paul Kossoff was, and he was extremely compatible with Paul Rodgers. In fact Paul Rodgers was really cool. One night, I believe in New Orleans, the crowd was calling out "Osibisa," "Osibisa"!

I did not know how to deal with it, but Paul Rodgers simply came and put the microphone to my mouth, "Go on Dell say hello, and talk to them!" And I did and they simply went quiet. Ginger Baker was Simone Kirke's hero, Otis Redding was Paul's hero, Tetsu a really fine player, and a great human being. Rabbit was having a kind of serious friendship with Southern Comfort and we seemed to clash. Traffic's dressing room was across the corridor from FREE; Steve Winwood said I could use his Stubor tuner, to tune my guitar, wherever it was.

The stage was over an ice rink, so they rolled away the canopy from the ice, and eagerly got me to run to the stage, I fell on the ice, knocked my guitar out of tune, and bended the complete neck. Pranks may be okay after the gig, but to damage my guitar was definitely goodbye to Free.

You have a new solo album from 2014 called Omowale Byter. *It has some really fine playing and it's great to see you still making new music. How did you feel about this latest album?*

My new solo CD *Omowale Byter* was recorded in Antigua, but was not released until 2014. The album before that was *Nail Byter* recorded in London.

Recommended solo: "Phallus C" from *Osibisa* with Osibisa (1971)
Further info: www.facebook.com/dellrichardson01
Photo credit: Naoki Takyo

CHAPTER 41

Uli Jon Roth
(Born Ulrich Roth, December 18, 1954, Düsseldorf, Germany)

One of the most spiritual guitar players ever to exist, Uli Jon Roth is a master craftsman with a complex language spoken through his guitar. His tone transcends and enraptures, his soul and emotion are within his music, and he has explored numerous possibilities with the connection between the electric guitar and classical music.

German hard rock/heavy metal band Scorpions had lost their brilliant lead guitarist Michael Schenker, who left to join the incredible British hard rock outfit UFO in 1973, essentially splitting Scorpions having released just one album in 1972 called *Lonesome Crow*. Another band called Dawn Road featured Roth and absorbed two members of Scorpions in vocalist Klaus Meine and guitarist Rudolf Schenker. This then became a new Scorpions lineup since Scorpions was a more established name.

Roth, drummer Jürgen Rosenthal, bassist Francis Buccholz, and keyboardist Achim Kirschning were now all Scorpions and the band signed a worldwide deal with RCA releasing *Fly to the Rainbow* in 1974. This album was leagues above the debut, and with songs like the freewheeling rocker "Speedy's Coming," the nearly ten-minute title cut, and another lengthy piece called "Drifting Sun," the band was creating something vibrant, new and exciting, largely due to the influence of Roth. Here was an intriguing record. Roth's guitar playing was unlike anything at the time and Scorpions was unlike any other band for the most part.

With Kirschning departing and Rosenthal drafted into the army, a new drummer was found in Rudy Lenners in time for *In Trance* (1975). The now infamously risqué album cover featured a woman sexually embracing Roth's guitar with boob exposed! The melodic, moving title cut showcased Meine's amazing voice and Roth's guitars in tandem in harmony. Heavy hitters like "Dark Lady" (sung by Roth), "Robot Man," and "Top of the Bill" were accompanied by the poignant "Life's Like a River" and the Roth-penned instrumental "Night Lights." Roth's writing, playing, and vocals were all very much of spirit and feel. Uli was not only a brilliant player, but his inspirations, whether it was Jimi Hendrix or classical music, added to his overall character and sound. There was nobody like him then or since, though many have tried to emulate his style and sound. Also, remember how early this was in terms of what we now know as modern heavy metal. Aside from Judas Priest, there really wasn't anyone doing things like this in the '70s; not even the godfathers of metal, Black Sabbath.

Upping the ante, *Virgin Killer* followed in 1976 with one of the most foolish and tasteless album covers ever. At least the music persevered and people did realize the musical prowess inside and did not judge a book by its (hideous) cover. Material from "Virgin Killer" and "Catch Your Train" to "Backstage Queen" and "Hell Cat" featured speaker-melting guitar work from Roth that continued to amaze. Some of Roth's most masterful moments, however, came with the fan favorite "Pictured Life" with wicked harmonies and a melodic sensibility and memorable chorus hook that have lived on for decades as a Scorpions classic. There is as much power in the melody and lyrics as the riff here, and the open verses with Buccholz's thumping bass and Meine's tremendous vocals give way to Uli's intoxicating, thematic lead fills that become ingrained in the listener's brain. "Polar Nights" features mesmerizing axe work as well, and has Roth on a higher plane than mere mortals. Again, this was 1976 people!

Herman Rarebell became the next drummer in time for 1977's *Taken by Force*. While this was a great album, Roth was at odds with a more streamlined sound and did not care for some of the material. Like the true professional and amazing player he was though, he shined yet again. It isn't crazy to say that "The Sails of Charon" might be five minutes and sixteen seconds of the most mind-altering guitar work you could ever hear. The riff is so insistent and uses a variety of vibrato, accents, arpeggios, rhythms, and a feel one cannot imitate. This playing coupled with Meine's vocals make this as supreme a moment as any in the Scorps' legendary career. And when it comes to complexities, such as harmonic minor and Phrygian dominant mode, one can see what an influence this man had on all the neo-classical shredders that would follow in the '80s.

This album also had cool tunes such as the dramatic "We'll Burn the Sky" and Roth's "I've Got to Be Free" and saw the Scorps modernizing their sound, which was a sign that perhaps this was the end of a chapter and the start of another. Thankfully, Uli stayed on for the tour that led to *Tokyo Tapes*, a splendid live double album in 1978 that captured the band on fire for their Japanese fans and was an excellent farewell for Roth.

Uli then formed Electric Sun and released the daring album *Earthquake* in 1979, which was dedicated to Jimi Hendrix, who is somewhere in Uli's soul—trust me. The ten-and-one-half-minute instrumental title track is like listening to classical music composed for electric guitar and takes the listener on many travels during its duration. "Earthquake" is every bit as important a guitar piece as something like Van Halen's "Eruption." "Japanese Dream" and "Still so Many Lives Away" (with a whirling dervish of a guitar solo) are also highly recommended.

The year 1981 saw Uli issue *Fire Wind* that was every bit as challenging and rewarding as the first Electric Sun LP. This fantastic effort included another ten-minute work of excellence in "Enola Gay (Hiroshima Today?)," "Indian Dawn," and the surprisingly infectious and decidedly oddball gem "Chaplin and I."

In 1985, *Beyond the Astral Skies* was another complex effort, and Uli's tones and playing were magnificent and all his own, as always. Listen to "Elesion" or "The Night the Master Comes," which even got a bit of MTV support, helping the album chart in the US. Ex-Jethro Tull member Clive Bunker handled the drumming chores.

Following the end of Electric Sun, Roth followed his passion for classical music by playing with symphony orchestras and composing four symphonies and two concertos. Among the most impressive albums were *Sky of Avalon—Prologue to the Symphonic Legends* (1996), *Transcendental Sky Guitar Vol. I & II* (2000), and the beautiful *Metamorphosis of Vivaldi's Four Seasons* (2003).

In 2006, he reunited with Scorpions to play the massive Wacken Festival in Germany (this, after a reunion in France in 2005), and it went so well that he has joined the band on stage several times since, putting a smile on many faces. Uli has visited his old pals in Scorpions several times now over the years, which has been a wonderful thing for the fans and the band. *Under a Dark Sky* (2008) with Sky of Avalon was another classical solo effort. Respect was paid by Smashing Pumpkins leader Billy Corgan, who has had Uli jam on stage with the band a number of times since 2007.

It was especially nice to see Uli revisit his past in a modern way with the double CD *Scorpions Revisited* in 2015 as he tackles all the Scorps classics he was a part of from 1974–1978 with an excellent band, including vocalist Nathan James. The reaction to the album from fans and critics has been very, very positive and the 2015 *Scorpions Revisited* tour has really brought in the audiences.

Uli also helped with the construction of the unique and quite unusual Sky Guitars that can provide the high notes of a violin and have extra frets (30 in fact, and actually 35 including half step frets) which is pretty damn wild. Watching Uli play one of these things is a real treat. He still tours for fans each year worldwide and has become a painter as well. There's just no player like Uli Jon Roth—a man who has as intense a connection to the guitar and all its possibilities as any player there has been.

In March of 2015, I was able to speak with Uli at length about a variety of topics and he was awesome to talk to.

You know, once guys like you stop touring and recording I shudder to think what happens to music in fifteen to twenty years.

I am fortunate that I am one of the few able to so. I don't know the future, but I can still tour. Guitar-wise there just aren't too many acts who can keep touring on just their own name.

Who were some of the musicians who influenced you even if it wasn't just from the guitar?

Oh, I was very influenced by the Beatles before I started playing the guitar and I used to know all their stuff by heart. There was also classical music that has played a big role for me.

Which composers in particular?

All of the greats to be honest. In my mind I kind of tried to fuse these two languages together in an organic way that didn't seem contrived.

Contrived it never sounded like, as you were one of the very few doing such a thing within the realm of hard rock in the early '70s. Now you were in a band before Scorpions called Dawn Road that essentially became Scorpions around 1973, correct?

Yes, it was more like an amalgamation as both joined each other. Rudolf Schenker was in effect the only remaining Scorpions member at that time and then Klaus Meine came back into it on vocals. However, Scorpions were a professional band who had toured and done an album, whereas Dawn Road was essentially a college band. So, we just called it Scorpions with a new lineup.

I suppose that helped with club bookings since Scorpions already had a reputation at the time.

Yes, but Scorpions was not a name I exactly liked. However, Scorpions had been a professional act and a bit of a name.

Fly to the Rainbow was the first Scorpions album you appeared on and the title cut especially was something I instantly noticed where the sound had become more complex. Were you able to blend your lead guitars with Klaus's vocals pretty quickly? There were very intriguing melodic combinations with his voice and your lead guitar.

Yeah, we got on really well right away and I thought we blended well despite coming from different backgrounds and we shared a love for the Beatles. Klaus's lead vocal line is where I would often add a counter melody in the background of a song like "In Trance" and also in the chorus lines.

That was a perfect musical marriage.

I used to play a cello line or a theme to augment his main vocal line.

Songs such as "In Trance" set Scorpions apart from any hard rock acts at the time, especially with those counter melodies you mentioned. It just took a while here in North America for people to catch on.

That came gradually. We did have a cult following. RCA Records wasn't really a big fan of the band and didn't support the band initially. America wasn't giving us a lot of support at first, but in Europe and Japan things were going very well. It took some time with America but it did finally happen right around the time of *Tokyo Tapes*.

Virgin Killer had one of my very favorite songs in "Pictured Life." This was a perfect example of the balance of melody and hard hitting riffs. Do you recall the genesis of that song?

Yes, it was a joint effort between Klaus and me. The intro lead came from an idea I had recorded on a 4 track.

I cannot get enough of that song. The melodies and the theme leads on guitar are just brilliant. It is truly one of the highlights of Scorpions' catalogue! The emotions of the song are very pure.

Really? [Laughs] It is catchy and slightly different, so I suppose it does stand out.

It also has that driving bass riff in connection with the drums in the verses.

Ah, that was typical Francis; he was very good at that.

It gave the song a very open sound, and thus when the guitars come back in it sounds even fuller.

Almost like a Tango feel in 2/4. It's the only song we ever did with a rhythm like that.

I can't recall anything else sounding like it. "Polar Nights" is another great composition.

That is very much a Hendrix-based song that I always thought Jimi could've written. I always thought it was a rip-off of "In from the Storm" because it's in the same key, and then someone pointed out to me, "No, no—it's actually like "Gypsy Eyes"! He was right, so I had the wrong song. [Laughs] I guess it's a cross between the two. When I came up with the song, it was just natural and I wasn't actually thinking about those Hendrix songs.

Now I know you've probably been asked many times about this song on Taken by Force, *"The Sails of Charon," but I could probably play that 100 times straight without tiring of it.*

Have you heard the new version on my new album?

I sure have; I bought it already!

Oh, you bought it, okay!

That song has influenced many guitar players, including Yngwie Malmsteen, among others, and he covered it. The chords are so unusual and very intoxicating; where did you even come up with those chords to go together on a piece of music such as that?

You see, the chords are really pretty much Flamenco chords and the rhythm and intro lead, that triplet; are inspired by Flamenco as well. It isn't technically Flamenco, but it could be. In fact, a friend of mine, Ben Woods, has a band called Flametal and he did a version that was great of "The Sails of Charon."

Was this a piece you knew was special?

No, not really. At the time I was writing so many pieces of all types, including "Earthquake," that it was a prolific year for me, 1977. I knew the guitar lead was special because I hadn't heard anything like that back then. And the rhythm was unusual. At first it did not stand out to me as much, as there were other things I was writing that I felt just as strongly about. But once the album was out, we started to get a lot of feedback on the song and I started to realize that it was something special.

I always felt it wasn't quite finished and didn't have a proper ending. In 2005, I did an orchestral arrangement and I was very happy about it. The way we do it now live is the way I feel it should be and I am happy with that.

It did feel a little abrupt on the album.

It really wasn't finished yet. I thought in the back of my mind there was more to do someday.

At that time I know you weren't so thrilled with some of the songs the band was doing.

That was a part of the issue. I didn't like "Steamrock Fever," but it wasn't so much the songs but just that my time was up. I felt I needed to explore these other avenues and play different music and write in a different kind of way in an increasingly commercial band. Success was inevitable for Scorpions; we all knew it. I certainly saw it coming and it was obvious; all the band needed to do was keep going and get better and that's exactly what they did.

I remember reading somewhere that you felt the first night—which was not recorded for Tokyo Tapes—was the best of the three nights. Is that true?

Yeah, that was a shame. Personally speaking, the first night was the finest show we ever did in my five years in the band. The second and third nights were undoubtedly good, but there was something magic and extra on that first night. For me personally, my guitar playing was better that first night. I can't speak for everybody, but we all felt very strong about that night. There is a bootleg recording of that night, but the guitars are so soft from the recording of where the person was in the hall it just doesn't translate well; it's just history I guess.

The first Electric Sun album has a breathtaking track called "Earthquake." To me, that is essentially classical music, but with electric guitars assisted by bass and drums. It is a dynamic, driving piece with several changes and colors. I feel this is an extremely important piece of music. Where did it come from?

Chronologically speaking, it was written in the fall of '77 as well as several other songs. The intro was inspired by Beethoven. The rest is a musical journey for me. The song wasn't called "Earthquake" at first; that wasn't even my own idea. I was trying to do something symphonic with the guitar and several overdubbed guitars and the four part harmony on the intro as well as the kettle drums.

Then the end part with the ostinato bass run that goes on ad infinitum, to me, had a Franz Lizst-styled left-handed run, although it wasn't; you won't find that anywhere—at least I don't believe so. It kind of had that vibe for me and also had that Spanish sequence on top. The whole thing was more or less just there for me; it didn't take a long time to write it.

And that album was recorded with a band that was just a trio, even though it sounded huge.

Yes, that's right, although there were the guitar overdubs. There were no keyboards on that album though.

At times, it sounded like keyboards but it was clearly the symphonic guitars overdubbed and such.

I did use an Electric Mistress flanger on there, which I used a few times, including when the drums come in on the 6/8 part. The flanger provided an echo and the chords were played backwards. I like that intro section.

I know you have done a lot of work with orchestras. Have you revisited that piece with an orchestra?

Yes, we did it once live in Germany at a concert that was essentially a rendition of a lot of my *Transcendental Sky Guitar* pieces and we played the entire "Earthquake" intro and all with orchestra.

When you made that first Electric Sun album, did you feel that this was a new beginning for you musically and anything was possible? Fire Wind *was the next statement and was just as good.*

Every Electric Sun album was a new step up the artistic ladder. They were explorations of what I felt like doing. They weren't meant to be commercial, and in fact, they are not commercial at all.

That is safe to say.

Those albums did not make the impact on the music scene like Scorpions albums, but they did well enough for me to be able to sell out large theaters in the UK that seated 3,000 people. Each album reflected different areas of where I was going and the first album was me spreading my wings, including as a producer. I wanted to go about in a purist manner and didn't use a lot of effects. I restrung the guitars with relatively hard strings and tuned up to concert pitch as with Scorpions we used to tune to E flat. That gave it a completely different vibe and the guitars had very little distortion compared to what I had done before. It wasn't flashy or brutal but was more a reflection of a search for something new. In places I think it hit the mark and in other places I could do much better nowadays.

Probably so, but the album still holds up and there shouldn't be much change at all. That first Electric Sun album remains a special album for me, especially for 1978.

It took some time for it to be accepted. I did catch flack because it wasn't the *Virgin Killer* revisited, which is exactly what people thought I would do. It was kind of like an anti-statement, and afterwards it became very respected. I got critiqued for the singing but other than that, like you said, it has held up.

Well, I'm fine with the singing too. In 1985 you released the third Electric Sun album Beyond the Astral Skies *and I remember seeing the video for "When the Master Comes" on MTV a few times and here was an album that was as different from* Fire Wind *as that was from Electric Sun.*

That was my favorite of the Electric Sun albums and it was the hardest to produce and took the longest amount of time. To this day I am not ashamed of that album.

You should not be—that was another interesting album. If I recall, you dedicated that to Martin Luther King Jr.?

Yes I did. I had a habit of dedicating my albums to people I admire and respect.

In 2006, you reunited with Scorpions at the massive Wacken Festival and have done so a few times since. Those events seem to have been fun for you I'd guess?

Yes, most of them. Sometimes the sound or framework was difficult, but most times they were very enjoyable. The first time in France in 2005 was wonderful and had a real family vibe to it. We also did some nice stadium shows in Athens, Greece, and more in France and Germany.

You've also played on stage with the Smashing Pumpkins.

Yes, quite a few times.

Billy Corgan is a huge Scorpions fan.

He really likes the early Scorpions like *In Trance*. We did some spectacular jams on stage.

I remember seeing you jam with them on "Gossamer" on an MTV show for the Rock Am Ring I believe around 2007 or 2008.

Oh, I love that song! I didn't even know it at the time though. It was such a big festival—over 80,000 fans and it was the encore and I didn't know what was coming and it turned into this massive jam. It was really exciting. Billy is such a natural and he's not afraid of letting things become musical no matter where it goes. I was also blown away by their drummer Jimmy Chamberlain. It was over twenty minutes long and the whole band was great.

We would play again together in a number of cities in Germany and we also jammed at the Glastonbury Festival in England about a year or two ago, which wasn't as long but was also excellent and I didn't know where it was going! [Laughs]

Exactly how did he reach out to you?

It was by email and usually is; he just invites me. He will just say, "We're playing here tonight so bring your guitar and meet us there." The first time was at a NAMM show and Rudolf Schenker was there and told me that Billy was there and wanted to talk to me. I actually didn't know who he was because most of the '90s I was doing classical music, and once I listened to their stuff, I understood why they were so successful.

With all the albums of classical music you have done, I'd have to say the one that intrigues me the most was Metamorphosis of Vivaldi's Four Seasons *because "The Four Seasons" was one of the first classical pieces I came to enjoy in high school and I thought Vivaldi was wonderful. How did you feel about the challenge of doing that and arranging the piece?*

It went very well. It wasn't easy to do. It was quite a challenge to technically play these pieces in such a way that the guitar will be out front and can rival or equal the violin on its own terms because it is very, very awkward to play on the guitar. After I had a good look at the score I figured it out. The violin is tuned in fifths and it is relatively easy and the stretches aren't as big and it is very well-written for the violin.

On the guitar this is an awkward piece, but I made it my own by finding the right fingerings. I am good with that, so once I knew what to do and what not to do, it became very enjoyable. We played *The Four Seasons* in its entirety all in one go with an orchestra in Germany at the same concert that we did "Earthquake." I also wrote a fifth season, so to speak, which was a concerto called "Metamorphosis" that was based on some of the main themes of the piece.

The idea was to do a little time travel and see what other composers such as Chopin or Wagner might have done with these themes filtered through the eyes of the guitar. The Sky guitar to be precise because that's the only guitar that allows me to play at that kind of pitch! [Laughs] I didn't want to play the violin parts an octave down because that sounded completely wrong and awful with the other string parts.

How many units are there now of the Sky guitars?

About 50 of the limited edition, which is approaching the end of that run now. A lot of them are in Japan and some are in Europe and America. I've got a few of them. The limited edition was put on the market by Dean guitars.

And what have been your preferred guitar models through the years?

The first electric guitar I had was a Framus. It was a cross between a Gibson and a Strat, though different from either. From 1971 onwards, I played predominantly the Strat. On *Fly to the Rainbow* I played half the songs on a Gibson Firebird that I bought from Rudolph. I believe Michael Schenker owned it first, then Rudolph, and then me. It is a 1961 model.

I continued to use that guitar live for a few songs in the early days of the Scorpions. As for the Strats, I had a sunburst, and then from 1975 on I had a white maple Strat, which became my main guitar without fail. I also used those on the Electric Sun albums. The Sky guitar did appear on *Beyond the Astral Skies* a little bit.

I have a sunburst Strat. It's a 1972 and I've had it since high school around 1985 or so.

Oh really? Well, that's fairly close to the one I had, which was a 1971.

Well, how about that! And on the new album Scorpions Revisited, *how did you choose what songs you would be recording?*

That was actually relatively easy. I looked at the tracks on the old albums and picked the ones that stood out the most to me. The ones that I remembered being my favorites and that lent themselves best to this project. A few others were suggested by friends such as "Crying Days."

It was cool to see songs like "All Night Long," "Yellow Raven," and "Drifting Sun," which gave it a nice balance. On top of that, Nathan James did a really nice job vocally.

Oh yes.

Not an easy job.

No, not an easy job at all. He really nailed it.

And the response on the live dates so far, including the US?

The live dates have been great. The response has been great, virtually all of them. People are often quite ecstatic. We recorded a live DVD at the Sun Plaza Hall in Tokyo and the audience was nothing less than ecstatic. The reaction was excellent. It was phenomenal. I've also written a new album and want to record that next, but in live shows after this tour I will continue to play Scorpions songs.

That's great to hear. And I love the idea that you can go back again.

For many years I wasn't interested in that ground that I had already covered. I became interested again because I saw a new way of doing those songs and bring it to a new kind of level and that was the goal for this new album.

I was happy to hear it and the reviews have been very good and the audience reaction has been great from the clips I have seen on YouTube.

Yes, it has been very nice and quite encouraging.

Recommended solo: "The Sails of Charon" from *Taken by Force* with Scorpions (1977)
Further info: www.ulijonroth.com
Photo credit: Sonia Ritondale
Roth will be part of the *Ultimate Guitar Experience Tour* with Jennifer Batten (also in this book) and Andy Timmons (2016).

CHAPTER 42

Steve Rothery

(Born Steven Rothery, November 25, 1959, Brampton, South Yorkshire, England)

Without question, one of the most tasteful guitarists you will ever hear, Steve Rothery has graced the British progressive rock band Marillion with his tones and talents since their inception in 1979.

The original Marillion lineup contained Rothery, bassist Doug Irvine, keyboardist Brian Jelliman, and Mick Pointer on drums. Marillion was formed at a time when prog rock was considered passe and "Dinosaur Rock" by short-minded critics who seemed to be unaware that Progressive bands were still highly successful in the late '70s/early '80s with many eschewing the long-winded compositions of the '70s and focusing on shorter, more concise, and accessible songs. Marillion was not doing that, however; in fact, they were brazenly wearing their musical sleeves on their shoulders by embracing the '70s style of the genre with long musical passages and lengthy solo segments and soon writing conceptual pieces.

It wasn't until 1981 that the band decided to ditch the instrumental format and brought in vocalist Fish and new bass player Diz Minnit. By 1982, Pete Trewavas on bass and Mark Kelly on keyboards brought the band the talent to match their musical ambitions. Although critics laughed the band off, they were filling clubs and even theaters without a record deal; that would change when EMI Records (Capitol Records in the US) signed the band and debut album *Script for a Jester's Tear* hit the UK Top 10 in 1983 (also reaching #165 in the US and providing a minor rock radio/MTV item in "He Knows, You Know").

The album was majestic, beautifully arranged progressive rock that echoed Genesis, Pink Floyd, Rush, and the Moody Blues, among others, and was most definitely not Taco, Kajagoogoo, or Naked Eyes, who were ruling 1983. Epic tracks such as "Chelsea Monday" and the title song were filled with drama and emotion as well as theatricality courtesy of Fish's Peter Gabriel-influenced style of singing (not to mention donning face paint live), Kelly's keyboards and snyths were heavily influenced by the sounds of Genesis great Tony Banks and the ethereal, atmospheric guitar sounds of Rothery, who was always more concerned about mood, texture, and sound, as opposed to flash, speed, and too many notes.

During the band's 1983 tour they went through a myriad of drummers (John Martyr was with the band when they opened a week at Radio City Music Hall for Rush in the fall of '83 and were heckled badly by surprisingly nasty Rush fans), which led them to Ian Mosley who had played with Curved Air and Steve Hackett. *Fugazi* was a challenging listen and at times rather dark and venomous. "Jigsaw," "Incubus," and "Fugazi" were all fairly dense and harrowing and the album rarely made a pleasant listen. Regardless, it hit the UK Top 5 and produced hit singles in the jaunty "Punch and Judy" and the aggressive "Assassing."

The band's crowning moment occurred with *Misplaced Childhood* that went to #1 in England and broke the band in the US reaching the Top 50. The gorgeous "Kayleigh" went to #2 in the UK and was to be the band's lone hit single in the States, also becoming a Top 20 video on MTV. For this one moment in time, Marillion ruled the world. The romantically soaring "Lavender" was another Top 5 single in the UK and, because the song was so short, Rothery had to go into the studio and add one of his patented beautifully aching solos to extend the song for the single. *Misplaced Childhood* was a concept album a la Pink Floyd, with all the songs running into one another and concluded the story of the Harlequin who had appeared on all the band's album covers. The band toured the world in 1985–1986 and opened dates for Rush again in the US.

In 1987, *Clutching at Straws* followed, rising to #2 on the UK charts but only #103 in America. Three hit singles came from the album with the raucous keyboard-led "Incomunnicado," "Warm Wet Circles," and the heartbreaking "Sugar Mice." The album was anything but an easy listen as listeners watched the character it was based on unravel in a sea of despair aided by booze after looking at his life—a deadbeat Dad, a failed marriage, and a failed career in a band. The music and lyrics are possibly the best Marillion ever created, and other songs such as "White Russian," Hotel Hobbies," and "Slàinte Mhath" are as intense musically as they are emotionally and lyrically. Rothery's guitars throughout are sublime with each note, each passage, each fill, each accent always of delicacy and artistry. Do you want the proof that Steve "gets it"? Man, just listen to the solo on "Sugar Mice." Can't you just feel the sadness and the pain of the lyrics pouring out through his guitar? It's more than enough to bring a tear to your eye, and in a good way.

The recording sessions for *Straws* were less than ideal and despite a hugely successful tour in '87–'88, Fish and the others were at odds and at each other's throats. Sessions for a new album were abandoned in 1988, and Fish left for a lengthy solo career he maintains to this day. Death was predicted for the band just as critics had done for Marillion's heroes Genesis when Peter Gabriel departed in 1975. There, Phil Collins was promoted from within and against all odds (yeah, I said it), Genesis became even bigger. Marillion went outside the box for singer Steve Hogarth from new wave act Europeans. Hogarth looked, sounded, and wrote nothing like Fish.

Despite this gamble, Marillion crafted one of their very best albums in *Seasons End* in 1989, yet another Top 10 in the UK. Three more hits came from the album and Marillion's musical colors and shapes were still very much in line with what they'd done before as well as some new ideas. There wasn't a dud in the batch, and the epic opener "The King of Sunset Town" is a ravishing song from the seductive buildup of the intro to the musical explosion it leads to before we hear Hogarth's angelic voice. Rothery unleashes some furious solos on here and elsewhere adds his usual shadings on the haunting "Seasons End" (about climate change), "Berlin" (about the city behind the Wall that, ironically, would come down weeks after the album's release!) and "Easter" (dealing with Northern Ireland's issues and sporting one of Steve's most memorable solos in all its grandeur). The '89–'90 tour confirmed that Hogarth had been accepted by the demanding fan base.

The run of British Top 10 albums continued with the more pop-oriented *Holidays in Eden* in 1991, which was uneven, but produced three Top 40 hits including the delightful "Cover My Eyes (Pain and Heaven)," "Dry Land," and "No One Can," which both somehow eluded US radio programmers. *Brave* was a full-fledged prog concept album that was as daring as any album in 1994 could be. "Bridge," "Brave," "Living with the Big Lie" (another Rothery solo of excellence is here), "Made Again," and "Goodbye to All That" (which had some ripping guitar solos) were among the many splendid songs tying this whole tale together. Listen to the splendor of "Made Again" and the combination of Rothery's languid acoustic guitars and Hogarth's delicate voice and try not to weep!

Brave was about a girl who had been found wandering a bridge in England. Taken into police custody, she didn't know who she was or where she'd come from and refused to speak. Hogarth took the story and created a fictitious account of how she could've gotten to the bridge. This is a startling album and was played in its entirety on the tour.

Afraid of Sunlight from 1995 was an album that dealt with fallen celebrities, such as O. J. Simpson and Mike Tyson ("Gazpacho"), Kurt Cobain and Elvis Presley ("King"), and the title cut (actor James Dean), and easily ranked as one of their best with "Beyond You" and "Out of This World" all featuring Rothery's pinpoint guitar textures (listen to the crazed madness at the end of "King" for intensity spoken through the guitar). "Beautiful" was to be the band's last hit for many years from the album reaching the UK Top 20, and by 1997's

This Strange Engine, the band would start a lost journey on various independent labels with albums that were very much hit and miss. Unable to tour the US due to funding issues in 1997, the band's rabid fans made headlines by using the still nascent Internet to raise enough money to bring the band over for a tour. Marillion would continue to be ahead of virtually any and all acts in music with their revolutionary way of using the Internet to not only survive, but thrive from the late '90s onwards.

In 2004, *Marbles* surfaced on the band's own label Intact Records and was a concept album that was rather good and available in both single disc and double disc forms. This was the group's best album for years and fans purchased enough legal downloads of the singles "You're Gone" (UK #7) and "Don't Hurt Yourself" (UK #16) that they became hits, despite sneers from the critics. The slow-building "The Invisible Man" was thirteen minutes of creativity (and borrows everything from Pink Floyd to Radiohead in a very good way), while "Ocean Cloud" clocked in at eighteen minutes (only appearing on the 2 CD version) and ranks as one of the highlights in Marillion's extensive oeuvre.

In 2012, after a few misfires, the band returned with *Sounds That Can't Be Made* that had nearly eighty minutes of music, including the politically charged seventeen minutes of "Gaza," the fourteen minutes of "Montreal," and ten minutes of "The Sky Above the Rain," each proving that Marillion still had it in them to challenge both themselves and their fans and do so successfully, all the while sounding totally modern. Naysayers claiming the band are stuck in the '70s and '80s clearly haven't been paying attention as the band has been totally forward-thinking for over the last twenty years or so, although sometimes that has led to some of their least enjoyable albums. The band's willingness to try new things each time out should certainly be acknowledged though.

Rothery got the British Guitar Academy going in 2011 and also formed a side project called The Wishing Tree with singer Hannah Stobart who created two albums in *Carnival of Souls* (1996) and *Ostara* (2009). More important than that though was Steve's first solo album, an instrumental affair called *The Ghosts of Pripyat* in 2014 that is an intriguing album from start to finish. Rothery lays down all the foundations fans would expect, but also uses disparate styles with ranging emotional spheres to great impact.

"Morpheus" features Steve Hackett of Genesis and is eight minutes of atmospheric beauty, while "White Pass" (which has some crunchy, ballsy riffs towards the end section) and the title song are equally as resplendent. "Old Man of the Sea" features both Hackett and Steven Wilson of Porcupine Tree and is a must hear. The whole album is tranquil and certainly echoes Pink Floyd (pun intended), but this work stands on its own. To hear Rothery playing guitar over these sonic escapades for nearly an hour is satisfying, but don't expect to be rocking out—that's not at all what Steve or this album is about. Hopefully the future will offer another solo album from Steve. Marillion is already working on another album as of this printing in 2016. [It is tentatively titled *M18* and will definitely be released in 2016 with a tour (dates are already on sale and I have tickets!), but the album title could change.]

Steve Rothery is truly one of the most refined players one could ever hope to hear and his solos and musical passages through the years have been like one wide-ranging lesson in poignancy on the guitar.

I was beyond happy that Steve welcomed being in the book and answering some questions when we connected in May 2015, and here's how that ended up:

Who were the musicians who influenced you as you started an interest in becoming a guitarist?

My three main influences were Steve Hackett, Andy Latimer of Camel, and Dave Gilmour.

What have been your preferred guitar models through the years?

I originally played a Yamaha SG 2000 (I was a big Santana fan at the time) but started playing Strat type guitars on our second album *Fugazi* in 1984.

Script for a Jester's Tear couldn't have been more out of place in 1983, and yet, after seeing "He Knows, You Know" on MTV, I immediately went and bought the album on vinyl. You took a ton of crap from snobbish critics but became a success rather quickly because fans gravitated to Marillion and the prog rock style of the music and lyrics. How rewarding was that and frustrating at the same time? Also, the emotional solos on songs such as "Chelsea Monday" and "Script for a Jester's Tear" were a perfect marriage with Fish's lyrics and voice. Did that come naturally, or did that take time to develop?

We were never in fashion with the media, so we ignored any criticism, we knew what we wanted to achieve musically. My style of playing was always very natural to me. The emotional and melodic aspects of my playing were a consequence of those three original influences.

Fugazi had some great guitar-based songs, such as "Emerald Lies" and "Assassing" (which has been one of my favorite solos by you), and the record was rather dark and nasty at times. Do you agree that this album seemed to have a heavier edge both lyrically and musically?

It was the difficult second album syndrome with *Fugazi* (also finding the right drummer took quite a long time). Maybe the darkness made it a lot less commercial an album than *Script*.

Misplaced Childhood was the moment worldwide but especially in the US where you were now a success in many countries for the first time. I finally got the chance to tell everyone in high school that THIS was the band I had been telling them to listen to all those years! Did the dates with Rush go well in the US? For some reason it seemed some Rush fans didn't understand Marillion.

"Kayleigh" was a well-deserved smash and songs like this have such lovely, lyrical solos. Do you remember constructing the solo for "Kayleigh" and was it a song you guys kinda had a feeling about as far as being a smash? And, were you aware that MTV and rock radio were now really playing the band in the States?

The Rush tour was a great success generally. We went back to one of the venues in Canada later and headlined it ourselves. There was only one show in the US where we had a very negative reaction (people throwing coins at us).

I can't remember the moment I wrote the "Kayleigh" solo but nearly all of side one of *Misplaced Childhood* came together in a week down at Barwell Court, a big old house near Chessington in London. I'd already written some of the guitar parts like the "Kayleigh" riff. The solo was recorded live with the track and was edited down for the single version by Chris Kimsey, the producer.

My favorite album is Clutching at Straws and that is a harrowing listen, yet utterly compelling. Your solos on "Hotel Hobbies," "Sugar Mice," and especially "Slainte Mhath" (so much power and spirit in that song) are such highlights and each has a different approach. Could you take me through the guitar parts on "Hotel Hobbies"?

All the guitar parts on the album, with the exception of parts of "Incommunicado," were recorded with my Strat (EMG pickups, Kahler tremelo) through various Boss, Rockman, and Roland effects into a Roland JC 120 combo. "Hotel Hobbies" starts with the Rockman clean compressed and chorused sound into a Quadraverb. The solo sound is a Boss DS-1 distortion pedal with a Roland digital delay.

Seasons End *was obviously a huge turning point in 1989, but right from the opening notes of "The King of Sunset Town," I knew all was well. How nerve-racking was it with Steve Hogarth coming in from a little-known new wave band and replacing such an iconic front man?*

We had complete confidence in the music we were writing when Fish left the band, a lot of which became the tracks on *Seasons End*. We were amazed at the reception the fans gave Steve when we performed the album live. It all felt very natural.

Afraid of Sunlight *was a real gem and seemed to tackle the subject of the price of fame. "Gazpacho" is still a song that gives me chills and the different musical passages are haunting. I'm guessing this was about O. J. Simpson? I could be wrong, but that was always my take; what guitars did you use on that song?*

Yes, that was based on O. J. Simpson. Most of the song is the 12-string part of my custom Steinberger double neck (three single coil pickups) into the Rockman/Quadraverb/JC 120 sound.

Marbles *and* Sounds That Can't Be Made *are evidence the band can still write inventive, yet modern material. Are you happy with how those came out and what could we expect from the next album?*

Yes, very happy with both those albums. The challenge for us now is to try and—if possible—surpass or match *Sounds That Can't Be Made*.

Your solo album The Ghosts of Pripyat *is such a pleasure. I have played this album repeatedly. "Morpheus," where you have Steve Hackett (also in this book) and "The Old Man of the Sea" with Steven Wilson are awesome enough, but the acoustic title track and "White Pass" are seriously well composed pieces as well. I love all the tones and textures you used on this album. You had to have been pleased with this album and I sincerely congratulate you on it.*

I really enjoyed making my solo album. I used a new guitar (Jack Dent Raven), new amp (Pitcher Shadow SE amp) and a new pedalboard to give me some tonal variation from the Marillion albums. I'm already planning the follow up album.

A final, stupid question I ask most players in jest: If you had to rename a Marillion album or song with a cat theme what would you come up with? My cats are curious—ha ha.

No idea! How about *Clutching with Paws?* [*Okay, this was my title, and not Steve's, but I am giving him credit because he's awesome.*]

Recommended solo: "Sugar Mice" from *Clutching at Straws* with Marillion (1987)
Further info: www.marillion.com and www.steverothery.com
Photo credit: Stefan Schulz

CHAPTER 43

Howard E. Scott

(Born March 15, 1946, San Pedro, CA)

Guitarist Howard E. Scott grew up in Compton, California, and began playing bass for a while and then switched over to guitar. Soon, he was playing in clubs and bars, usually playing blues or R&B. In the mid-'60s he toured as a backing musician with the Drifters and was then drafted into the US Army in 1966. When he returned home, he formed a band called the Night Shift with his cousin Harold Brown.

In 1969, Animals front man Eric Burdon stopped in and saw the Night Shift playing and he and harmonica player Lee Oskar jammed on stage with them, which led to a musical pairing formed the very next day, also including Thomas "Papa Dee" Allen (percussion), Leroy "Lonnie" Jordan (keyboards), B. B. Dickerson (bass), and Charles Miller (sax), alongside both Scott and Brown. Just like that, a musical alliance was forged between Burdon and this band, now called War.

Live gigs followed and then came the album *Eric Burdon Declares "War"* in 1970, a Top 20 Gold album in the US fondly remembered for the hit "Spill the Wine," which imbibed its way to #3 on the US singles charts. "Spill the Wine" is one of those timeless songs. It has elements of Latin, jazz, pop, and R&B, and Burdon even talks his way through some parts like a hip lounge singer wasted, which in itself is an early, musical form of rap. Doing his thing in the guitar department is Howard E. Scott, all smooth and subtle.

Their next release was a double album *The Black-Man's Burdon* that was a bit out there with elongated jams and explorations with political themes. The label was less than thrilled and did little promotion. Burdon left during the tour and War completed it without him.

The self-titled debut album in 1971 didn't sell well and was inconsistent. A few songs stood out though, including "Sun Oh Son" which starts deceptively mellow, laced with dreamy harmony vocals, organ, flute, and harmonica, but then come a few tasty notes from Scott and the pace quickens and grooves are executed to perfection. Listen to the subtle picking and playing from Scott and you will see how cleverly he fit into this ensemble. "War Drums" is a percussive chant of the band's name and also stands out.

All Day Music featured the quality hit "Slippin' into Darkness," which is a tale with some funk from the streets at its finest and also highly topical. And yeah, you can hear a reggae vibe here that predates Bob Marley & the Wailers' classic "Get Up, Stand Up." This is such amazing music with intense lyrics and an undercurrent that has that darkness yet somehow finds the brightness. The song became a million selling Top 20 smash single. Here, Scott slinks around the groove with some sweet picking techniques.

With *The World is a Ghetto* in 1972, War confirmed they were one of the biggest musical acts in the US. The album went to #1 and provided two Top 10 hits in "Cisco Kid" (another million seller with an irresistible slow-burning funk sound that accented the band's vocals and allowed Scott to play some wah-wah riffs low in the mix) and the title song which ran ten minutes on the LP but was trimmed for single release. Scott's guitars are in wah-wah mode and in tandem with the bass and horns in a mellow setting, allowing the music to set the tone for another real-life tale. The outro features some delicious soloing from Scott in a rare turn.

In 1973, *Deliver the Word* became another Top 10 album. The hits this time around were "Gypsy Man" which made the Top 10 as an edit from the eleven-and-one-half-minute jam that was the song itself and remains one of War's finest moments. "Me and Baby Brother" would reach the Top 20 as well.

Why Can't We Be Friends? was another Top 10 album in 1975 and provided the world with two undeniable classics in the honking grooves of "Low Rider" and the feel-good title song. Both of these tunes have lived on for decades and forever will. This album also had the amazing seven minutes of "Heartbeat," which is a groovin' track filled with sunny, tropical sounds and a beat and main musical theme not too far removed from reggae. A Platinum-selling album *Greatest Hits* followed in 1976 including one lovely new song "Summer," which has a beautiful, simple, and understated sound with insistent melodies.

In 1977 came the release of *Platinum Jazz* a double album featuring lesser-known album tracks of the past and new jazz-oriented material, including the title cut and "L.A. Sunshine." The record was issued on Blue Note Records, the famous jazz label. Later that year came the album *Galaxy* that contained the slammin' dance-oriented title song, a Top 40 hit. The album was another Gold seller as was the 1979 release *The Music Band* that featured "Good, Good Feelin'" a track much like "Galaxy" with one foot in the classic War sound and another in the burgeoning disco and funk movements. Scott added his groove and tasty licks on songs such as this by playing slinky staccato riffs accenting the dance beats. The title song was a mix of R&B and pop sounding a bit like Earth, Wind & Fire, and like all songs here, was a very long piece of music.

The Music Band 2 did not sell well later that year, but some more cool material came out of this album like "Night People," which was supremely funky and exuberant. But like its predecessor, this album was inconsistent. In 1982, War returned with *Outlaw* and a minor hit in the horn-laced dance floor cut "You Got the Power." The title song was also a minor hit and was another dance track. These latter-day War albums were far removed from the band's classic sound and could not compare to the glory days, but War did show they could create dance hits too in the '80s as others like Earth, Wind & Fire, the Gap Band, and the Dazz Band had done.

War would continue to record and perform sporadically in the rest of the '80s and more or less became inactive, but in 1993, Scott, Brown, Jordan, Oskar, and latter-day members Pat Rizzo (sax) and Ron Hammon (drums) were back and issued a new album *Peace Sign* in 1994 that had a more organic sound much closer to what War used to be all about.

By 1996, things unraveled due to legal complications and Scott, Brown, Oskar, and a returning Dickerson became the Lowrider Band and still tour to this day playing the songs by War from War members the way they should sound. Jordan formed his own version of War using the name that was still owned by former manager Jerry Goldstein, which sadly has hurt the War name and legacy and has misled fans into thinking they are seeing the real War members who are forced to use the Lowrider Band name that many people don't realize is actually War. The music business proves all the time it's just that: a business, and an often ruthless one. Nonetheless, it is the Lowrider Band you want to see in 2015 and these guys still get it done.

Nothing can detract from the fact that War was one of the biggest bands in America creating an amazing run of monster hits few bands have ever attained. War were nominated for the Rock and Roll Hall of Fame in 2015, but didn't get in (as soooo many other great bands have not).

Howard E. Scott may not have been the flashiest guy with a guitar and rarely offered up lengthy solos, but close inspection of the band's numerous songs and albums will reveal a tremendous rhythm player with special feel, who could also play quality solos when required and his sense of timing and his writing and singing were also integral to the band's sound. Hats off to ya, Howard!

On a frigid, snowy day in February 2015, Howard and I hooked up for a great conversation that was fascinating to be a part of.

So, who were some of the players that influenced you growing up?

I'll tell ya what; there were two main players who were a big influence on my playing. One of them was my cousin Jack Nelson Jr. and he was a Texas-based blues guitar player from San Antonio and another guy who was from Southern California was a player by the name of P. J. Somerville, who really showed me what showmanship was about. He was absolutely a great guitar player.

What style?

He was a blues player. When I first started as a player I was a bass player and then I switched over to guitar later on. I played in blues bands in San Pedro, California.

And did you play in bands with your cousin?

Oh yeah, for sure I did. These guys taught me how to play guitar. I played bass behind them to pay the bills.

Would you say playing bass behind these guys helped your rhythm skills? I ask because of the fact that your style in War featured a lot of great rhythmic ideas.

It gave me a very different style of playing guitar; it sure did.

That connection makes sense to me. What types of guitars have you preferred through the years?

The Gibson ES-335 and that's what guitar I played all through War.

One of the best guitars ever created.

For me it is.

Is it true you guys actually backed up Deacon Jones, the football player of the Los Angeles Rams? Did I read that right a while ago?

Yeah, you read that right. We had a band called the Night Shift that was one of the hottest bands in LA, and before we met Eric Burdon, we were backing up Deacon Jones. We had a twelve-piece band with horns when we met Eric Burdon and Lee Oskar, and Eric had this idea in his mind of a small horn section with just sax and harmonica, so we dropped the other horn players and kept Charles Miller on sax and Lee on harmonica.

The idea of sax and harmonica together was a little odd, but it created a cool sound.

That was all Eric's idea. I learned so much playing with Eric Burdon. He was such a great showman. I had been the band leader for the Night Shift and I remained so with Eric Burdon and War and then just War and I learned so much from Eric about showmanship, stagecraft, and timing—he taught me a lot.

"Spill the Wine" was such a unique song and one could easily say that Eric was doing an early version of rap the way he spoke lines in that song.

Exactly! I think Eric Burdon and War was one of the most exciting acts around at that time; I really do. If you go back and listen to the Animals and what led to Eric Burdon and War with the arrangements, the fury, the roughness, the ass-kickin' playing, I tell ya we were on fire.

We were ready for anybody at that point. We were even ready for Deacon Jones. We played behind him for about half of a year and then we made the transition to Eric Burdon. Deacon was not a really good singer but a helluva football player and a great guy. Burdon was a total rock star.

And why was the collaboration so short lived?

With Eric Burdon?

Yes.

Good question.

And you did do a second album.

Yeah, we did *The Black-Man's Burdon* and that was a very political album. MGM Records thought they had War signed when they signed Eric Burdon, but they only had Eric. The label went ballistic about the album and more or less canned it. I'll bet there's a warehouse out there somewhere that has about half a million copies of *The Black-Man's Burdon* with dust all over them. MGM buried it.

So it's safe to say MGM didn't do a lot of promotion for the album?

Not at all! The guy who was head of the label was a guy named Mike Curb, who was the lieutenant governor of California. He promoted "Spill the Wine" and was happy with it, but not *The Black-Man's Burdon*. And when Eric left, it was now just War the band.

And that led to the first War album, a self-titled record around 1971 or so.

And that was not a good album at all.

It was hard to get into. The band was clearly in transition.

We weren't ready for that album. When Eric left the band we were on a European tour. We woke up one morning and he was gone! He left us in the UK and we went on stage that night and I was shaking and thinking, "He's gonna show up, I know he is." But he never showed up, so we went on stage simply as War.

The people that showed up that night were told Eric Burdon wouldn't be there and they had the choice of getting their money back or staying and just watching War play. Most people stayed to see War and we were totally unprepared and we lit that place on fire!

So who sang that night?

[Laughs] Oh man! I must've sang and other guys in the band. We did some covers and originals that we had in our set. The first War song I wrote was "Sun Oh Sun" and it did nothing as a single when it came out, but we played that. I really liked that song. And "Lonely Feelin'" and "That's What Love Will Do"; we did things like that that ended up on the first and second album. The second War album is where you could really hear what we were capable of, like "Slippin' into Darkness."

I was going to ask about that song because that was the first big song for War and an unlikely hit when you think about it. That is one great song.

I wrote that one. As a matter of fact that was from the time when we were with Eric Burdon.

That song really captured the public's attention at that time and became a million-selling single, breaking War into the mainstream.

It really did. I totally was surprised that "Slippin' into Darkness" did so well. We were in Paris and I wanted Eric to listen to it and I hummed it to him and...he didn't like it! [Laughs] So, I put back and when it came time to put out the War album *All Day Music* it was time and we were ready and I was starting to come into my own as far as playing and writing goes.

The writing and the vocal arrangements, the percussion, and your guitar playing, which had those subtle fills; there was just so much going on with all your songs and albums. I also liked that you weren't wailing away with a three-minute solo even on the really long songs.

The thing is War wasn't that kind of band. The songs made things flow, so it was more of a rhythm thing and the rhythm led to a chord structure that had to work for a War song and style. It required a different kind of guitar structure.

I think that's commendable. I can tell you had the chops to wail away, but it just wasn't necessary for War's songs.

In my early bands, I was the featured guitar player, so when you mention wailing—yeah, I was wailing away. P. J. Sommerville was showing me how to play like Jimi Hendrix and be a showman. That was me at that time, but when it came to playing in War, I had to change my style of playing to suit what War was doing. So I had to play a different type of guitar.

And to me that's a guitar player.

[Laughs] And that's what I did. I wasn't thinking of being a star player. I was just the guitar player for the band War. When it came to "Slippin' into Darkness" I did take the guitar to a different level and that was my chance to say this is what I can do on the guitar. That song gave me a chance to show what level I was at now as a player.

I don't think too many people realize that quite a few of your hit singles were edits of songs that were actually seven, eight, maybe even ten minutes or more in length.

Yeah, War was probably one of the first Jam Bands. We would go into Wally Heider Studios in Hollywood and we'd just let the 24 track machine start rolling and we'd have a ten- to fifteen-minute song, and we would build and build until you could identify where the main point was. I would come in with the whole song written and it would be in the middle of this jam and we'd find the song that way. I did a lot of that writing.

With so many endless, monster million-selling hits like "Low Rider," "Why Can't We Be Friends?," "Cisco Kid," "The World is a Ghetto," and "Gypsy Man" you guys were on such a ridiculous roll and pulling from all kinds of influences and sources to create all this music.

It could've kept going but internal stuff started happening. I think with all bands there is a growth pattern and with Eric we were all in our twenties and all of a sudden you have more money than you can even look at to spend and then people got lazy and they didn't want to go on the road or record, so it caused friction and every band goes through that I'm sure and it happened to us.

I think every group of human beings goes through that. When you get more than one personality and one opinion it all changes.

True. Bands always break up or have problems when they have this great roll going.

What was the Platinum Jazz *album all about in 1977?*

That was a Steve Gold thing to get a Platinum record on Blue Note Records. We had done some movie work and they put some of that in there, along with some old songs and new things and Blue Note had never had a Platinum album before even though they were a legendary jazz label.

How were you able to do that with another label while still on your old one?

I don't know! Somehow they worked it all out though.

One of your late '70s Top 40 hits was a funk tune called "Galaxy" that showed that War could adapt to some of the styles of the time, such as funk and disco. Do you remember that song?

I do remember that well. "Galaxy" came out around the same time as *Star Wars*.

There was that whole sci-fi explosion, also including Close Encounters *of the* Third Kind *and there were disco versions of that theme and* Star Wars!

I know man, it just happened in a big way! "Galaxy" came out and it had that line, "Take me to your place in space, I'm sick and tired of the rat race, on a rocket ship no time to wait, I just want to gravitate." B. B. Dickerson came up with that whole thing.

That makes sense, since the bass is so funky and prominent in that song that he came up with that.

Exactly, and those lyrics—I mean, I was writing "Why can't we be friends, why can't we be friends" and "Gypsy man, they call me a gypsy man" and stuff like that and "Me and baby brother." That wasn't me writing about outer space! I wasn't there that day, but I jumped in on it with them.

Another song I wanted to ask about was "The World is a Ghetto." Lyrically and musically that is a pretty mind-blowing song. Do you remember how that came into being?

I do, I do. Everybody's going to have their version of how it came about, but I will tell you exactly what happened. We used to rehearse in Long Beach, California, and we were on a Friday and it was just me and Papa Dee. I had that wah-wah lick on guitar and Papa Dee recorded it on his tape recorder and took it home. Then he came back with the "Don't you know that it's true, that for me and you, the world is a ghetto" and I said, "That's the worst thing you could've done. You just tore that song apart" and I was against that, but that's what made it happen.

And how about "Gypsy Man"?

"Gypsy Man" came from a jam I put together when we were on the road. Why it made sense was, we had been on the road for so long and we had a gig in Des Moines, Iowa, and for some reason we missed Des Moines and ended up in Detroit. The promoters from Des Moines called and asked where we were and we said we were in Detroit and they asked if we could get to Des Moines and we said no way. I felt like a gypsy man being on the road for so long so that's where that came from.

Just like gypsies always traveling, I get it.

And I love that song, man.

It's one of my top choices from War. I think so many people hear all those classic War songs in commercials and films and TV shows and don't identify with who actually wrote and recorded them, which is why War should be recognized more after such a massively successful career.

I know. With War, everyone knows the songs, but try to connect the songs with who actually did those songs with the public and there's a disconnect there. It was pretty much done by design by the people in management.

I feel that has happened to big bands that were ensembles and were known more as a group as opposed to individuals. That happened with Chicago, one of the biggest bands of all time. Chicago had the logo on every album but no band photos until many, many years later, so the public identified with the group and the logo but not the players. And, as I always do, I mention Terry Kath's name as one of the most brilliant guitar players ever and too many people look at me and ask who that is, rather than go, "Hell yeah, he was amazing!"—which is what they should be saying. I think this also happened with War.

Let me ask you something: I remember playing in the late '60s with a band called CTA; was that Chicago? That was Chicago wasn't it?

Yes it was! They were known as Chicago Transit Authority the first few years, which is also what their first album was called. They became known as Chicago in 1970.

I remember playing in Chicago with them and he tore it up. We also played a gig I remember at the Fillmore West as Eric Burdon and War with Santana, The Grateful Dead and It's a Beautiful Day for $9! Nine bucks!

And I bet that was a lot of cash at the time! $9 now might get you...

A Big Mac!

I was going to say an Arby's beef n' cheddar but I think we're on the same wavelength! [Laughs]

[Laughs] This was a night of entertainment for $9. Are you kidding me?

Another song of yours that takes me back is "Summer."

That was a Papa Dee song. He wrote that one. He and I did a lot of the writing in War. Papa was a wordy guy and he wrote some epic stuff.

And Jimi Hendrix played his last set ever with Eric Burdon and War. I believe he came on stage and jammed with you guys for about thirty-five to forty minutes and passed away a day or two later in September 1970.

That's exactly right. Oh man...I'll never forget that night. That was so historic. Jimi came two nights and he was not himself that first night so he didn't come up on stage; this was at Ronnie Scott's Jazz Club in London. The second night he showed up and his eyes were ice-white. He looked good and he was ready to go up there and jam.

When he came up on stage, I handed my guitar to him and said to the guys, "I'm outta here. Jimi Hendrix just came on stage!" so I bailed. He grabbed me and said, "No man, stay. I want you to play with me." He is still the greatest guitar player ever. After that, they're all #2 because there can only be one #1 and that was Jimi. He told me to stay, so we jammed, and we kicked ass and traded licks and jammed and I played on "Third Stone from the Sun" and he did a fantastic solo, which I guess was his first farewell solo.

Wow.

Yeah, and then he played a solo, and I came right behind and played another blues lick. And then we started trading blues licks, and that night was so much fun. Back stage there was a great vibe and everybody was having fun and laughing, and I remember walking back to the hotel in the rain so elated at what had happened. That next night he didn't show up.

He was supposed to come back again?

Yes, he was supposed to come back and play again, but he never showed up and he had passed away.

And that night did you actually have the details or officially know what had happened? Did somebody call you?

They called Eric Burdon and our tour manager. I believe that Jimi was still alive when the call was made, but by the time the paramedics got there he had aspirated. So, Jimi died just like that and I had his Strat in my hotel room for two nights with the case open. I wouldn't even touch the guitar. I just looked at it and couldn't and wouldn't even touch it. I just could not touch that guitar.

I don't even know what to say to that. And you still had to play the gig that night.

We did play, but all we knew at that point was it wasn't good and something was wrong. He hadn't died just yet. It was afterwards that it turned for the worse.

And who would've known just how bad it was for him you know? He was only twenty-seven years old and, like you said, he was still having these good moments, but there were ominous signs.

I know, and he was such a great guy. He was just a victim of this whole industry. You take a person who is all about his music and his love for spreading that to people, and then these others come along and manipulate him and use him so they could control him. He was all about the music and loving and giving and he was taken advantage of. I think some of the people around him put Jimi in very bad situations, and the drug use was so prevalent at that time and those people around him were a terrible influence.

It's quite clear there were too many who cared about Jimi Hendrix the entertainer and not Jimi Hendrix the man.

For sure, for sure, but they also cared about themselves more than Jimi Hendrix.

Recommended solo: "The World is a Ghetto" from *The World is a Ghetto* with War (1972)

CHAPTER 44
Eric Stewart
(Born Eric Michael Stewart, January 20, 1945, Droylsden, Lancashire, England)

Eric Stewart is yet another one of the players who makes me proud to listen to guitar players. With all of the people in this book, it's just as much what these guys are not doing as what they are doing. Eric is such a tasteful, creative player (not to mention singer/writer/producer/ engineer/keyboardist), that it's always a pleasure to discuss this man's guitar skills.

In 1968, Stewart founded Strawberry Studios in Stockport, UK, which is where he honed his craft in a multitude of ways. Prior to that, in 1963 or so, Stewart became guitarist for Wayne Fontana and the Mindbenders who would score some massive hit singles both in the UK and the US. Eric landed the gig only because he was at the Oasis Club in Manchester when Fontana had an audition for a record label and the guitar player and drummer hadn't shown up. Fontana knew Eric was good enough and asked him and drummer Ric Rothwell to sit in. They did so well, that it was a condition of the label that the new guys be included with Fontana and bassist Bob Lang.

Wayne Fontana and the Mindbenders had eight UK Top 40 singles, none bigger than "The Game of Love" (UK #1, US #2), and simply as the Mindbenders without Fontana, they scored another mammoth hit with "A Groovy Kind of Love," which Stewart sang on (UK #2, US #2). This was later a #1 hit for Phil Collins in 1988. A few more minor hits followed, but the Mindbenders disbanded in late 1968 after a lack of success.

Stewart put together his studio and also formed the band Hotlegs with Graham Gouldman, Kevin Godley, and Lol Creme and scored something of a novelty hit in 1970 with the bizarre "Neanderthal Man" based around caveman-like drums and acoustic guitars. The song hit #2 in the UK and #22 in the US and sold over 2 million copies worldwide. The band didn't really actively do much after the single, and when they finally issued a follow-up, "Lady Sadie," it bombed badly. The group folded, but this led to the formation by the four members of Hotlegs of the splendid, creative, warped band 10cc.

Neil Sedaka's album *Solitaire* was released in 1972 and did well. The album featured the four guys who would become 10cc and it was also engineered by Stewart and recorded at Strawberry Studios. The band recorded a song called "Waterfall" that Apple Records rejected, but after recording another tune called "Donna," they sent it to producer Jonathan King, who loved it and signed the band to his label UK Records. "Donna" was a mid-tempo song with high falsetto vocals and was also partially tongue-in-cheek. It went to #2 in the UK in the late summer of '72.

The debut album *10cc* came out in summer 1973 and made the UK Top 40 and produced further hits with the upbeat rocker "Rubber Bullets," which shot to #1 and featured some blazing guitar work, and "The Dean and I" also made the Top 10. Do you know how clever "The Dean and I" is? If you're a fan, then you do. This is wacky, art-pop genius that goes all over the place and remains catchy and quirky with enough spaces for great guitar harmonies and melodies that only sophisticated '70s pop could provide.

Sheet Music was their first UK Top 10 album and one of the greatest albums of the '70s. Again, this was high art and sophisticated, with each song playing like a mini-musical. The creativity was at an all-time high and the band produced the album with Stewart engineering and mixing. "The Wall Street Shuffle" was a UK Top 10 hit and "Silly Love," which sounded like a warped combo of Queen and Monty Python, hit the Top 25 and had some hot guitar work by Stewart. "Clockwork Creep," "The Worst Band in the World," and the lengthy "Somewhere in Hollywood" are out of this world.

Mercury Records signed the band for $1 million based on a new song the band had composed in 1975: "I'm Not in Love." We all know this song, unless you've never listened to music. "I'm Not in Love" is a deceptively simple-sounding song laced in electric piano, mini-Moog snyths, awash in loads of vocal treatments. The song would top both the UK and US charts and has been covered by plenty of acts since. Over 600 voices were used in this masterpiece. The song would appear on the album *The Original Soundtrack* that graced the UK Top 5 and US Top 15. The saucy "Life Is a Minestrone" was another UK Top 10 and wholly unique and original as ever, and was laced with those heavenly guitars from Eric Stewart. The eight-minute faux-opera of "*Une Nuis A Paris* (One Night in Paris)" was totally outlandish and wonderfully so.

10cc continued to dazzle with *How Dare You!* in 1976, scoring two more UK Top 10 hits with the amazing "I'm Mandy, Fly Me" (with outrageous soloing by Stewart along with some wonderful acoustic strumming) and "Art for Art's Sake" with some more seriously crackling good guitar that rocks. Bizarre tunes like the jazzy "Iceberg" and the remorseful "Don't Hang Up" (that has the line "When the barman said what are you drinking, I said marriage—on the rocks") are more examples of the song-craft at hand. This is warped genius, people!

When Godley and Creme departed, it was a huge blow, but Stewart and Gouldman kept the band going with drummer Paul Burgess who had filled in earlier and issued *Deceptive Bends* in 1977, which continued the success against the odds as the infectious "The Things We Do For Love" became a runaway hit (UK #6, US #5) and featured smooth vocals and guitars from Stewart in this, one of 10cc's greatest songs. "People in Love" was also a US Top 40 single and "Good Morning Judge" another UK Top 10 hit adding some more dark humor and funk into the mix. The guitars on this track are white hot. The tour added guitarist Mick Fenn, keyboardist Tony O'Malley, and drummer Stuart Tosh.

Bloody Tourists followed in 1978 and provided a UK #1 (and US Top 50) in the whimsical reggae of "Dreadlock Holiday," another divine slice of warped, sophisticated pop rock with hooks galore. Duncan Mackay was now on keyboards and the band continued to fascinate with the hilariously titled "Everything You Wanted to Know!!! (Exclamation Marks)."

"Reds in My Bed" and the warped song "The Anonymous Alcoholic" (with loads of nasty slide guitar) that sounds like Randy Newman, Little Feat, and Frank Zappa before going disco/funk were also wonderfully crafted and quite demented songs. Seriously! The album made #3 in the UK, but things would soon unravel as Stewart was in a bad car accident in 1979 and was out of commission for a while.

Look Hear? barely reached the UK Top 40 in 1980, only sniffing the lower rungs of the charts in the US, and though fans and critics, and even the band, were down on the album, the opener "One-Two-Five" is great fun and clever as always, and "It Doesn't Matter At All" is a beautiful song. How both of these failed to chart as singles is a mystery, but tastes were changing.

Ten Out of Ten went nowhere in 1981 and featured new keyboardist Vic Emerson and a more Americanized sound. That being said, it was hardly as bad as its reputation. I mean, c'mon, this album has "Action Man in a Motown Suit" (complete with killer solo) and "Don't Turn Me Away."

A final effort, *Windows in the Jungle* surfaced in 1983 with drumming by the great Steve Gadd and Simon Phillips, and although it was ignored, it was really good and featured some long Prog-styled songs (it started as a concept album) and some more pop gems. "24 Hours" was an eight-minute epic to open the album and featured an excellent set of solos from Stewart. The lengthy, jazzy track "Taxi! Taxi!" closes the album in outstanding fashion with hints of Steely Dan, Pink Floyd, and the Alan Parsons Project (whom Stewart would later sing with) and "City Lights" is a snappy tune that could've been a hit with an irresistible feel. 10cc folded soon after another tour with drummer Jamie Lane, but Stewart was not hurting for work.

From 1982–1986, Stewart was in Paul McCartney's band appearing on the excellent *Tug of War* album in 1982 with the big hit "Take It Away," 1983's *Pipes of Peace, Give My Regards to Broad Street* (1984) and *Press to Play* (1986), the latter of which he wrote a lot of material for.

The original 10cc re-formed and issued *…Meanwhile* in 1992, Godley and Creme only appeared on a few tracks making this more of a Stewart/Gouldman album. A tour followed and, in 1995, a final album was released called *Mirror Mirror,* which was not a bad album, although sales were modest. The album featured a beautiful acoustic song "The Monkey and the Onion" and the mournful "Ready to Go Home," which Asia did a wonderful version of in 2001 on the *Aura* album.

10cc folded again shortly thereafter and Stewart has continued along with solo projects *Do Not Bend* (2003) and *Viva la Difference* (2009) that were both very good. Eric has previously released solo albums with *Girls* (1980) and *Frooty Rooties* (1982). Stewart also sang on several Alan Parsons albums in the '90s and he has produced and/or engineered albums for Neil Sedaka, Sad Café, the Blue Jays, and more. A book about Eric's career is due out at some point and he's in this book too!

In January 2015, I had the honor of hearing the man's answers to my questions and he even did a self-portrait for me.

Who were some of the guitarists that influenced you as you developed an interest in playing guitar?

There was Scotty Moore (Elvis Presley), James Burton (with Rick Nelson then), Cliff Gallup and Johnny Meeks (Gene Vincent), Chet Atkins, Ry Cooder, Lowell George (Little Feat).

What are the types of guitars you've preferred over the years live or in the studio?

There's a Les Paul 1958 split maple Flame Top for live work (my best one was nicked from the Hammersmith Odeon London in the 1970s) and a Les Paul Junior TV model, great for slide guitar work. Also, there's a Gibson 1962 ES335 for studio work; I couldn't really use this one live because of feedback problems in those days. As well, I have a 1957 Fender Stratocaster for studio work, too. The D.I. sounds were quite magical for me.

Looking back on your time with the Mindbenders, was it a good learning experience, especially in terms of the industry and what you had to deal with? Also, "A Groovy Kind of Love" remains an absolute classic and the guitars and vocals really work despite how short the song was. I suppose there wasn't much time to explore the spaces in a song such as this back then?

We were tending to record things very quickly in those days, a whole album in two days, mostly in Mono to begin with, and we really didn't think about overdubbing anything that we couldn't play "live"!

The Sheet Music album from 10cc was one of the greatest albums of the '70s and incredibly diverse and challenging with a true uniqueness. I always considered 10cc a British Steely Dan in some ways if that makes sense. "Wall Street Shuffle" is something in particular that reminds me of their style, and you played lead guitar, piano, organ, and sang lead on that—a pretty wild feat, yes? And "Silly Love" sounds like Bowie meets Queen meets Monty Python—I mean, who wrote like this?

Steely Dan certainly influenced my work in the studio, and when I engineered and mixed the 10cc songs. I loved their "close miked" sounds, and tried to emulate them when we recorded our stuff. *Sheet Music* is my favorite collection of diverse directions that 10cc took at that time. We had the luxury of four people in the band who could write well, and three of us who could sing really good lead vocals.

Is it true that based on "I'm Not in Love" you were able to land a new deal with Phonogram and ended up doing the The Original Soundtrack album? And, just how long did it take to record all of those voices for that track? It's almost classical or choir-like in terms of arrangement, and there's such sparse instrumentation, too.

We had recorded "I'm Not in Love," and "One Night in Paris," *before* we approached Phonogram, but initially they didn't see "I'm Not in Love" as a single; they thought it was too long! The 625 voices took us three weeks to record!

Can you take me through the solo on "I'm Mandy, Fly Me"? I have always found this to be a seriously underrated slice of crafted guitar genius. Same goes for the solo on "Art for Art's Sake"; I love the riff and solo there.

The solos in "Mandy" were recorded by myself and Lol Creme on separate occasions; neither of us were in the studio at the same time. I laid down my bits first, and Lol Creme went in the studio after me one night, with our assistant engineer, Martin Lawrence, and laid down his bits.

"Art for Art's Sake" was a fun track to record, I never thought of it as a single though, and I had a ball just soloing stuff wherever I thought the song could take it. One riff came from my vocal melody on the "down down" part. It was a great track to perform live as well, and I could extend the solo on stage for as long as I wished.

"The Things We Do for Love" is a pop gem but has some very creative chord changes, hooks, and vocal arrangements as well as a lovely guitar solo that is quite lyrical and has stuck in my head for decades. I think that's a lost art in pop music: to be able to get all those aspects right and still make a very human song while doing it with musical talent that does not overwhelm the song. Do you have fond memories of this one because it also came at a critical time for the band in 1977?

Yes, I do have fond memories of this track. It was the single 10cc released after Godley and Creme had left the band, and I was out to prove something to myself. I did all the lead and backing vocals myself, except for the bass vocal that Graham Gouldman did on the answer vocals over the end fade out. I actually sang the guitar solo before I played it!

You played with Paul McCartney from 1982–1986 or so and played a pretty significant role in the band, especially on certain albums. And I believe that's you in the video for the wonderful "Take it Away" in 1982, as well as "So Bad." I felt there were some fine albums by Sir Paul during this time frame; you were there with Tug of War, *an especially good album. Was this a good time for you after the breakup of 10cc?*

Yes it was very inspiring for me to be asked by Paul, who was a friend by then, to sit in on those sessions, and, getting to work with a genius like George Martin producing, and Geoff Emerick engineering, was a thrill for me, too!

What can fans expect from your forthcoming book and anthology CD?

The book is "my life story." My life has been involved in many, many more creative things than the music I was involved with most of the time. The Anthology CDs will be the best bits from my four solo projects, re-mixed.

Last silly question I ask most guitarists: if you had to change a 10cc album or song title to a cat-based theme, what would you come up with? My cats are curious—ha ha!

My wife and I have loved and owned many cats while traveling around Europe in our forty-nine years of marriage. We have only one dog now, however, called Truffle. The "cat" song would have to be "Good Mews," after "Good News," on the "B" side of "Second Sitting for the Last Supper."

Recommended solo: "Art for Art's Sake" from *How Dare You!* with 10cc (1976)
Further info: www.ericstewart.uk.com
Photo credit: Eric Stewart

CHAPTER 45

George Thorogood

(Born George Lawrence Thorogood, February 24, 1950, Wilmington, DE)

As nasty a slide guitar player as there ever was, "Lonesome" George Thorogood defines the blues and boogie as only one man can.

George started as a solo acoustic performer around 1970 but moved on to a full band situation by 1974 forming George Thorogood & the Delaware Destroyers (usually said without the "Delaware" part). The band became a hit on the college and club circuit and did some demos for MCA Records that year. They were not picked up and it took a few more years before Rounder Records signed them, and the debut album *George Thorogood and the Destroyers* was recorded in 1976 and released in 1977 to excellent reviews, though it somehow failed to chart. With Billy Blough on bass and Jeff Simon on drums (along with some additional guitar by Ron Smith), the band was on fire in a simple setting. Virtually no overdubs, no frills, and pure blues, boogie, and old time rock 'n' roll.

George's guitar work is the highlight here and his solos are authentic and pure. The Elmore James tune "Madison Blues" is a blast, the "Delaware Slide" will have you rockin' and features wicked slide appropriately, and the eight minutes plus of "One Bourbon, One Scotch, One Beer" (a medley of tunes by John Lee Hooker and Amos Milburn) will getcha drinkin'. It's an album of purity, sincerity, and attitude, and it eventually went Gold without ever charting.

In 1978, *Move it on Over* moved into the US Top 40 and featured such classics as the Hank Williams cover in the title cut, which they totally owned, and a shufflin' take on Bo Diddley's "Who Do You Love?" that sees George gettin' down and nasty on the guitar behind a backbeat that works wonders (the band was just a trio of George, Jeff, and Billy). Chuck Berry's "It Wasn't Me" rocks with fun and abandon, another Elmore James tune "The Sky is Crying" is enough to make anyone weep, and "New Hawaiian Boogie"? Well, it boogies for sure and is another Elmore James tune done up Thorogood style. This was another Gold record and the band were starting to become a household name.

With Hank Carter added on sax, the band released *More George Thorogood and the Destroyers* in 1980 to decent, but lesser sales. There were many strengths here though, including a downright stomping take on "Night Time," Willie Dixon's "I'm Wanted," a fantastic version of Muddy Waters's "Bottom of the Sea," and the original "Kids From Philly." Carter added more of that old rock 'n' roll feel and the band was now one of THE top live acts around, as evidenced in their performance in Germany on the concert TV series *Rockpalast* that year, which is a must-see show.

In 1981, things were nuts for the band. George and the boys opened stadium shows for the Rolling Stones, which was an amazing thing for them. But…the *50/50 Tour* saw the guys play 50 shows in 50 states in 50 days. Utterly nuts and utterly fantastic! From October 23 in Honolulu, Hawaii, to December 11 in Pasadena, California, they did indeed accomplish this insane feat. Oh, and for good measure they played two shows on November 25: Catonsville, Maryland, and Washington, DC. This goes down as one of *the* craziest and coolest tours in rock history.

This was followed by a major label deal with EMI and the release of *Bad to the Bone* in 1982 to rave reviews and another Gold album. Of course, the title track needs no introduction as it has lived on in rock infamy. And as overplayed as it is, it remains an awesome song with one of George's wickedest solos.

The MTV video (with appearance by Bo Diddley) is still charming and clever and is deservedly iconic. The song has been used in numerous films, commercials, TV shows, and at sporting events. The album also produced a hit in a buoyant take on the Isley Brothers classic "Nobody but Me," and with "Blue Highway," Bob Dylan's "Wanted Man" (showing a mellower, folkier George), John Lee Hooker's "New Boogie Chillun," and Chuck Berry's "No Particular Place To Go" there was a lot to enjoy. Rolling Stones keyboardist Ian Stewart also played on the album and the headlining tour of arenas was the band's first. An appearance on *Saturday Night Live* also happened that year.

In 1983, the seasonal "Rock and Roll Christmas" was issued as a single and a video was done with the MTV cast and crew, and John Lee Hooker as Santa Claus! In 1985, *Maverick* was another Gold album and possibly the best album yet. The hit single "Willie and the Hand Jive" was accompanied by radio smashes like "Long Gone," the hilarious, yet dark "I Drink Alone," and the supremely kick-ass "Gear Jammer," which saw George scorching his guitar like never before. On July 13, the band appeared at the massive Live Aid concert in Philadelphia and even brought out Albert Collins and Bo Diddley to jam with them.

Soon after, guitarist "Sleeveless" Steve Charisma joined the band and the explosive concert set *Live!* went Platinum in 1986 and remains one of the finest rock live albums of the '80s, especially the rendition of Chuck Berry's "Reelin' and Rockin'," which George simply owns here.

Born to Be Bad was another Gold album in 1988, pumping out major radio faves like "You Talk Too Much," the title cut, and a take on Roy Head's "Treat Her Right," whilst covers of Elmore James's "Shake Your Money Maker" and Howlin' Wolf's "Smokestack Lightning" were excellent.

The '90s saw sales fade a bit, but 1991's *Boogie People* and 1993's *Haircut* were both really good albums, and the latter contained three more radio hits with the biggest being the humorous rocker "Get a Haircut," complete with hilarious animated video for MTV.

The band continued to remain a live force and George hasn't lost a damn thing with his playing. Charisma departed later that year and Jim Suhler replaced him in 1999. Buddy Leach took over from Carter in 2003.

Rockin' My Life Away (1997), *Half a Boy/Half a Man* (1999), *Ride 'Til I Die* (2003), *The Hard Stuff* (2006), and *The Dirty Dozen* (2009) are all recommended. Just because they weren't huge sellers doesn't mean you won't get good results. With *2120 South Michigan Avenue* in 2011, George tackled songs only recorded at the infamous Chess Records in Chicago where so much legendary music was created. Both Buddy Guy and Charlie Musselwhite made guest appearances.

George is as pure a guitarist as possible, and makes no pretense about what he does best and what he doesn't do best. His dedication to the blues, rock 'n' roll and boogie remains as strong as ever. And, there ain't too many slide players that can rival Lonesome George Thorogood.

I was happy to speak with George in January 2015 and here's how that chat went:

How are you?

Bad.

...to the bone?

You got it!

Excellent! Thanks for taking part in this.

Sure. So what's the book about?

Primarily it's about guys who I think are every bit as good, if not better, than the typical names we endlessly hear about. I've never understood why guys have to fly "under the radar" just because they aren't talked about as much when they are incredibly talented and, in some cases, more so than whom we always hear about.

Like cats who aren't household names but are a force to be reckoned with in their own right.

Exactly.

I've always been a big Bruce Dern fan. In terms of acting he's someone to me who was just as good as the big names. He was nominated for an Oscar for *Nebraska* last year. Outstanding character actor, just never got the recognition until all these years later. So that's kinda what you're talking about—guys who still got it goin' on, still deliver, but they aren't gonna be on the front page of the magazines.

Yes, and they've had success, these players. They've sold records, sold concert tickets, but just weren't routinely multi-million sellers and not front page news.

Well, you couldn't get a better candidate than yours truly!

[Laughs] Well, there's my clever intuition I guess. Plus, I'm in South Jersey ten minutes from Philly, so I know your career very well.

We're practically neighbors since I'm in Northern Delaware.

I know, and I've seen you live a few times over the years as well. Who were some of your primary influences?

Well, one of the people that got my attention when I first got serious about playing guitar was John Lee Hooker. He could do so much with one chord and had a very basic style. It wasn't complicated, but it was different and very exotic and very rhythmic, which caught my ear.
   That's my style—I will never be as flashy as Jeff Beck or Eric Clapton or those kinds of people. But later when I heard Bo Diddley, he was the one who really did it for me, and when I met him, he told me that John Lee Hooker was the reason he started playing guitar and I said to him, "That's funny because you're the reason why I started playing guitar." These guys could do so much and almost sound like an orchestra with what they did in such a simple way. When you asked me who my influences were, of course there are those who everybody mentions like Keith Richards, Hendrix, and those cats.
   But when I sat down and got serious about this, and said to myself, "What are you going to do? What are you close to? What's something that you know you can master?" I started away. John Lee Hooker was a guy I thought I could get started on copping, because even though there were a few others I could try and copy and do it well, he was the guy that got me on the path.

I love that you mention rhythm as being a key, because I've talked to some other players who also value that aspect of guitar playing too often overlooked.

If you listen to his playing and there are great solos and everything, one of the great artists in terms of rhythm guitar is Steve Miller. They call him Stevie "Guitar" Miller, but there's a lot more than being able to solo like Clapton on the version of "Crossroads" by Cream. There's a lot more to it.

And if people ask who am I close to in playing I usually say Brian Jones of the Rolling Stones or John Kay of Steppenwolf. They play both rhythm and slide guitar and they were so good at both. I'm not much of a lead player in the conventional way. I once asked Bo Diddley, "If you could tell me the one person who copped your rhythm and your style as good or better than Bo Diddley, who got the closest?" and do you know who he said?

I could guess, but I won't—who was it?

Brian Jones.

That's so surprising. I'm such an enormous Stones fan and Brian Jones was brilliant and played a load of instruments. He brought so much into the overall sound of the Stones, but doesn't get discussed enough, especially for rhythm playing. the Stones' 1963–1964 recordings clearly show a heavy Bo Diddley influence and they covered some of his tunes.

Yeah, and the thing about Brian is, when he left the Stones in '69 they weren't quite the same. They remained a great band and in fact still are, but he was missed. He brought a certain element with whatever he played and he added something strange and if you listen to Bo Diddley's music, I feel there's something strange there as well. This is some real exotic stuff, and I'm not even sure he knows how he's doing it and Brian Jones fit that.

Listen to John Kay's playing on rhythm and slide in Steppenwolf and there's so much great rhythm work in Creedence Clearwater Revival with John Fogerty's playing.

Without a doubt! Both he and his late brother Tom from CCR are some of the finest rhythm players we've had.

There's fantastic stuff that goes on in those songs! I've heard some people say CCR were just a high school Garage Band who were really simplistic and I say, "Are you out of your minds? This is one of the greatest rock bands of all time."

Fogerty and his rhythms are something else. Not to mention his leads, vocalizing, and writing.

John Lennon once said about his own guitar playing when he was asked about it, "You know, people don't think that I'm much of a guitar player, but I can drive a van." He was right! With the Beatles he played that second guitar like a drummer. It was tremendous, driving rhythm guitar on a lot of those songs.

That's why I like your playing—very rhythmic and percussive.

Well, that's why we hired Jim Suhler to play, because he's fantastic at slashing out those leads, which is something I just can't do. I'm the rhythm guy—I keep it together with that for the songs; that's my contribution to what we do. A lot of times people come up and say to me, well he's not much of a guitar player and I say it's not all about flashy stuff [*note—who the hell would say that to George? Morons!*]. Look at how great Chuck Berry is at rhythm guitar and lead guitar! Isn't that fantastic! That is amazing, that is just amazing! He can play both styles in the same song!

And he hopped around like a maniac and sings and entertains.

Yeah, he's a freak of nature!

No chance there will ever be another one like him again.

No, there never will be.

What are the types of guitars you've preferred over the years?

There's only one I can really play due to my style and the fingerpicking I have, and my hands are very small and I have problems with other guitars, especially acoustic guitars. When I fell into the Gibson ES-125, it worked for me; it was very light and the fretting is very small and gave me a unique sound, and it has the archtop and it's what they used to call a semi-electric. That's the one I feel most at home with.

And how about acoustic guitars?

You know, I'm still searching there. Acoustic is a real mother to play. I have a real aggressive style and my hands and wrists are small and I play a driving style. So when I pick up an acoustic, I'm spent after one song.

No matter what anyone says, playing acoustic, especially if you want to drive the guitar, isn't easy and can be a little painful. My shoulder always hurts and my wrists, too.

I hear ya! I picked up Taj Mahal's acoustic one time and I couldn't even press the strings down! How him and John Hammond do that all night I have no idea. Taj also plays that big Dobro—he must have the hands of Wilt Chamberlain or something. I admire anybody that can get up there and really deliver. There are singer/songwriters who accompany themselves on acoustic guitar like Paul Simon and Gordon Lightfoot. Then there are others who really blast. And I'm not even gonna try that.

As part of the very first MTV generation I was an MTV junkie and it's how I learned about music. No matter how overplayed the video is, the clip for "Bad to the Bone" from 1982 was fantastic and was like a humorous mini-movie. Plus, you had Bo Diddley and pool-playing legend Willie Mosconi in the video. I live in Haddon Heights, New Jersey, which is where Mosconi is from, and he was my Mom's next door neighbor!

[Laughs] Are you kidding?

No! He was indeed my Mom's neighbor for many years on Prospect Ridge in Haddon Heights.

That's pretty wild.

How fun was that video to do? It became iconic, but did you know it would be as you were filming it?

I don't think so, because nobody does know that until it becomes iconic. We knew it came out great. What we did know was, by 1982, MTV had become the big thing and it was a giant advertising thing. It was a lot more fun then, because the market was wide open and you could experiment with ideas more. MTV was on twenty-four hours a day and there was more demand than supply.

We had a lot of fun doing that and having Bo Diddley and Mosconi was a huge part of it. It helped promote the record and did what it had to do. Capitol Records wanted a video to go along with the single and I was a company man doing what I needed to do.

It really did come across as fun, even though I know those shoots can become quite tedious. Were all those trick pool shots really by you?

No, there were trick shots. We did them, but Mosconi set them up for us.

Oh, so you did actually have to shoot then?

I did some of them, but he'd say just do this with the shot and put the cue here, use some English there, etc. He taught Paul Newman how to play for *The Hustler.*

I know—that's really cool.

He worked with me for six months actually to get that right. It had to look authentic when I did it.

The song itself is as classic a rock tune as there is. "Bad to the Bone" has lived on in movies, commercials, and TV shows. It still sounds so damn good after all these years and it's not just the guitars.

We got fortunate that we found something that stuck around for a while.

The Maverick *album has a killer song that is one of my favorites from you in "Gear Jammer." Can you recall the origins of that song?*

I'd been monkeying around with the riff on that one for so long and everybody in the band heard it and asked what possible lyrics I was gonna come up with for that song. Usually, when you have a groovy riff that gets everyone's attention, the rest of it all falls into place.

The phrase "gear jammer" means truck driver as you know. At that time, the world was changing, Peter, and in the past, if a truck driver was listening to any music at all, it was usually country and western. By the late '70s and early '80s, truck drivers were now listening to rock songs. So, I figured if I created a rocker with a Led Zeppelin kind of riff to it, then I could appeal to another market that was wide open around 1985.

There were people at the label saying we had to target certain markets that were already being done over and over, so I said why not go after some untapped markets? Why go after the same people listening to the Who and the Stones? Why not try something untapped? For lack of a better term, "Gear Jammer" was aimed at those people. It was the '80s version of "Six Days on the Road."

Funny you mention that because to me in some ways it was an update on Deep Purple's "Highway Star," one of the ultimate driving songs. You can't slow down when those songs are on!

Neither did they! If you're going from Albuquerque to Fresno in a day and a half, you need to be a "gear jammer"!

The song just kicks it.

Once again, we just got lucky with another one that worked.

Later that year, you played at Live Aid, which I'm sure was over in a blur. What do you recall about that day, and how did you get invited?

I remember being tired and hot. We usually get invited to those big gigs because someone else cancelled and this was no exception. That's usually how Thorogood and his boys get a big gig! [Laughs] Someone cancelled and then someone else cancelled and then we got the call. I just remember having no sleep and it was very hot.

I think it was 95 degrees that day.

It felt more like 195 degrees.

You were glad you participated in the end though?

Of course I was. It was for a great cause; feeding starving people and especially the children.

And you are on the official DVD.

Yeah, at least we didn't get edited out like we usually do [Laughs].

The 50/50 tour in 1981—what were you thinking playing 50 shows in 50 days in 50 states?

Good question [Laughs].

Where did it begin?

It started in late October and ended in mid-December. We started in Hawaii, then Alaska, then Oregon and then traveled all over.

Has anybody tried that since?

I hope not! And it was actually 51 shows because we played one day in the afternoon in Baltimore and the evening in DC. The whole thing ended in Pasadena, California.

Where did you find the song "Get a Haircut" in 1993? Was it some guy in Australia I believe?

That's correct, we heard a comedy team doing it. Our bass player asked these guys if they wrote it and they said no, it was a cover of a song by a band from Melbourne who put it out as a single. Our bass player got it and it had only sold like 100 copies. I thought how is that possible? This song's a classic—it's something Neil Young should be doing, you know like Crosby, Stills, Nash & Young did that song "Almost Cut My Hair." It was just a fun rock song, and it was the story of rock like Keith Richards.

Was the 2120 South Michigan Avenue album a chance to pay homage to all those legendary Chess Records artists?

I've been paying homage to those guys since 1965! I thought it was very outdated because so many people did those songs before and did them better than me. Why they asked me to do that album I don't know. The Stones and Clapton had done them all and done them well, so I wondered what the point was. Capitol was hot on the idea and I wanted to stay with a major label so I went along with the project.

On the debut album with "One Bourbon, One Scotch, One Beer," was that actually a combo of two separate songs from John lee Hooker and Amos Milburn?

Yeah, that was "House Rent Blues" by John Lee Hooker and we just connected one with the other. We had been doing "One Scotch…" on its own and that had been going over Okay, but once we connected the two, it took off.

Did that develop from the live shows?

No, that was purely by accident. It happened at a club show and there were about five to ten people watching us play. Nobody else was paying any attention because they were watching the World Series on TV. I started playing the intro by myself on guitar and before I started singing the line "one bourbon, one scotch and one beer" the bass player and drummer jumped in right behind me and kicked it off and everybody watching the game left the bar and jumped on the bandstand and I said, "Well, we got something here"!

When you signed with Rounder Records in 1976, were they primarily known as a folk label or something?

It was mostly bluegrass and old-timey music.

So how did the deal come about and did you think it was worth taking a shot to get the music out there?

When a baby cries long enough and loud enough, you're gonna do somethin' to shut that baby up! That's how I got that deal. Squeaky wheel gets the grease.

Well, I'd say that's a wrap.

It's been nice talking to you, Peter; most of what I've said has been true.

[Laughs] *I will keep that in mind.*

I have all the faith in the world that when you're done writing about me in your book, you'll keep me under the radar where I belong.

Recommended solo: "Gear Jammer" from *Maverick*
with George Thorogood & the Destroyers (1985)
Further info: www.georgethorogood.com
Photo credit: Rebecca Blissett

CHAPTER 46

Bernie Tormé

(Born Bernard Tormey, March 18, 1952, Dublin, Ireland)

Irish guitar player Bernie Tormé began professional gigging in clubs in his mid-teens in Ireland before relocating to London in 1974. There he was part of a band called Scrapyard, who went into the scrapyard before he formed the punk outfit the Bernie Tormé Band in 1976 who would put a few songs on a compilation album before landing a deal with Jet Records, the label owned by Don Arden, also manager of Black Sabbath and ELO.

They were able to record an album but it went unreleased. However, Bernie's talents were not forgotten, as he was invited to join the odd but powerful band Gillan led by ex-Deep Purple singer Ian Gillan in 1979. Over the next three years plus, Tormé was an integral part of this highly interesting, oddball outfit who enjoyed massive success in the UK, Europe, and Japan but went largely unknown in the US.

Mr. Universe, Tormé's first album with the band narrowly missed the UK Top 10 in 1979 and 1980's *Glory Road* soared to #3 and included the seven-minute track "If You Believe Me" that contained a vicious, aggressive solo by Tormé that has stood the test of time and is raw power at its finest. Gillan went the unusual route by including a second bonus album called *For Gillan Fans Only* with copies of *Glory Road* as well.

Future Shock would hit the #2 spot in the UK in 1981 and had such awesome material as "No Laughing in Heaven" (a Top 40 single), "Sacre Bleu" and the title cut. The arrangements were unusual for the most part and the playing through the roof. By this point "Trouble" had become a Top 20 UK single and a cover of Gary U.S. Bonds' hit "New Orleans," a Top 40 hit showing Ian Gillan's love of old time rock 'n' roll. Live, the band cut it even better than in the studio, and Tormé, bass player John McCoy, keyboardist Colin Townes, and drummer Mick Underwood understood each other and had a true chemistry.

By 1981, Bernie had grown frustrated with the business side of things and during a tour in 1981 left the band, refusing to take part in a taping for the BBC's *Top of the Pops* TV program. He does appear on a number of live tracks issued on the next Gillan album that was a half live, half studio double-album *Double Trouble*, which also introduced Bernie's replacement: future Iron Maiden guitarist Janick Gers.

Just as Bernie had a record deal for his new band Bernie Tormé & the Electric Gypsies in 1982, came a series of requests to replace the late Randy Rhoads in Ozzy Osbourne's band. In a short time, Rhoads had established himself as one of the most brilliant players on the planet and his reputation was continuing to build. He had tragically perished in a plane crash on March 19, 1982. After the funeral services, the tour had to resume, and Tormé received numerous phone calls from Ozzy's management. Having already started booking gigs for his new band, he was reluctant to commit and also hadn't really heard any of Ozzy's material. Nonetheless, Bernie ended up flying out, auditioning, and getting the pressurized gig. After about two weeks, he left the band, and Brad Gillis of Night Ranger completed the tour.

Bernie had gotten Ozzy and his band through an incredibly difficult, dark period of time and did so with little chance to learn the material properly. That being said, he pulled it off. He really did. It was different playing than Randy, but it worked and it saved Ozzy personally and musically. It was a wonderful thing Bernie did, and was a true sacrifice. He was then able to resume his solo career.

Two albums followed in *Turn out the Lights* (a UK Top 50 album in 1982) and *Electric Gypsies* (1983). Bernie also joined veteran psychedelic/progressive rockers Atomic Rooster for a tour in 1983 and appeared on their album *Headline News*. A new band called Tormé issued a few albums in the late '80s with Phil Lewis later of L.A. Guns singing.

Around 1988, Bernie became part of a new band called Desperado with ex-Twisted Sister front man Dee Snider, former Iron Maiden drummer Clive Burr, and bassist Marc Russel. Signed to major label Elektra, the label foolishly spent a ton of money on the album and shelved it (the album would finally surface in 1996 as *Bloodied, but Unbowed*). Bernie went on to issue a number of albums in the '90s and 2000s, including three records with the band GMT (Guy/McCoy/Tormé) that included drummer Robin Guy and Bernie's former bandmate in Gillan, bass player John McCoy. Each album was raw, hard-hitting rock as you would want.

A solid, raunchy new solo album *Flowers and Dirt* graced our presence in 2014. Bernie released another new album, *Blackheart,* in the fall of 2015 and hit the road once more for tour dates.

In November 2014, Bernie and I had a chat in which he gave me wonderful, detailed answers to my questions and is truly a first-class player and human being.

Who were some of your influences that made you want to play guitar? Can I assume some Thin Lizzy players would be in there or Rory Gallagher coming from Ireland?

Like everyone else of my age, it was initially George Harrison, Keith Richards, Chuck Berry, and slightly later Jeff Beck with the Yardbirds. Then I got into Bluesbreakers-era Clapton, Peter Green, Cream, and, of course, Hendrix when he broke here at the beginning of '67. In terms of Irish guitar players, it was a bit later, I saw Rory with Taste first in '68 I think, playing a club in Dublin with four people in the audience! He was astounding, but obviously not yet a big draw! I saw him so many times after that, totally brilliant, unspoilt, real. I played just before him with Gillan at the Reading festival in 1980 to 35,000 people; he was headlining, and we were special guests. He was brilliant.

Dublin was great to be an aspiring guitarist in around '68/'69/'70; there was Rory blowing in from time to time, Gary Moore with Skid Row, Eric Bell with Thin Lizzy—they were all big influences because I could go and watch them and see what they were doing with their hands. Lots of others too who did not become as well known, like Ed Deane, Jody Pollard, lots more. There were lots of great acoustic pickers, too: Paul Brady being one, and Louis Stewart who was a killer jazz player. It really was a guitar town!

What guitars do you prefer on stage or in the studio?

I always play Fender Stratocasters. I occasionally have used other guitars in the studio: Gibsons, Epiphones, Danelectro electrics, Guild, Washburn, Martin acoustics usually for a specific thickening or sparkle or whatever, but the basic guitar track for me is always a Strat—it was and is my weapon of choice, and I'm a one woman sort of guy! I can get more varied workable sounds out of a Strat than anything else, I love 'em.

Was it tough with the Bernie Tormé Band in the late '70s? You guys got a deal and then nothing happened with Jet Records? And did you enjoy playing what was essentially punk rock?

Tough? Well I suppose it wasn't easy, but I would not say tough, just a good, hard learning process! Jet signed us at the end of '77 and put us in to record, and put us out on tour with the Boys, Bethnal, Billy Idol's Generation X, and on our own. It was non-stop and very educational. We also did a lot of one-off's; it was a really great opportunity to learn how to deal with audiences, all types, all sizes, ones who loved you, ones who hated you. The recording situation we did not do so well with; Jet had an anti-producer stance, so they put us in on our own, and we were clueless! They put out a single and an EP, and we also recorded an entire album that they did not release. The records did not sell.

Jet tried pretty hard with us, but we probably were not right for the label and vice-versa. On the other hand, they did do pretty well with ELO! I did enjoy playing punk rock, I was a huge Sex Pistols fan—still am, but I was always going to play guitar solos! That did not go down so well with some of the hardcore punk rock hipsters at the time. Guitar solos not allowed…

Your long tenure with Gillan produced some truly visceral, exciting hard rock that went into some unusual areas. To me, the best albums were Glory Road *and* Future Shock. *It certainly seemed like you had a large hand in the sound of the band—were you given some free rein in what and how to play?*

Completely. There never were any comments or interference with anyone's playing or how they saw it unless they asked for an opinion. It was very much a band, and in that context, Ian was a great boss; he trusted his band to do the right thing, never ever got involved in telling people what to do when I was there. We played like a band of equals.

Could you take me through the solos on "If You Believe Me" and "No Laughing in Heaven"? Those are some really great moments.

"If You Believe Me" is just one of those blues/psychedelic solos that is intentionally very raw and primitive; it's the kind of thing I do without thinking. To be honest, I love doing that sort of thing; it's very natural for me, the space and the crudeness, a Strat into a Marshall plexi in the room at Kingsway—where Hendrix recorded "Red House" by the way. Probably one or two takes. It's kind of inspired by Clapton's bluesbreaker stuff and Hendrix's many slow blues jams. Just a straight E Blues Pentatonic sliding into a Dorian and a major Blues/Ionian in places. So that gives you a large choice of notes, too. Personally, I could never make a straight Blues Pentatonic work. The song is basically major with a flattened 7th-Mixolydian really, with that blues flattened 3rd creeping in from time to time.

The "No Laughing in Heaven" solo is virtually a straight Blues Pentatonic workout in F sharp, which is the relative minor of what the song key is, which is A. It's very Clapton-esque with again touches of Hendrix and Peter Green. It sounds good—Strat, big muff, plexi, love it! I had an auto trigger wah wah pedal that I was trying out; it didn't do anything until about two-thirds of the way in the solo, and then it does this lovely throaty swallow sound! That was all it did! It was a complete accident, so that was one take and had an instant magic about it! Not technically complex at all, but nice timing and phrasing, and it worked. The construction of the solo was very early Jeff Beck/Yardbirds, start low and build it up—sound-wise too.

I understand you had some serious reservations about joining Ozzy Osbourne's band after Randy Rhoads had passed away in 1982. Can you describe how it all came about and why you felt it wasn't a proper fit musically, if that was the case?

I had no problems about it being a good fit musically; it was a pretty good fit. The problems for me lay in other areas, which are long-winded and pretty boring: when they first asked me (through David Arden at Jet), they thought I was out of a job and looking for a gig. I wasn't. I had just signed a deal for my first solo album *Turn Out the Lights* and that was being released in the UK and throughout Europe in a few weeks' time, and I also had a month-long tour booked to promote it that was about to start.

So when they asked me, I said I couldn't do it, that I would have liked to help out, but I just couldn't in the circumstances, and I explained why. They kept on calling me, called Gillan's manager, and he eventually talked me into trying to move my release and the gigs.

At this point, all I was being asked by David Arden was to "stand in" and get the tour rolling again, David promised me a silly amount of money ($2,000 per week), which again I had never asked for, and he said they would find someone to replace me permanently in Ozzy's band within a month at most. He also told me that I did not have to audition, but I knew that I would have to. You always have to. There was always this surreal quality about dealing with Jet, reality seemed to vary from minute to minute. Gillan's manager then arranged for me to get a week's pay up front: he said David would say anything to get me to do it and not to trust him, and that had indeed been my previous experience of Jet Records, so I had no objection; it was insurance of sorts.

I still hadn't heard any of the material; I thought it would be Sabbath-y—I knew some of that. So, next day I went in to London and got the vinyl albums, I was blown away by Randy and the great songs.

So, two days later I flew to LA and auditioned (thanks David!) and met Ozzy and Sharon and the band (bassist Rudy Sarzo, drummer Tommy Aldridge, and keyboardist Don Airey) for the first time, and got the gig: Sharon told me the pay was $200 a week or something! After some initial surprise and hilarity at the promised amount of $2,000 versus the real one of $200 (because this was absolutely typical of Jet), I said, "Well you don't have to pay me for quite a while!" Ridiculous! They were nice people, I wanted to help, and I honestly couldn't give a fuck about money anyway. There also seemed to be completely crossed lines: whereas I thought I was standing in for a few weeks, Sharon, Ozzy and the band seemed to think I had agreed to stay. Weird.

Thing is, I don't expect anyone to understand this, but I had just spent nigh on three years in Gillan, a very egalitarian band where I had been one of the main writers; I had chosen to leave that because I wanted to do a solo album. I was thoroughly sick of the whole rock 'n' roll circus of touring, big crowds, being a sideman; I wanted to do what I wanted to do: nothing to do with money, I was a '60s hippy, I wanted to do my own thing in my own time. I was so tired of being the dream guitar slinger and getting two cents at the end of packed-out tours doing something that had frankly turned into more than a bit of a drudge. So I really did not want to step back into that world. I know it was and is a lot of people's dream, and that's fine too, but it was not my dream, then or now. It was also quite strange for me at that stage to be playing an entire set on stage of which I had written nothing: great songs definitely, but nothing to do with me.

The other rather pressing problem for me was that I had about thirty to forty gig contracts that I had signed that the promoters wanted fulfilled within a matter of months—if I didn't, I would have court cases from there to kingdom come, so I had to bail out; it was not possible for me to stay.

So having got the gig playing three songs that I half- knew, I had no chance to rehearse any more until the first gig in Allentown, Pennsylvania. We only ever played the whole set once without Ozzy during the soundcheck. There was no way on the planet I was even getting close to Randy's wonderful playing, I was just trying to remember the chord progressions and the arrangements; that was hard enough, and trying with difficulty to work out what Randy was doing on a shitty Walkman cassette tape, because no one in the band knew, there was no tab, no video's, no nothing. Very, very difficult. Not fun. I obviously fucked up repeatedly—plenty of mistakes by me, but no complete pile-ups, no train crashes; the gigs ran as normal and improved as we rolled on.

If I played anything, especially horrific or especially good onstage, the others would look across at me and then think, "Oh shit, it's not Randy." It was not a good situation—people had died, people were missed, I was happy to help out, but it was a weight I was not interested in carrying. And looking at the nastiness and lies and shit that has emanated from various sources since the tragedy of Randy's death, the purveyors of most of the lies not even having been present, I am glad I left when I did.

Everyone there was very kind to me in what was more than difficult circumstances, and that includes Ozzy, Sharon, Tommy, Rudy, Don, and the crew. The shit and lies and nastiness have been spread about people following the awful event of Randy and the wardrobe lady's (Rachel Youngblood) death is shameful.

So I was very glad when Brad Gillis showed up and they auditioned him. That few weeks changed my life totally. Since then, I am happy just to wake up on Earth and have another day to play and write and love my family: no interest at all in the megastar music business; I'll stick with the music. But it was a good fit musically, it worked for what it was, but it was not the time or place for me. I was very glad to have helped and very proud to have been asked.

I have heard the bootleg of the concert from Madison Square Garden in New York in 1982, and I was very, very impressed with how you added your own style in those difficult to play Ozzy songs. What you did in songs like "Mr. Crowley," "Flying High Again," "I Don't Know," and "Crazy Train" worked for me. I'd imagine the fans were perhaps quite demanding at that point, however, and wanted to hear Randy. How do you look back on it now and do you have any recordings yourself of the shows you were with the band for?

Very kind of you to say that. That's not true about the fans though; nobody at that point seemed to want to do anything other than support Ozzy—probably because of that they were also very supportive to me. The thing is that though Randy has rightfully become a legend following his death, he was not at that level at that point. This was the tour that was really going to turn him into a fully-fledged legend. He really wanted to play MSG; that was apparently the one gig that he really wanted to do. And I ended up doing it. That really does not make me feel good. He deserved it, I didn't. He also wanted to leave at the end of the tour. He never got that chance.

I don't have any recordings of the gigs, and generally I don't listen to any recordings I've done; I just hear the mistakes and how I could've done it better! That includes everything, not saying they are shit or anything, but I enjoy the process, and once it's done, it's in the past. I'd rather listen to someone else or nothing; it would be a bit too much like talking to yourself.

What was it like working with Vincent Crane in Atomic Rooster? He was a pretty wild guy.

It was great. I loved Vinny; he was one of a kind, unrepeatable, wonderful musician, great writer, storyteller from hell—loads of tales about jamming with Hendrix and Jim Morrison, and mad as a hatter, of course! I had a lovely chat with Arthur Brown (Crazy World of Arthur Brown) about a year ago about Vinny. Vin was the crazy in the Crazy World! We had so many things to say about Vin; it was really nice to have a laugh and compare notes! Playing with Vinny was like being transported back to the late '60s. Every time we played a song it was different; you had to listen, like having a conversation. Wish they could teach that at music colleges.

Why did the Desperado album with Dee Snider not get released for so long (it was originally scheduled for 1990)? That was a good album and what a cool choice to cover the great Tom Waits on "The Heart of Saturday Night"! Record label crap I assume is why it didn't get issued.

Elektra Records decided they didn't like it, and therefore having spent $500,000 or $1,000,000 on it, I can't remember exactly, some crazy amount, they decided they'd rather destroy everyone's career and home lives along with destroying the band and not release it. And they call that an industry.

They didn't like "The Heart of Saturday Night"; that incidentally wasn't originally destined for the album, but for an Elektra compilation, twenty years, or twenty-five years as a label or something like that, I don't remember. Elektra wanted us to record "Spirit in the Sky," for that—Lenny Kaye was working as A&R on that album at that time under Derek Shulman. We didn't want to record "Spirit."

Can you describe your new solo album Flowers & Dirt?

I haven't done a solo studio album for fifteen years, did lots of others, three Guy/McCoy/Tormé (GMT) albums and three Silver albums with Gary Barden on vocals. So I wanted to do something different, bigger, a double album, with rock 'n' roll grooves on it and not too continually high energy, up and down. I had no financing to do it, so I did it on a crowdfunding thing, Pledgemusic; I had no idea how that would go, but I was completely humbled; I had 100% of what I needed in twenty-four hours! Mind blowing! Having had that success, it was like terrifying, I had just undertaken to complete a twenty track double album in three months! I had to work my ass off, but it was a good thing having a time limit, like the old days. It really worked, had great reviews on it, selling well, currently on tour promoting it, what more can you ask for?

It's my thing: rock, lots of guitar, blues, blues rock, psychedelic, bits of acoustic, very old school, Zeppy even in places (obviously without Robert Plant!), its gone down really great.

Silly question I ask most players: if you could rename a Gillan or Ozzy song or album after a cat what would it be? My cats are dying to know—ha ha.

Well I have a black cat called Ozzy, so I think it would have to be *Diary of a Mad Cat*? He is.

Recommended solo: "If You Believe Me" from *Glory Road* with Gillan (1980)
Further info: www.bernietorme.co.uk
Photo credit: Mick Gregory (from Bernie Tormé collection)

CHAPTER 47

Pat Travers

(Born Patrick Henry Travers, April 12, 1954, Toronto, Ontario, Canada)

Bad-ass. That's Pat Travers in two words (or is that one?), and listening to this guy play is a true joy after all these years.

The Toronto native quickly became an ace guitarist in his early teens and before long he was playing with rockabilly legend Ronnie Hawkins. Travers signed his first solo deal with Polydor records after relocating to London, England in 1976 and issued his first album *Pat Travers*. *Makin' Magic* followed in 1977 (including awesome cuts like the moody epic "Stevie" and "Hooked on Music") as did *Putting it Straight* which cracked the US Top 100.

This latter album is a perfect example of why '70s hard rock is still so damn good and holds up so well. The band included Travers, bassist Peter "Mars" Cowling, and future Iron Maiden drummer Nicko McBrain, and they were a powerful trio indeed. The opening one-two punch of "Life in London" and "It Ain't What It Seems" is as quality as it gets. Toss in the Skynyrd-styled "Speakeasy" (with a guest appearance from Thin Lizzy's Scott Gorham) and "Gettin' Betta," among others, and this album will please the masses.

Even better was *Heat in the Street*, another Top 100 album from 1978 that opens with the sinister title cut—a slammin' opener if there ever was one. A new band maintained Cowling and added guitarist Pat Thrall for Travers to trade licks with and future Ozzy and Whitesnake drummer Tommy Aldridge. The grooves were tighter and a bit funkier, but the guitars, bass, and drums were all still ablaze in hard rock synergy. The title track is such a clever, creative blend of hard rock and an almost Progressive fusion without ever getting fancy-pantsed; it's a vision of excellence. Who wouldn't crank this to 11 in their car then or now? And what about "Killer Instinct" (great guitar harmonies, too), the instrumental speed metal of "Hammerhead" or "Evie," "I Tried To Believe" and the nasty guitar funk of "Go All Night"? What an album this is.

It all culminated with *Live! Go for What You Know* in 1979, a Gold-selling live album that was as exciting as a concert album could be. The '70s gave us some of the greatest live albums ever made, and this was one of them. The connection between audience and band is palpable and the vibe is warm. The cover of Stan Lewis's "Boom Boom (Out Go the Lights)" is balls-out party rock with smokin' guitars, popping bass, and thrusting drums with loads of double-bass fills and Pat's deep, killer rock voice. The song became a US hit single and FM rock radio smash and deservedly so.

In 1980, *Crash and Burn* continued the success reaching the US Top 20 and producing a hit with a light cover of Bob Marley's "Is This Love?" Far better was the Albert King cover "Born Under a Bad Sign." The album also featured the snarling "Snortin' Whiskey," a big radio hit with rip-roaring guitars galore, go for the throat vocals, a funky key change in the solo section, and drumming with double-bass work galore that would tire any air drummer. The synth and organ laced title cut was anything but what fans were expecting and a cool departure sonically.

Radioactive was a US Top 40 album, but an overreliance on keyboards and the loss of Thrall and Aldridge (with Sandy Genarro taking over on drums) made this a dalliance with mixed results. A lawsuit with Polydor didn't help either, but 1982's *Black Pearl* was a rather enjoyable album and contained the MTV hit "I La La La Love You," which provided hooks as did the sardonic "I'd Rather See You Dead" with a perfectly morbid (and quite amusing) video. Album sales declined but 1984's *Hot Shot* did have "Killer," which was a great song.

After being dropped by Polydor, Travers drifted into the clubs and could only release albums on small indie labels into the '90s, though a few fine blues albums were issued during this low-key period. The 2000s and beyond have been much more kind as Pat continues to tour regularly and record with the Pat Travers Band. Imaginative cover songs appeared on some of the albums and Pat's playing and tone were really, really in a good way again.

In 2009, *Fidelis* showed plenty of life (and included one of Pat's best songs ever, in the emotionally filled "Stay") and the 2012 release *Blues on Fire* was a clever album of 1920s songs cranked up for today in a raunchy blues style. In 2013, *Can Do* was a damn fine effort and his best in years. The title cut is an oddly arranged, blazing song and the album never lets up. The current lineup features Travers, Genarro, Kirk McKim (guitars/vocals), and Rodney O' Quinn (bass/vocals). *Retro Rocket* kept up the string of good albums in 2015.

Pat has also teamed up with drumming legend Carmine Appice as Travers & Appice, releasing several very cool albums (the best being *It Takes a Lot of Balls* in 2004, which also happens to have a great title) and he will not only crush you with his guitar and voice but with his black belt in karate. So there!

And, just before the New Year in late 2014, Pat and I were able to have one of those cool talks that just make your day better.

And how are you today, Pat?

I'm good. I'm sittin' outside, but it's kind of a gloomy day here in Florida.

I am not outside—it's thirty degrees! How long have you been in Florida now?

I've been here since around 1978. I left Canada in 1975 and moved to England, which is where I got my first record deal.

That's right, with Polydor. The purpose of this book is to feature players who simply don't get the constant accolades all the time like Hendrix, Clapton, Page, etc., as awesome as they all are and I love Page. But, here is a chance for me to talk about Terry Kath and guys of that nature.

That is amazing! What a coincidence you mention Terry Kath. We were playing the first Chicago album yesterday and not only did he play his ass off, but he sang a lot of songs and was so damn good.

I always thought of him as a white Ray Charles if that make sense!

You just took the words right out of my mouth! I don't think people realize his voice and his lightning guitar playing made him out of this world. Jimi Hendrix said he was a favorite of his.

I think part of the problem with Terry's identity was that Chicago always were an ensemble and many people knew the horns and the band but not the players as they didn't even have their faces on an album cover until the mid-'70s.

Exactly; he didn't really have a face like the others. I was such a big fan of his. I was in Ottawa, Canada, at the time and I think it was frickin' cold in like February or so, and a bunch of us drove in a van to Toronto to see Chicago at Maple Leaf Gardens. It was about a 250-mile drive and we froze our asses off to see him play in his hockey jersey. He had a rough mid-rangey kind of tone, but he played so amazing it didn't matter. That's so great you've got him in there. My son, who is eighteen, and I were really enjoying his playing yesterday. So who else ya got in there?

Oh man, so many wonderful players. Martin Barre from Jethro Tull…

Fuck! I love that guy! I got to hang out with him a few years ago at the NAMM show and it was so great because I was a big fan of his sound and his riffs. He had an awesome vibrato and tone and to find out he was a funny and awesome guy was great. Those first three Tull albums have so many classic, iconic guitar riffs.

As a massive Thin Lizzy fan, I also have Eric Bell in there.

Yeah, I was pretty tight with those guys when Brian Robertson and Scott Gorham were the guitar duo.

And Scott was on one of your albums.

Yeah, and Brian, too. They were the first band I saw in the UK I thought was any good when I got there. I saw them at the Roundhouse and got in touch with their management, which is how I got to know those guys.

So who were some of the players who influenced you?

We've been talkin' about some of them [laughs]. Martin Barre definitely, Terry Kath for sure. I stopped using a wah-wah a few years ago because I was getting' too much like Terry [laughs]. I have a lot of Terry's musical DNA in me for sure. I was lucky as I started playing guitar around 1966 and we had Hendrix, Cream, Jeff Beck, Johnny Winter, Carlos Santana—and all of these guys were brand new at the time. I had been playing bars since I was fifteen playing five sets a night five to six days a week.

And what have been the go-to guitars through the years?

Basically there's three: the Les Paul, the Stratocaster, and the Telecaster. Those are really the three for me, but there's a Gibson ES-335 as well. There's a Rickenbacker, too, so maybe four I really use and I guess five with a PRS. When I go in the studio, I turn to my Telecaster because I don't have to do much with it. I just plug in, mic it up, push up the fader, and I'm good. It fits right in the mix. Live, I mostly use a PRS Custom 22 and I've got 57/08 pickups on it.

Do you use that in the studio as well?

Yeah, I use it both but mostly live. It's a great guitar. Solid as rock and it looks good, too.

Did you know early on you guys had found your sound?

I don't know really, because I winged it for quite a few years. I really seem to get the same sound no matter what guitars or effects I'm using. So, whether that was my signature sound or not, I don't know actually. Now I'm really down to just some delay and a bit of chorus.

At this point, you don't really need all that extra stuff anyway.

Nah, I just feel I can get more out of my hands and fingers rather than a bunch of effects. I just trust my cable and people don't realize how important that is.

The cable?

Yeah, you have to spend some bucks on your cable. You can hear a huge difference if you use the proper cable from your guitar to whatever it is. A nice big thick cord and I try to get as much as I can out of my guitar. I've never really used fuzz boxes. I've always used a 50 watt Marshall and a 100 watt Marshall in the early days. Now I use a Black Star preamp and it just sounds awesome. In the studio it's super clean and punchy with a lot of tone. They can be a little finicky. To me they're one of the best in the studio and live.

In the late '70s, the Pat Travers Band were becoming a huge live attraction, and Live! Go for What You Know *became one of those great, iconic hard rock live albums of that time. You had to know you had something special with those recordings?*

No! As a matter of fact, I was kind of indifferent to the whole thing and we had been touring non-stop for a good three to four months and we were just at the end of the tour and I was going to get the time to record the *Crash and Burn* album. So they wanted me to mix the live album right away, and we did the last show in Miami, Florida, and I was living there at the time. And Tom Allom of Judas Priest came in and basically did everything. I was so sick of that material, that I left it up to him to get a good mix and I went out and got some sun on the roof since the studio was right on Coconut Grove in Miami.

I'd come down and hear what he had done and then I went, "Okay, that sounds good." I'd heard the songs so much that each playback I'd hear mistakes and just wanted to move past that material [laughs]. It was a total surprise because all of a sudden we had a big radio hit with "Boom Boom (Out Go the Lights)" and I was like, "are you kidding me?"

Did you even know that was going to be issued as a single?

No, I really didn't. I was totally disinterested in the live album. Its only purpose was to give me time to work on the next album *Crash and Burn*. Now I can hear what people are talking about though—it sparkles, it's got all kinds of energy and the band busts out of the speakers.

Getting to Crash and Burn, *that went Gold, and you had a hit with the Bob Marley song "Is This Love."*

We may have played that live once or twice, but it just never seemed to work for me, and now we play it again and it's so much fun to perform.

It works on the album because it is a different treatment.

Yeah, I loved Bob Marley, thanks to Pat Thrall exposing me to his music. I can't sing a lot of his songs because I can't relate to where he's coming from and what he dealt with, but that one, it's such a simple song, with a nice message that repeats and I can make it work.

"Snortin' Whiskey" still leaps out no matter how many times I hear it on the radio.

There's another one that just jumped out. It came out of nowhere. It was Pat Thrall who coined the term after showing up three hours late for rehearsal. In fact, he was in no condition for rehearsal, and I said, "What the hell have you been doing?" He replied, "Snortin' whiskey and drinking cocaine." We all laughed and I said right there, "That's a song," and I had that riff lying around and it took about seven minutes to put together.

And what about that funky mid-section with the cowbell and the key change? Was that always meant for that song or was it a separate idea that you blended in?

I always liked trying to go somewhere different key-wise in the mid-section, so you could create some tension when you came back to the original key. That's all that was about really. To tell you the truth, Tommy Aldridge the drummer had the cowbell on the left side so he hit it on the upbeat instead of the downbeat and I just didn't wanna argue with him, so now I have Sandy play it on the downbeat because it's so odd.

That's why I always liked it so much—it is odd. You've had some killer drummers through the years.

I've been cursed and blessed with drummers. I've played with some of the best ever. Nicko McBrain who went on to Iron Maiden, my first one was Roy Dyke from Ashton, Gardner & Dyke. Then there's Tommy Aldridge, of course. I've been fortunate to play with Ansley Dunbar live and in the studio and a great one now in Sandy Genarro.

Once it hit 1981–1982 with the explosion of MTV, you began doing music videos, some of which were morbidly humorous. Was that a scene you wanted no part of but had to play the game, or something you were up for? And did you have a say in how these came out?

It was collaboration and I wasn't thrilled about having to do these things because I thought it was kinda ridiculous. There was some tension because we're not actors, we're just musicians and we're being told what to do and how to look and there was a lot of standing around. I did have a say as to how these videos came out though. And I thought with "I'd Rather See You Dead" it was a good chance to do something funny with black humor.

It came out well and got into pretty good rotation.

It did okay, but it came out way, way after we had done the tour with Aerosmith in 1982, and it should've come out months before that tour began, but they screwed everything up and issued it several months after that tour had ended, so there ya go.

The other one "I La La La Love You" was also in good rotation on MTV and scored airplay on radio. That was also on the Valley Girl *soundtrack wasn't it?*

Yeah, it did really well with that movie and it was showcased pretty well. "Snortin' Whiskey" was in *Sideways*, remember?

I loved that movie! And when that song came on I couldn't believe it. I started rockin' out in my seat and my wife asked what the hell song it was and I said, "I'll tell ya later." She had no idea anyway.

[Laughs] I loved how it just jumped out at you in the film.

Did you know about that in advance of the film's release?

Yes we did, a little bit anyway. My wife and I went to see it before it hit mainstream theaters and halfway through the film, I leaned over and said, "Someone's pulling our leg, because the movie is half over and I don't see any place the song could pop up and be used." When it did, it was white trailer trash—that's what my music is used for I guess! [Laughs] It was funny and it was a good scene.

The video for "I La La La Love You" had you in a towel and singing into a hair dryer or something and there was a model.

Yeah, we never really got the concept for that one solidified. There were things going on and I just didn't want to be there, but the one thing that we had was that Victoria's Secret model in the video.

Hell yes! And that part of it was quite eye-catching.

I liked the idea of having an African-American girl in the video. They were showing me a bunch of 8 x 10 photographs and I recognized her and went, "Bingo! That's her," but she wasn't all that friendly [laughs].

For 1982 that was very daring to have an interracial couple in a video.

Yes, I thought it was cool.

Moving into some of your more recent albums, Fidelis *has a song called "Stay" that is awesome—one of your best.*

It's become a big one for me, even though I didn't write it. I did have some lyrics, but not many. I sang it three different times and I really just wanted to get to bed because it was three o'clock in the morning and the producer asked me to do it one more time and that's the take that went on there. The two solos—there's one at the end, too—I used a PRS Modern Eagle and it sounds so good.

It's a real treat to hear. And the title cut on the most recent album "Can Do" is so cool, but a strange one rhythmically.

Yeah, I agree. I'm not sure what was going on there when I thought of it. I had the music and was trying to find the chorus rhythmically before I had written lyrics and I remember driving to a show somewhere and I needed a pen because it hit me and came together in my head! Live it's even better.

There's no doubt that there are some artists still recording some great material, and these last few just have you in a groove and the reviews have been overwhelmingly positive. Have you been getting good feedback?

Yes. I even got some of the best reviews I've ever received for *Can Do*. I was very determined that the songs would be super-strong on that one. We worked off and on for eight months on that one and I had time to think about things. It came out the way I wanted and I had the time to make good decisions. I have another studio album coming out early in 2015. [Update! The new album did come out in 2015 titled *Retro Rocker*.]

You've done some interesting covers through the years and there's a version of "Spanish Moon" by Little Feat that is a knockout on the Don't Feed the Alligators *album from 2000.*

I love that tune! Some years ago, the first time I had XM satellite radio for the car, that came on and I heard the bass and the guitars and I thought, "Damn, who is doing this great version of that song?" and it was me! [Laughs] I was like, "Oh yeah, I forgot I covered that."

Hilarious! That was true?

Yeah, true. There are some good covers on that album.

And you've also tackled and done a stellar job on "Green Eyed Lady" by Sugarloaf.

Yeah! Everyone seems to like that one, but I've not been able to make it go down well live, at least not for myself. The song doesn't go anywhere—you're locked into this riff and you can't deviate from it. I've gotten a good response though, so maybe we should give that a go live.

Well, it's another clever arrangement because that song has distinctive keyboard parts and you're replicating that on guitar.

We just swapped out the keyboards for the guitars and it came out cool.

Back in the late '70s, the Pat Travers Band opened for Rush a few tours. Did that kind of break the door open for you guys?

That was the best tour for us—the winter of '78. Rush didn't have much radio play yet, but a huge following and we were able to play in front of 7,000–12,000 people a night, and even though we only had thirty minutes or so, it went down very well. We were just a three-piece then, so we didn't need much equipment, which helped as well. It was just Tommy Aldridge, Mars Cowling on bass, and me, and we really got to hit a lot of the US for the first time. That was fun.

Well, I thank you so much for doing this and making all that great music.

Absolutely. I had fun chatting!

A final stupid question: if you could rename an album or song of yours after a cat what would you come up with? My cats want to know.

A cat? As in c-a-t, cat?

Yep! Told ya it was stupid!

Ha! How about "Boobala"? We had a cat by that name—that was my first cat my wife and I had, so there we go. [Laughs] Oh, man…

[I have no idea if I spelled that cat's name right!]

Recommended solo: "Snortin' Whiskey" from *Crash and Burn* with Pat Travers Band (1980)
Further info: www.pattravers.com
Photo credit: Margriet Cloudt

Carl Verheyen

(Born Carl William Verheyen, April 3, 1954, Santa Monica, CA)

Sometimes it's just not fair how good certain players are, and it makes me want to just put my guitar down and walk away. Then, I embrace my mediocrity and pick the guitar up again because I realize it's okay not to be a guitar genius because there are only so many. Carl Verheyen is one of those guys.

With a gift for composition, teaching, unique styling and picking, a great voice, and as well as being a teacher/instructor, to say the least Carl Verheyen is a wonderful asset to the guitar world. Carl has written instructional booklets (and filmed DVDs as well), articles for top music magazines, and is an adjunct instructor of Studio Jazz Guitar for the Thornton School of Music of the University of Southern California (USC).

A renowned session player, Carl issued his first solo album *No Borders* in 1988. *Garage Sale* was his next release in 1994, and the song "Garage Sale" is a colorful exhibition of Carl's uncanny taste, sense of harmony and tone. His solos have purpose and are extremely musical and take different twists and turns. The musical backing from his fellow musicians is also excellent and sympathetic to Carl's playing. One can hear some Eric Johnson in his playing and perhaps even Jan Akkerman, Steve Morse, Lowell George, Jeff Beck, and Eddie Van Halen. Yeah, he's that good! Those names are just reference points because Carl has a style all to his own and a dynamic one at that.

In 1985–1986, Carl was a touring guitarist with Supertramp on their *Brother Where You Bound* tour, and this would not be the last time Carl was with Supertramp.

Slang Justice and *Slingshot* were album releases in the late '90s that were once again a pleasure for guitar fans. A 2011 collaboration with Austrian jazz guitarist Karl Ratzer entitled *Real to Reel* was recorded in just two days. Carl's album *Six* followed in 2003, and he went on an extensive tour.

Every album has something special to offer, but *Trading 8's* from 2009 was a real treat with Carl trading off with other guitar greats, such as Joe Bonamassa (you must hear their jam here called "Highway 27," good lord!), Robben Ford, Scott Henderson, Steve Morse, Albert Lee, and Rick Vito. With the double live CD *The Road Divides* (2011), Carl and his trio simply called the Carl Verheyen Band (with bass player Dave Marotta and drummer Walfredo Reyes Jr.) created an intense album with vibrancy and "The Road Divides" is one mother of a song: beautiful melodies and harmonic sound, insanely complex soloing that despite the technical expertise never loses sight of feel (this isn't as easy as it sounds) and a bounce and spirit in both Carl's guitar and his vocals (and man, does he have an excellent voice). There's plenty of groove, too, and the band is hot. This might be my favorite Carl moment.

"Riding the Bean," "Fusioneers Disease" (hilariously titled, but the groove here is wicked, as are the drums—do not be fooled by the brief mellow intro!) and a rendition of "Bloody Well Right" acknowledging his tenure with Supertramp are all money from *Mustang Run* (2013). "Mustang Run" is a great tune as well with a solo to appreciate and then some, and the soulful "Spirit of Julia" is beautiful with a tone and feel best described as being from above.

In 1997, Carl joined Supertramp as a permanent member, which was quite interesting as Supertramp has never been a guitar-based band. The album *Some Things Never Change* sold moderately and contained the minor hit "You Win, I Lose." There were some very long songs, such as the title cut, "It's a Hard World" and "C'est What?" The latter cut allowed Carl to record a very cool solo, but throughout much of the album he was relegated to some light jazz chords and R&B phrasings. The double-live album *It Was the Best of Times* from 1999 was a chance to really hear how Carl fit in with Supertramp so well on classics like "Bloody Well Right," "School," and "Goodbye Stranger." Not only that, the nearly ten minutes of "Another Man's Woman" sees Carl follow up original keyboardist/vocalist Rick Davies' amazing improved piano solo with a rip-roaring solo that takes the song to the stratosphere.

A new Supertramp album called *Slow Motion* was finally released in 2002 and featured the engaging single "Over You," along with "Little By Little" and "A Sting in the Tail." After the tour, the band folded until Davies re-formed the group for more touring in 2010 and 2011 albeit in limited capacity, mainly in Europe and Canada. Since then, the band has been inactive once more, but Carl remains a member—and an important one.

Ah, but it is Verheyen's trio where you must enjoy the full experience of seeing him at his finest. The live performances by the Carl Verheyen Band continue to draw audiences worldwide in numerous countries, and if you have an opportunity to see them, do yourself a favor and go! A splendid new solo acoustic album *Alone* was released in 2015.

And, to no surprise, Carl is a quality human being, and he answered all of my questions with the class and humility I expected when we connected in January 2015.

Who were some of the players that have influenced you through the years?

Roger McGuinn and George Harrison got it all started for me back in '65. I progressed through Clapton, Hendrix, Bloomfield, all three Kings, Duane Allman, Alvin Lee, and Stephen Stills, until I arrived at Wes Montgomery, John Scofield, Mike Stern, and especially Pat Martino. Then I checked out Joe Pass and Joe Diorio, Lenny Breau and Chet Atkins before coming full circle back to rock and blues. I play a lot of country guitar and have studied all the greats. Currently, I listen to a lot of slide guys like Sonny Landreth and Derek Trucks and attempt to achieve that level of expression on normal fretted guitar.

What are the types of guitars you've preferred during your career on stage and in studio?

I have a good example of every important guitar made, all the essential tools. But my heart and soul is in the Stratocaster; it's the instrument with which I can best express myself. You have to jump through a few more hoops to make it sustain and distort in a singing, saturated way like a Gibson, but I believe that makes for a more personal and individual tone.

I know you have a pretty extensive background in music for television shows—what exactly did you get to play or write for Cheers *and* Seinfeld?

All those TV shows, especially sitcoms, have short little cues no more than ten seconds long. Occasionally there will be longer *source music* to record. These cues are usually songs emanating from a radio, a nightclub, or an offstage source. It's often cheaper for the production to record an original disco tune by the show's composer than to license a Bee Gees tune.

You cover an awful lot of ground live with complex playing and wonderful singing, especially with the Carl Verheyen Band. How hard was it to find that balance?

I think of it like this: the music I write starts with the guitar. Something new and interesting on my instrument is essential for every one of my songs. But I also prefer vocal music to pop or rock instrumentals, so I've spent a lot of time driving around in my car writing lyrics to my riffs or melodies. And I must admit I love to sing! It's a guilty pleasure because I know so many great studio singers here in LA, and I have nowhere near their chops, but neither does Bob Dylan, and he gets it across.

Supertramp is not a guitar-dominated band, and you have had to pick your spaces for the appropriate times to solo in your own fashion. It has worked wonderfully well and has added another dimension to the music of the band, especially on "Another Man's Woman" (what a solo you play on that one!), "Bloody Well Right," and "School," among others. How did the gig come about, including the first bout of touring in 1985? And, have you enjoyed the shows as they are so different to your solo activities?

The beautiful thing about that band is that they all appreciate improvisation. Most giant arena-touring bands insist on the parts, including solos, to be played exactly like the record. But early on I was able to convince them to let me hit a few integral points at the beginning of the solo and then take off from there. So I start the "Goodbye Stranger" solo with the iconic wah-wah lick and then burn it down! The ability to stretch out like that in front of 20,000 people is a real privilege, but I do believe it makes the music live and breathe every night, as opposed to static, scripted solos. I really do enjoy those shows!

How has teaching and instructing affected your career? I teach and there's nothing more rewarding than making a difference to someone trying to learn something. It must be a gratifying feeling.

I have a strong feeling of responsibility to pass down the knowledge to the next generation. We want people playing instruments, not typing music into computers. Teaching can truly enrich one's life. It also provides an income stream that I'm grateful for. And when I do master classes out on the road, I feel it brings me closer to that super appreciative fan base of guitar players.

Can you take me through the composition of the riff on the song "The Road Divides"? That is my favorite piece by you and the guitar work really makes my head spin. It is catchy, yet complex. Not an easy thing to create, plus your vocals are so good on this song!

There's a certain hybrid picking technique I use when playing country music and bluegrass. Over the years I've expanded the range of that concept to include not just 2 strings, but 4 and sometimes 5. "The Road Divides" uses this hybrid, string skipping country technique and slams it into a rock-type song. It's hard to play and sing at the same time, especially the bridge. But with practice on my own and a few rehearsals with the band, anything is possible! I once had a guy come up to me before a show and ask, "Are you going to play 'Chinatown' tonight?" He was extremely disappointed when I said yes because he'd bet his friend I couldn't play and sing it at the same time. It cost him $50!

The Trading 8's *album sees you playing with guitarists like Robben Ford, Joe Bonamassa, Rick Vito, Scott Henderson, Steve Morse, and Albert Lee. This must have been a blast, and the song with Bonamassa ("Highway 27") is out of this world. Was anything pre-arranged for these guys at least in skeleton form or did you basically say "plug in and play your ass off"?*

Nothing was pre-arranged as these guys are all great musicians and can enter the studio with fresh ears and nail it. Joe and I shared the same European agent at the time and always talked about doing a project together. I called him and said, "When will you be in town? I have a track I'd like to play on with you!" He said, "Tomorrow!" So I booked time at Sunset Sound and had about thirty-five of my amps delivered. Joe picked a 100-watt Marshall of mine from 1969 and I played out of a 50-watt plexi from '68. His Les Paul and my Strat traded back and forth, we did three takes and the entire session took ninety minutes! It was effortless, inspiring and a lot of fun! I enjoyed doing that CD a lot and when it was finished a lot of other heavy players came out of the woodwork wishing they'd been called. So a volume 2 is in order for some time in the future!

The Mustang Run *album continues the wonderful quality of album you are putting out consistently. Of particular note is "Spirit of Julia." The tone on that is something else. How did you get that tone and your tone in general?*

That song was my '65 Gibson ES-335 and a '66 plexi JTM-45 Marshall head. In general my guitars are set up with medium action because I believe action height has more to do with tone than string gauge. I pay careful attention to everything in my signal chain from strings and picks to cables, pedals, tubes, and speakers. Over the many years of playing on other artist's records, I've amassed a solid collection of gear, and certain combinations, like that 335 and JTM-45 fall into my category of "secret weapons."

Final silly question I usually ask players: If you had to rename a song or album of yours (solo or in Supertramp) with a cat theme, what would you come up with?

"Hairball Harmonies"!

Recommended solo: "The Road Divides" from *The Road Divides* with Carl Verheyen Band (2011).
Further info: www.carlverheyen.com
Photo credit: Peter Figen

CHAPTER 49

Rick Vito

(Born Richard F. Vito, October 13, 1949, Darby, PA)

Truly one of the greatest slide guitar and blues players of now and then, Rick Vito has played behind the scenes and upfront with some seriously big names, as well as some lesser-known names but no less talented than those more discussed.

Rick's grandmother owned a corner bar in Wildwood, New Jersey, down the seashore, and he was able to see his first concert at the Steel Mill in Atlantic City in 1959, which was an Everly Brothers show, and by age fourteen, he began playing guitar in front of people. Through the mid- to late-'60s Rick immersed himself in the blues and started learning to play songs from all the greats of the genre. After playing in various college bands, Rick kept at it, and he recorded some songs. A guest spot with Delaney & Bonnie convinced Rick that a career might happen and he relocated to Hollywood in 1971.

After touring with Delaney & Bonnie, Rick did sessions for Todd Rundgren on the *Something/Anything* album and then worked with John Prine, Little Richard, Bobby Whitlock, and Dobie Gray among others into 1974. Late that year, Vito was invited to join John Mayall in his band and stayed there for four albums (check out his subtle blues work on "Who's Next, Who's Now" from the album *Notice to Appear* from 1975).

Rick would also form an alliance with legendary ex-Byrds member Roger McGuinn playing on the album *Thunderbyrd* in 1977, and that led to him writing a song for the self-titled album by supergroup McGuinn, Clark & Hillman in 1979 called "Surrender to Me," one of many excellent songs on the album that made the US Top 40.

In 1982, Rick joined Bonnie Raitt's band appearing on the *Green Light* album and that's him with the band in the video for a spirited, swampy take on the Equals' (Eddy Grant of "Electric Avenue" fame's old band, by the way) classic "Baby Come Back." That same year, Rick began playing with Jackson Browne and appears on Jackson's Top 10 smash hit "Somebody's Baby" from the *Fast Times at Ridgemont High* soundtrack album.

Rick also played on Browne's 1983 *Lawyers in Love* album as well as with Dolly Parton and on another Browne LP *Lives in the Balance* from 1986. *Lawyers in Love* has some great guitar work, especially on the hit title song and "Tender Is the Night," while *Lives in the Balance* saw Vito playing on the painfully beautiful "In the Shape of a Heart," which is one of Jackson Browne's best songs musically and lyrically.

Also in 1986, Rick played on Bob Seger's *Like a Rock* album and on the song "Like a Rock" laid down what is now one of the most famous guitar solos ever recorded on a rock song. That is not too much hyperbole. Vito's two slide solos on this track are the stuff of legend, particularly the emotionally stirring outro solo. The guitars perfectly marry Seger's excellent lyrics about looking back and wondering whether enough was achieved in one's life. I still get the same chills hearing it now as I did when I was in high school when the album came out and the song became yet another monster hit for Seger. There was something very special about this one though, and it was those biting slide solos. Sure, millions have heard these solos on those incessant Chevy commercials, but consider it a gift!

And then things really changed for Rick after touring with Seger and the Silver Bullet Band. In 1987, he received an offer to join Fleetwood Mac from Mick Fleetwood, who was a fan of Rick's playing. Mac legend Lindsey Buckingham had recently quit the band and the core of Fleetwood, bassist John McVie, keyboardist/vocalist Christine McVie, and vocalist Stevie Nicks decided to push forward, adding Vito and guitarist/vocalist Billy Burnette and toured to support the massively popular *Tango in the Night* album. A concert video from this tour in San Francisco shows that the band was still fantastic live, but Buckingham's absence was hugely noticeable. That being said, with Vito on board, the band played a few songs from their blues-era as Vito was a huge Peter Green fan, even having seen Fleetwood Mac with Green in concert in Philadelphia way back in the late '60s.

Rick also found time that year to play another memorable slide solo on Bob Seger's excellent version of "Little Drummer Boy" from the *A Very Special Christmas Album* and he would also play on Seger's albums *The Fire Inside* (1991) and *It's a Mystery* (1995).

In 1988, Fleetwood Mac released *Greatest Hits* a best-of with two new tracks, the first with the new lineup. The gorgeous "As Long as You Follow" became a sizeable hit falling just shy of the Top 40 and sported a lovely Christine McVie vocal performance. The song also featured a lovely, eloquent solo by Vito immediately proving his worth to the band. The guitar playing is very distinctive and refined. The album sold over 8 million in the US, so loads of fans got to hear the two new songs.

Behind the Mask followed in 1990 topping the UK charts, but stalling in the US Top 20 and only going Gold. Worse yet, only "Save Me" made the singles charts, edging into the Top 40. Truth be told, this album is far better than what critics and some harsh fans said, and Vito shines with co-writing credit on tracks like "Love is Dangerous" and "Stand on the Rock." Throughout, his signature guitar sound appears and this album also contained one supreme gem in the beautiful "Affairs of the Heart," which was one of Stevie's very best vocal turns. After another rather good tour, the band took some time off and turmoil followed with Nicks quitting and Vito soon followed, though an excellent jaunty new song "Paper Doll" co-written by Vito would appear on the box set *25 Years: The Chain* in 1992 and became a minor hit.

By 1992, Vito issued a solo album on Atlantic called *King of Hearts* that had great songs like the raunchy blues of "I Still Have My Guitar" and "Knock Me Down." In 1994, Vito toured with Nicks for her *Street Angel* album. Rick would also rejoin Raitt's band for a tour in 1998–1999. Listen to Rick get down and dirty on "Long Black Car" from his excellent *Lucky Devils* album in 2001. This is fabulous playing and so is Rick's vocal. The guitar on this track is scrumptious (look, I can only use the same adjectives over and over again), and it is an example of his great picking style and feel. Vito has released further solo albums including *Band Box Boogie* in 2003, which incorporated swing, R&B, jump blues, and even some Latin to great results.

In 2009, *Blue Again!* was issued with the Mick Fleetwood Blues Band, a tremendous live recording of old blues material with a four-piece band, including Fleetwood on drums and Vito on guitar and vocals. New songs, including the Vito-penned "Fleetwood Boogie" blend with vintage Mac classics like "Black Magic Woman," "Stop Messin' 'Round" and "Rattlesnake Shake." On "Black Magic Woman," Vito displays total respect for this classic with phenomenal blues playing with a perfect tone and also sings wonderfully. A bonus EP was included with a sterling take on the Fleetwood Mac UK #1 instrumental hit from 1968 "Albatross." Peter Green's masterpiece of sea-like tranquility is handled with grace and taste by Vito like nobody else could. Yes, it's that authentic and real. *Blue Again!* would earn a Grammy nomination.

In the 2000s, Vito has also played with John Fogerty and Boz Scaggs among others and has also released several DVDs. A new studio album *Mojo on My Side* was released in the summer of 2015.

One of the very finest American blues rock slide guitar players around, Rick Vito is a guy you should know more about, and now I hope you do.

Who were some of your primary influences as you started playing the guitar?

Elvis Presley, Ricky Nelson, James Burton, Duane Eddy, Chuck Berry...early rock and roll. Later on, it was Keith Richards, George Harrison, B. B. King, Mike Bloomfield, Elmore James and ALL the bluesmen.

What have been your preferred guitars through the years?

I used to like old Telecasters, then I got a '58 Les Paul, so I've always liked those two. But I love so many different kinds of guitars and I design my own, too. I have a "Rick Vito Signature" model out with Reverend Guitars in Michigan.

Congratulations on the success of the Blue Again *album with the Mick Fleetwood Blues Band. That is an outstanding album and features some of your best singing and playing.*

Thank you very much; I'm proud of it. The CD was recorded at our very first gig and was nominated for a Grammy!

You've also played many years with Bonnie Raitt, who I respect very much, and I'm sure you feel the same. Do you guys click well in regards to your styles on guitar?

We both listened to a lot of the same artists coming up. I was into Son House a bit and she, Fred McDowell, both country/blues artists. Then we both got into electric slide as played by guys recording out in LA, like Jesse Ed Davis, Ry Cooder, and Lowell George of Little Feat. We both like a lot of the same stuff.

As a devotee of the blues, I assume getting invited into John Mayall's Bluesbreakers had to be an honor and a thrill. Were you able to express yourself during that tenure and grow more as a blues player? And what is your connection to the blues and your slide playing? It's as authentic as it gets.

I couldn't believe it when John heard me play two songs at his house with Larry Taylor and said, "You're in!" (Thanks again Larry, for recommending me.) The records he made with Peter Green and Eric Clapton, etc., were such classics and changed the way guys played blues and rock, so to be in that company was a real honor. I started playing slide in college up at Kutztown University after being shown "Walking Blues" by my friend Rick Valenti from Springfield, Pennsylvania. I just got captivated and have always tried to keep taking it further and further, because it's like a voice and you can get very expressive with it. When I joined Mayall, he encouraged you to do everything you could do and more. So, naturally I played some slide with him.

You played on some of Jackson Browne's finest songs in the '80s, including the engaging "Somebody's Baby" single in 1982 and the Lawyers In Love *and* Lives In The Balance *albums. Do you have good memories of working on that material and what songs that you played on stood out?*

I never understood Jackson's music (except for "Doctor My Eyes") until I started working with him. He's a poet from the Bob Dylan school and I'd always been drawn to the music rather than the lyrics. I started listening to lyrics more after that. We worked five days a week on a downtown LA loft making "Lawyers in Love" and going on tours, too, for two years. So it was really finely crafted work and it was all recorded LIVE! So if it sounds inspired or good to you, it's because it's something called "real music." I liked, "Tender Is the Night," "For A Rocker," and "In the Shape of a Heart," as I recall.

The era of Fleetwood Mac from 1987–1991 you were a part of is an underrated one. I especially love your solo on "As Long As You Follow" and the Behind The Mask *album had some fine material as well. Can you describe how you approached that solo, especially knowing that this would be the first song heard by the public from the new lineup and your experience overall with the band?*

Thank you. I never know what will make the cut, so I never think about it going out to the public; I just try to play everything well, as best I can. As it happens, it WAS the first thing I recorded with them and it was a #1 adult contemporary hit (whatever that meant). The solo just came out, but I remember trying a couple two-note bends on part of the solo as Peter Green had done. It reminded the band of Green they said, so that was a plus. Obviously, my favorite era of the band was the original lineup from the later sixties, way before pop rock came into it.

I know it's been much discussed, but I don't care—the solo on Bob Seer's "Like A Rock" is extraordinary. From the first moment I heard the song in 1986 (I was a Junior in high school) I tried to find out who played it. The second half of the solo is so emotional and ties in perfectly to Bob's lyrics. I don't think there's too many slide solos, or solos in general, better than this in rock history. Could you take me through the composition of the solo, and that is *you in the video with some wheat in your teeth—ha ha?*

Again, thanks. I agree that the blend of the sound of the slide guitar over the mood and lyrics of the song is just a perfect accidental marriage. I recorded that in '85, so that's thirty years ago, and have seldom come close to doing anything that reached that ethereal point musically since. I just had met Bob, he put the song up...I said I thought slide would be good and he said, "No." I asked for one pass and nailed it the first time, just working off of inspiration and somehow allowing myself to be in the moment. The video was done much later in 1986, and it had reached the middle of the night, and I was exhausted from waiting around. I just picked up a strand of wheat and was chewing on it to pass the time and it was the take they used. When Bob goes out on tour they get guys who can play it note for note, which makes me feel like, "why don't you just call the original man who created it?" I'll never figure those guys out I guess.

Congrats again on the Grammy nomination for Blue Again *album with the Mick Fleetwood Blues Band! That is one fun, outstanding record. "Red Hot Gal" and "Fleetwood Boogie" (great swing to this one) are killer compositions by you. How did that record come about and how satisfying was it for you?*

Yes, thanks for mentioning the Grammy again, ha ha. As I said, it was our first gig and Mick wanted to record it for posterity. Later, I took the tapes and mixed it at my studio, and everybody went, "Gah!" "Red Hot Gal" was about my wife and was originally done on my CD, "Rattlesnake Shake" as "My Baby's Hot." With Mick, I just put it slightly more in the Elmore James style that hearkened back to the original Mac sound a bit.

"Fleetwood Boogie," was originally called "Cadillac Boogie," but again, I tailored it for Mick. I got a release for the album in Europe on Hypertension Music in Hamburg. They put my solo work out over there. Then one of Mick's managers got it to Savoy Records in the states. It's always gratifying when your work gets recognized, because it doesn't happen that often, if at all. It was a big surprise.

Final silly question I ask most players for my cats: if you could rename an album or song you've played on with a cat theme (solo or with Fleetwood Mac, Jackson Browne, Stevie Nicks, Bob Seger, etc.) what would you come up with? (i.e., "Like As Long As You Meow"—I know that was terrible, but you get the idea).

Mew stumped me on that one.

CHAPTER 50
Robb Weir
(Born Robert Weir, May 4, 1959, Takoradi, Ghana, West Africa)

In 1979, a musical movement dubbed the NWOBHM (new wave of British heavy metal) emerged, and loads of guitar-based bands were getting snatched up by record labels. Some of these bands were simply fantastic and have had monumental success, and others had a very nice run, and some were simply cult bands. Many of these acts have proven to not only be influential and successful but also have a back catalog that has remained relevant with albums from the golden era of the late '70s and early '80s that still sound fresh. Among these acts were names like Iron Maiden, Def Leppard, Saxon, Angel Witch, Demon, Diamond Head, Venom, Nightwing, and many more.

One of the best of the lot was the Newcastle-based band Tygers of Pan Tang that featured Robb Weir (guitar), gravelly throated Jess Cox (vocals), Rocky Laws (bass), and Brian Dick (drums). The Tygers landed a deal with indie label Neat Records and issued their first single "Please Don't Touch Me There." Red-hot live gigs, sales of the single, and a sizeable local following led to the big leagues and a major label deal with MCA Records in 1980.

The band's debut album *Wild Cat* was issued in summer 1980 and clawed its way into the UK Top 20. The album was a rough 'n' ready set of hard rock songs played raw with few overdubs and a very live-sounding feel. From start to finish *Wild Cat* is an album any hard rock fan should enjoy for this simple reason: it kicks ass! The ferocity of "Wild Catz," "Badger Badger," "Euthanasia," and "Fireclown" is cool enough, but then you've got the slamming "Suzie Smiled" with a simple chord progression that instantly makes one want to rock and the lengthy "Insanity" where Weir uses harmonics and tremolo and a chugging rhythm to great effect.

The band toured and played the prestigious Reading Festival as well making a huge impression. Blazing guitarist John Sykes was added later that year, but Cox would soon leave and Jon Deverill (ex-Persian Risk) would become the new singer, adding a more melodic-based sound. In 1981, *Spellbound* became a Top 40 album and contained the minor hit "Hellbound." Songs like "Gangland," "Take It," "Tyger Bay," and "Blackjack" were as hard hitting as ever, but the band's sensibilities changed with the haunting track "Mirror" and the dramatic "Don't Stop By" that had a muted, staccato intro heightening the dramatics and new sound.

In late 1981, the band quickly released *Crazy Nights,* which continued a tradition of awesome album cover artwork. The LP felt rushed, however, and many of the songs sounded the same. The production was also very raw, almost demo-like. Despite this, some tracks stood out, such as "Running Out of Time," "Never Satisfied," "Make a Stand," and especially the catchy title song. The guitars were the primary force here, and as on the previous album, Weir and Sykes proved an excellent tandem trading off solos with ease. The album would stall at #51 on the UK charts as the band toured into 1982 and made some UK TV appearances as well.

In 1982, the band scored a Top 50 UK hit single with a cover of the old Clovers tune "Love Potion No. 9." This track also had a stupid but fun video that scored them airplay on MTV, giving the band their first serious US exposure. Sykes had a ripping solo, but this was his last appearance with the band as he took a can't-refuse offer to join Thin Lizzy. Fred Purser replaced him on guitars and keyboards as the band went to work on *The Cage* (which also included the recent single).

The Cage was a daring album as the band went for a pop sound utilizing keyboards and electronic drums, cover tunes, and songs from outside writers. This was tough to get used to at first for most fans, but further listens revealed a sophisticated approach with some subtle nuances that worked quite well.

Additional minor hits were achieved with the blatant pop of "Rendezvous" and the semi-acoustic pop of "Paris by Air." "Making Tracks" was dance/pop metal with clattery electronic percussion and the catchy "Letter from L.A." even had a voice box solo. "Tides" was a real highlight, awash in melancholy chords and melodies. This was as far away from *Wild Cat* as could be, yet it somehow (mostly) worked. The album sold extremely well moving over 200,000 and reaching the outskirts of the UK Top 10. MCA tried to push the band even further, insisting on more covers (most awful choices) and outside writers. The band refused to be told what to do and a battle of wills would ensue that sadly saw the group disband in 1983.

In 1985, Deverill and Dick re-formed the band for two forgettable hair metal albums, but Weir and Cox played the popular Wacken Festival in Germany with three new faces as the Tygers of Pan Tang in 1999 and released a live album. Cox left again, but Weir decided to keep the band going in 2000 with drummer Craig Ellis, bassist Brian West, guitarist Dean Robertson, and singer Tony Liddell. In 2001, there was a new studio album of decent quality called *Mystical*. Richie Wicks took over on vocals in 2002 and *Noises from the Cathouse* followed.

Italian vocalist Jacopo Meille joined later in 2004, and his dynamite voice got the band going for real. A strong album called *Animal Instinct* came out in 2008 with some meaty tracks like "Dark Rider" and "Bury the Hatchet." The guitars and vocals were very solid and Weir proved that keeping the band going was indeed a good idea after all. Gavin Gray came back on bass in 2011 (he had been there in 1999), and *Ambush* was an even stronger album in 2012. No way Weir and company should have put out an album this slamming at this stage, but choice cuts "Mr. Indispensable," "Man on Fire," "Rock & Roll Dream," and especially "She" and "Speed" are so good, it's really impressive. The fire is still there from Robb.

In 2013, Micky Crystal replaced Robertson who had been a great foil for Weir, but there's been no noticeable slippage. The 1980–1983 era of Tygers was golden, but these last six years or so have shown that Weir and his cats have a lot more meowing to do (did I really just say that? Well, as you know, I'm a cat nut, so forgive me)!

Robb was also gracious enough to go into great detail about his career with the Tygers and his guitar playing in January 2015, so here are the results from that cat chat (I did it again).

Who were some of your main influences as you started to learn the guitar?

My first guitar was nylon strung Spanish affair that my dad bought for me in a junk shop on his way home one day from surgery; he was a doctor! If he was alive today, he would tell you it was one of the biggest mistakes of his life! (You see I kinda forgot the importance of school and discovered the importance of rock 'n' roll!). I loved that guitar and although I started to learn playing left-handed (which felt very uncomfortable!), I soon figured out I was a right-handed player and things progressed from there.

That guitar was painted in army camo colors and the strings stood off the fret board by at least an inch! So on went the Elvis, ZZ Top, Hendrix, and Status Quo records and the learning began! Guitar heroes never really struck me until I started going to live shows in the early seventies when I saw and liked Mick Box of Uriah Heep, Manny Charlton from Nazareth, Glenn Tipton of Judas Priest, and Alex Lifeson of Rush. As a rule I'm not a big guitar hero person. In my book, less is more! Simple songs "ROCK" and complicated songs...well you make your own mind up!

What have been your preferred guitars over the years, live and in studio?

Do you know I have been very lucky to have owned some fantastic guitars over the years, into the hundreds I would guess, (not all at the same time, of course!). My favourite shape guitar is the Explorer. In the late seventies I had an endorsement deal with the American firm Mighty Mite. They made me a custom Explorer guitar with a whammy bar; it had a maple Strat neck and boy did it play well! They also made me my other favorite shape guitar, a Les Paul with three pickups. I used this one when we played Reading Rock Festival in 1980 with Whitesnake.

I've always liked the slightly unusual shape guitar and, with this in mind, Mighty Mite made me a BC Rich Bich-style guitar with a maple Strat neck. I used this guitar to record most of the backing tracks for the *Spellbound* album at Morgan Studios in London in 1981. Today, I have guitars made for me by Tim Ellis from Cardiff in Wales. Tim also makes guitars for Phil and Lemmy out of Motorhead. I currently have two fantastic, three pickup Les Pauls, which I love. Wherever I go they turn heads! I also am lucky enough to have a company called Warman Guitars supply my pickups and hardware for all my guitars. They have also made me a cracking custom Telecaster guitar to my design!

The Tygers of Pan Tang were a major part of the new wave of British heavy metal movement in that key 1979–1982 period. Did you guys realize what was happening or were you just doing your own thing in Newcastle? And then all of a sudden there you were on MCA Records and a success!

I think the divining moment the metal mist cleared, was when Geoff Barton, one of the journalists from *Sounds* newspaper wrote an article about all these new rock bands appearing on the scene in 1979. Geoff called it the "new wave of British heavy metal" and so a new piece of metal history was created! The Tygers were included in Geoff's BIG four he wrote about. The BIG Four being Iron Maiden, Def Leppard, Saxon, and the Tygers of Pan Tang. The Tygers at that point were recording our first single, "Don't Touch Me There" on the soon-to-become famous label called Neat Records up in the Northeast of England. With the phenomenal record sales generated by our first single, it wasn't long before the big record companies came looking to sign us. Sure enough, late '79 we signed to MCA Records; they re-released "Don't Touch Me There" and the rest is history as they say!

Wild Cat remains one of the greatest hard rock albums of the 1980s. It is raw, visceral, no frills, and hard hitting. I always thought it showed more of an American influence and sound (I hear bits of ZZ Top, Ted Nugent, Aerosmith, Iggy pop, etc.). Was anything from here in the States soaked up in your sound? For 1980, this album really stands the test of time and features very few overdubs and sounds pretty live.

Thank you for your kind comments! *Wild Cat* has been described as an iconic album amongst other fantastic critique over the years. To be honest, there are lots of references in the music on *Wild Cat* from my early influences. But in my defense, I think you can hear influences in every artist's music from their early listening!

Chris Tsangarides, our record producer who guided us through the *Wild Cat* recordings, was very subtle with the overdubs. Because we were a one guitar band, he wanted the music to be able to be reproduced faithfully live. I remember when we had done a "take" in the studio, Chris would say, "Come in and have a listen." He had two monster speakers he used to listen to the takes back. Trouble was, he played the take so loud he kept blowing the speakers' fuses. Beside him he had a large jar with hundreds of the damn things ready to replace the blown ones! Chris was a master at work and together we managed to produce a number 13 hit album with *Wild Cat*. Not a bad effort for your first album, eh?

The solos on Wild Cat *are all very distinctive, such as "Slave to Freedom," "Badger Badger," "Insanity," and my favorite "Suzie Smiled." "Suzie Smiled" has one of my favorite hard rock riffs ever, and your choice of solo was interesting as it was mostly what sounded like a few notes here and there with some volume-knob control. It showed taste—how did you come about playing that part as well as the solo and fills on "Insanity," which also utilizes some cool harmonics and tremolo?*

Again thank you for your kind comments. I'm one of these odd musicians who never actually sits down with the intention of writing anything! It just happens. I don't know how or where it comes from, but the ideas I get just "jump" into my head and out of my fingers! It's always happened like that, I don't really think about it to be honest. If I did, I might freak myself out!

For "Slave to Freedom" I pretty much had the solos mapped out as we had been playing the song for about two years on the circuit before we recorded it. Same goes for "Suzie Smiled," although the volume swells were Chris's idea in the studio. In my book, "less is more." Why waste time playing a hundred notes when ten choice ones will do! So many guitar players from yesteryear have the same approach, and do you know what? The songs that feature a few notes or maybe a guitar theme are the songs people can sing and remember instantly.

How tough was it replacing Jess Cox on vocals at first? It was such a surprise to see him leave after a successful debut album, but Jon Deverill was a great choice and opened things up melodically on tracks like "Mirror" and "Don't Stop By." Was this by design to change the sound a bit? It worked so well.

To be very honest, when Jess left we were a pretty big band in the making. Just having completed a major sell out UK tour and a number 13 British chart album, we were on fire! So when we advertised for his replacement we had 120 or so hopefuls! Auditions were held in Newcastle-upon-Tyne and there was one star that shone way above the rest...Mr. Jon Deverill.

Jon's vocal range was like no other and instantly the *Wild Cat* songs that sounded great sounded even better; in fact, they sounded absolutely amazing! So songwriting instantly took place and the much revered *Spellbound* album was created. John Sykes wrote half of the album music wise, and I wrote the other half music wise, with Jon Deverill creating the melodies and lyrics. Rocky and Brian of course were also an integral part of the writing process and arrangements. All in all, a massive band effort that achieved a number 18 album in the British charts for us in 1981. Although we didn't set out to change the Tygers sound, it happened for us and a new chapter in NWOBHM and Tygers history began!

The addition of John Sykes was a huge one. It must've been clear what an undeniable talent you had added on guitar. Did you two work well as a tandem? Both Spellbound *and* Crazy Nights *were damn good albums and it seemed to work well live.*

In the spring/summer of 1980, we toured as a four piece, opening up for Magnum, Scorpions, Saxon, Def Leppard, and Iron Maiden. Van Halen were also touring here, late summer of '80 and I *so* wanted the Tygers to open up for them, but MCA, our record company, said "No" as we were booked to go into Morgan Studios in Willesden, London, to start recording our first album *Wild Cat*.

While we were recording, there were talks going on as to whether we should strengthen up the lineup with the addition of another guitar player to help me out. After *Wild Cat* was finished, we held auditions at a rehearsal studio next to London Bridge. Once again out of all the great guitar players that auditioned, John Sykes was the cream of the crop! While I was showing John all the guitar work involved, we ended up writing "Take It" together, which was the first song recorded on the *Spellbound* album. It was the only song John and I wrote together. Because of our personal circumstances, we always ended up writing separately. On tour, John and I always shared a room, which was a laugh a minute. I laughed so much in two years, I developed asthma!

The Cage *was a daring step into a pop-oriented, slick sound, yet it became your biggest album in 1982 and showed a different side, although the heaviness was gone. Also, MTV picked up on the "Love Potion No. 9" video in the US—were you aware you were finally getting a presence over here and did the label then mess too much with a good thing and ruin things for the band?*

The Cage was a huge bone of contention for me at the time! This was the start of MCA wanting us to play outside songwriters' material. John Sykes had left the band at this point, (although he had already recorded "Love Potion No. 9" and "Danger in Paradise" in preparation for the new album!). John's replacement was Fred Purser. Fred had come from the punk band Penetration and his musical pedigree was quite superb. Classically trained pianist, great vocalist, producer, and a monster guitar player! MCA wanted a different angle on *The Cage*.

They started by drafting in a pop producer, Peter Collins. His previous track record included hits with the likes of Matchbox and the Lambrettas in the late seventies. This was the first time Peter had worked with a hard rock band, so we were the "test run," if you will, the new metal guinea pigs! Hey good name for a band that! Peter gave us a softer edge, more in line with the American AOR scene.

On the surface it was great, but in truth, I didn't like it—gone were the crunching guitars and pounding bass lines, and in was the super-polished sound. As for the songwriting, we had four band-written songs on the album, the rest were from outside writers. We had to try and Tygerize these "covers" into our style. I think we did a pretty damn good job, but at the end of the day, they were not our songs. In the end, 1983, the band walked away from MCA. What's the point of being a creative songwriting musician and playing other people's songs? Answer...there is no point!

Although I was skeptical of a comeback in the 2000s, your recent albums, Animal Instinct *and* Ambush *with Jacopo Meille on vocals are fantastic. In fact,* Ambush *(from 2012) is one hell of an album with kick-ass riffs, solos, vocals, and production. Congrats for defying the odds, and how have you been feeling about the band and your playing the last few years? It seems to be going so very well.*

The Tygers are a family, and as with all families, members there are fall-in's and fall-out's! There has never been any bad blood throughout our history and today sees a very strong bond between the five of us. Craig Ellis our drummer has been in there from the re-formation in 2000, so fifteen years for Craig. Jack Meille our Italian stallion vocalist has been with the band for eleven years. Gav Gray, the big bass boss has been with us for four years, and Micky McCrystal our new "hot shot lead guitar player" has been with us two years, so not so new really! We are as they say, "on fire!" at the moment. I've had to raise my game because, with Mick in the band and his amazing guitar playing technique, I'm getting left behind! "The Tygers are roaring louder than ever,"—these are not my words but our critiques. Praise indeed for a thirty-seven-year-old band of catz!

My last question and a silly one: I ask most players (it's also very appropriate here) if you could rename a Tygers album or song with a cat theme what would it be? My cats want to know ha ha, and Wild Cat *is ruled out and any other cat songs you've used, sorry!*

How about these? "Making Katz" ("Making Tracks") (*The Cage*); "Black Cat" ("Blackjack") (*Spellbound*); "Love is a Tyger" ("Love Is a Lie") (*The Cage*).

Recommended solo: "Insanity" from *Wild Cat* with Tygers of Pan Tang (1980)
Further info: www.tygersofpantang.com
Photo credit: from Robb Weir's personal collection. Robb (L)
and John Sykes (R) in Tygers of Pan Tang, 1981.

CHAPTER 51

Kyoji Yamamoto

(Born March 23, 1956, Matsue, Shimane, Japan)

Without a doubt, one of the finest and most original hard rock/heavy metal guitarists in the world, Kyoji Yamamoto is a guitar genius. After honing his skills at guitar playing and writing as a teen, Kyoji entered the Yamaha Music School and would soon form Bow Wow, a hard rock outfit, which immediately allowed his talents and creativity to show.

Yamamoto was one of the first guitar players in the world to utilize finger-tapping and developed a wild style that would be copied by loads of players over the years. Bow Wow's self-titled debut album (1976) as well as the two follow-up albums *Signal Fire* and *Charge* (both from 1977) were loose, rocking affairs with ingenious guitar work and energetic almost punk-like rhythms and elements of power pop and early heavy metal. The band was hard to categorize at times, but the musicianship was exemplary. The vocals were a mix of both English and Japanese and perhaps were a turnoff to American audiences, but these albums are truly a joy.

From the debut album, "James in My Casket" is a nine-minute opus dedicated to Yamamoto's guitar hero Jimi Hendrix. The playing is through the roof; it is truly hard to believe this was 1976 and it was a debut for arguably the first true heavy band from Japan. The emotion and sincerity of Yamamoto's playing is undeniable here. One can also hear moments of Ritchie Blackmore, especially from the mellow Rainbow classic "Catch the Rainbow."

From the first wah-wah heavy notes, you'd swear it was indeed Jimi himself playing. *Signal Fire* even had a song called "Rainbow of Sabbath" just to let you know their influences aside from Hendrix! The heart-rending "Still" is a spine-tingling, sublime example of the quality here. Yamamoto rips away a beautifully emotional blues-based solo to this mid-tempo ballad and then furiously adds textured guitar harmonies within the solo that prove the man's compositional skills were second to none.

In 1978, *Guarantee* is where more of a power pop sound joined the hard rock and the album was recorded in California. This was really fun stuff, but not as challenging as what came before. In 1980, there were three catchy, fun albums with *Glorious Road* and *Telephone*, as well as the soundtrack to a cool puppets-in-space movie called *Kumikyoku X-Bomber* that was predominantly instrumental.

The following year's *Hard Dog* was another stellar album with a much tougher sound. The style changed with 1982's *Asian Volcano* and *Warning from Stardust* where their albums were now available in the UK, Europe, and North America. These albums were more straight-ahead heavy metal and the respect garnered to the band for their live shows (and in particular *Asian Volcano*) saw them playing both the Montreux Jazz Festival in Switzerland and Reading Festival in the UK.

The classic lineup of Yamamoto, Mitsuhiro Saito (guitar/vocals), Kenji Sano (bass), and Toshihiro Niimi (drums) came to an end as did Bow Wow in 1983. Yamamoto then formed a new band called Vow Wow with Niimi, Sano, vocalist Genki Hitomi, and keyboardist Rei Atsumi. The style was more hair metal than the classic hard rock sound of Bow Wow, but it landed the band attention with the album *V* in 1987. They scored some airplay with "Don't Leave Me Now," which was written for them by Asia bassist/vocalist John Wetton. By this point, with the band now relocated to the UK, Sano went back home and ex-Whitesnake bassist Neil Murray joined. Kyoji's guitar playing was as great as ever, but his old '70s sounds had gone away sadly. It was the late '80s after all.

In 1989, the album *Helter Skelter* even made the UK Top 75 and the Beatles-cover title track was a minor hit. Murray left for Black Sabbath later that year and Mark Gould joined for 1990's *Mountain Top* co-produced by the legendary Bob Ezrin. But not achieving that massive breakthrough, Vow Wow disbanded.

Yamamoto would re-form Bow Wow in the late '90s and released six more rather solid and heavy, modern albums with *Era* (2005) being one of the best. Kyoji has also issued numerous solo albums of varying styles showcasing his versatility. Among these are such gems as *Mind Arc* (1998), *Requiem* (2000), *Time* (2004), *The Life Album* (2010), and *Philosophy* (2014). Of importance is *Requiem* that features "Sea of Tears," "Spanish Pirates," and "Mother Ocean," among others, as Kyoji's playing is both intense and tranquil emoting images of the beauty of the sea and nature acting almost as a soundtrack to the mysteries of the ocean and its contents.

Kyoji also put out some superb solo albums while he was still in Bow Wow and these records, such as *Horizon* (1980), which is where you can fight the regal genius of "Dog Fight," *Guitar Man* (1982) and *Electric Cinema* (also 1982) stand with anything else he's done in or out of Bow Wow.

A 2010 US compilation entitled *Voyageur: The Essential Kyoji Yamamoto* is evidence to the man's awesomeness. A heady mix of hard rock/jazz fusion and blues will make you weep with joy. Check out live versions of "Dog Fight" (Kyoji and his band are off the charts here), "Mother Ocean," "Mars," or his renditions of "Little Wing" and "Ave Maria" on YouTube and you will be better off for it. This man has provided me so much musical joy I can't even begin to describe it, but if you've never heard his playing, thank me later. There are also several outstanding live DVDs of Kyoji and his band where one can witness this man's excellence on screen.

In October 2014, I received some early Halloween candy in the form of an interview in Japan with a man who has truly meant a lot to me with his playing. I must say, this was an absolute thrill that we were able to connect. Gotta love the magic of the Internet at times.

Who were some of the guitar players that inspired you to play guitar? I am guessing Jimi Hendrix and Ritchie Blackmore were influences?

Yes, they gave me great influence. I loved thrilling guitarists such as them and Jeff Beck and Roy Buchanan. I didn't copy Hendrix licks so much, but I learned the freedom of expression from Jimi a lot. I was also influenced by Leslie West of Mountain. I really loved his tone.

You play with amazing spirit. It sounds like you play from the soul, like Carlos Santana or John McLaughlin. Do you feel a spiritual connection with the guitar?

I and guitars are connected very tightly. I always say that my guitar is one of the organs of my body, and spiritually connected as well. I talk to my guitar without using any particular words, my guitar talks back with its beautiful tone and melodies. I still don't know how it works!

Can you describe the solo on "James in My Casket"? I am still amazed at that solo to this day.

It was a magic moment. "James in My Casket" was on Bow Wow's first album. I really didn't know about the guitar overdubbing stuff then. So I played it just twice with members playing solo parts together. Of course the solo was improvisation. And the take 2 was what you hear. Maybe Jimi came down to Tokyo and played a trick on me!

How did you come across the finger-tapping technique back in the 1970s long before Eddie Van Halen and others took it further?

I used tapping technique in early '70s. But it was just touching stuff, not like Eddie's trill one. I think I was the first guy who did "Touch and Slide" using the pick. You can hear the sound in the "Gonna Be All Right" solo off of the *Hard Dog* album. I have tried to find new, original techniques and I have quite a few.

I was such a fan of the Glorious Road to Hard Dog *era. It sounds like there were some power pop influences in those songs. I also feel those albums had some of your best playing like "Hot Rod Tornado" and "Ai No Kusari." Did you enjoy making those albums even though they were different from the first three classic albums?*

Really? There are much better albums and songs in my history though. To be honest, I didn't like those pop-era albums. I prevented a re-release of those albums for a long time. You know re-mastered stuff...but when a friend of mine played those albums when we went on a trip, I thought they are not so bad...especially some certain songs were great! So now you can get them on Amazon.com.

And what was it like opening for KISS in 1977?

Bow Wow was the opening act of KISS's Japan tour in 1977 and 1978. It was my first time watching their show and listening to their songs. I was thunder struck by their performance. I don't think there are lots of influences in my writing, but we got a lot of influence on stage performance.

Your solo career has involved some amazing jazz fusion and blues material. Your song "Dog Fight" is intense. Is this a style you enjoy as much as the hard rock of Bow Wow?

Yes, I love to play any genres of music. Actually, I don't want to play one particular music style. I would be frustrated if I have to do the same thing. To keep my musical brain healthy, I need to play different kinds of music in a good balance, just like food you eat.

What was it like working for Bow Wow on the X-Bomber *soundtrack in 1980? That seemed so fun!*

It was TV stuff using dolls and puppets just like *Thunderbirds Are Go*! I love writing music imagining some specific scenes. Just like my current solo albums. I play music as if I were drawing pictures in the air.

What are your favorite guitars to play?

Yamaha HR special custom is my favorite and also my signature model.

Is there ever a chance you will play in the USA any time soon?

No, I hope I can go and play one day in the near future. Thank you!

Recommended solo: "James in My Casket" from *Bow Wow* by Bow Wow (1976)
Further info: www.kyoji-yamamoto.com

Acknowledgments

I want to thank all the guitar players I spoke to for being able to relate to me in their own words about their amazing careers. Reaching out to anyone through their websites was always a mystery, and while there were plenty of guitarists who never got back to me, there were so many who did and were thrilled and honored that I wanted to feature them, that I am still overwhelmed by who I was able to speak with.

Also, I happen to be blessed with a ridiculously large amount of friends who have been very supportive of me as well as what is left of my immediate family through an especially rough time in my life and also for keeping me focused on this book.

I can't thank everyone, and I wish that I could, but I can single out some names that I feel were most important, including my sister, Susan, who is far more than a mere sister to me; my father, Ray, who certainly has kept us entertained through the years and has been a damn good Dad; and all the loyal pets, including the current batch of Krimpet, Wilbur, and Uncle Steve (don't ask); and to my family who really has endured more than enough tragedy over the recent years.

The friends who I must mention include Craig Kline for being the brother I never had, but I would've been honored to call my brother and his adorable family; Matt Miller for being that other brother I should've had; Brian McRory for the visits to help me format this thing and send it off properly as well as sarcastically answering my texts (thanks, jack-ass!); Amber Lauff, for being such a great friend, listener, and craft beer fan; Mike Whilleson for making me hate fantasy baseball and football every year (except for the rare times when we win); Jack Trout for taking care of my sister and my car (not in that order, ha ha); Joe Briglia, Frank Moran, and Rick and Mike Veneziani for being like family; Ryan "Doot Doot" Toogood, Melissa McConville, Nicole DeFeo, Sue and Chris Tracey; Dave Manuele, who knows he's always wrong even if he's right; Nick DeMatteo and Mike Pallante for being the best musical partners ever who shared my demented vision all these years; Gwen Dade, Lehcar my cousin, Patti and her husband Dennis, who have been above and beyond what family means; and Kevin Agnew for loving ham and being one.

Also, I'd like to thank all of my co-workers at the Phillies, who always asked about the book's progress and made me smile from the time I walked in the ballpark; plus the wonderful teachers and kids in Audubon and Haddon Township, even the kids who have driven me nuts. And as well, I thank all my fantasy football and baseball pals who know I'm a genius regardless of what place I finish!

And, thanks to other music geeks like myself at the wonderful sanctuary that is IMWAN/ICE where each and every one of us is a music obsessive: Alan, "Smiff", John G, Dan O, "Dr. Evil," "Jimbo," Rich, Steve, Kym, Rick, Geff, and Linda, our "den mother," and plenty more of you.

And, I can't forget all my "children" who weren't mine but I watched grow up hanging out at my stores and for whatever reason became a father figure to. Now they have developed into amazing adults who will make this world a much better place, especially the four who have become such fine musicians themselves in Taylor and Connor Lenahan, Pete Sarubbi, and Neale Demento, as well as Dillon Knoettner, Allison Herens, Bryan Donahue, Eric Leonard, and many others.

There are so many more friends, but I can't possibly name them all and believe me, I'd like to. Every one of you means the world to me. If a man is judged by the amount of friends he has then I'm pretty high up there.

I also want to thank my ex-wife Nicole, because most of our eighteen years together were wonderful and I treasure those years still; as well as our cats Nibbles, Cuddles, Felix, Squeak, and Chester, and no, we were not crazy cat people.

There were an awful lot of publicists, webmasters, agents, connections, and such who were very nice, interested, helpful, and excited about this project and made things happen with the artists. Among those are Anne Leighton, who I have been proud to know for about fifteen years now, Dara Crockett, Rick Wharton, Denise Kovalevich, John F. Higgins, Bernie Finkelstein, David Spero, Patti "The Webmistress," Melissa Kucirek, Harold Brown, Tamara Yajia, Frankie Wilde, LaDonna Gales, Gillian Hewer, Rodney O'Quinn, Lori Lousararian, Amanda Stone, Beth Fieger Falkenstein, Jo Hackett, Amanda Lehmann, Jimmy Smith, Ben Hylands, Petter Stene, Steven Winterhalter, Leighsa Montrose, Jill Meniketti, Nathan Parsons, and Chris Hewlett.

I also especially thank Bob Biondi at Schiffer Publishing for reaching out to me after seeing my blog at https://chudbeagleblog.wordpress.com.

About the Author

Peter Raymond Braidis

was born January 8, 1969, in Bristol, Pennsylvania, but was raised in Haddon Township, New Jersey. He graduated from Haddon Township High School and earned a BA in history and journalism from Rutgers-State University of New Jersey-Camden. He has written and been published in *Metal Rules Magazine*, *Goldmine Magazine*, Indie-music.com, and the *Philadelphia Inquirer* newspaper. Pete has also co-owned and operated Watchdog Video from 1995 to 2006 and the Watchdog/Cool Beans Café from 2006 until 2008.

Author Peter Braidis with drumming legend Carl Palmer.

Pete currently works part-time as a teacher in grammar school and middle school in the Audubon and Haddon Township, New Jersey school districts and also works for the Philadelphia Phillies Major League Baseball Club. Additionally, Pete has a humor blog at https://chudbeagleblog.wordpress.com in which he mocks awful album and book covers as well as cheesy monster movies from the '70s and '80s and music videos from the '80s. He plays guitar and writes for the not-so-legendary "studio project" Business of Ferrets. This is his first book—and it won't be his last.